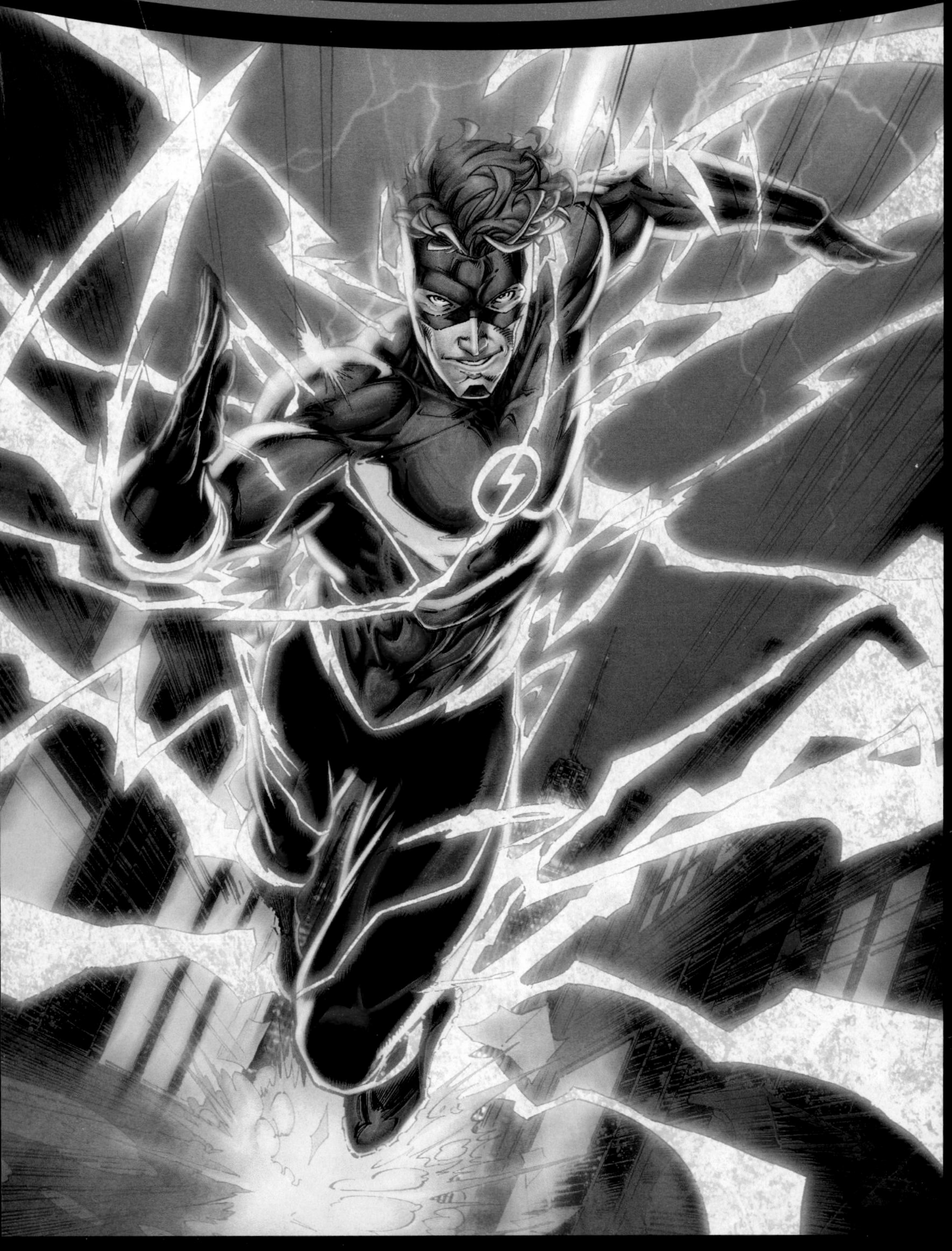

TITANS

VOL. 1 THE RETURN OF WALLY WEST

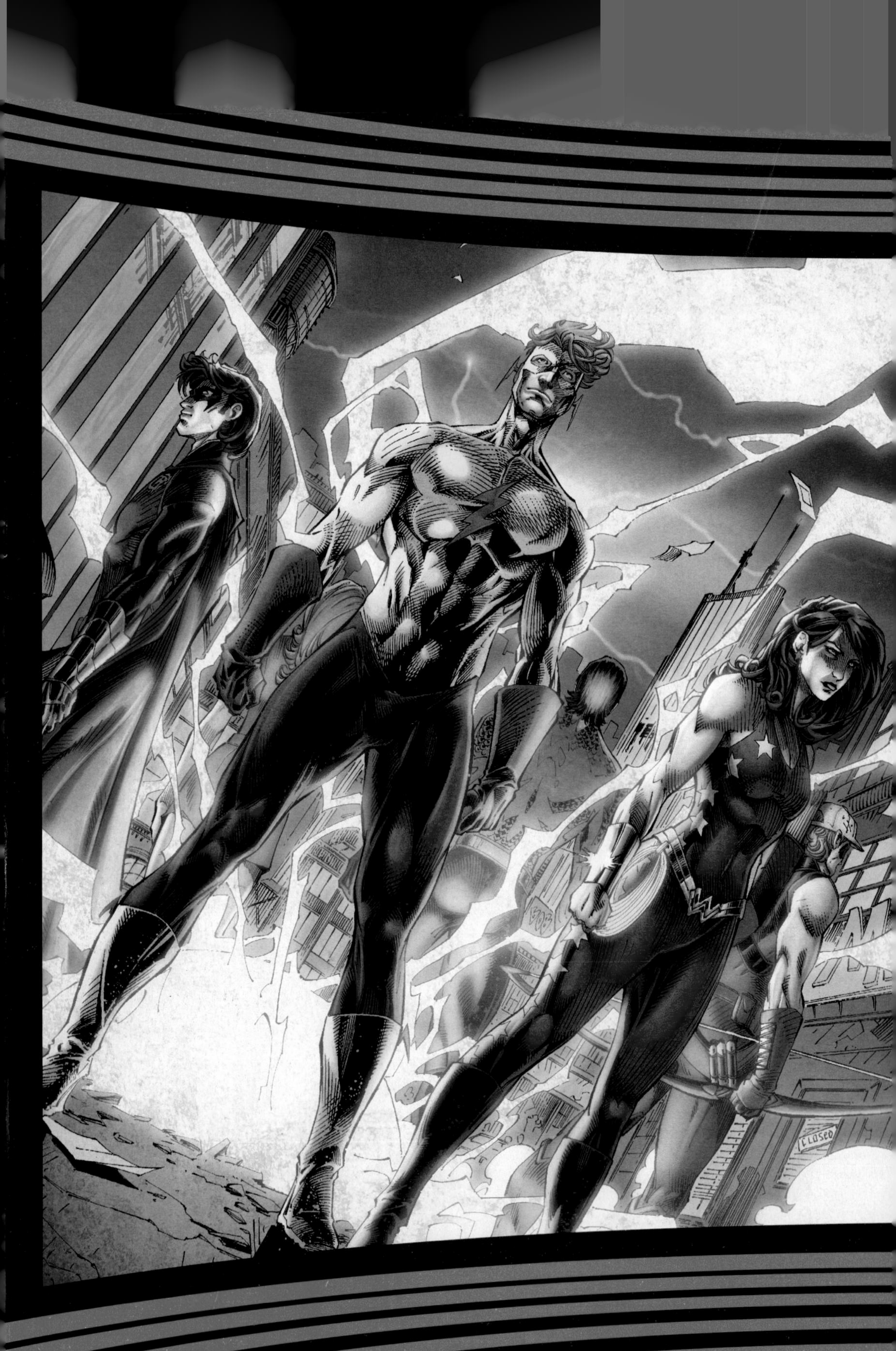
CLOSED

TITANS

VOL. 1 THE RETURN
OF WALLY WEST

DAN ABNETT
writer

BRETT BOOTH
penciller

NORM RAPMUND
MARC DEERING
inker

ANDREW DALHOUSE
CARRIE STRACHAN
colorists

CARLOS M. MANGUAL
letterer

BRETT BOOTH, NORM RAPMUND
& ANDREW DALHOUSE
collection cover artists

ALEX ANTONE Editor - Original Series • **BRITTANY HOLZHERR** Assistant Editor - Original Series
JEB WOODARD Group Editor - Collected Editions • **ROBIN WILDMAN** Editor - Collected Edition
STEVE COOK Design Director - Books

BOB HARRAS Senior VP - Editor-in-Chief, DC Comics

DIANE NELSON President • **DAN DiDIO** Publisher • **JIM LEE** Publisher • **GEOFF JOHNS** President & Chief Creative Officer
AMIT DESAI Executive VP - Business & Marketing Strategy, Direct to Consumer & Global Franchise Management
SAM ADES Senior VP - Direct to Consumer • **BOBBIE CHASE** VP - Talent Development • **MARK CHIARELLO** Senior VP - Art, Design & Collected Editions
JOHN CUNNINGHAM Senior VP - Sales & Trade Marketing • **ANNE DePIES** Senior VP - Business Strategy, Finance & Administration
DON FALLETTI VP - Manufacturing Operations • **LAWRENCE GANEM** VP - Editorial Administration & Talent Relations
ALISON GILL Senior VP - Manufacturing & Operations • **HANK KANALZ** Senior VP - Editorial Strategy & Administration
JAY KOGAN VP - Legal Affairs • **THOMAS LOFTUS** VP - Business Affairs • **JACK MAHAN** VP - Business Affairs
NICK J. NAPOLITANO VP - Manufacturing Administration • **EDDIE SCANNELL** VP - Consumer Marketing
COURTNEY SIMMONS Senior VP - Publicity & Communications • **JIM (SKI) SOKOLOWSKI** VP - Comic Book Specialty Sales & Trade Marketing
NANCY SPEARS VP - Mass, Book, Digital Sales & Trade Marketing

TITANS VOLUME 1: THE RETURN OF WALLY WEST

DC Comics, 2900 West Alameda Ave., Burbank, CA 91505
Printed by LSC Communications, Salem, VA, USA. 1/27/17. First Printing.
ISBN: 978-1-4012-6817-6

Library of Congress Cataloging-in-Publication Data is available.

PEFC Certified

Printed on paper from
sustainably managed
forests, controlled
sources

PEFC/29-31-337   www.pefc.org

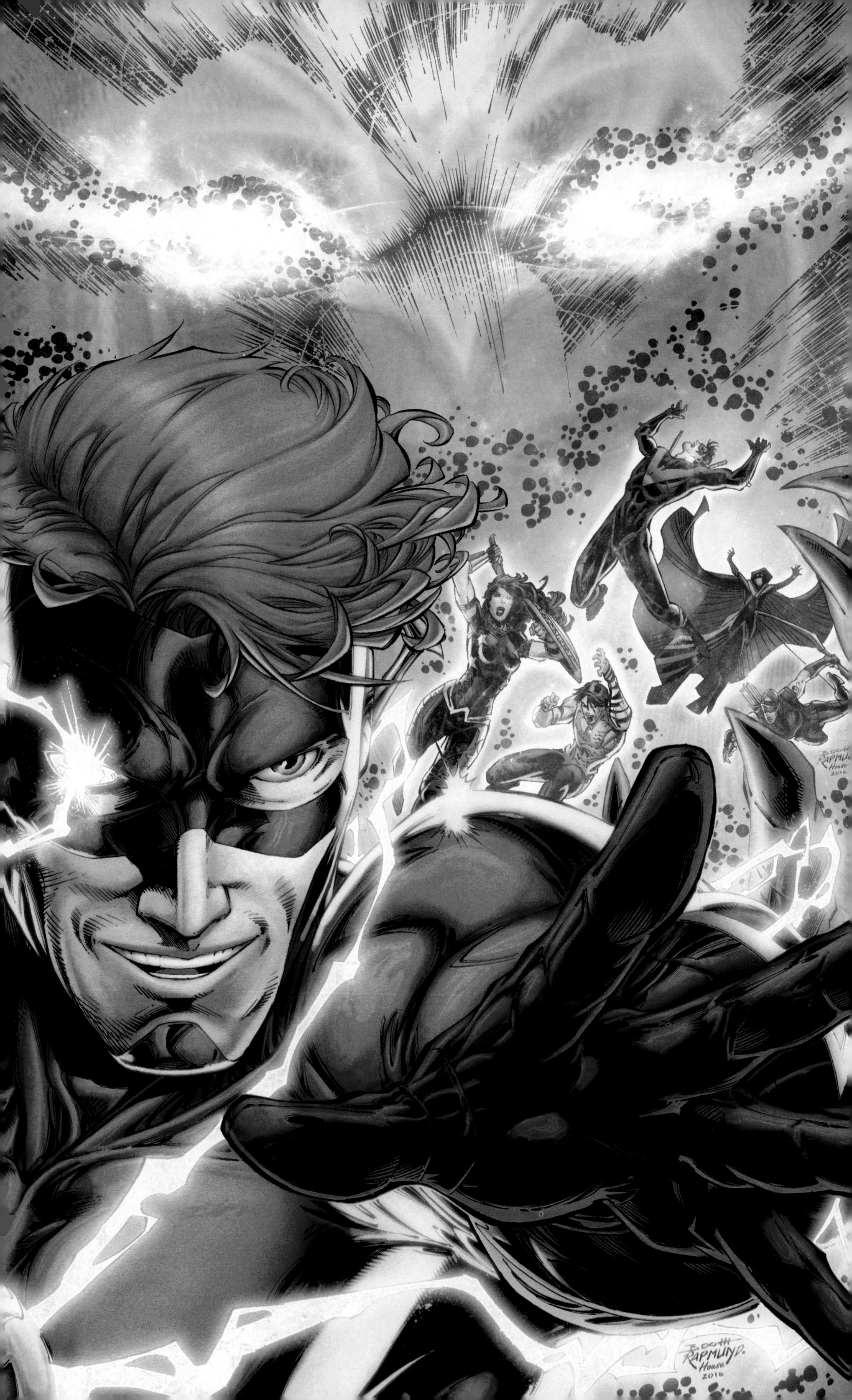
BOOTH RAPMUND House 2016

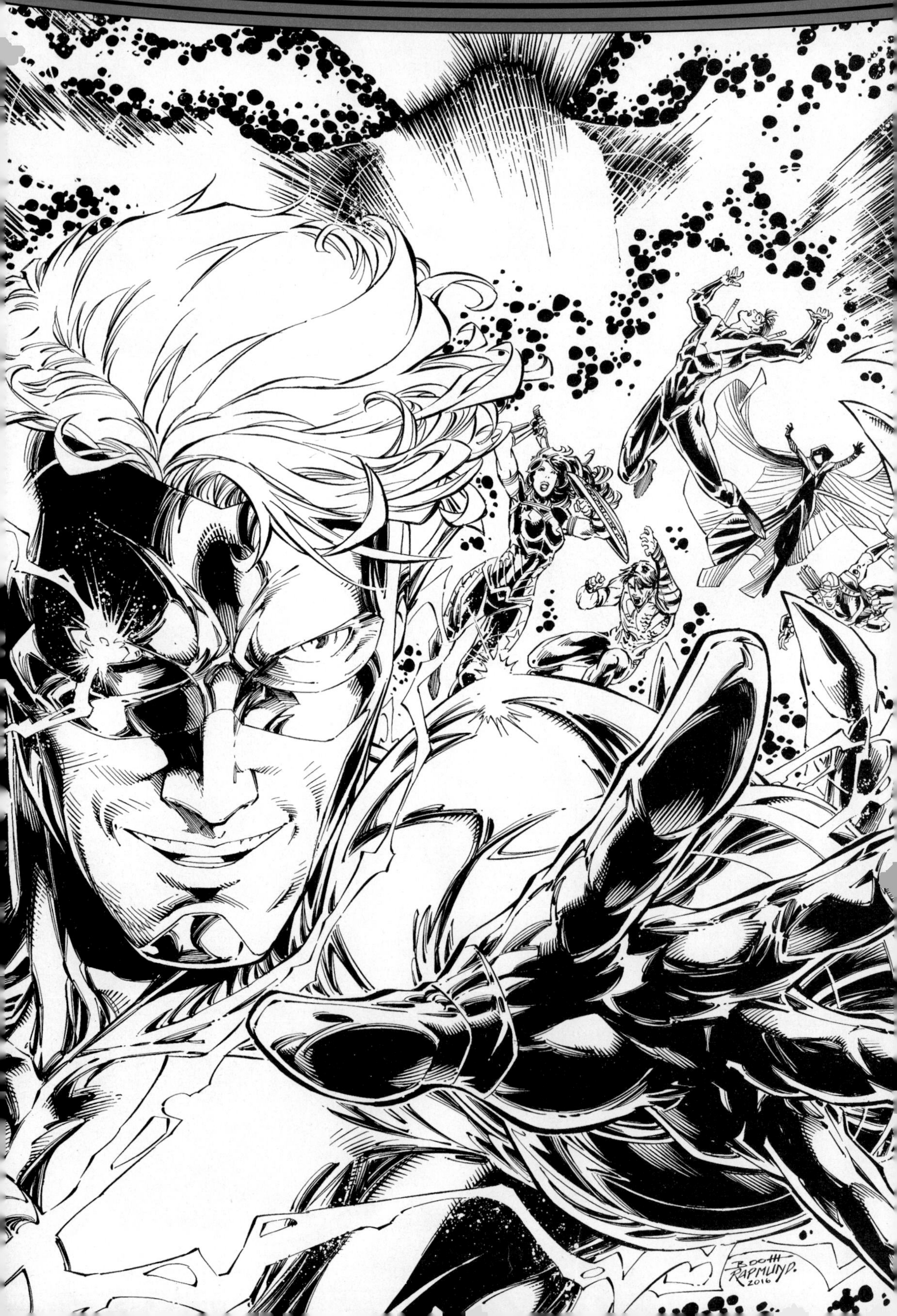
BOOTH
RAPMUND.
2016

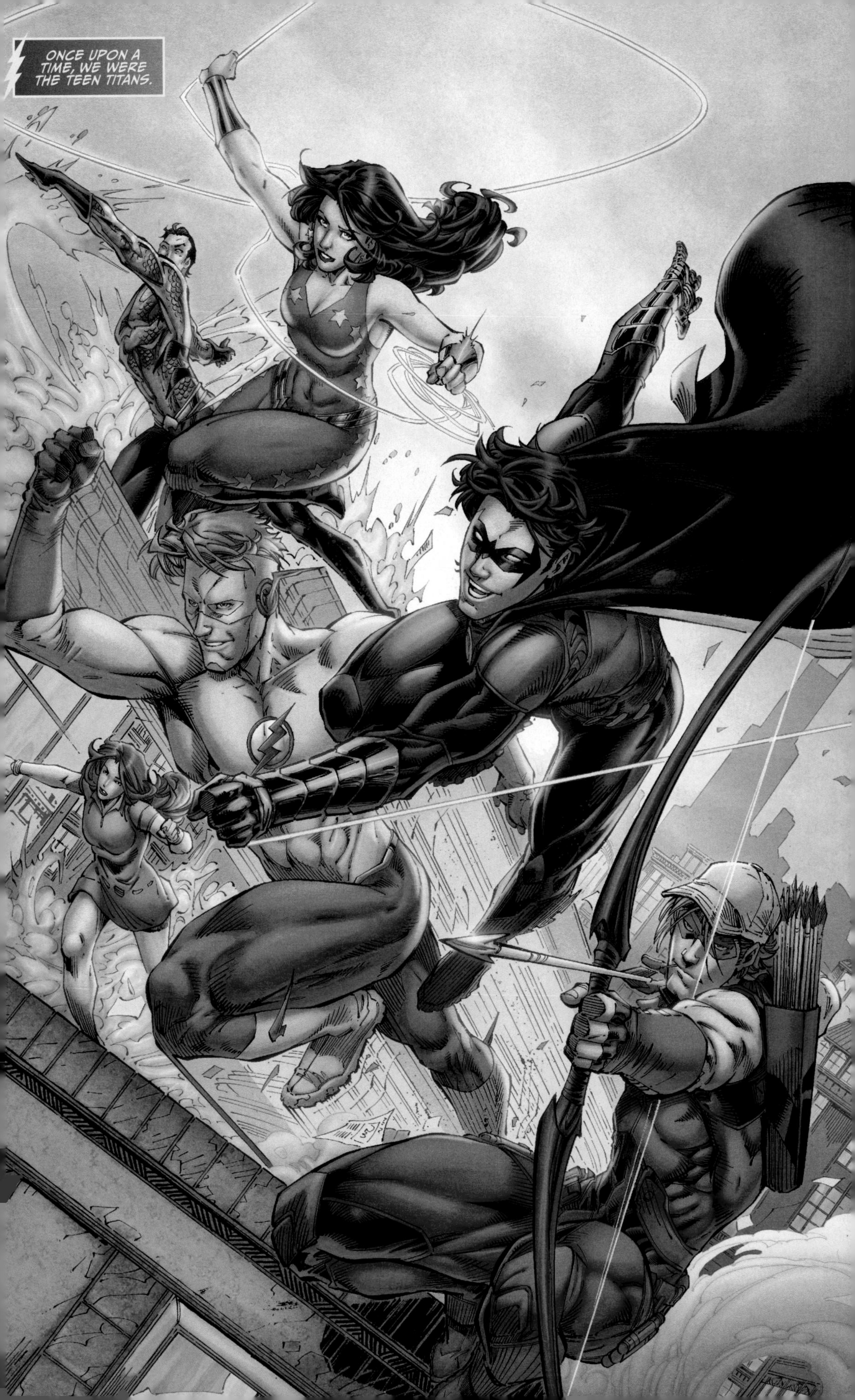
ONCE UPON A TIME, WE WERE THE TEEN TITANS.

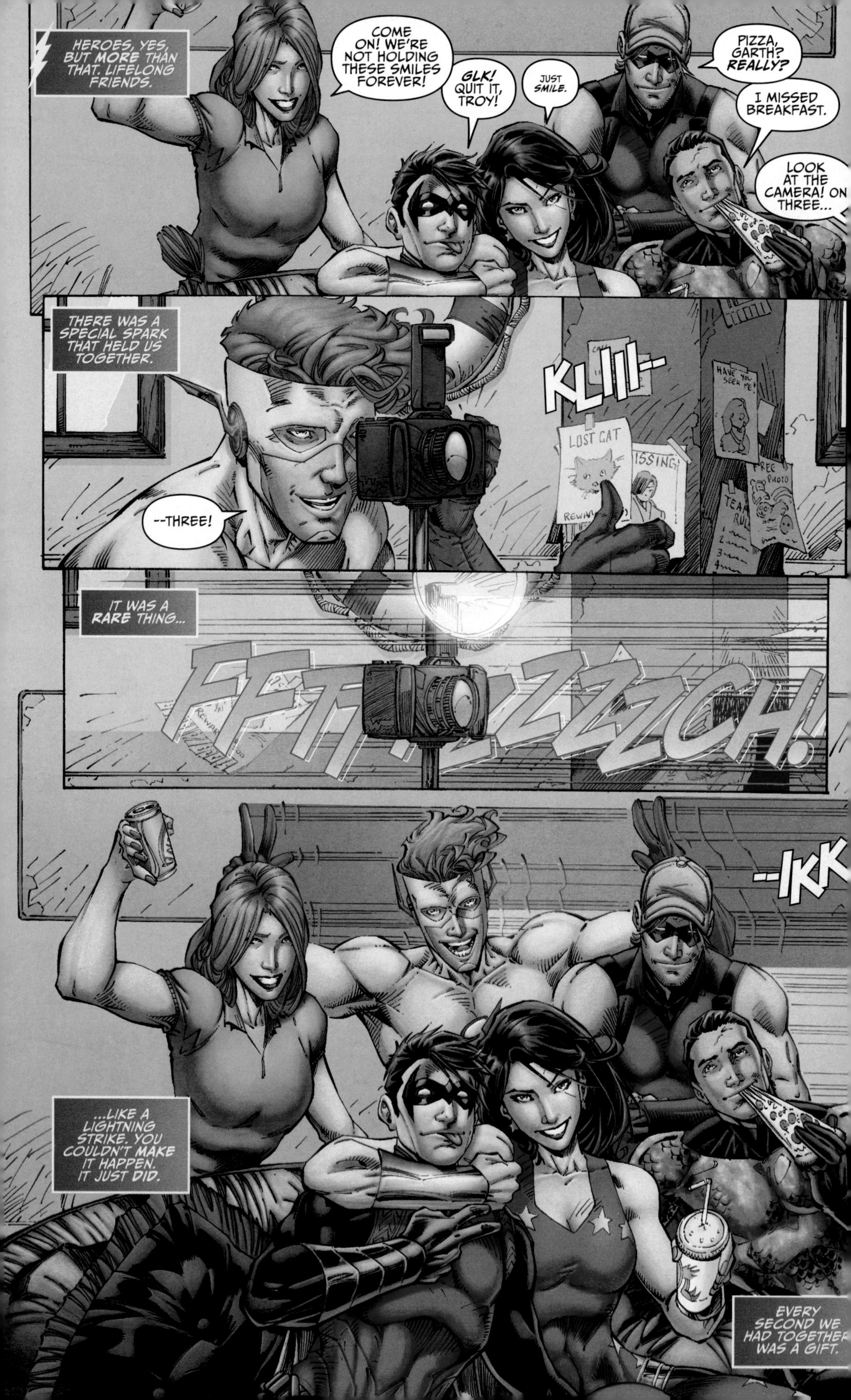
HEROES, YES, BUT MORE THAN THAT. LIFELONG FRIENDS.
COME ON! WE'RE NOT HOLDING THESE SMILES FOREVER!
GLK! QUIT IT, TROY!
JUST SMILE.
PIZZA, GARTH? REALLY?
I MISSED BREAKFAST.
LOOK AT THE CAMERA! ON THREE...
THERE WAS A SPECIAL SPARK THAT HELD US TOGETHER.
KLIII--
LOST CAT
HAVE YOU SEEN ME?
--THREE!
IT WAS A RARE THING...
FFT!-ZZZZCH!!
--IKK
...LIKE A LIGHTNING STRIKE. YOU COULDN'T MAKE IT HAPPEN. IT JUST DID.
EVERY SECOND WE HAD TOGETHER WAS A GIFT.

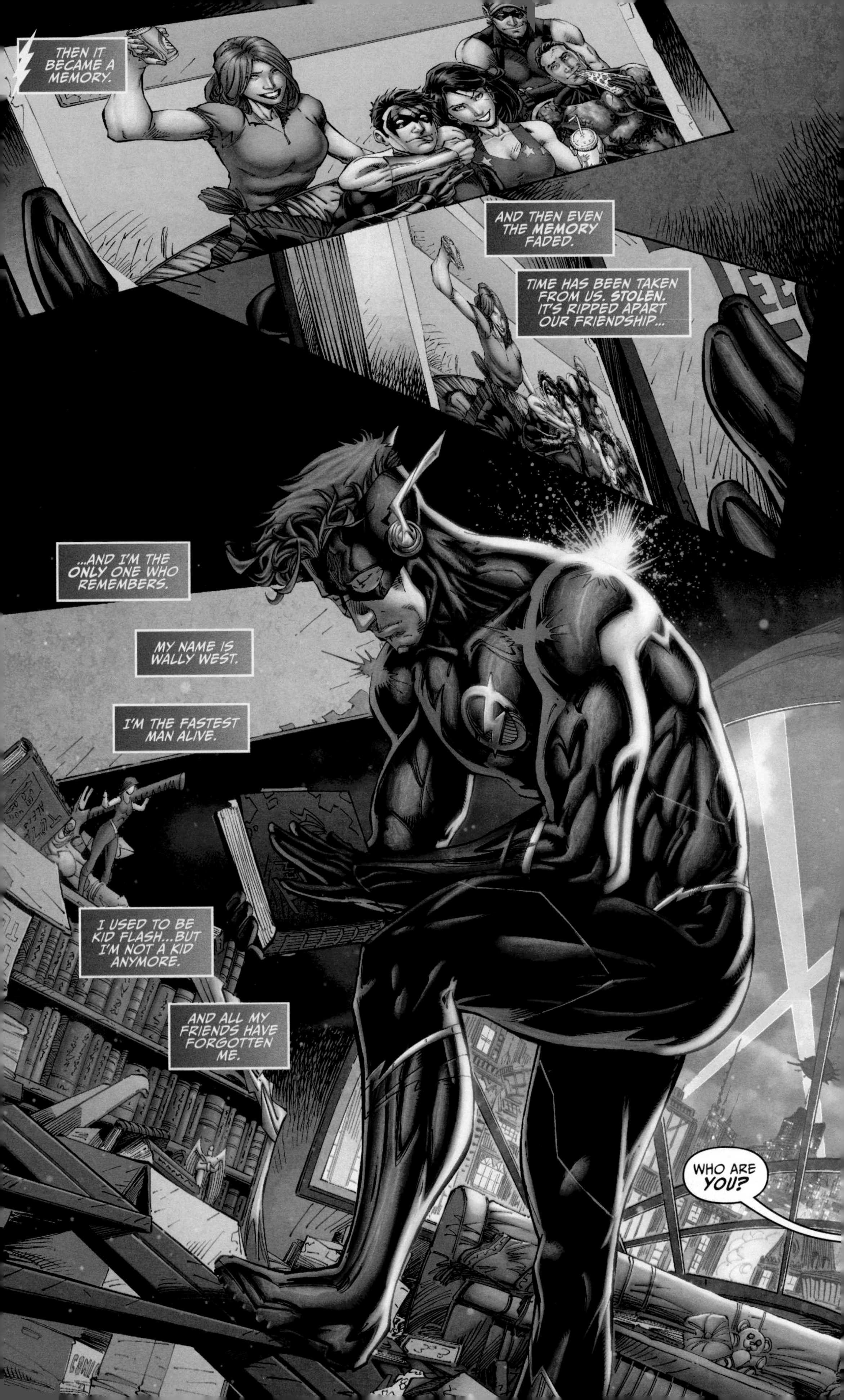
THEN IT BECAME A MEMORY.
AND THEN EVEN THE MEMORY FADED.
TIME HAS BEEN TAKEN FROM US. STOLEN. IT'S RIPPED APART OUR FRIENDSHIP...
...AND I'M THE ONLY ONE WHO REMEMBERS.
MY NAME IS WALLY WEST.
I'M THE FASTEST MAN ALIVE.
I USED TO BE KID FLASH...BUT I'M NOT A KID ANYMORE.
AND ALL MY FRIENDS HAVE FORGOTTEN ME.
WHO ARE YOU?

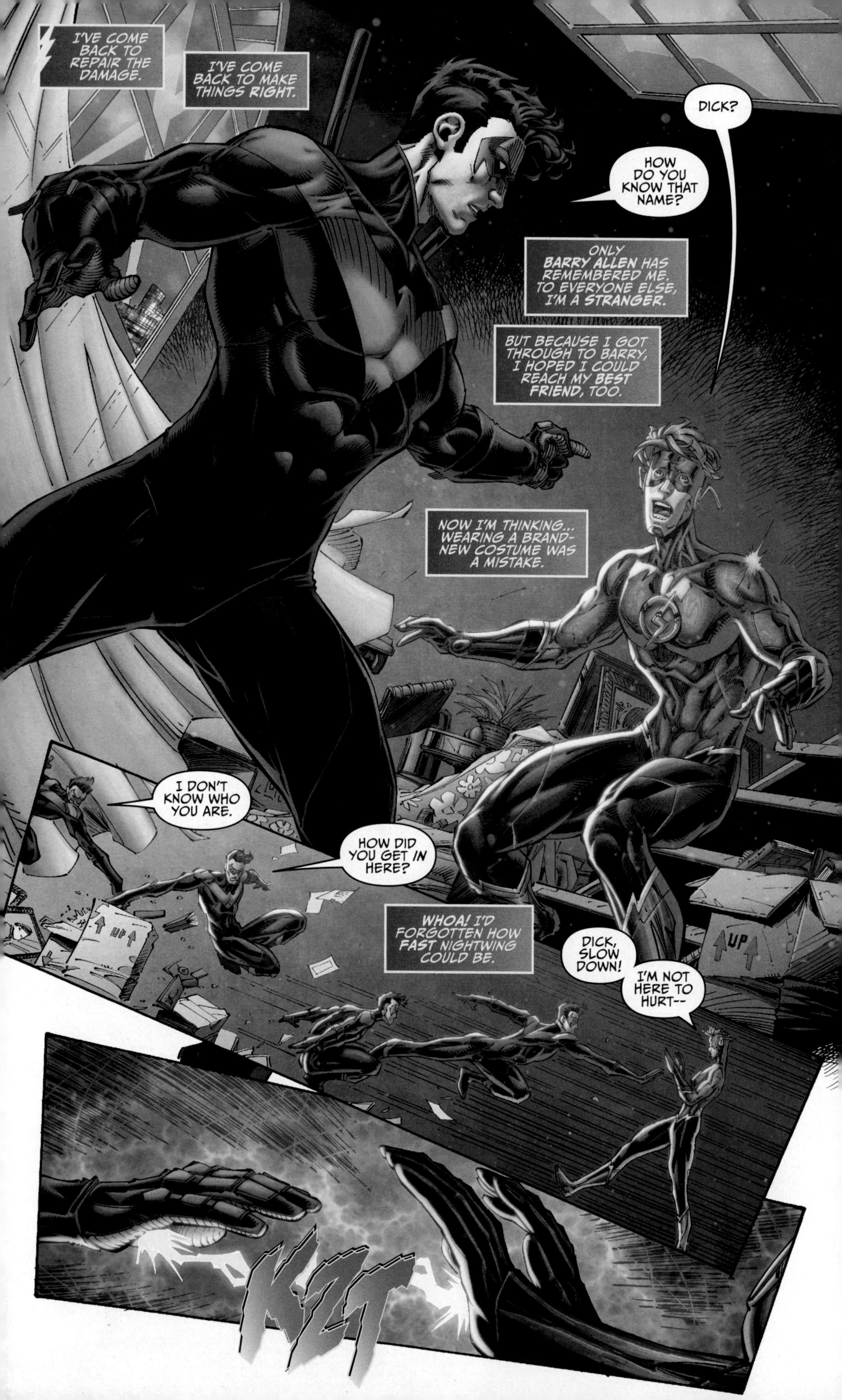

I'VE COME BACK TO REPAIR THE DAMAGE.
I'VE COME BACK TO MAKE THINGS RIGHT.
DICK?
HOW DO YOU KNOW THAT NAME?
ONLY BARRY ALLEN HAS REMEMBERED ME. TO EVERYONE ELSE, I'M A STRANGER.
BUT BECAUSE I GOT THROUGH TO BARRY, I HOPED I COULD REACH MY BEST FRIEND, TOO.
NOW I'M THINKING... WEARING A BRAND-NEW COSTUME WAS A MISTAKE.
I DON'T KNOW WHO YOU ARE.
HOW DID YOU GET IN HERE?
WHOA! I'D FORGOTTEN HOW FAST NIGHTWING COULD BE.
DICK, SLOW DOWN!
I'M NOT HERE TO HURT--
UP
UP
KZZT

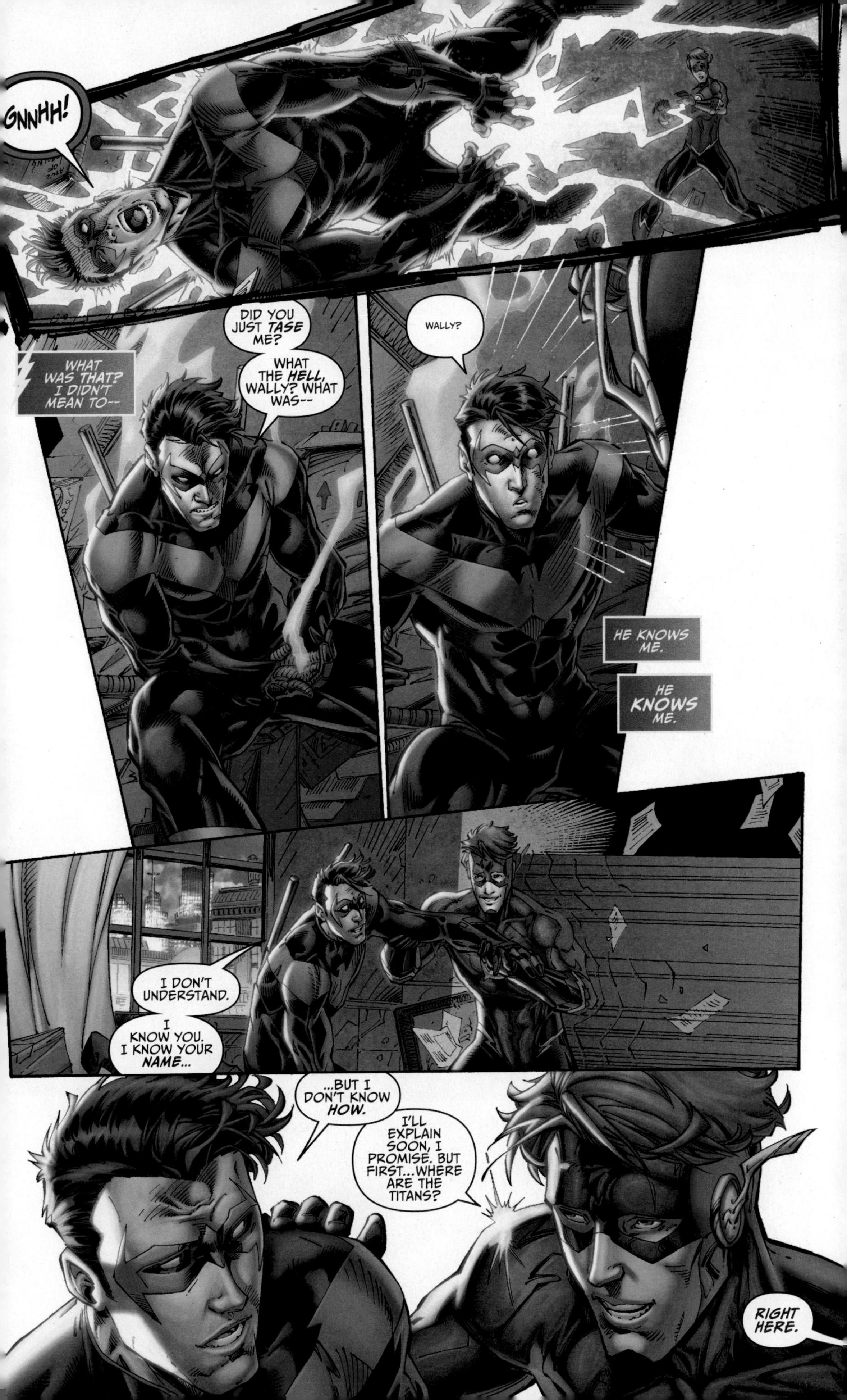
GNNHH!
DID YOU JUST TASE ME?
WHAT THE HELL, WALLY? WHAT WAS--
WHAT WAS THAT? I DIDN'T MEAN TO--
WALLY?
HE KNOWS ME.
HE KNOWS ME.
I DON'T UNDERSTAND.
I KNOW YOU. I KNOW YOUR NAME...
...BUT I DON'T KNOW HOW.
I'LL EXPLAIN SOON, I PROMISE. BUT FIRST...WHERE ARE THE TITANS?
RIGHT HERE.

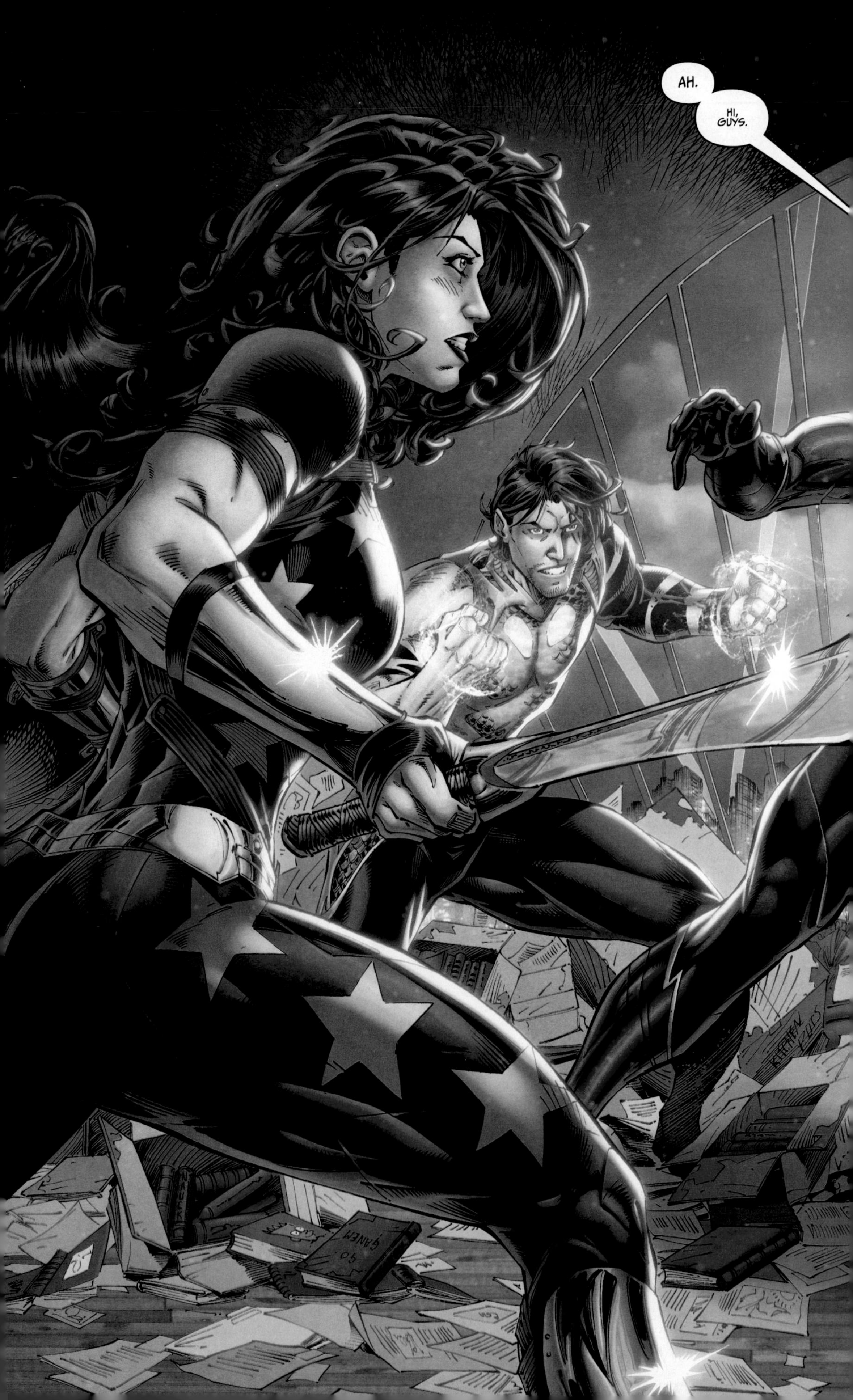
AH.
HI, GUYS.

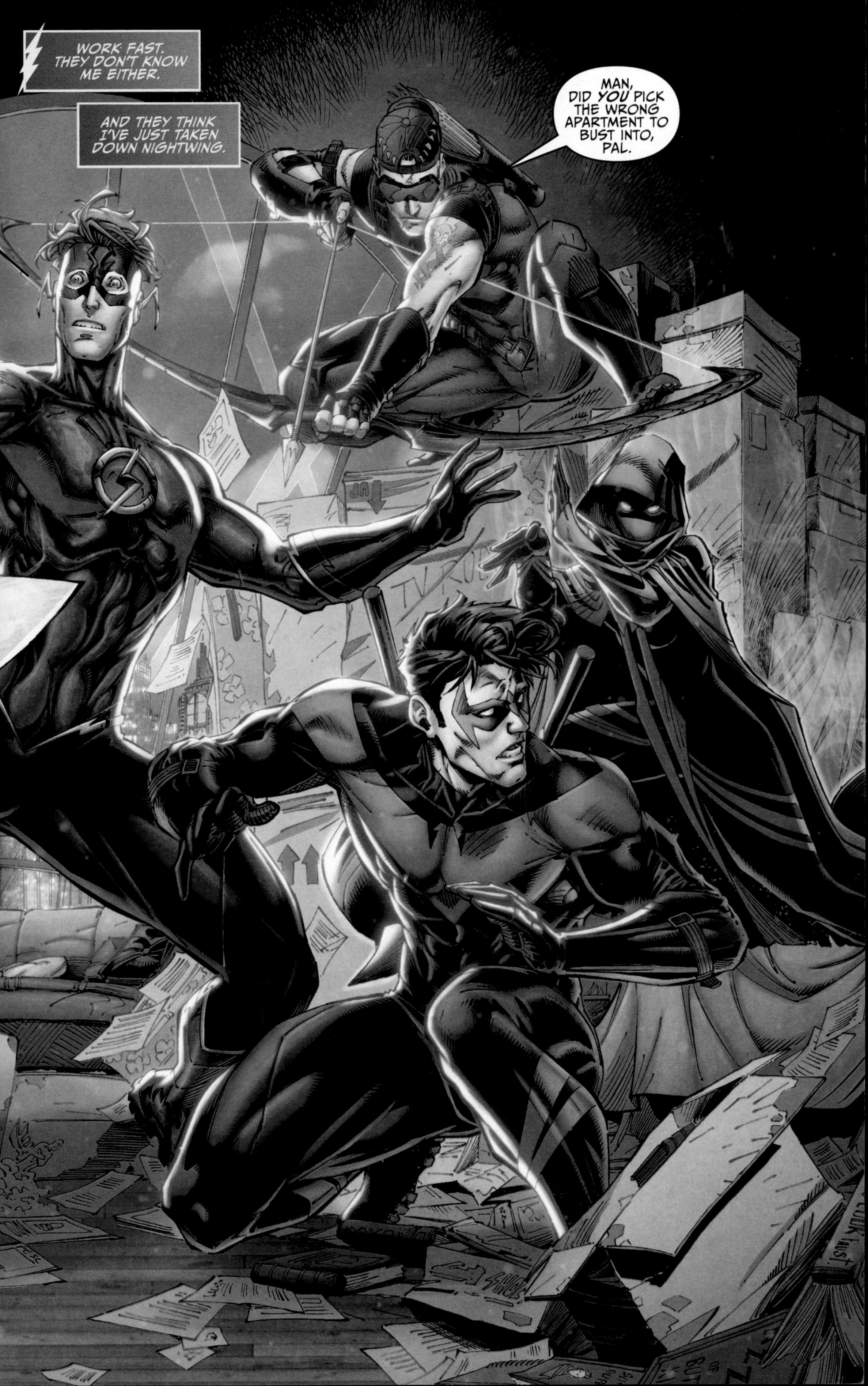
WORK FAST. THEY DON'T KNOW ME EITHER.
AND THEY THINK I'VE JUST TAKEN DOWN NIGHTWING.
MAN, DID YOU PICK THE WRONG APARTMENT TO BUST INTO, PAL.

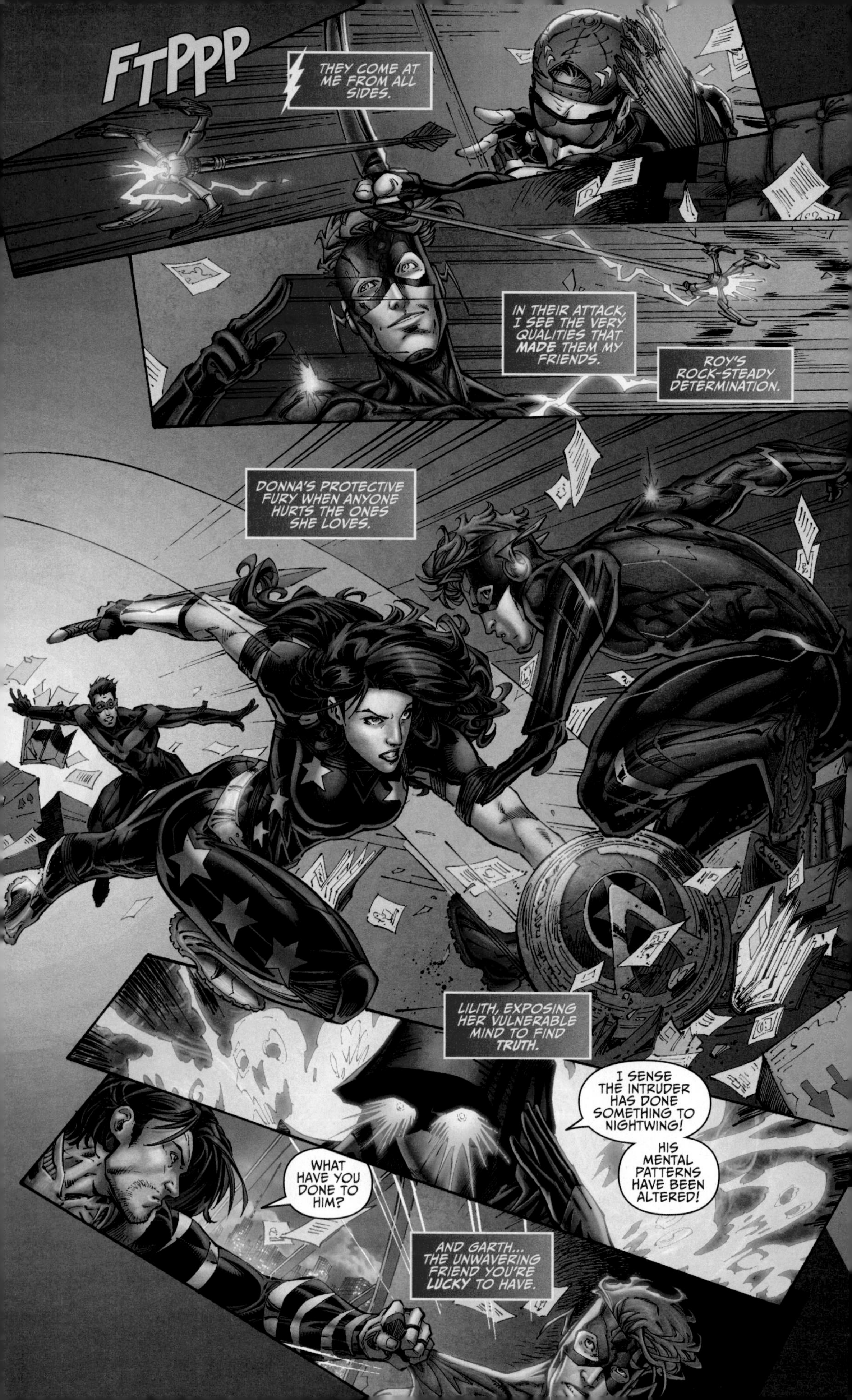
FTPPP
THEY COME AT ME FROM ALL SIDES.
IN THEIR ATTACK, I SEE THE VERY QUALITIES THAT MADE THEM MY FRIENDS.
ROY'S ROCK-STEADY DETERMINATION.
DONNA'S PROTECTIVE FURY WHEN ANYONE HURTS THE ONES SHE LOVES.
LILITH, EXPOSING HER VULNERABLE MIND TO FIND TRUTH.
I SENSE THE INTRUDER HAS DONE SOMETHING TO NIGHTWING!
HIS MENTAL PATTERNS HAVE BEEN ALTERED!
WHAT HAVE YOU DONE TO HIM?
AND GARTH... THE UNWAVERING FRIEND YOU'RE LUCKY TO HAVE.

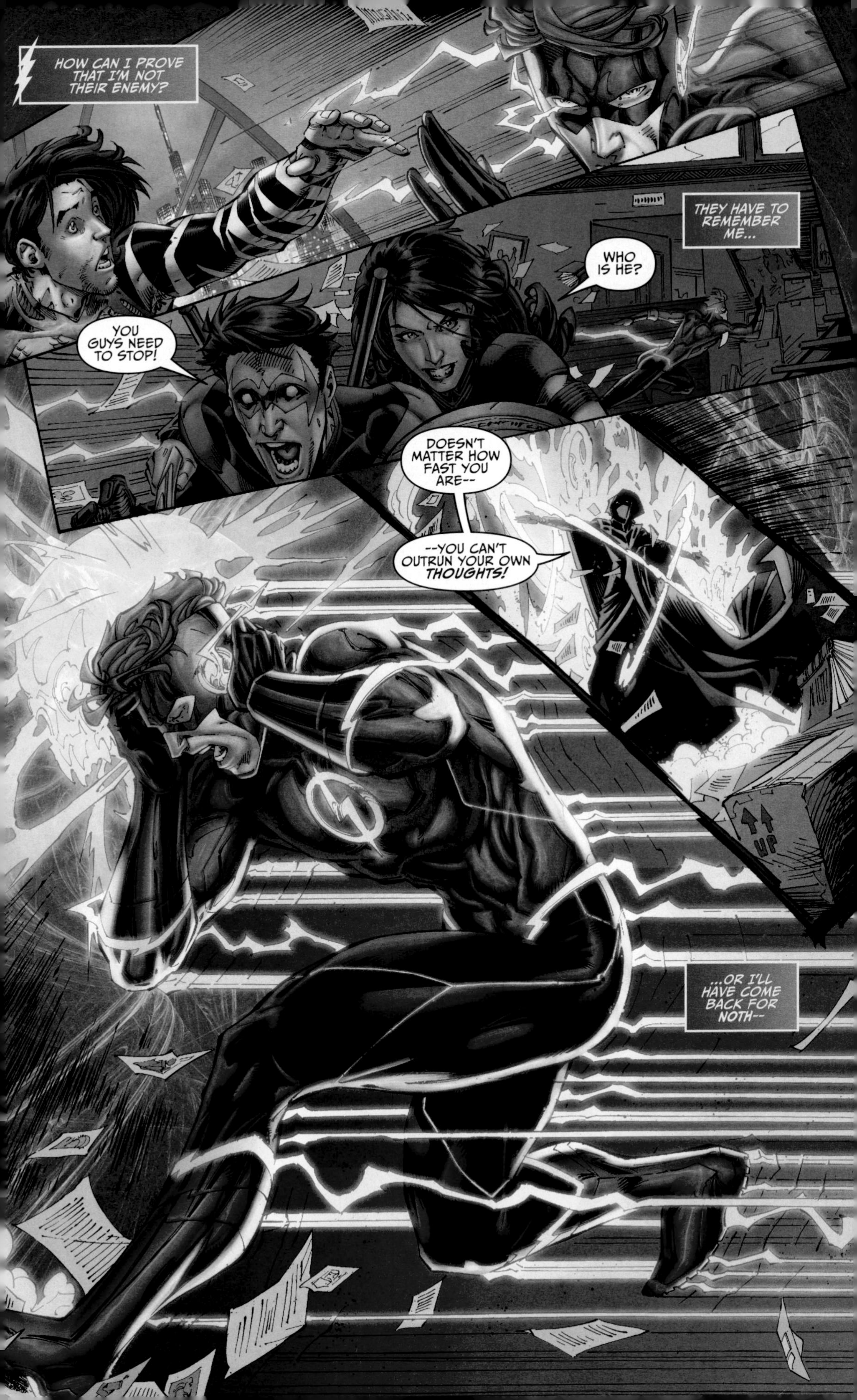
HOW CAN I PROVE THAT I'M NOT THEIR ENEMY?
THEY HAVE TO REMEMBER ME...
WHO IS HE?
YOU GUYS NEED TO STOP!
DOESN'T MATTER HOW FAST YOU ARE--
--YOU CAN'T OUTRUN YOUR OWN THOUGHTS!
...OR I'LL HAVE COME BACK FOR NOTH--

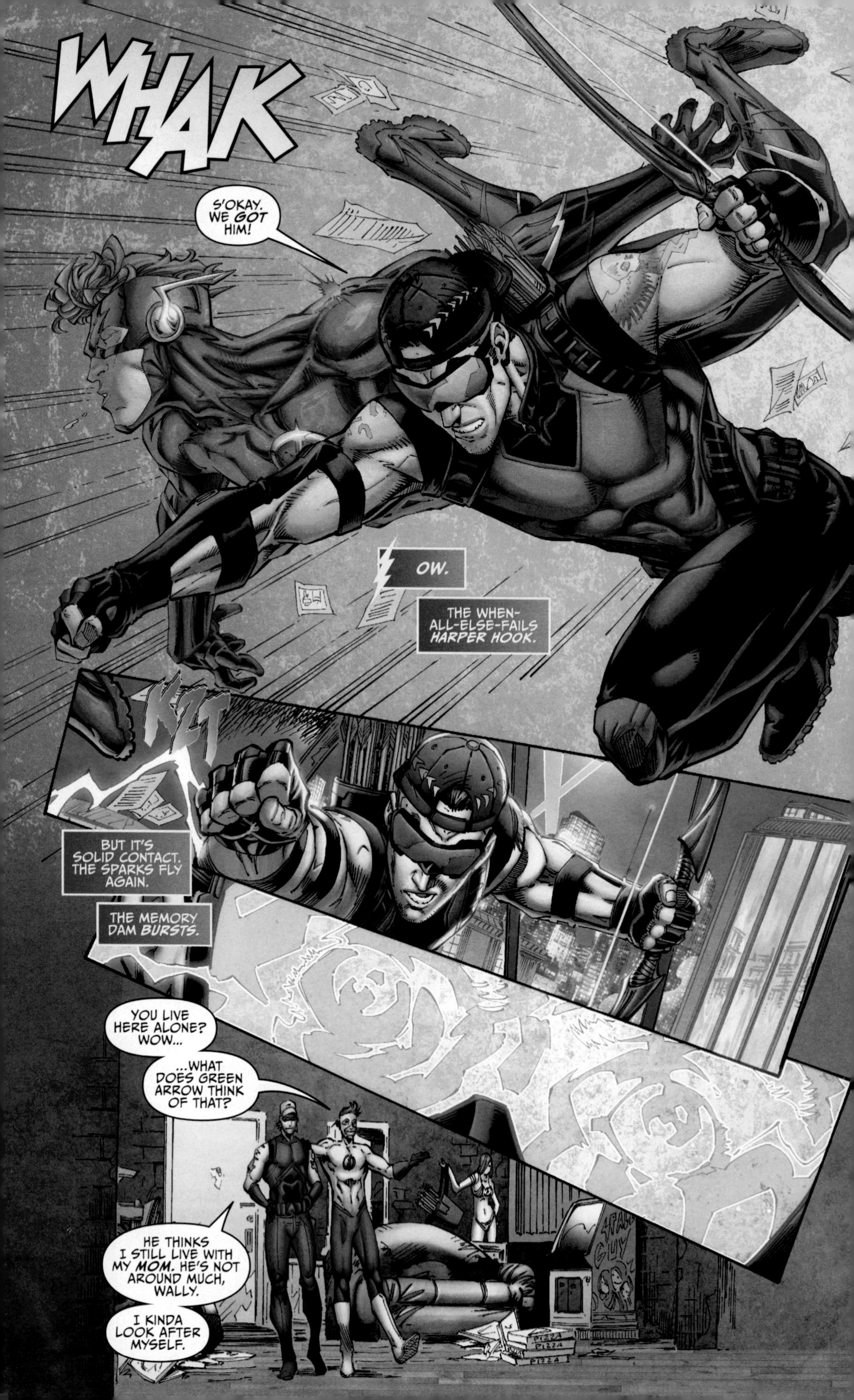
WHAK
S'OKAY. WE GOT HIM!
OW.
THE WHEN-ALL-ELSE-FAILS HARPER HOOK.
KZT
BUT IT'S SOLID CONTACT. THE SPARKS FLY AGAIN.
THE MEMORY DAM BURSTS.
YOU LIVE HERE ALONE? WOW...
...WHAT DOES GREEN ARROW THINK OF THAT?
HE THINKS I STILL LIVE WITH MY MOM. HE'S NOT AROUND MUCH, WALLY.
I KINDA LOOK AFTER MYSELF.
PIZZA
PIZZA
PIZZA

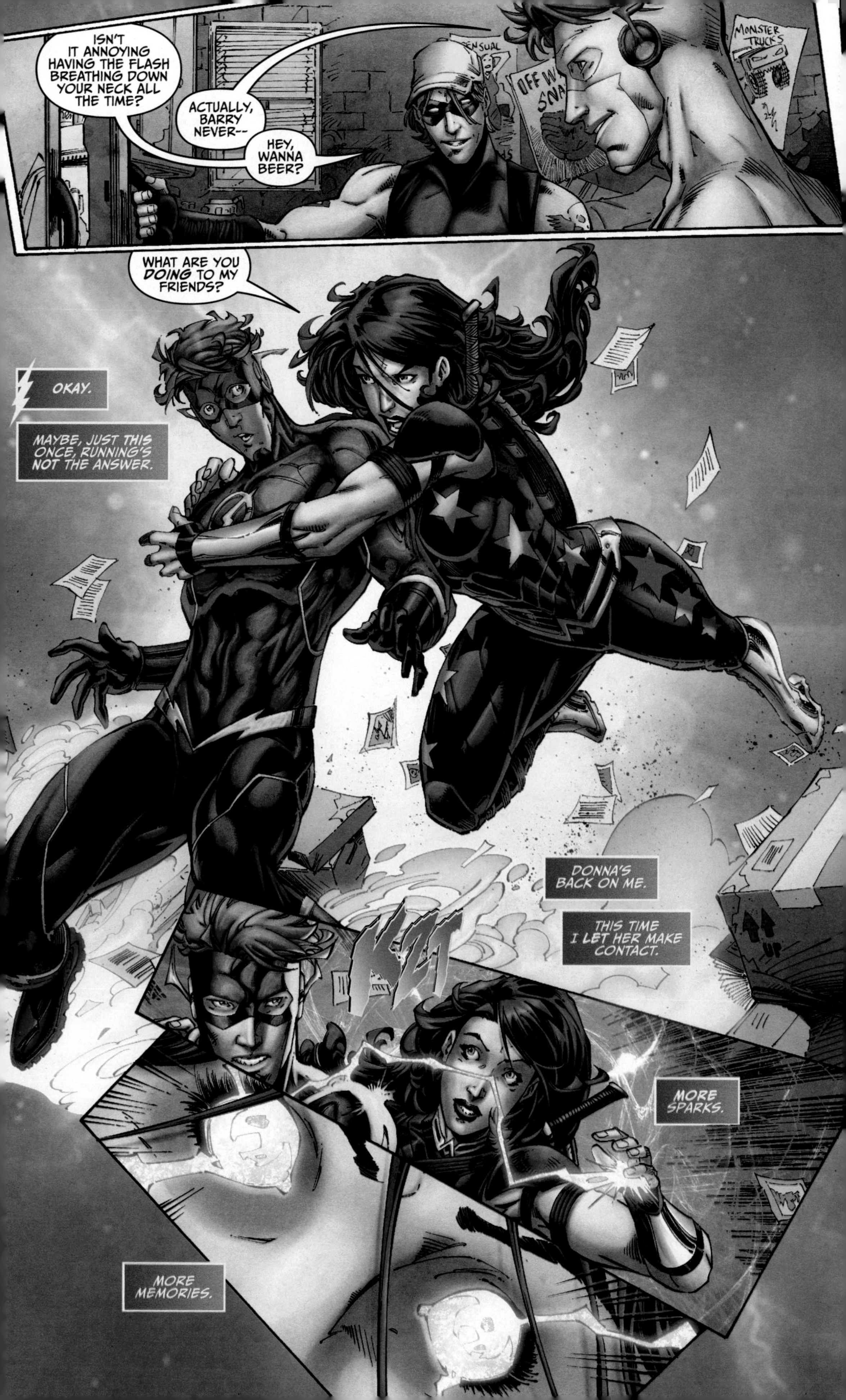

ISN'T IT ANNOYING HAVING THE FLASH BREATHING DOWN YOUR NECK ALL THE TIME?
ACTUALLY, BARRY NEVER--
HEY, WANNA BEER?
SENSUAL
OFF W SNA
MONSTER TRUCKS
WHAT ARE YOU DOING TO MY FRIENDS?
OKAY.
MAYBE, JUST THIS ONCE, RUNNING'S NOT THE ANSWER.
DONNA'S BACK ON ME.
THIS TIME I LET HER MAKE CONTACT.
KZT
MORE SPARKS.
MORE MEMORIES.

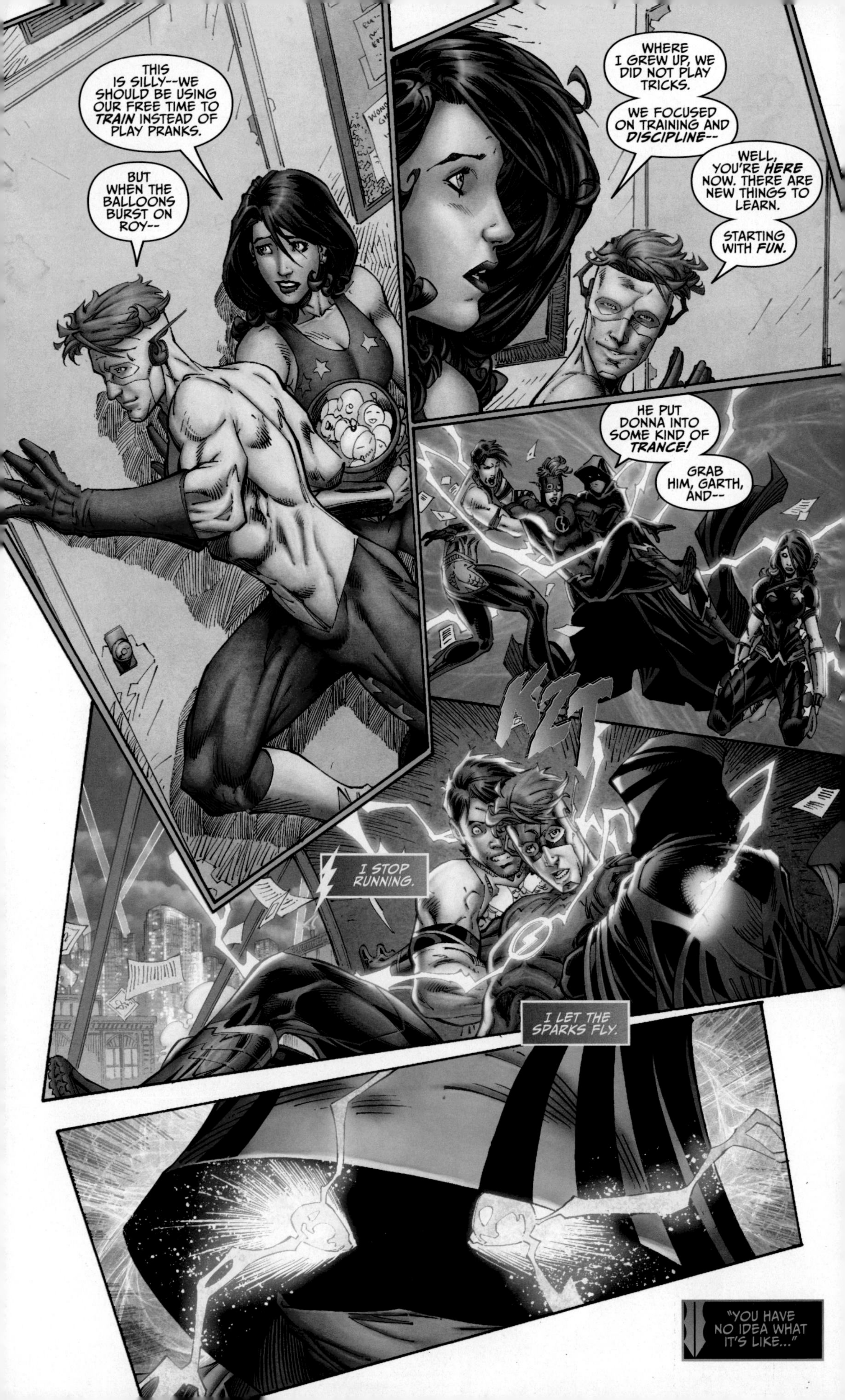
THIS IS SILLY--WE SHOULD BE USING OUR FREE TIME TO TRAIN INSTEAD OF PLAY PRANKS.
BUT WHEN THE BALLOONS BURST ON ROY--
WHERE I GREW UP, WE DID NOT PLAY TRICKS.
WE FOCUSED ON TRAINING AND DISCIPLINE--
WELL, YOU'RE HERE NOW. THERE ARE NEW THINGS TO LEARN.
STARTING WITH FUN.
HE PUT DONNA INTO SOME KIND OF TRANCE!
GRAB HIM, GARTH, AND--
KZT
I STOP RUNNING.
I LET THE SPARKS FLY.
"YOU HAVE NO IDEA WHAT IT'S LIKE..."

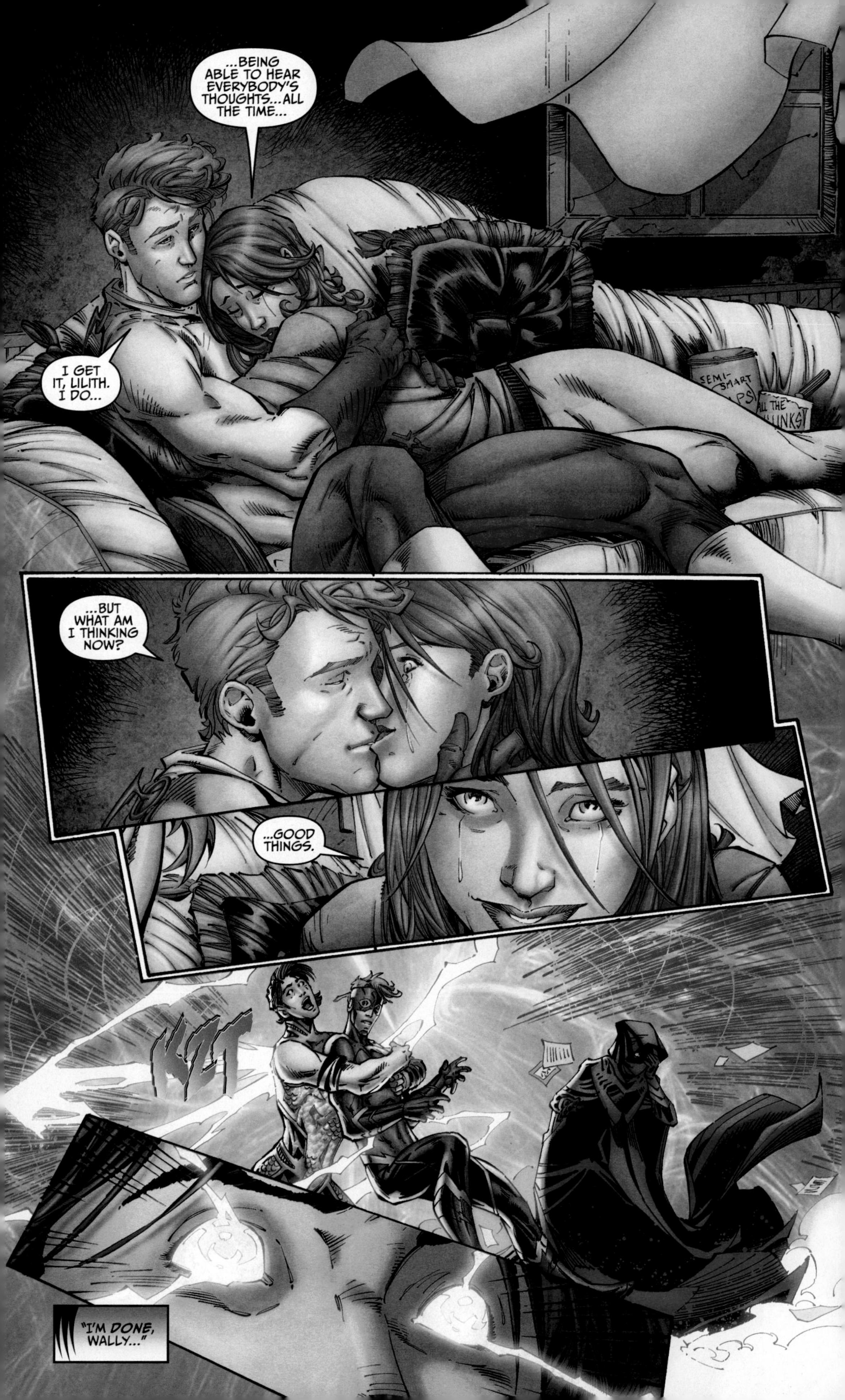

...BEING ABLE TO HEAR EVERYBODY'S THOUGHTS...ALL THE TIME...
I GET IT, LILITH. I DO...
SEMI-SMART
ALL THE
...BUT WHAT AM I THINKING NOW?
...GOOD THINGS.
KZT
"I'M DONE, WALLY..."

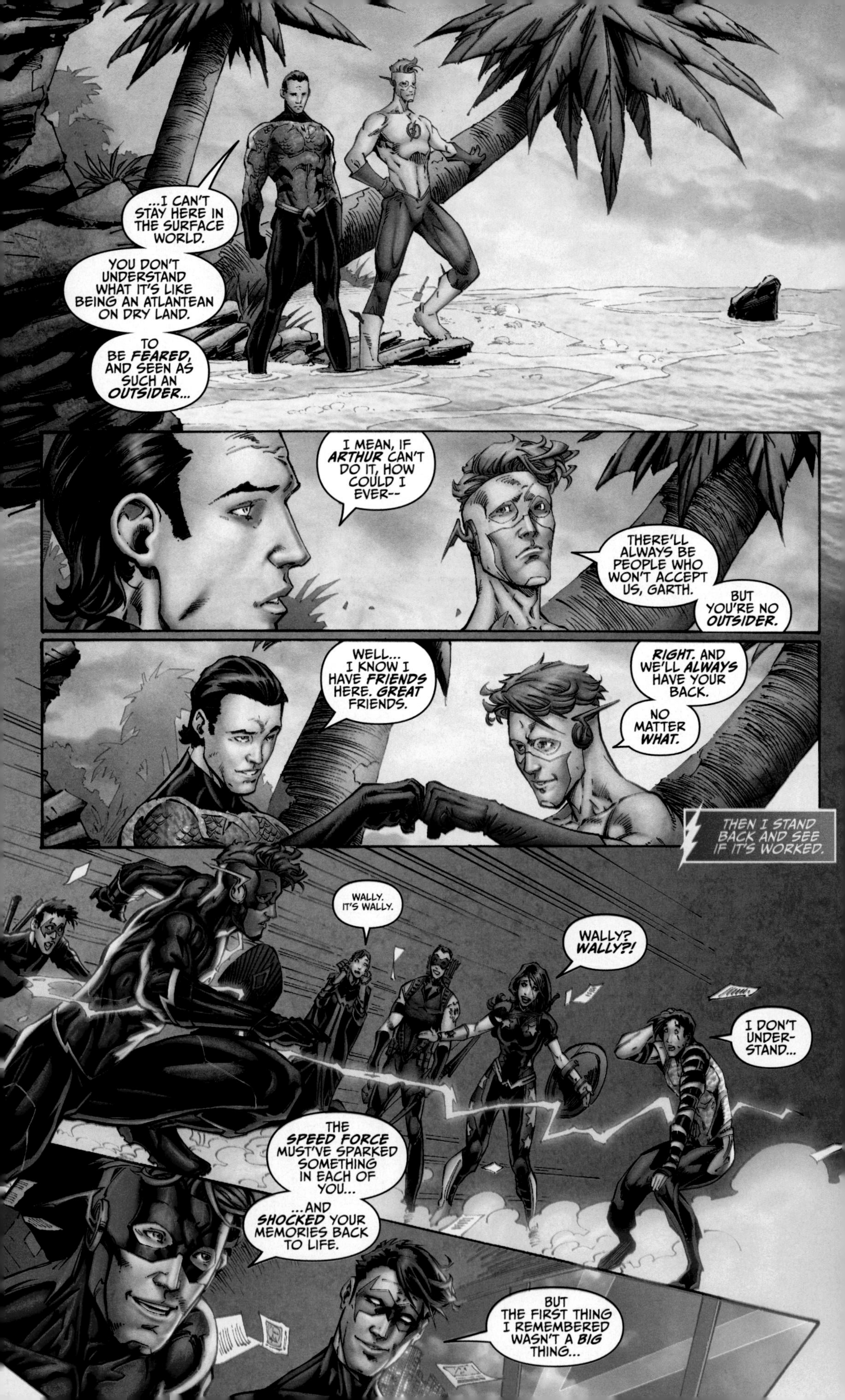

...I CAN'T STAY HERE IN THE SURFACE WORLD.
YOU DON'T UNDERSTAND WHAT IT'S LIKE BEING AN ATLANTEAN ON DRY LAND.
TO BE FEARED, AND SEEN AS SUCH AN OUTSIDER...
I MEAN, IF ARTHUR CAN'T DO IT, HOW COULD I EVER--
THERE'LL ALWAYS BE PEOPLE WHO WON'T ACCEPT US, GARTH.
BUT YOU'RE NO OUTSIDER.
WELL... I KNOW I HAVE FRIENDS HERE. GREAT FRIENDS.
RIGHT. AND WE'LL ALWAYS HAVE YOUR BACK.
NO MATTER WHAT.
THEN I STAND BACK AND SEE IF IT'S WORKED.
WALLY. IT'S WALLY.
WALLY? WALLY?!
I DON'T UNDER-STAND...
THE SPEED FORCE MUST'VE SPARKED SOMETHING IN EACH OF YOU...
...AND SHOCKED YOUR MEMORIES BACK TO LIFE.
BUT THE FIRST THING I REMEMBERED WASN'T A BIG THING...

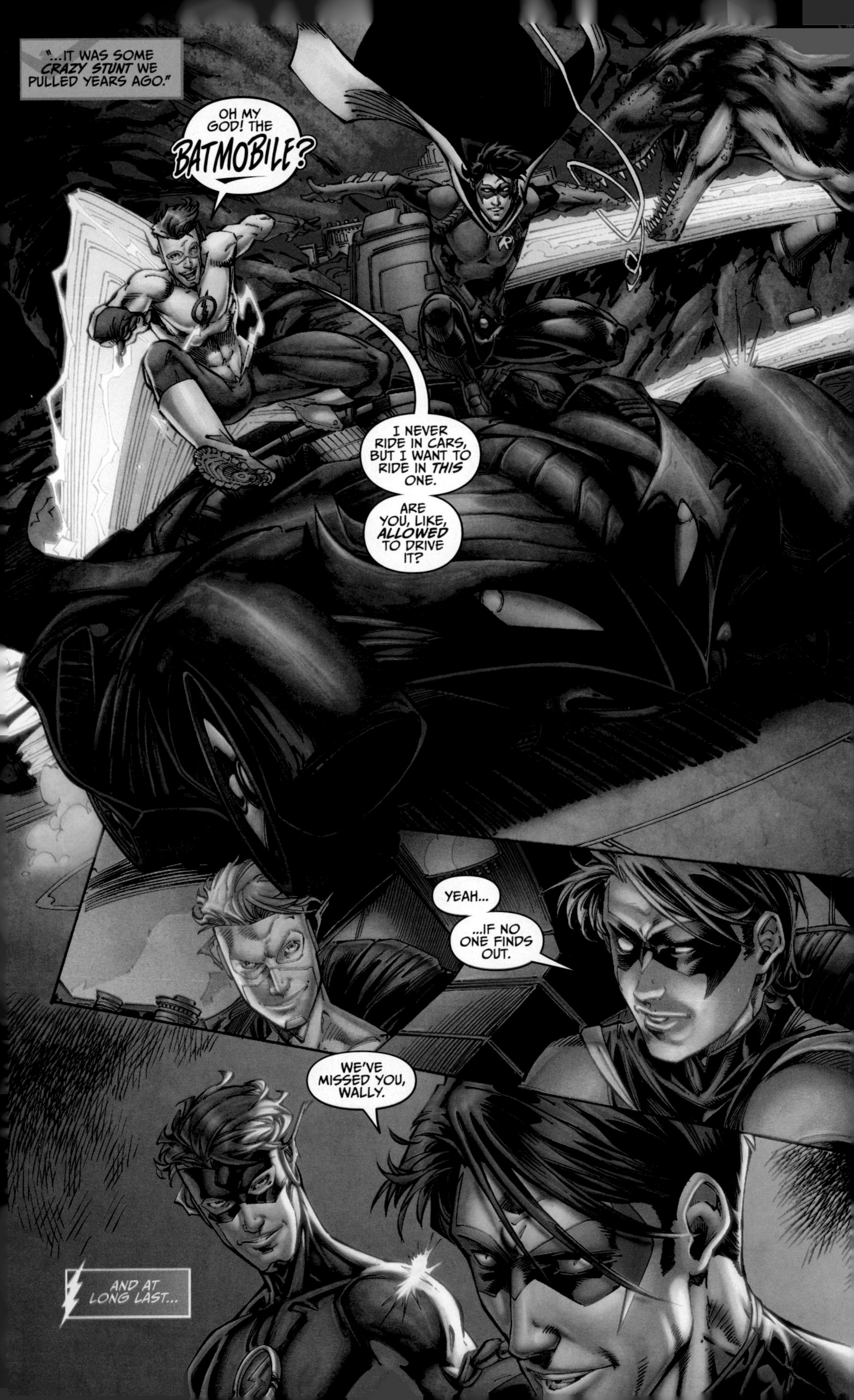
"...IT WAS SOME CRAZY STUNT WE PULLED YEARS AGO."
OH MY GOD! THE BATMOBILE?
I NEVER RIDE IN CARS, BUT I WANT TO RIDE IN THIS ONE.
ARE YOU, LIKE, ALLOWED TO DRIVE IT?
YEAH...
...IF NO ONE FINDS OUT.
WE'VE MISSED YOU, WALLY.
AND AT LONG LAST...

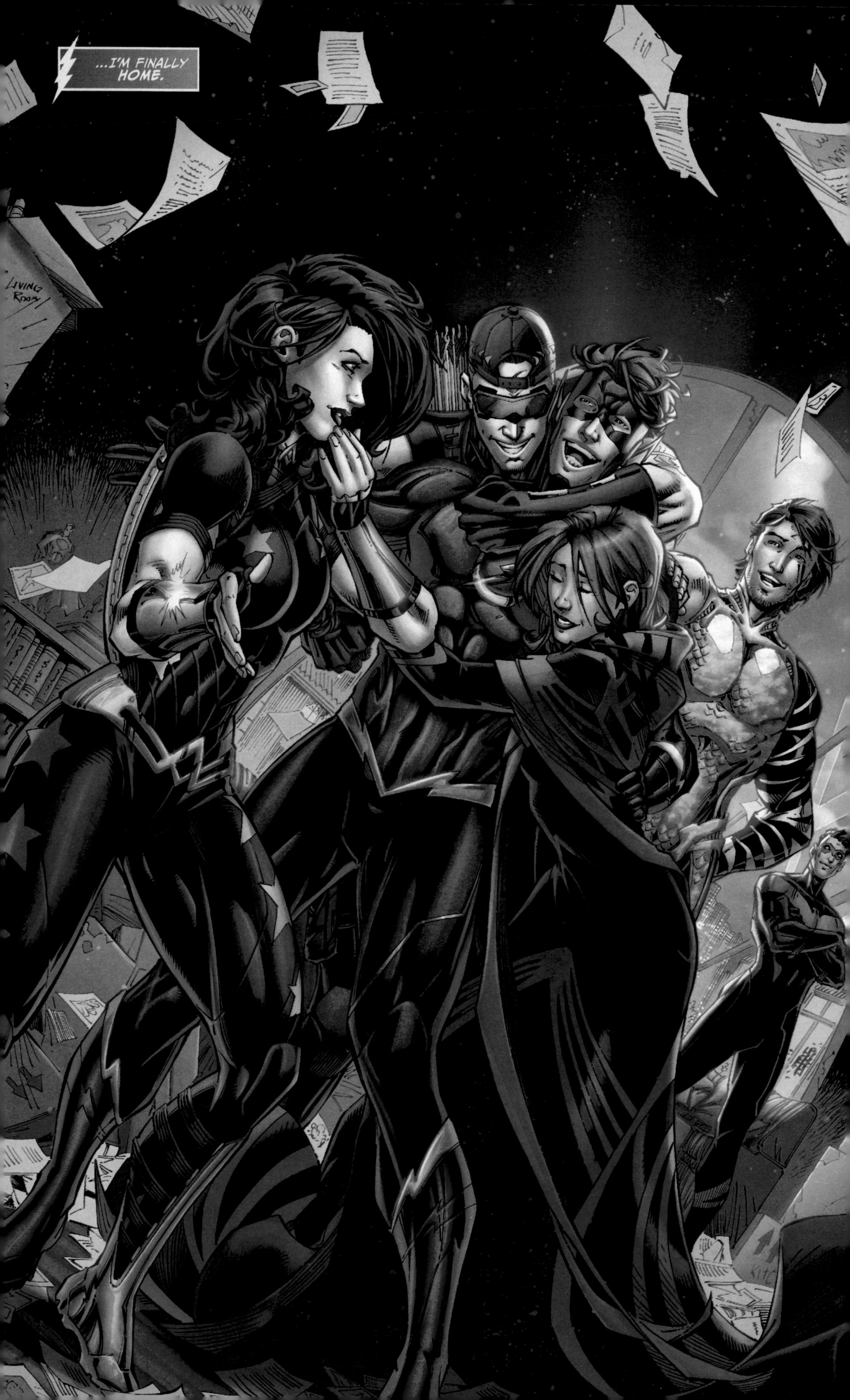
...I'M FINALLY HOME.

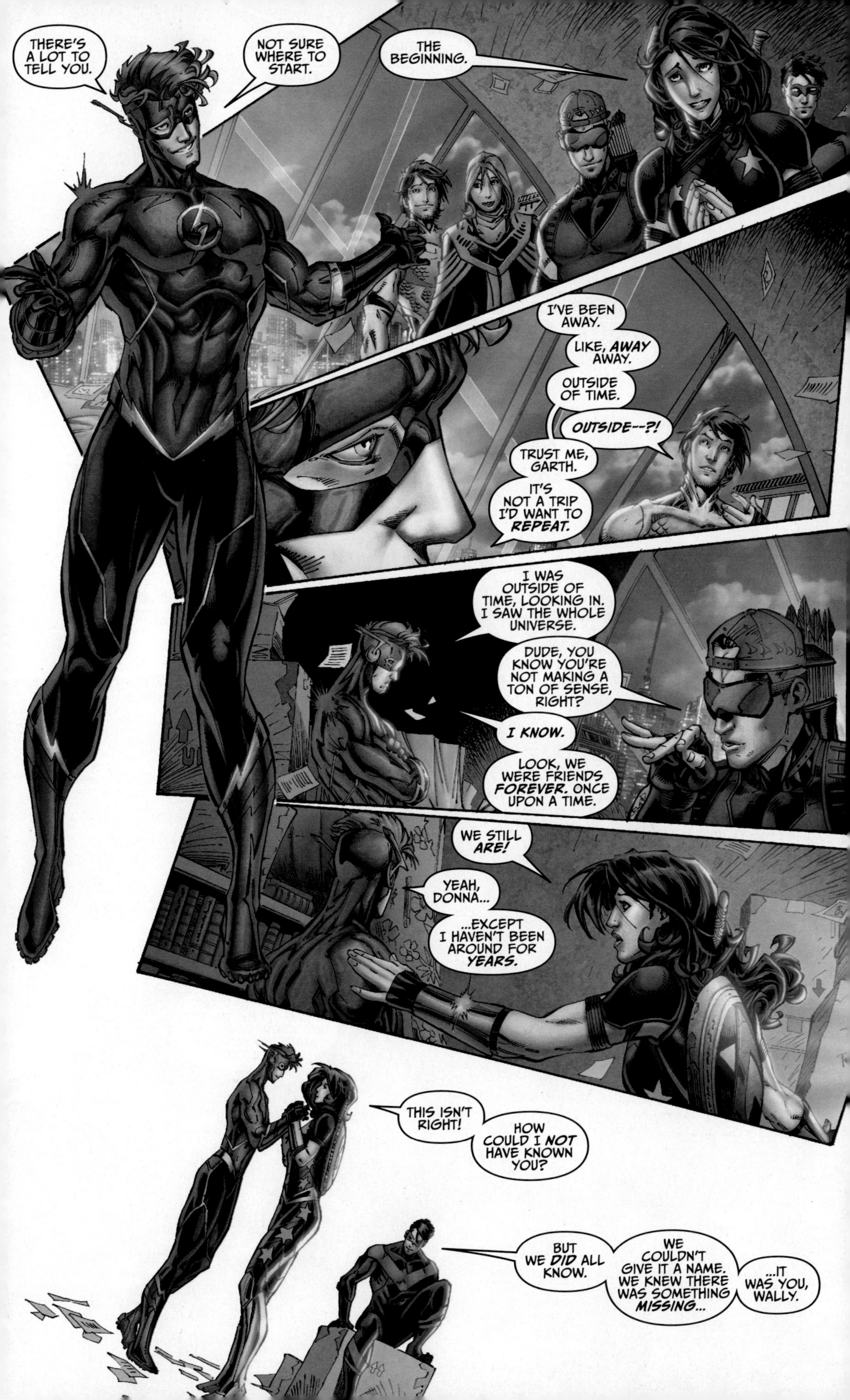
THERE'S A LOT TO TELL YOU.
NOT SURE WHERE TO START.
THE BEGINNING.
I'VE BEEN AWAY.
LIKE, *AWAY* AWAY.
OUTSIDE OF TIME.
OUTSIDE--?!
TRUST ME, GARTH.
IT'S NOT A TRIP I'D WANT TO *REPEAT.*
I WAS OUTSIDE OF TIME, LOOKING IN. I SAW THE WHOLE UNIVERSE.
DUDE, YOU KNOW YOU'RE NOT MAKING A TON OF SENSE, RIGHT?
I KNOW.
LOOK, WE WERE FRIENDS *FOREVER.* ONCE UPON A TIME.
WE STILL *ARE!*
YEAH, DONNA...
...EXCEPT I HAVEN'T BEEN AROUND FOR *YEARS.*
THIS ISN'T RIGHT!
HOW COULD I *NOT* HAVE KNOWN YOU?
BUT WE *DID* ALL KNOW.
WE COULDN'T GIVE IT A NAME. WE KNEW THERE WAS SOMETHING *MISSING...*
...IT WAS YOU, WALLY.

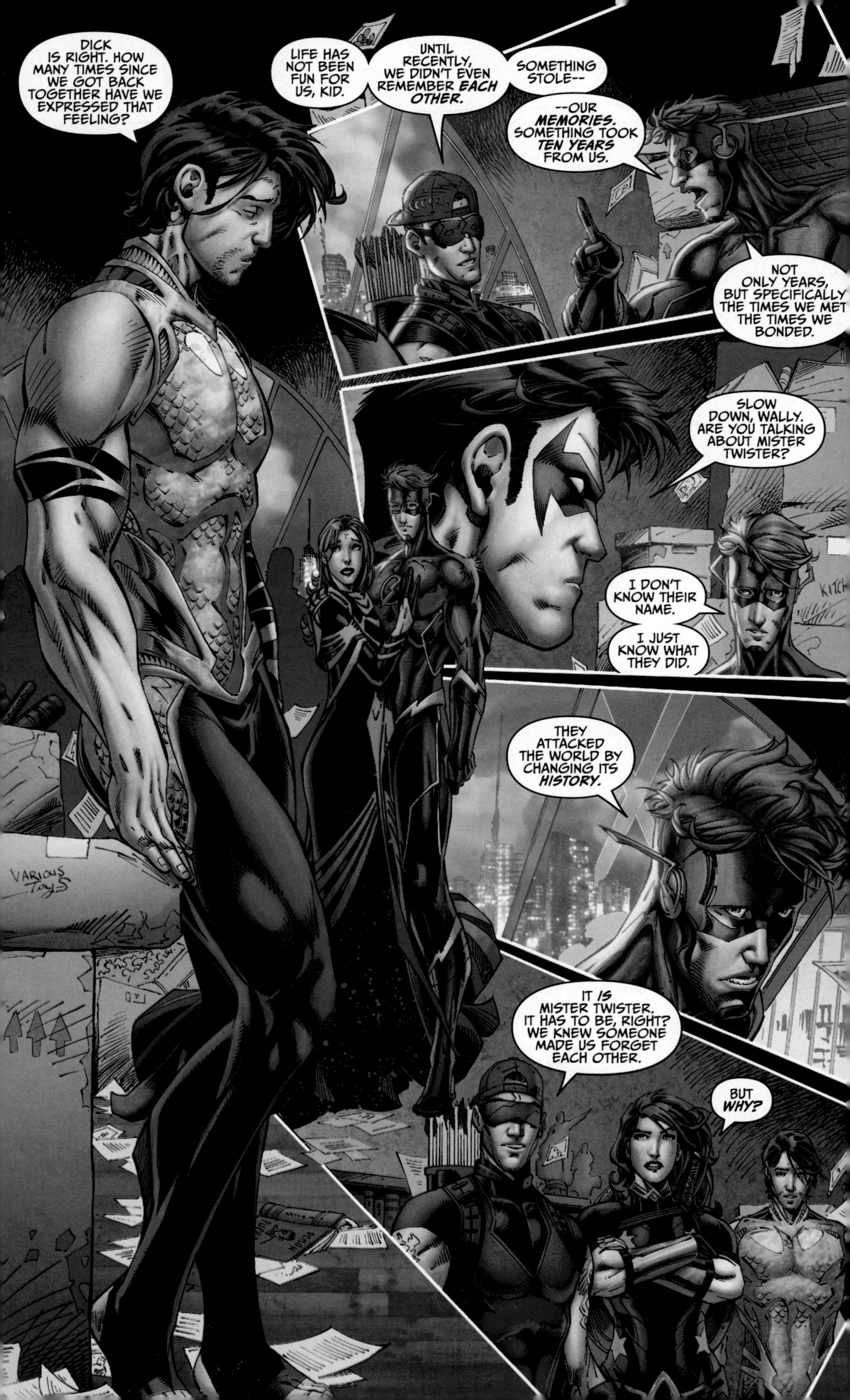
DICK IS RIGHT. HOW MANY TIMES SINCE WE GOT BACK TOGETHER HAVE WE EXPRESSED THAT FEELING?
LIFE HAS NOT BEEN FUN FOR US, KID.
UNTIL RECENTLY, WE DIDN'T EVEN REMEMBER *EACH OTHER.*
SOMETHING STOLE--
--OUR *MEMORIES.* SOMETHING TOOK *TEN YEARS* FROM US.
NOT ONLY YEARS, BUT SPECIFICALLY THE TIMES WE MET THE TIMES WE BONDED.
SLOW DOWN, WALLY. ARE YOU TALKING ABOUT MISTER TWISTER?
I DON'T KNOW THEIR NAME.
I JUST KNOW WHAT THEY DID.
THEY ATTACKED THE WORLD BY CHANGING ITS *HISTORY.*
IT *IS* MISTER TWISTER. IT HAS TO BE, RIGHT? WE KNEW SOMEONE MADE US FORGET EACH OTHER.
BUT *WHY?*
VARIOUS TOYS

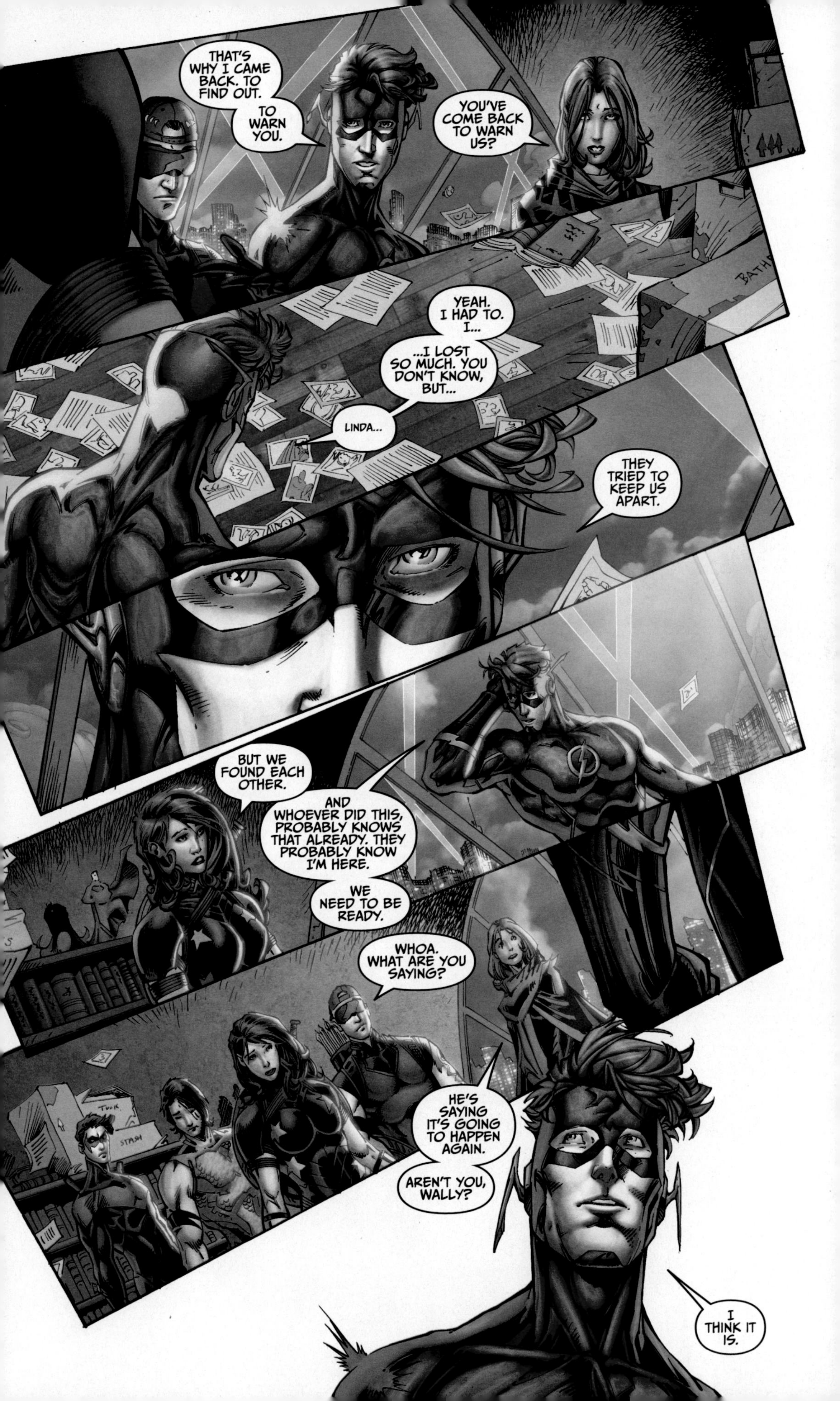
THAT'S WHY I CAME BACK. TO FIND OUT.
TO WARN YOU.
YOU'VE COME BACK TO WARN US?
BATH
YEAH. I HAD TO. I...
...I LOST SO MUCH. YOU DON'T KNOW, BUT...
LINDA...
THEY TRIED TO KEEP US APART.
BUT WE FOUND EACH OTHER.
AND WHOEVER DID THIS, PROBABLY KNOWS THAT ALREADY. THEY PROBABLY KNOW I'M HERE.
WE NEED TO BE READY.
WHOA. WHAT ARE YOU SAYING?
HE'S SAYING IT'S GOING TO HAPPEN AGAIN.
AREN'T YOU, WALLY?
I THINK IT IS.

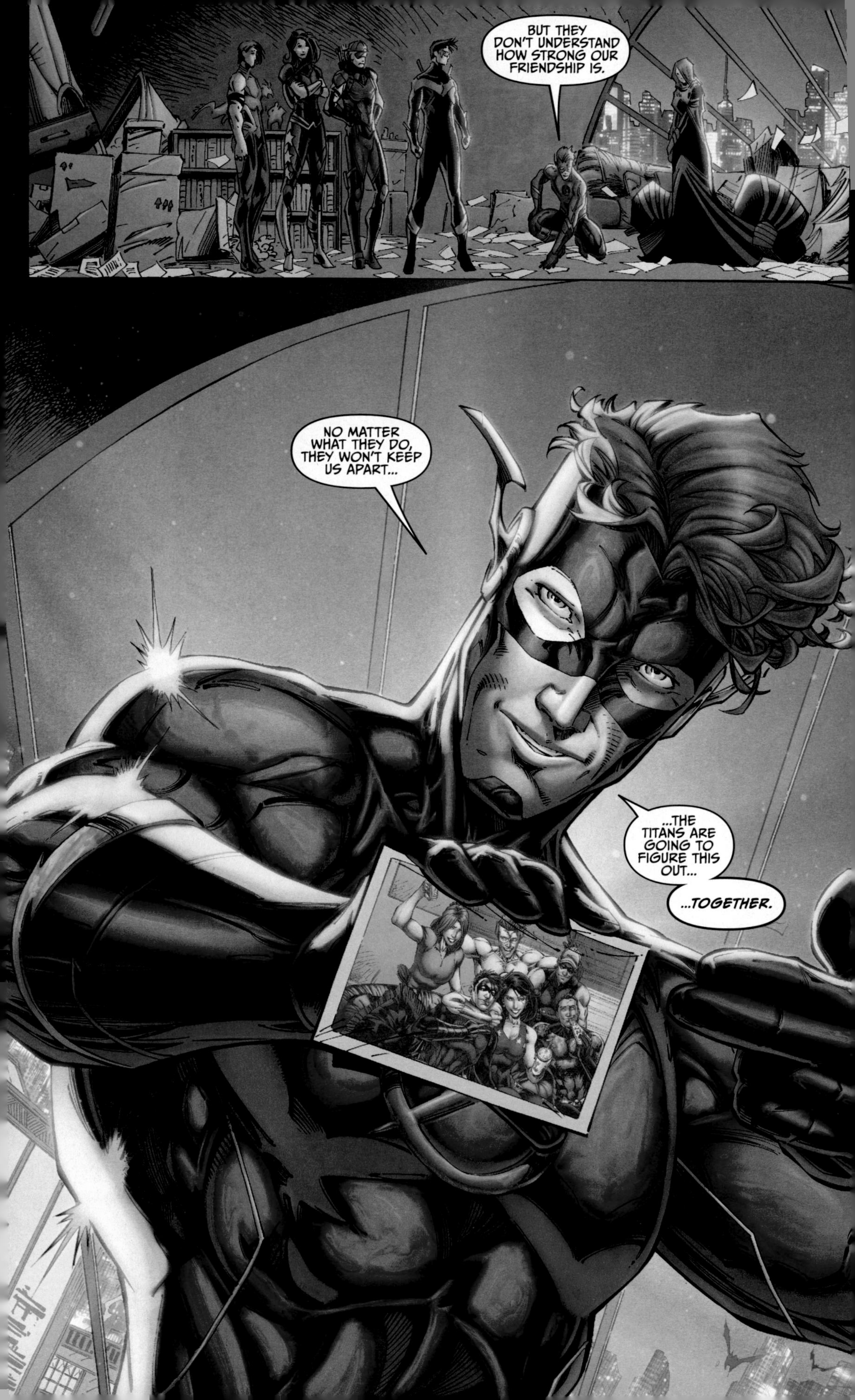
BUT THEY DON'T UNDERSTAND HOW STRONG OUR FRIENDSHIP IS.
NO MATTER WHAT THEY DO, THEY WON'T KEEP US APART...
...THE TITANS ARE GOING TO FIGURE THIS OUT...
...TOGETHER.

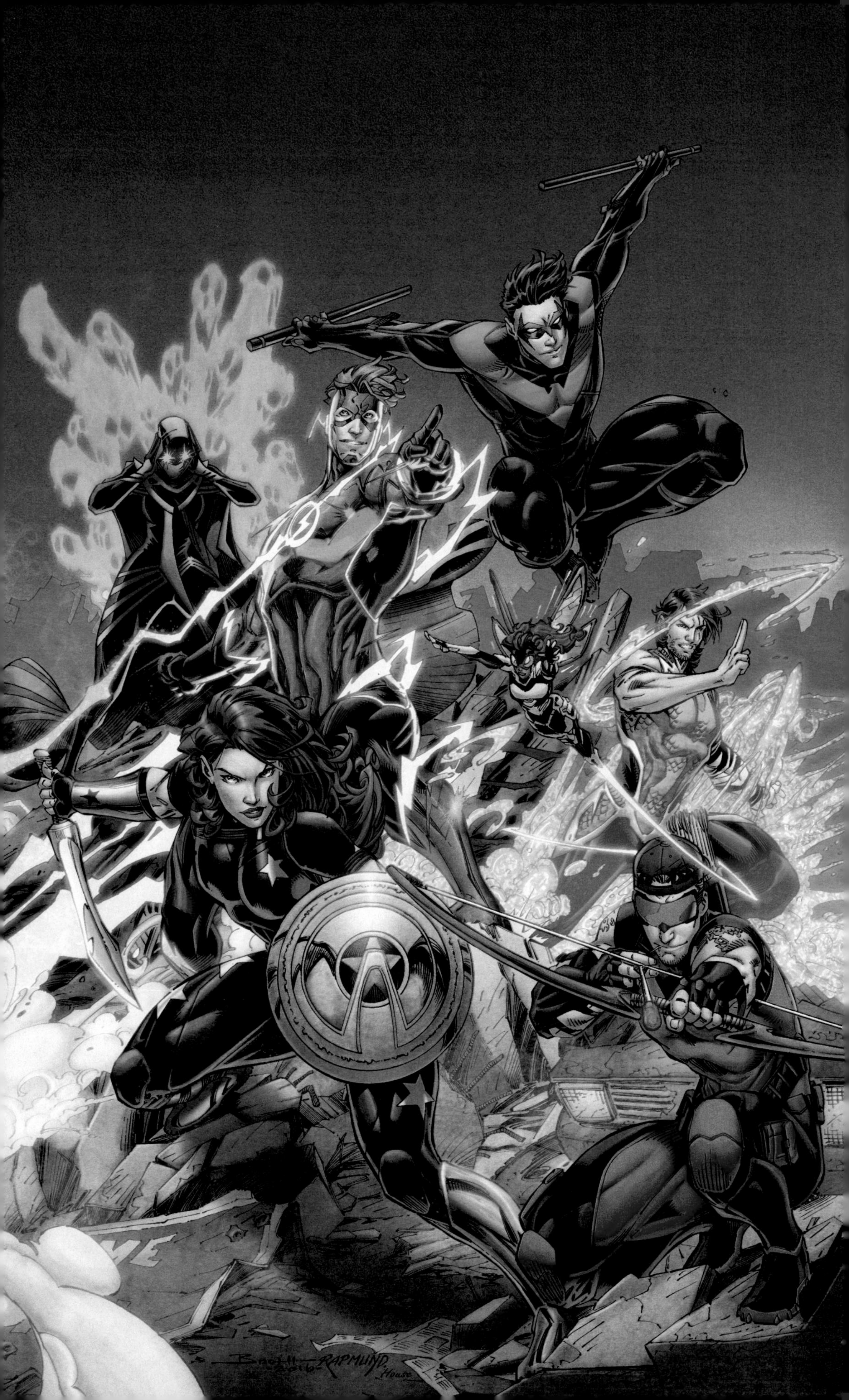

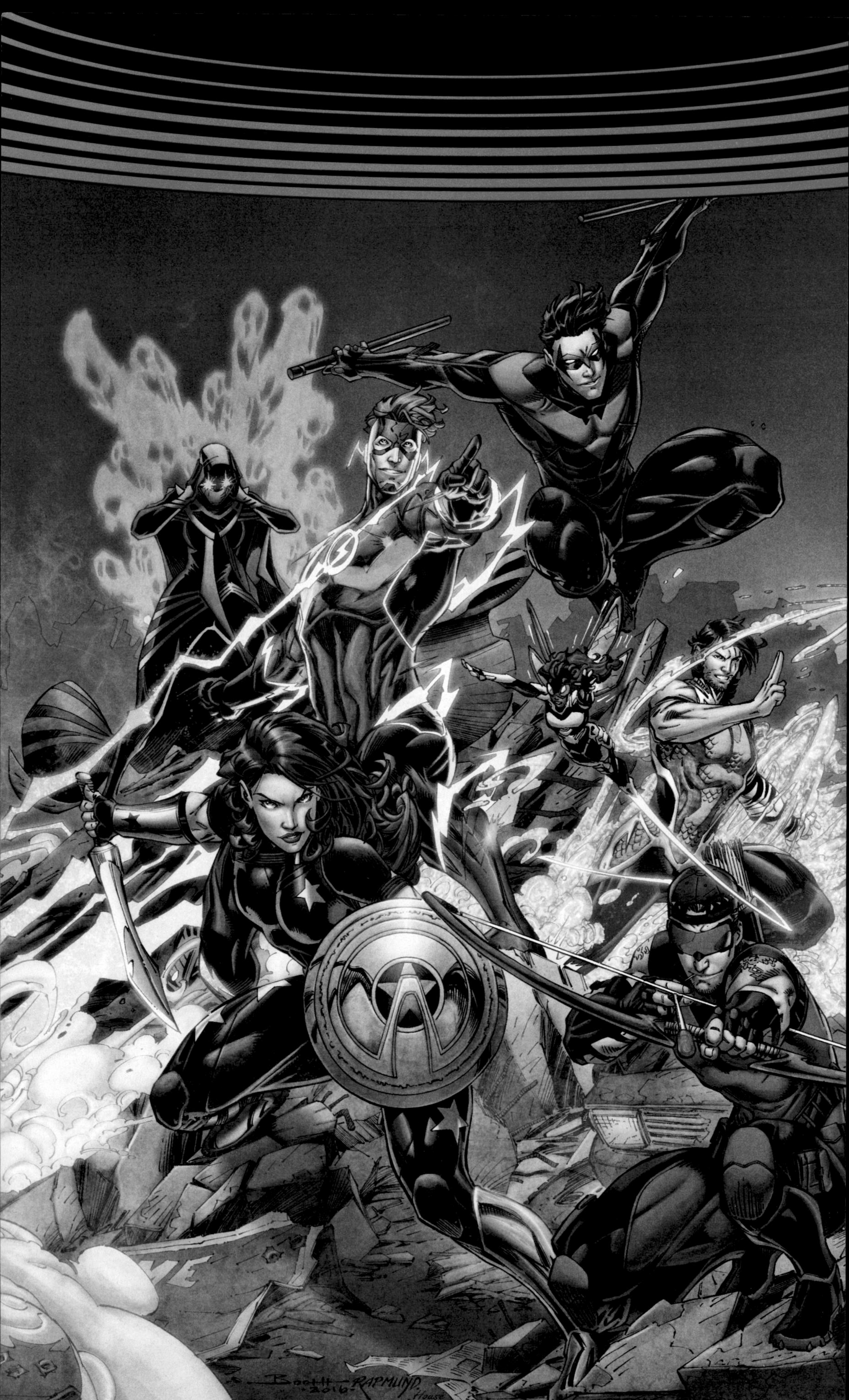
Booth 2016
RAPMUND
House

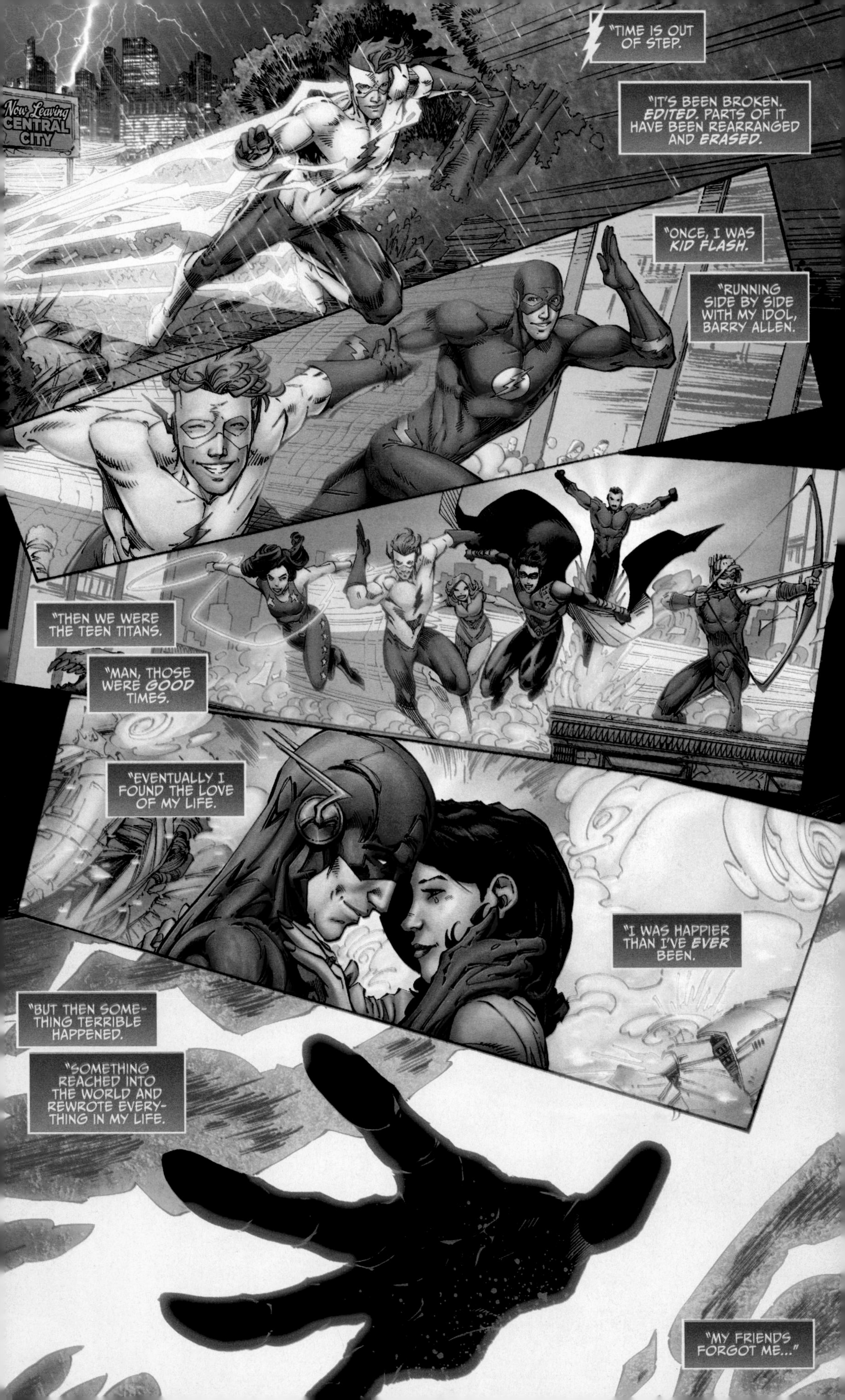
Now Leaving CENTRAL CITY
"TIME IS OUT OF STEP.
"IT'S BEEN BROKEN. EDITED. PARTS OF IT HAVE BEEN REARRANGED AND ERASED.
"ONCE, I WAS KID FLASH.
"RUNNING SIDE BY SIDE WITH MY IDOL, BARRY ALLEN.
"THEN WE WERE THE TEEN TITANS.
"MAN, THOSE WERE GOOD TIMES.
"EVENTUALLY I FOUND THE LOVE OF MY LIFE.
"I WAS HAPPIER THAN I'VE EVER BEEN.
"BUT THEN SOME-THING TERRIBLE HAPPENED.
"SOMETHING REACHED INTO THE WORLD AND REWROTE EVERY-THING IN MY LIFE.
"MY FRIENDS FORGOT ME..."

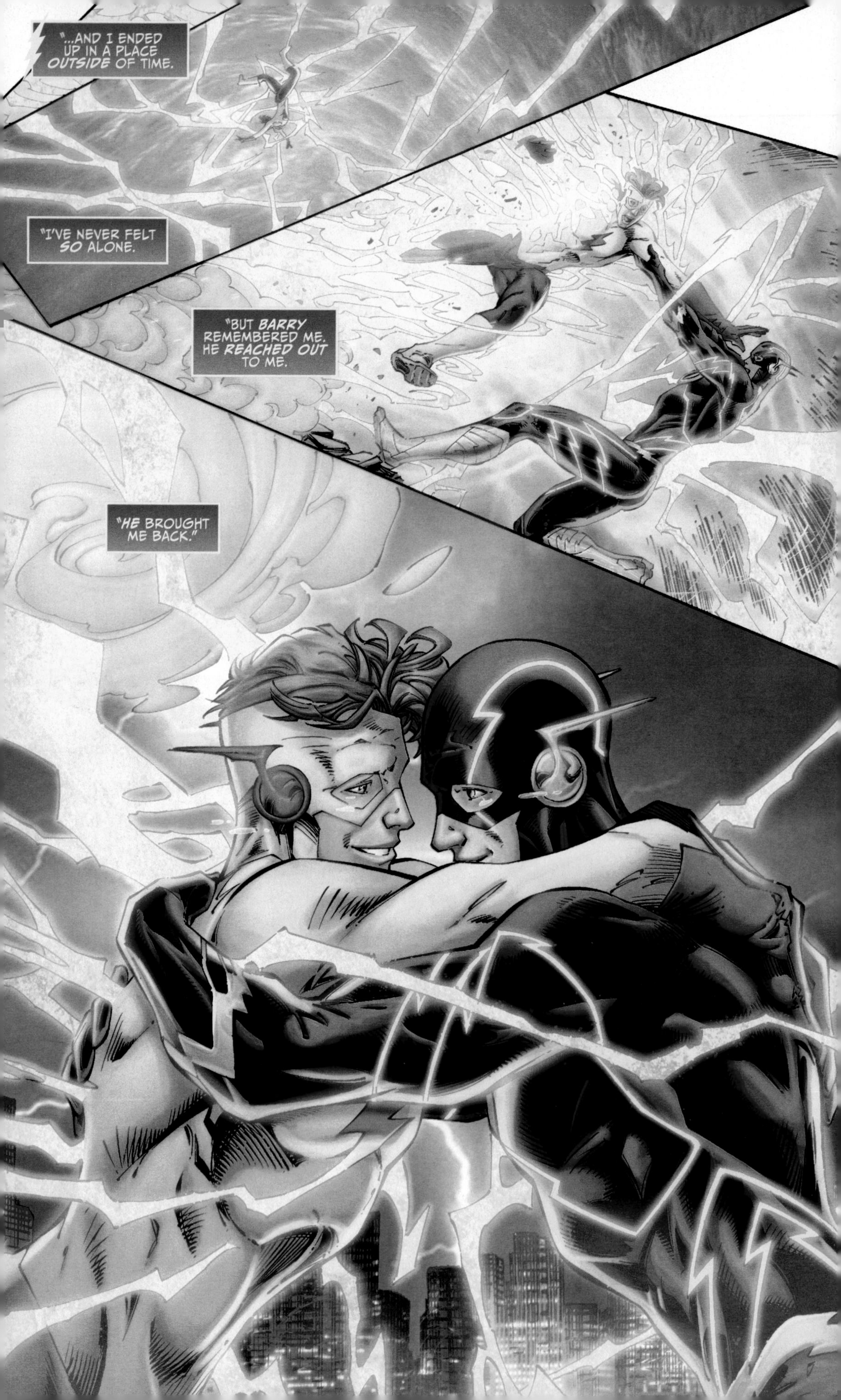
"...AND I ENDED UP IN A PLACE OUTSIDE OF TIME.
"I'VE NEVER FELT SO ALONE.
"BUT BARRY REMEMBERED ME. HE REACHED OUT TO ME.
"HE BROUGHT ME BACK."

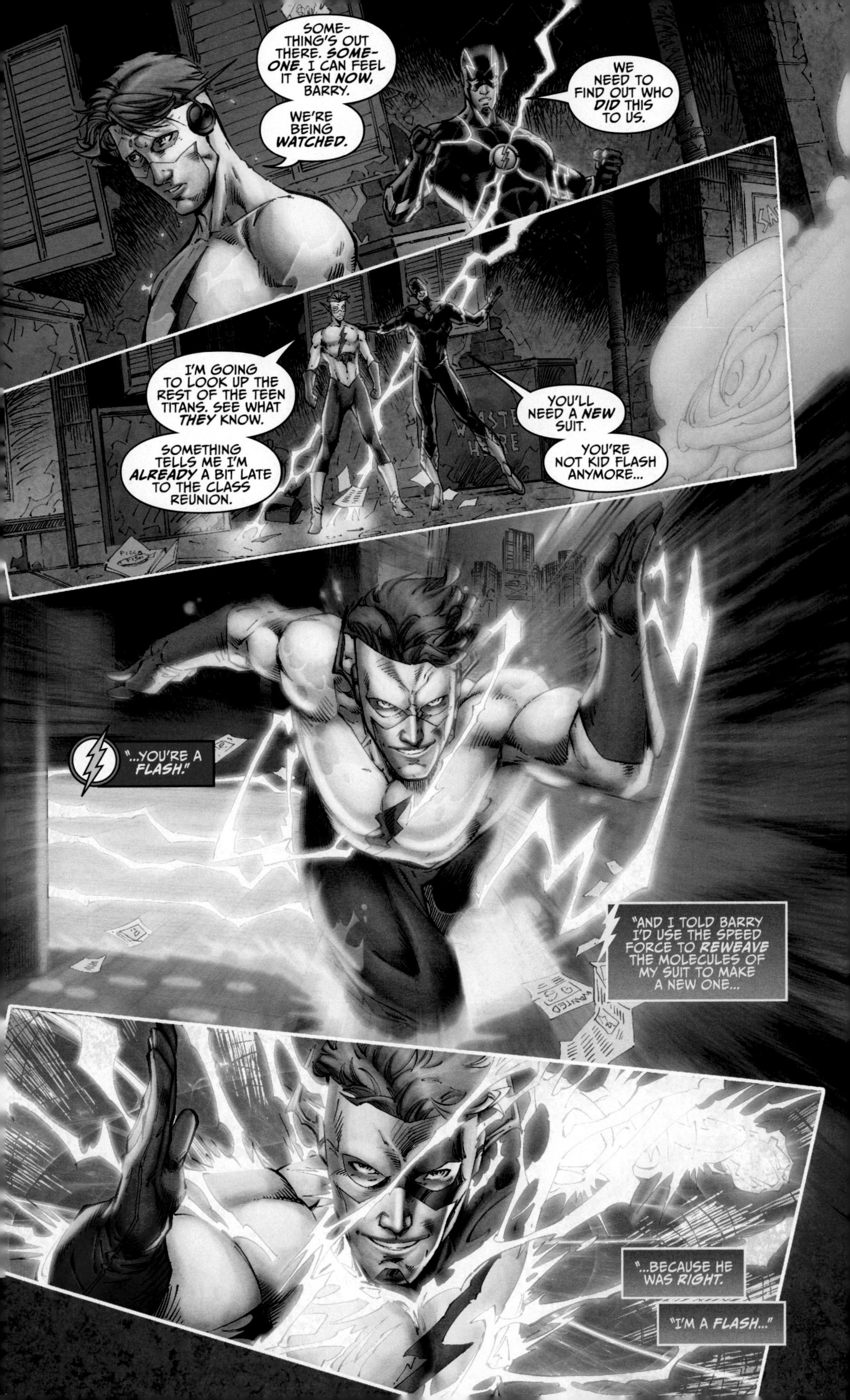
SOME-THING'S OUT THERE. SOME-ONE. I CAN FEEL IT EVEN NOW, BARRY.
WE'RE BEING WATCHED.
WE NEED TO FIND OUT WHO DID THIS TO US.
I'M GOING TO LOOK UP THE REST OF THE TEEN TITANS. SEE WHAT THEY KNOW.
SOMETHING TELLS ME I'M ALREADY A BIT LATE TO THE CLASS REUNION.
YOU'LL NEED A NEW SUIT.
YOU'RE NOT KID FLASH ANYMORE...
"...YOU'RE A FLASH."
"AND I TOLD BARRY I'D USE THE SPEED FORCE TO REWEAVE THE MOLECULES OF MY SUIT TO MAKE A NEW ONE...
"...BECAUSE HE WAS RIGHT.
"I'M A FLASH..."

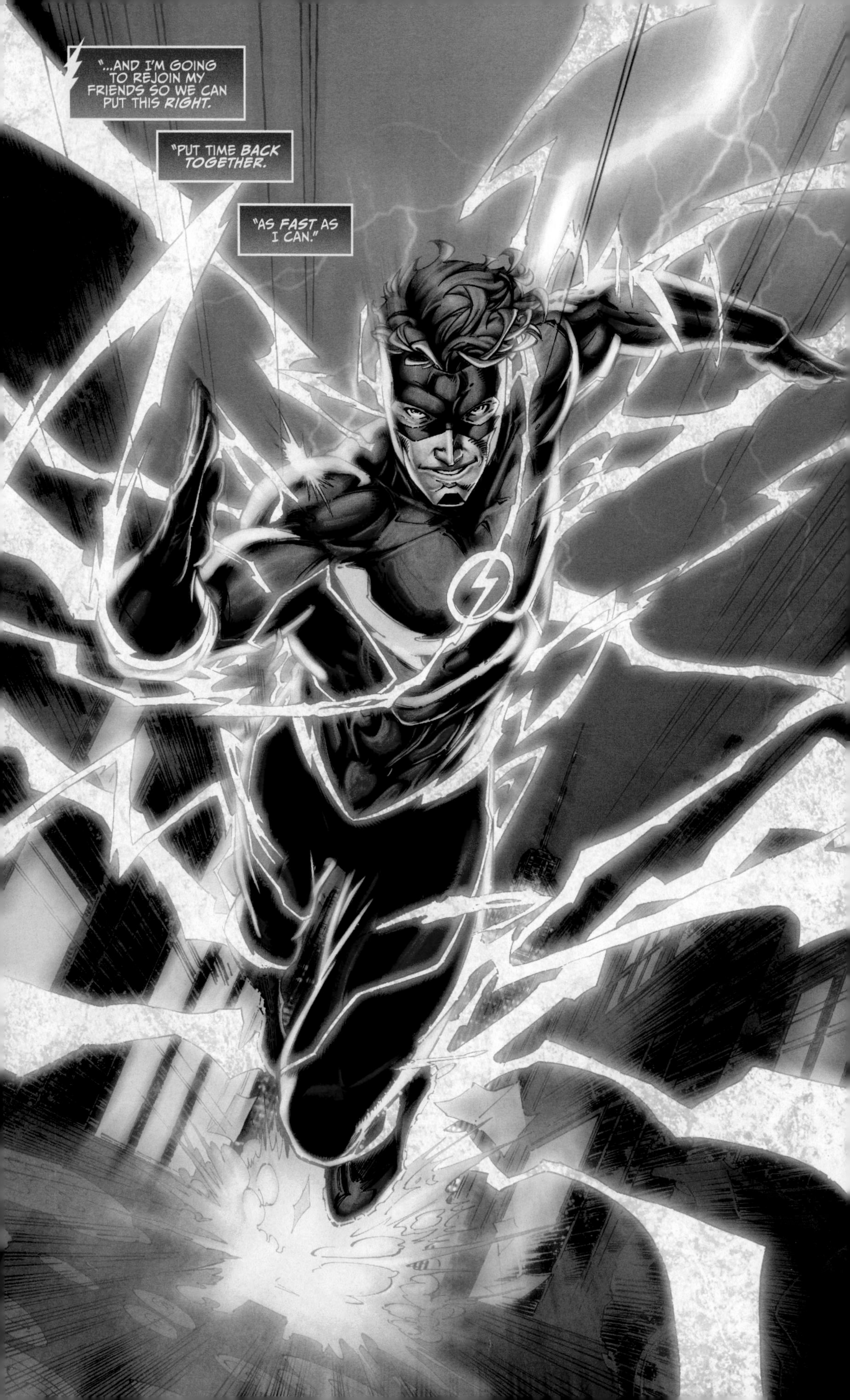
"...AND I'M GOING TO REJOIN MY FRIENDS SO WE CAN PUT THIS RIGHT.
"PUT TIME BACK TOGETHER.
"AS FAST AS I CAN."

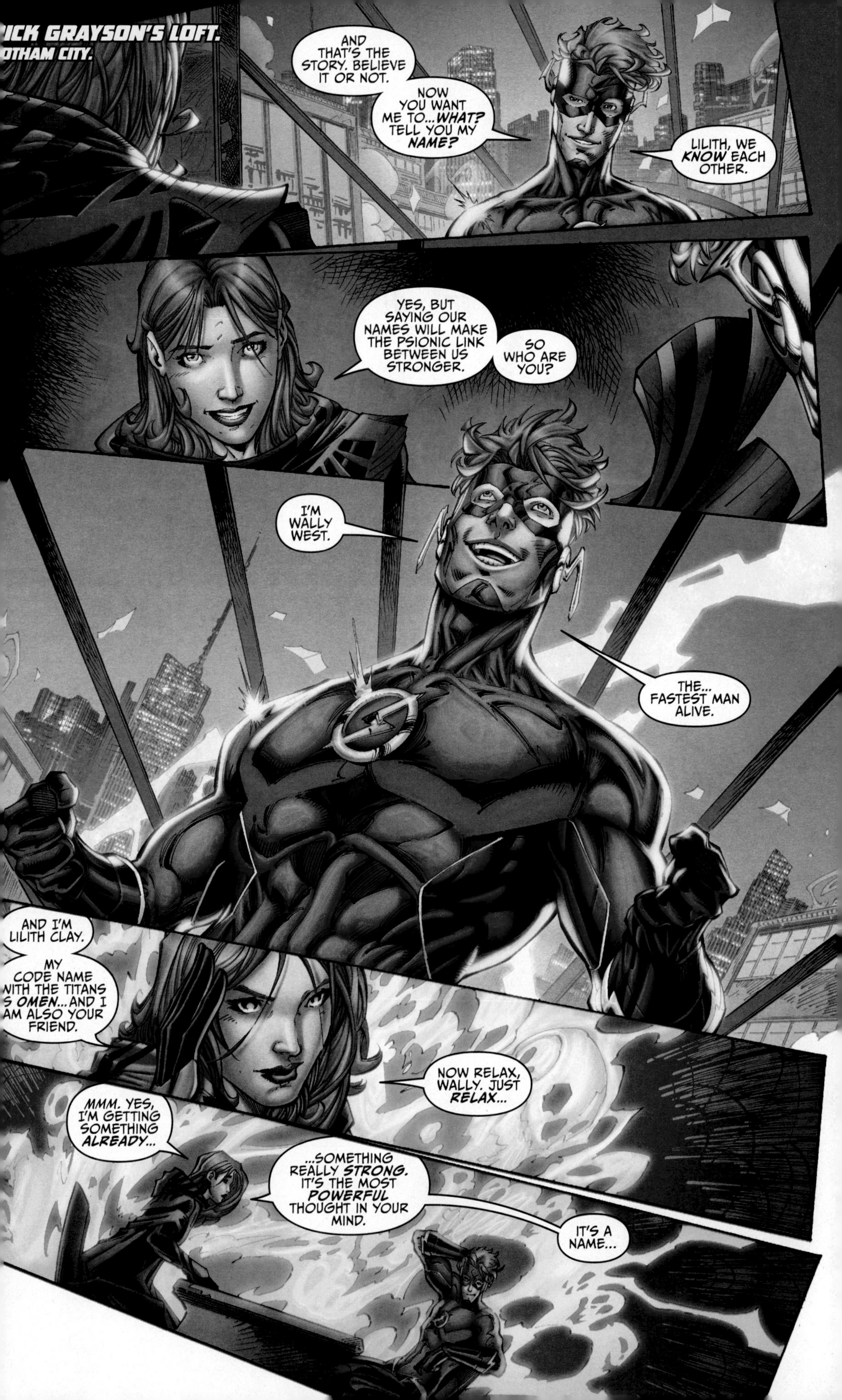

ICK GRAYSON'S LOFT.
OTHAM CITY.
AND THAT'S THE STORY. BELIEVE IT OR NOT.
NOW YOU WANT ME TO...WHAT? TELL YOU MY NAME?
LILITH, WE KNOW EACH OTHER.
YES, BUT SAYING OUR NAMES WILL MAKE THE PSIONIC LINK BETWEEN US STRONGER.
SO WHO ARE YOU?
I'M WALLY WEST.
THE... FASTEST MAN ALIVE.
AND I'M LILITH CLAY.
MY CODE NAME WITH THE TITANS S OMEN...AND I AM ALSO YOUR FRIEND.
NOW RELAX, WALLY. JUST RELAX...
MMM. YES, I'M GETTING SOMETHING ALREADY...
...SOMETHING REALLY STRONG. IT'S THE MOST POWERFUL THOUGHT IN YOUR MIND.
IT'S A NAME...

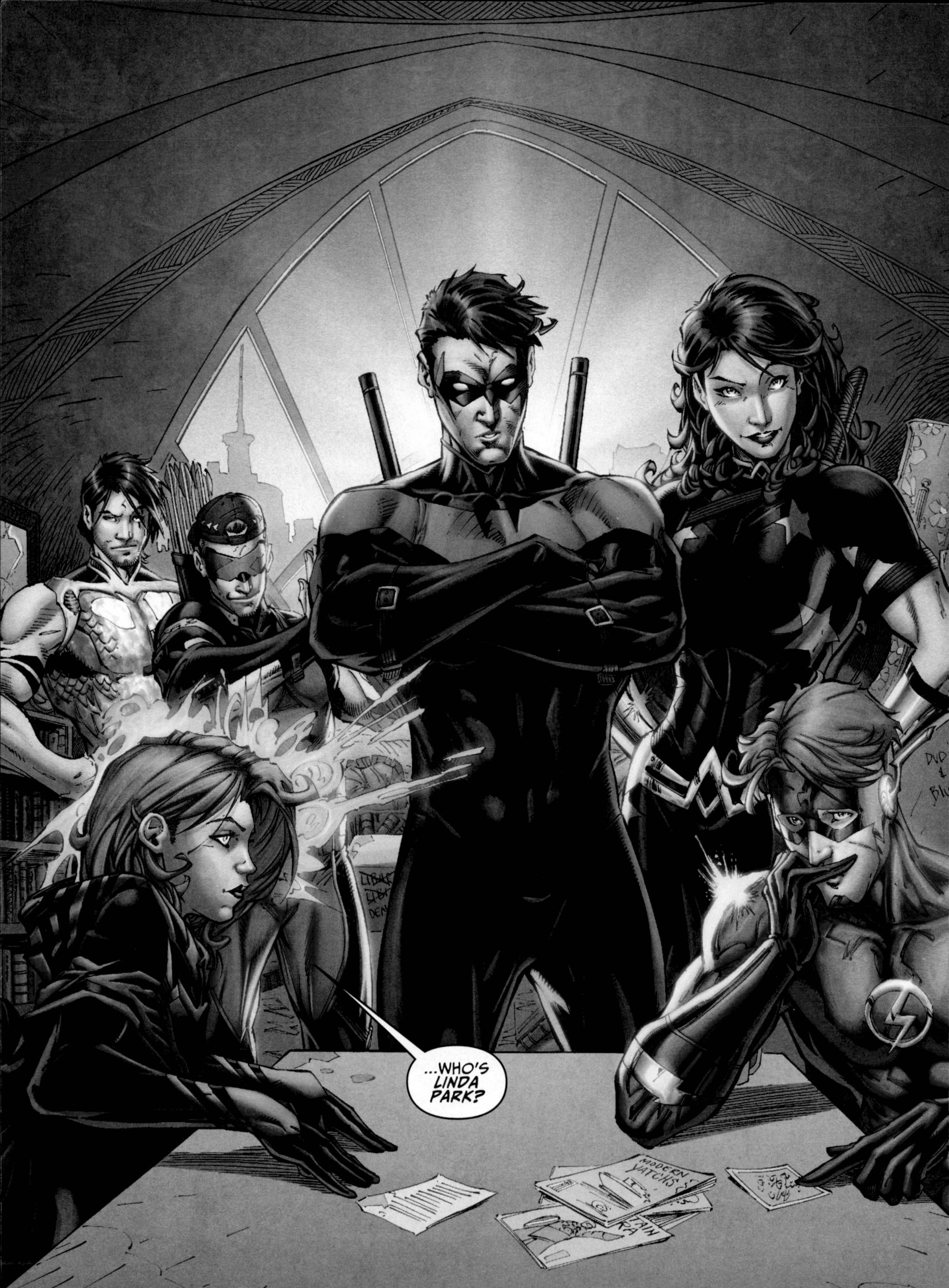
...WHO'S LINDA PARK?

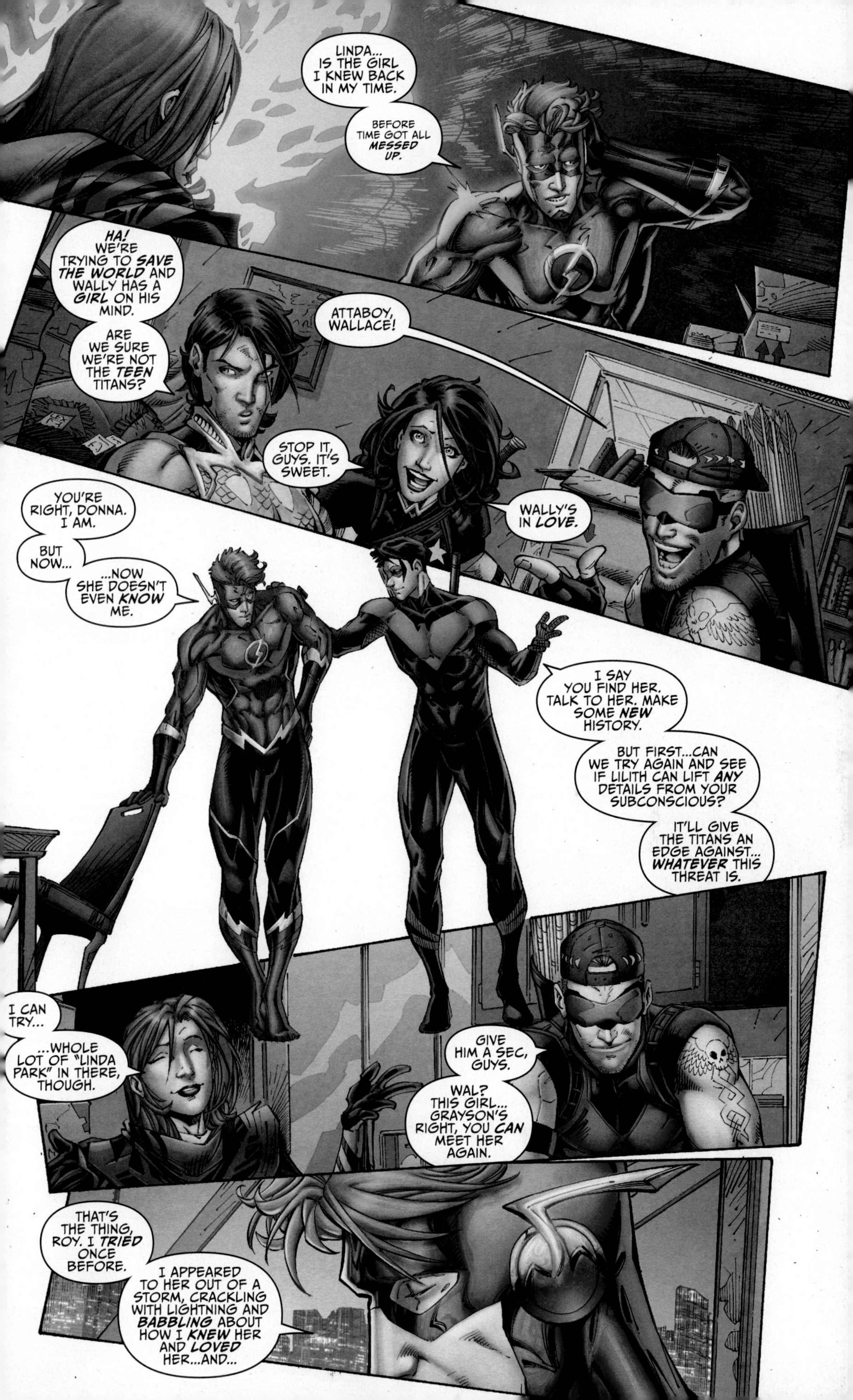
LINDA... IS THE GIRL I KNEW BACK IN MY TIME.
BEFORE TIME GOT ALL MESSED UP.
HA! WE'RE TRYING TO SAVE THE WORLD AND WALLY HAS A GIRL ON HIS MIND.
ARE WE SURE WE'RE NOT THE TEEN TITANS?
ATTABOY, WALLACE!
STOP IT, GUYS. IT'S SWEET.
WALLY'S IN LOVE.
YOU'RE RIGHT, DONNA. I AM.
BUT NOW...
...NOW SHE DOESN'T EVEN KNOW ME.
I SAY YOU FIND HER. TALK TO HER. MAKE SOME NEW HISTORY.
BUT FIRST...CAN WE TRY AGAIN AND SEE IF LILITH CAN LIFT ANY DETAILS FROM YOUR SUBCONSCIOUS?
IT'LL GIVE THE TITANS AN EDGE AGAINST... WHATEVER THIS THREAT IS.
I CAN TRY...
...WHOLE LOT OF "LINDA PARK" IN THERE, THOUGH.
GIVE HIM A SEC, GUYS.
WAL? THIS GIRL... GRAYSON'S RIGHT, YOU CAN MEET HER AGAIN.
THAT'S THE THING, ROY. I TRIED ONCE BEFORE.
I APPEARED TO HER OUT OF A STORM, CRACKLING WITH LIGHTNING AND BABBLING ABOUT HOW I KNEW HER AND LOVED HER...AND...

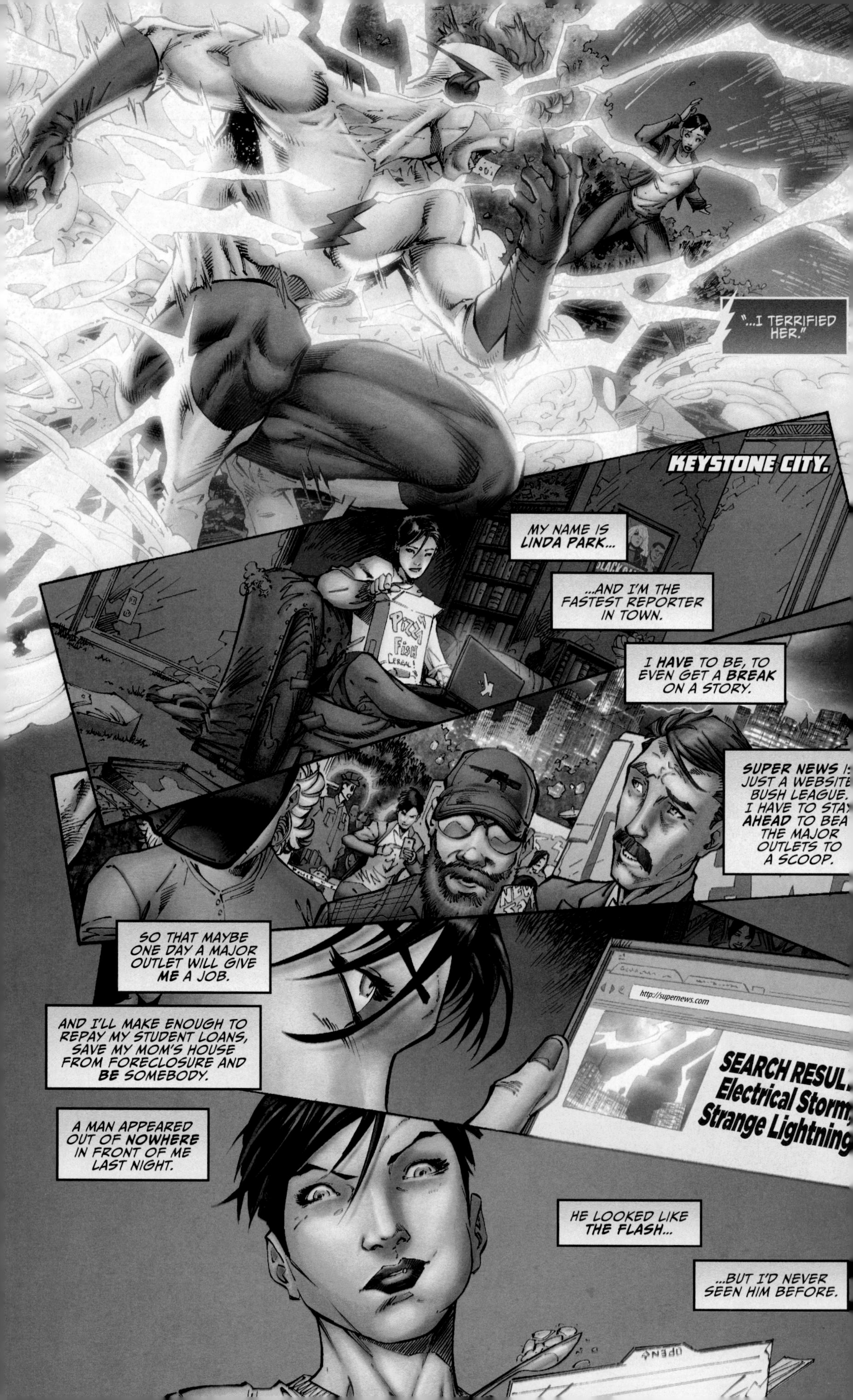
"...I TERRIFIED HER."
KEYSTONE CITY.
MY NAME IS LINDA PARK...
...AND I'M THE FASTEST REPORTER IN TOWN.
PIZZA FISH CEREAL!
I HAVE TO BE, TO EVEN GET A BREAK ON A STORY.
SUPER NEWS IS JUST A WEBSITE BUSH LEAGUE. I HAVE TO STAY AHEAD TO BEAT THE MAJOR OUTLETS TO A SCOOP.
SO THAT MAYBE ONE DAY A MAJOR OUTLET WILL GIVE ME A JOB.
http://supernews.com
SEARCH RESUL
Electrical Storm,
Strange Lightning
AND I'LL MAKE ENOUGH TO REPAY MY STUDENT LOANS, SAVE MY MOM'S HOUSE FROM FORECLOSURE AND BE SOMEBODY.
A MAN APPEARED OUT OF NOWHERE IN FRONT OF ME LAST NIGHT.
HE LOOKED LIKE THE FLASH...
...BUT I'D NEVER SEEN HIM BEFORE.

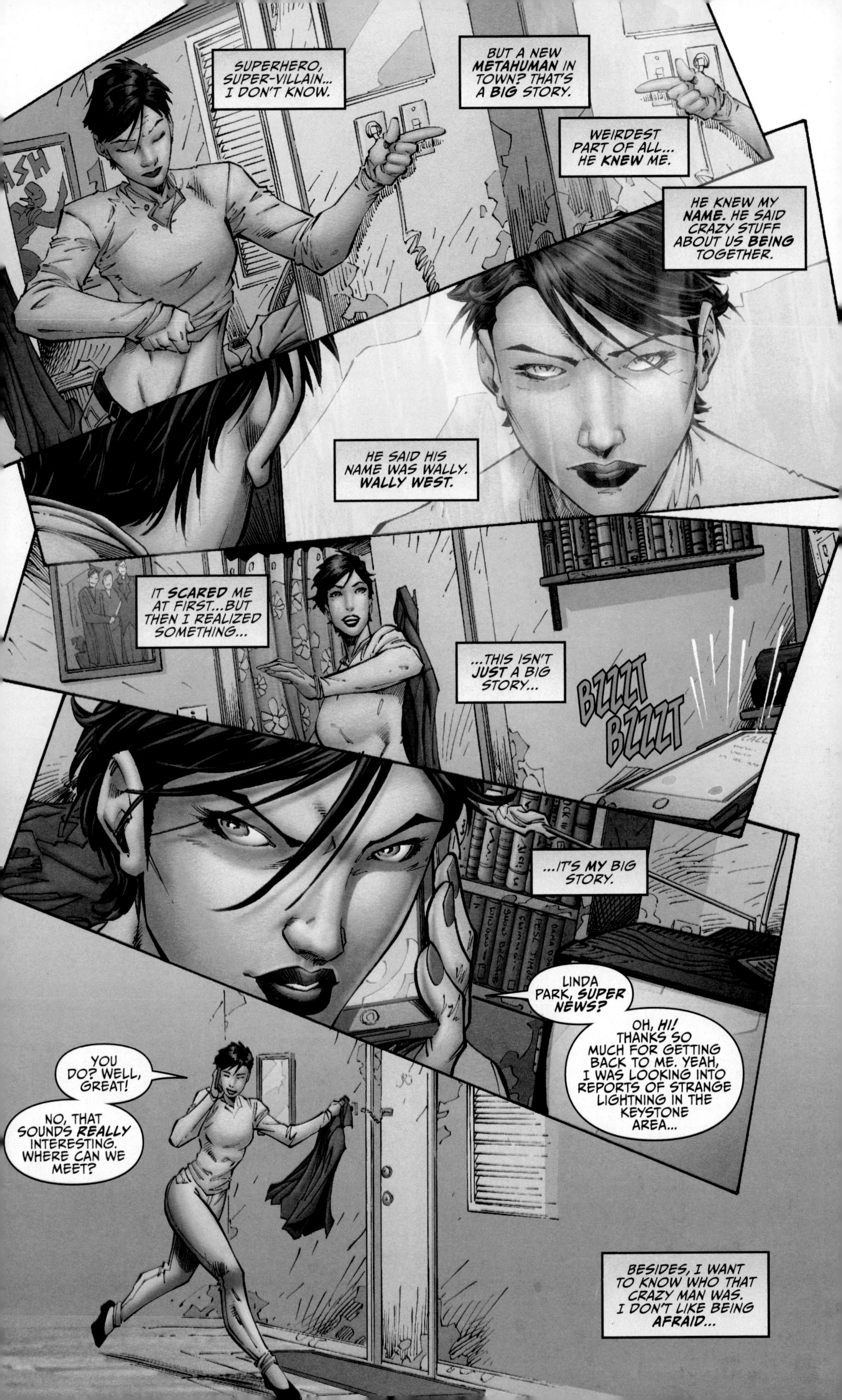

SUPERHERO, SUPER-VILLAIN... I DON'T KNOW.
BUT A NEW METAHUMAN IN TOWN? THAT'S A BIG STORY.
WEIRDEST PART OF ALL... HE KNEW ME.
HE KNEW MY NAME. HE SAID CRAZY STUFF ABOUT US BEING TOGETHER.
HE SAID HIS NAME WAS WALLY. WALLY WEST.
IT SCARED ME AT FIRST...BUT THEN I REALIZED SOMETHING...
...THIS ISN'T JUST A BIG STORY...
BZZZT BZZZT
...IT'S MY BIG STORY.
LINDA PARK, SUPER NEWS?
OH, HI! THANKS SO MUCH FOR GETTING BACK TO ME. YEAH, I WAS LOOKING INTO REPORTS OF STRANGE LIGHTNING IN THE KEYSTONE AREA...
YOU DO? WELL, GREAT!
NO, THAT SOUNDS REALLY INTERESTING. WHERE CAN WE MEET?
BESIDES, I WANT TO KNOW WHO THAT CRAZY MAN WAS. I DON'T LIKE BEING AFRAID...

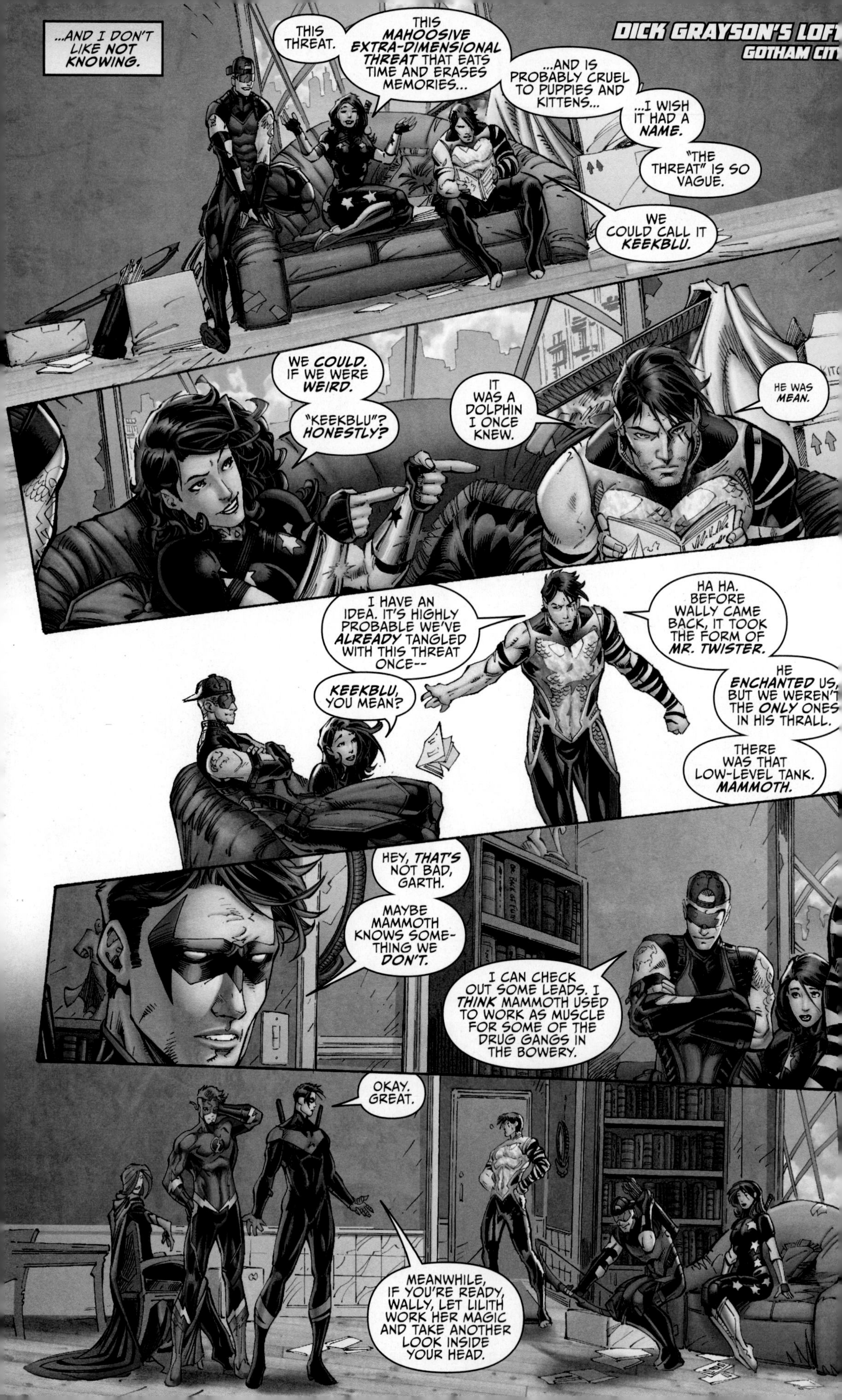
...AND I DON'T LIKE NOT KNOWING.
DICK GRAYSON'S LOFT
GOTHAM CITY
THIS THREAT.
THIS MAHOOSIVE EXTRA-DIMENSIONAL THREAT THAT EATS TIME AND ERASES MEMORIES...
...AND IS PROBABLY CRUEL TO PUPPIES AND KITTENS...
...I WISH IT HAD A NAME.
"THE THREAT" IS SO VAGUE.
WE COULD CALL IT KEEKBLU.
WE COULD. IF WE WERE WEIRD.
"KEEKBLU"? HONESTLY?
IT WAS A DOLPHIN I ONCE KNEW.
HE WAS MEAN.
I HAVE AN IDEA. IT'S HIGHLY PROBABLE WE'VE ALREADY TANGLED WITH THIS THREAT ONCE--
KEEKBLU, YOU MEAN?
HA HA. BEFORE WALLY CAME BACK, IT TOOK THE FORM OF MR. TWISTER.
HE ENCHANTED US, BUT WE WEREN'T THE ONLY ONES IN HIS THRALL.
THERE WAS THAT LOW-LEVEL TANK. MAMMOTH.
HEY, THAT'S NOT BAD, GARTH.
MAYBE MAMMOTH KNOWS SOME-THING WE DON'T.
I CAN CHECK OUT SOME LEADS. I THINK MAMMOTH USED TO WORK AS MUSCLE FOR SOME OF THE DRUG GANGS IN THE BOWERY.
OKAY. GREAT.
MEANWHILE, IF YOU'RE READY, WALLY, LET LILITH WORK HER MAGIC AND TAKE ANOTHER LOOK INSIDE YOUR HEAD.

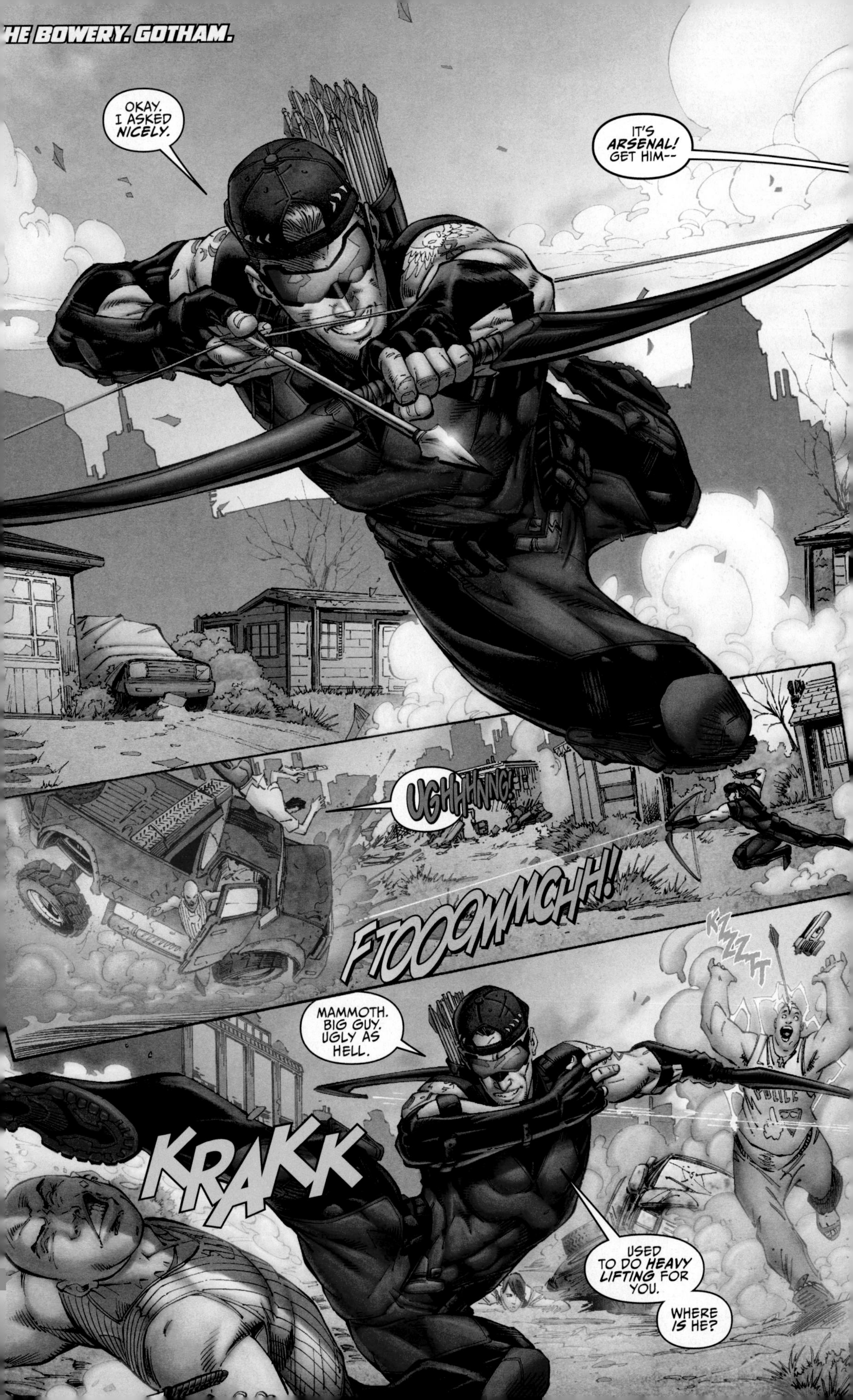
HE BOWERY. GOTHAM.
OKAY. I ASKED NICELY.
IT'S ARSENAL! GET HIM--
UGHHHNNG!
FTOOOMMMCHH!
KZZZZT
MAMMOTH. BIG GUY. UGLY AS HELL.
KRAKK
USED TO DO HEAVY LIFTING FOR YOU.
WHERE IS HE?

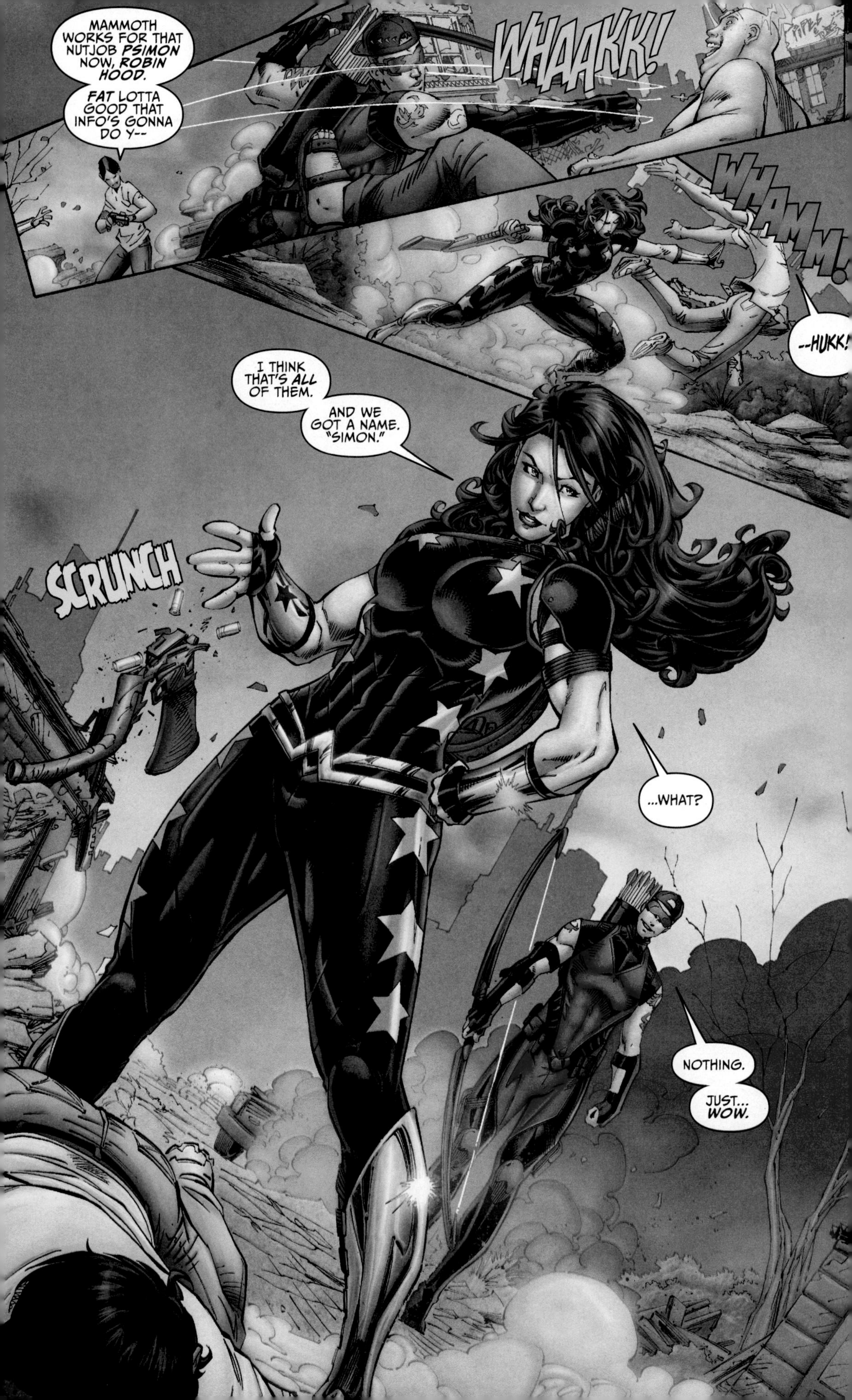

MAMMOTH WORKS FOR THAT NUTJOB PSIMON NOW, ROBIN HOOD.
FAT LOTTA GOOD THAT INFO'S GONNA DO Y--
WHAAKK!
WHAMMM!
--HUKK!
I THINK THAT'S ALL OF THEM.
AND WE GOT A NAME. "SIMON."
SCRUNCH
...WHAT?
NOTHING.
JUST... WOW.

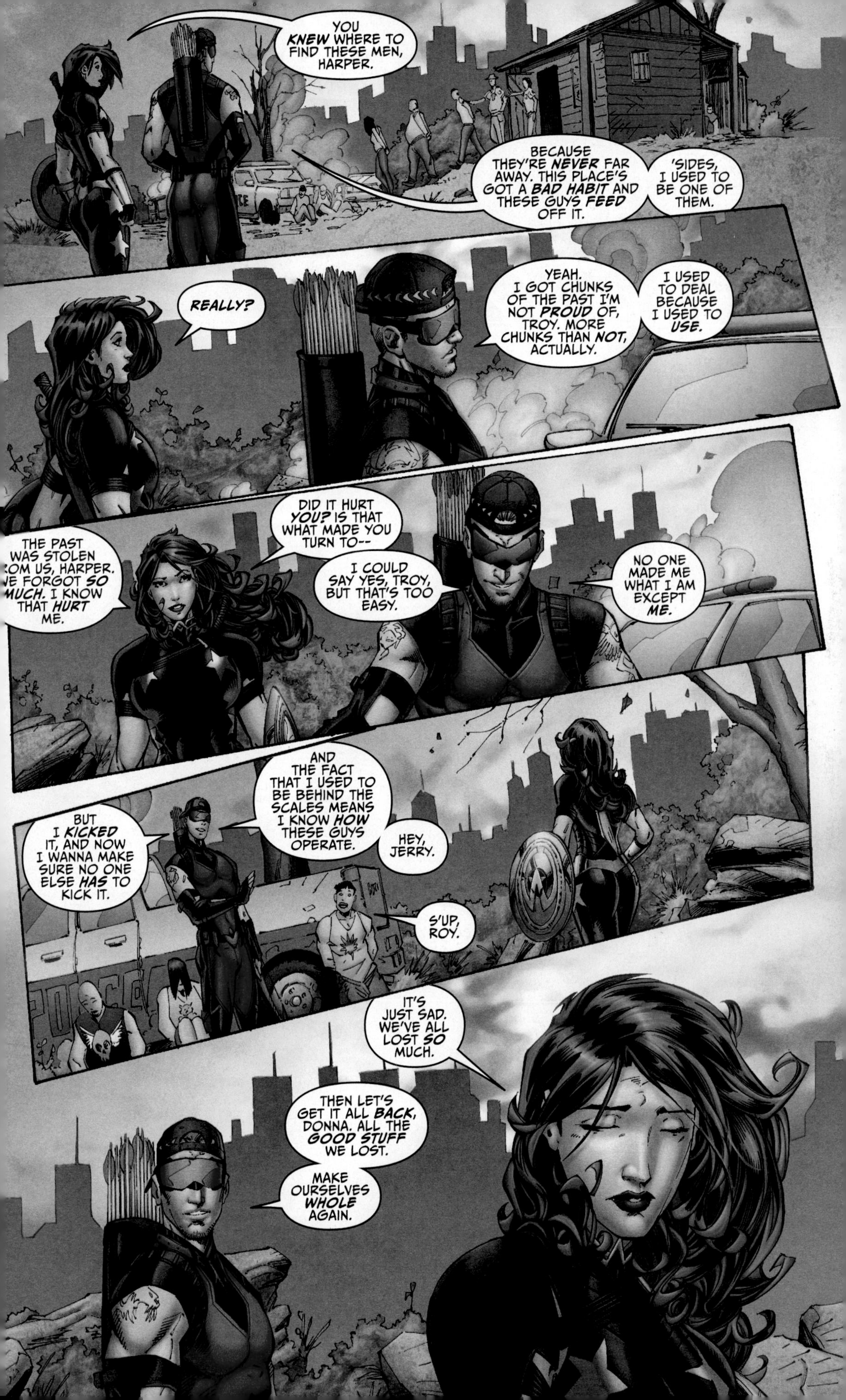
YOU KNEW WHERE TO FIND THESE MEN, HARPER.
BECAUSE THEY'RE NEVER FAR AWAY. THIS PLACE'S GOT A BAD HABIT AND THESE GUYS FEED OFF IT.
'SIDES, I USED TO BE ONE OF THEM.
REALLY?
YEAH. I GOT CHUNKS OF THE PAST I'M NOT PROUD OF, TROY. MORE CHUNKS THAN NOT, ACTUALLY.
I USED TO DEAL BECAUSE I USED TO USE.
THE PAST WAS STOLEN ROM US, HARPER. E FORGOT SO MUCH. I KNOW THAT HURT ME.
DID IT HURT YOU? IS THAT WHAT MADE YOU TURN TO--
I COULD SAY YES, TROY, BUT THAT'S TOO EASY.
NO ONE MADE ME WHAT I AM EXCEPT ME.
BUT I KICKED IT, AND NOW I WANNA MAKE SURE NO ONE ELSE HAS TO KICK IT.
AND THE FACT THAT I USED TO BE BEHIND THE SCALES MEANS I KNOW HOW THESE GUYS OPERATE.
HEY, JERRY.
S'UP, ROY.
IT'S JUST SAD. WE'VE ALL LOST SO MUCH.
THEN LET'S GET IT ALL BACK, DONNA. ALL THE GOOD STUFF WE LOST.
MAKE OURSELVES WHOLE AGAIN.

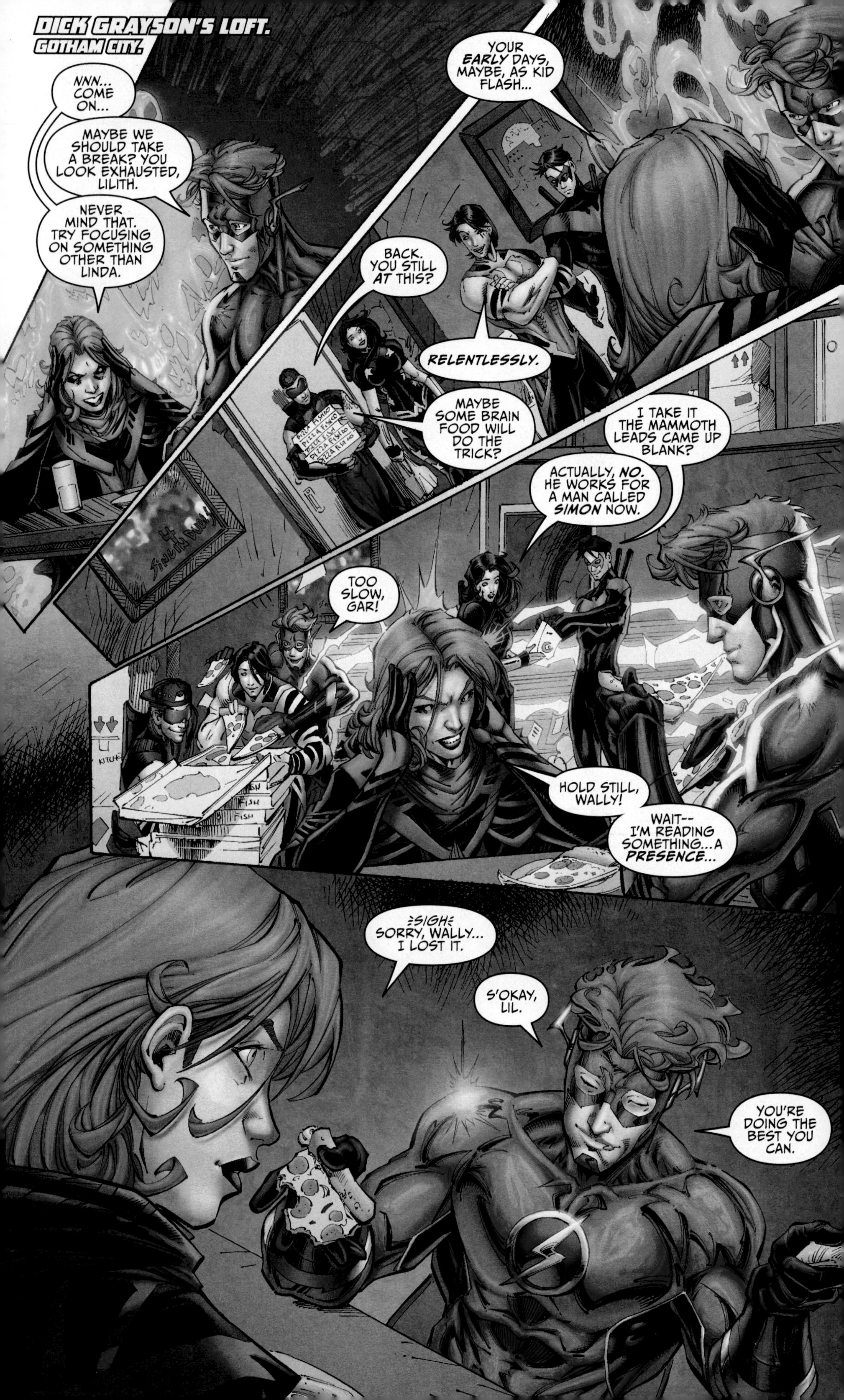
DICK GRAYSON'S LOFT.
GOTHAM CITY.
NNN... COME ON...
MAYBE WE SHOULD TAKE A BREAK? YOU LOOK EXHAUSTED, LILITH.
NEVER MIND THAT. TRY FOCUSING ON SOMETHING OTHER THAN LINDA.
YOUR EARLY DAYS, MAYBE, AS KID FLASH...
BACK. YOU STILL AT THIS?
RELENTLESSLY.
MAYBE SOME BRAIN FOOD WILL DO THE TRICK?
I TAKE IT THE MAMMOTH LEADS CAME UP BLANK?
ACTUALLY, NO. HE WORKS FOR A MAN CALLED SIMON NOW.
TOO SLOW, GAR!
HOLD STILL, WALLY!
WAIT-- I'M READING SOMETHING...A PRESENCE...
SIGH SORRY, WALLY... I LOST IT.
S'OKAY, LIL.
YOU'RE DOING THE BEST YOU CAN.

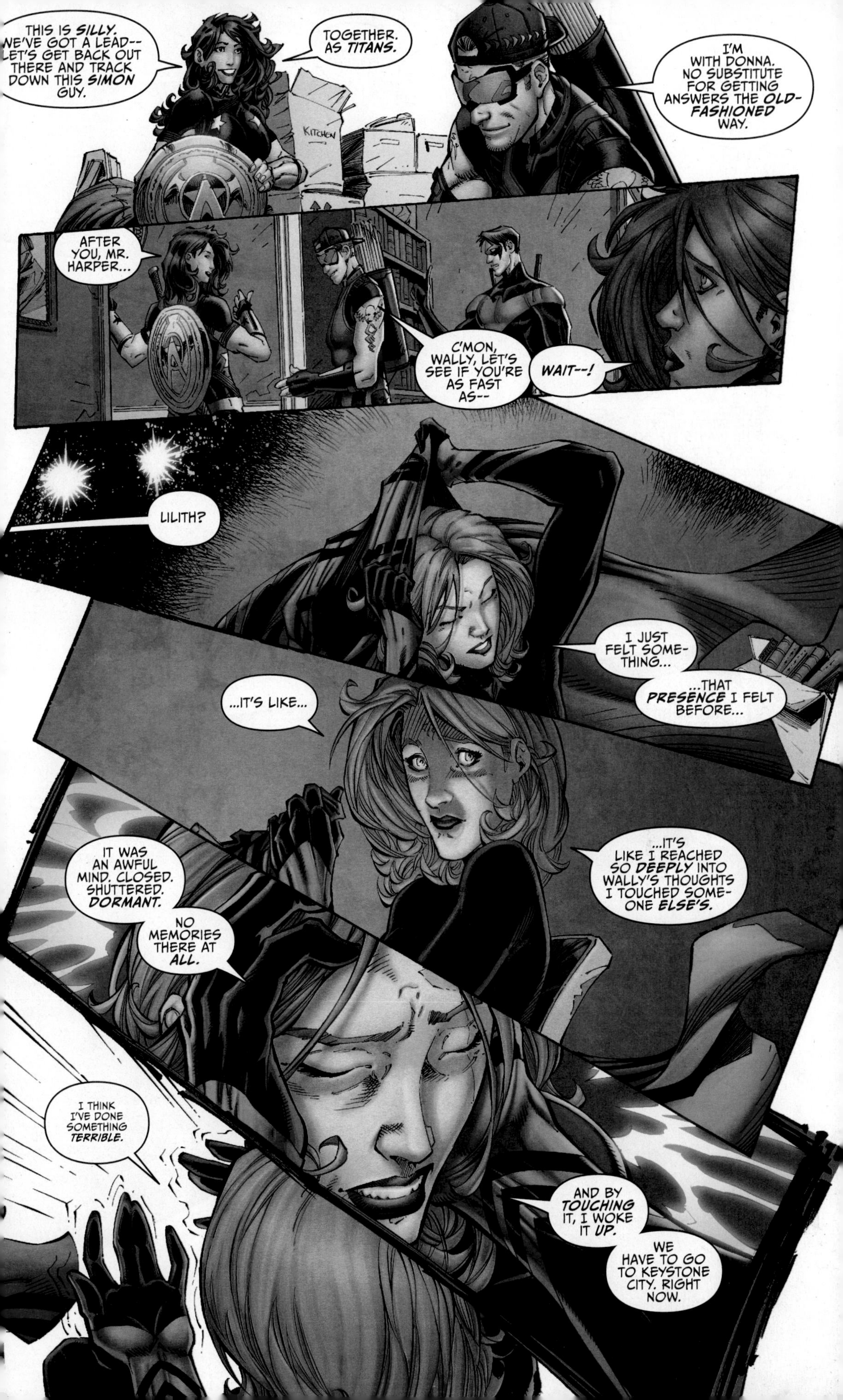
THIS IS SILLY. WE'VE GOT A LEAD-- LET'S GET BACK OUT THERE AND TRACK DOWN THIS SIMON GUY.
TOGETHER. AS TITANS.
I'M WITH DONNA. NO SUBSTITUTE FOR GETTING ANSWERS THE OLD-FASHIONED WAY.
KITCHEN
AFTER YOU, MR. HARPER...
C'MON, WALLY, LET'S SEE IF YOU'RE AS FAST AS--
WAIT--!
LILITH?
I JUST FELT SOME-THING...
...THAT PRESENCE I FELT BEFORE...
...IT'S LIKE...
...IT'S LIKE I REACHED SO DEEPLY INTO WALLY'S THOUGHTS I TOUCHED SOME-ONE ELSE'S.
IT WAS AN AWFUL MIND. CLOSED. SHUTTERED. DORMANT.
NO MEMORIES THERE AT ALL.
I THINK I'VE DONE SOMETHING TERRIBLE.
AND BY TOUCHING IT, I WOKE IT UP.
WE HAVE TO GO TO KEYSTONE CITY. RIGHT NOW.

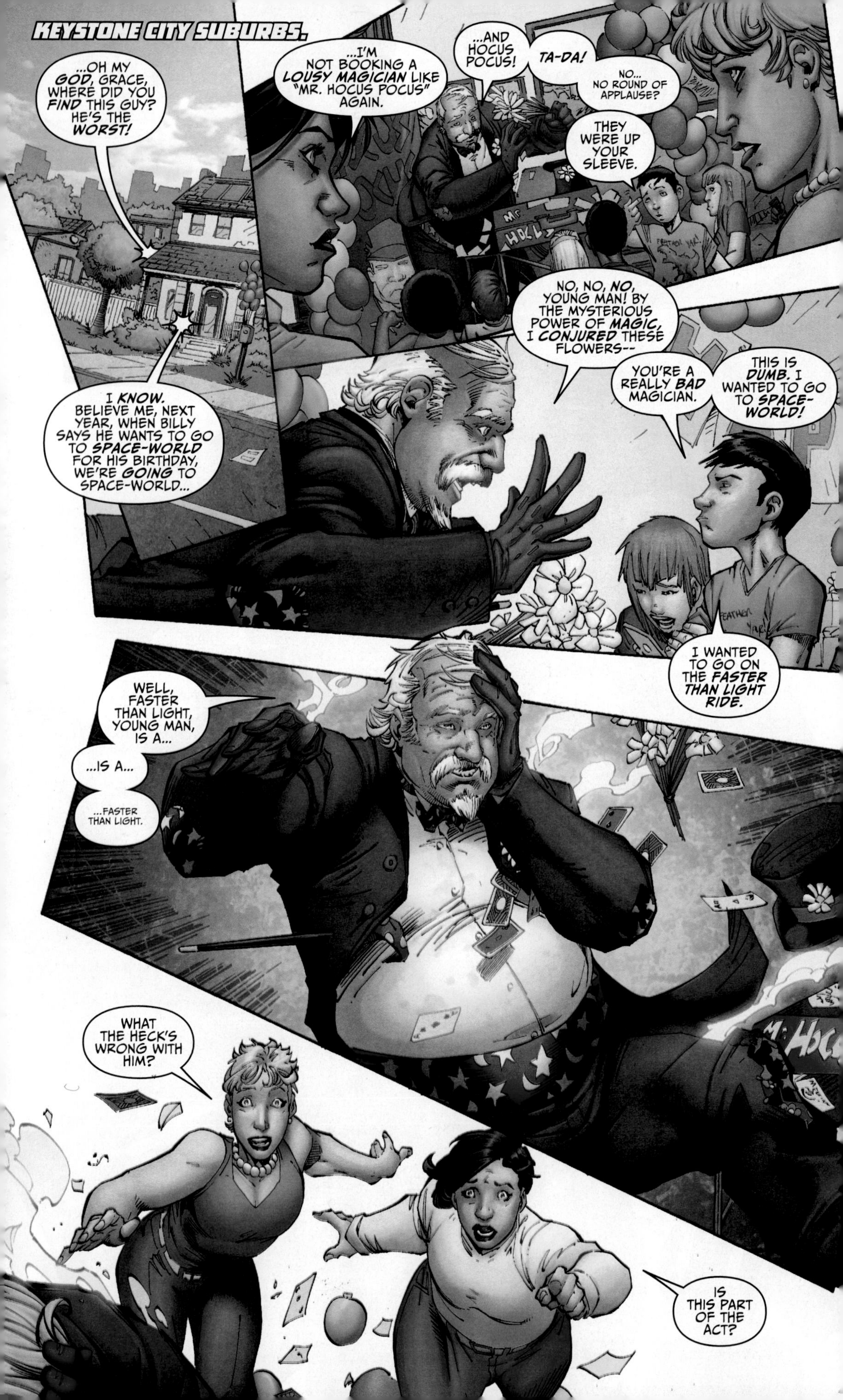
KEYSTONE CITY SUBURBS.
...OH MY GOD, GRACE, WHERE DID YOU FIND THIS GUY? HE'S THE WORST!
I KNOW. BELIEVE ME, NEXT YEAR, WHEN BILLY SAYS HE WANTS TO GO TO SPACE-WORLD FOR HIS BIRTHDAY, WE'RE GOING TO SPACE-WORLD...
...I'M NOT BOOKING A LOUSY MAGICIAN LIKE "MR. HOCUS POCUS" AGAIN.
...AND HOCUS POCUS!
TA-DA!
NO... NO ROUND OF APPLAUSE?
THEY WERE UP YOUR SLEEVE.
NO, NO, NO, YOUNG MAN! BY THE MYSTERIOUS POWER OF MAGIC, I CONJURED THESE FLOWERS--
YOU'RE A REALLY BAD MAGICIAN.
THIS IS DUMB. I WANTED TO GO TO SPACE-WORLD!
I WANTED TO GO ON THE FASTER THAN LIGHT RIDE.
WELL, FASTER THAN LIGHT, YOUNG MAN, IS A...
...IS A...
...FASTER THAN LIGHT.
WHAT THE HECK'S WRONG WITH HIM?
IS THIS PART OF THE ACT?

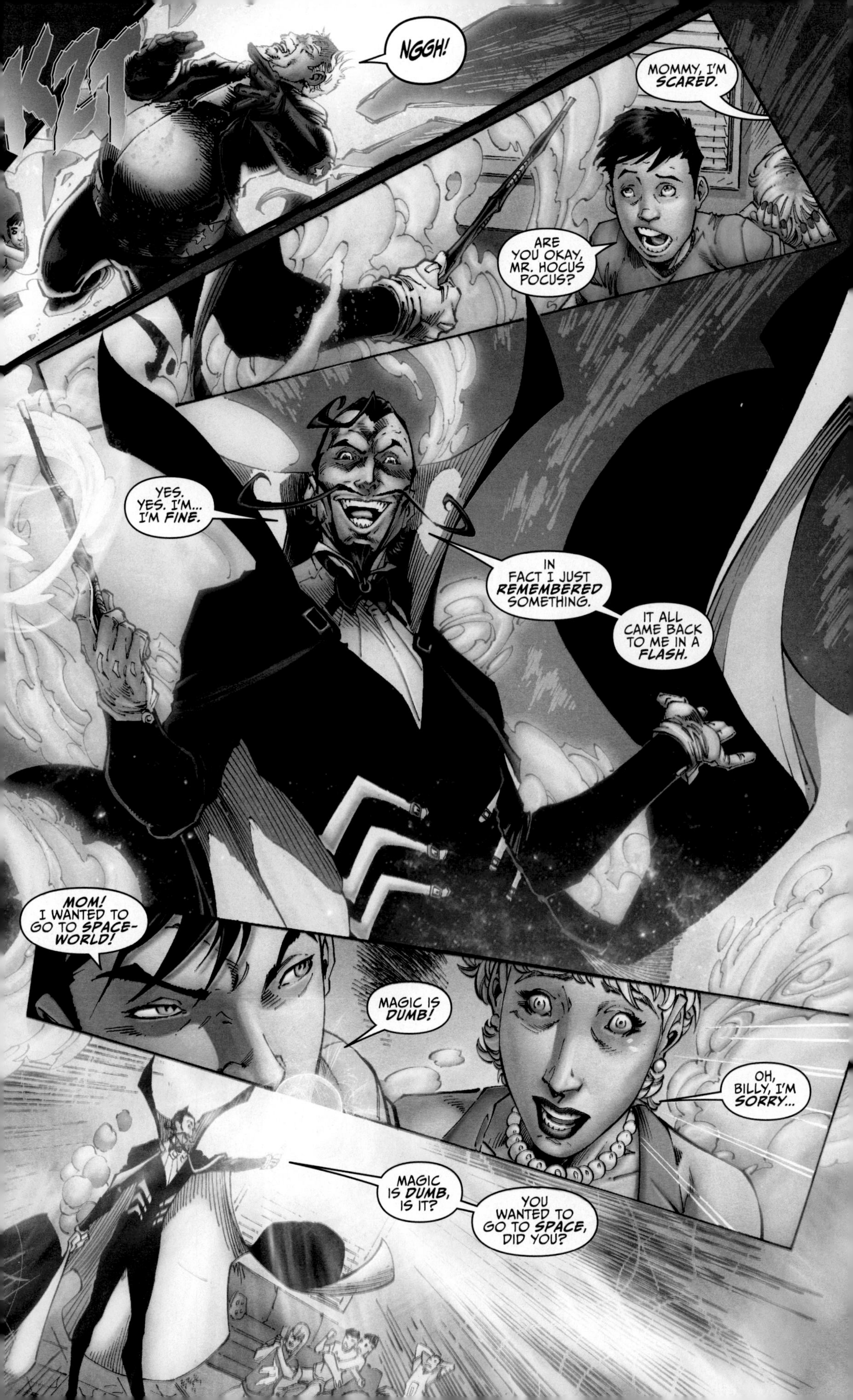

KZZT
NGGH!
MOMMY, I'M SCARED.
ARE YOU OKAY, MR. HOCUS POCUS?
YES. YES. I'M... I'M FINE.
IN FACT I JUST REMEMBERED SOMETHING.
IT ALL CAME BACK TO ME IN A FLASH.
MOM! I WANTED TO GO TO SPACE-WORLD!
MAGIC IS DUMB!
OH, BILLY, I'M SORRY...
MAGIC IS DUMB, IS IT?
YOU WANTED TO GO TO SPACE, DID YOU?

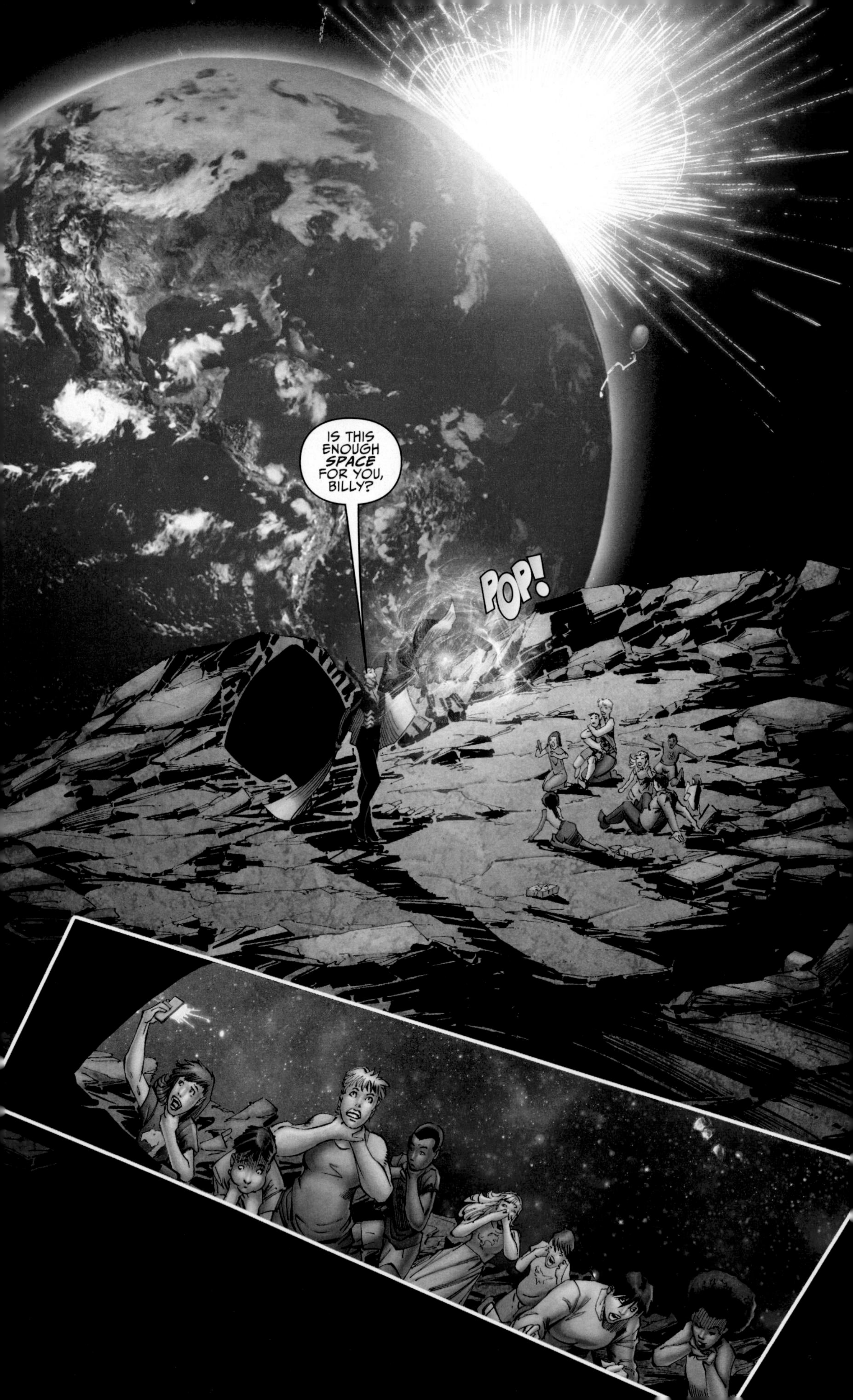
IS THIS ENOUGH SPACE FOR YOU, BILLY?
POP!

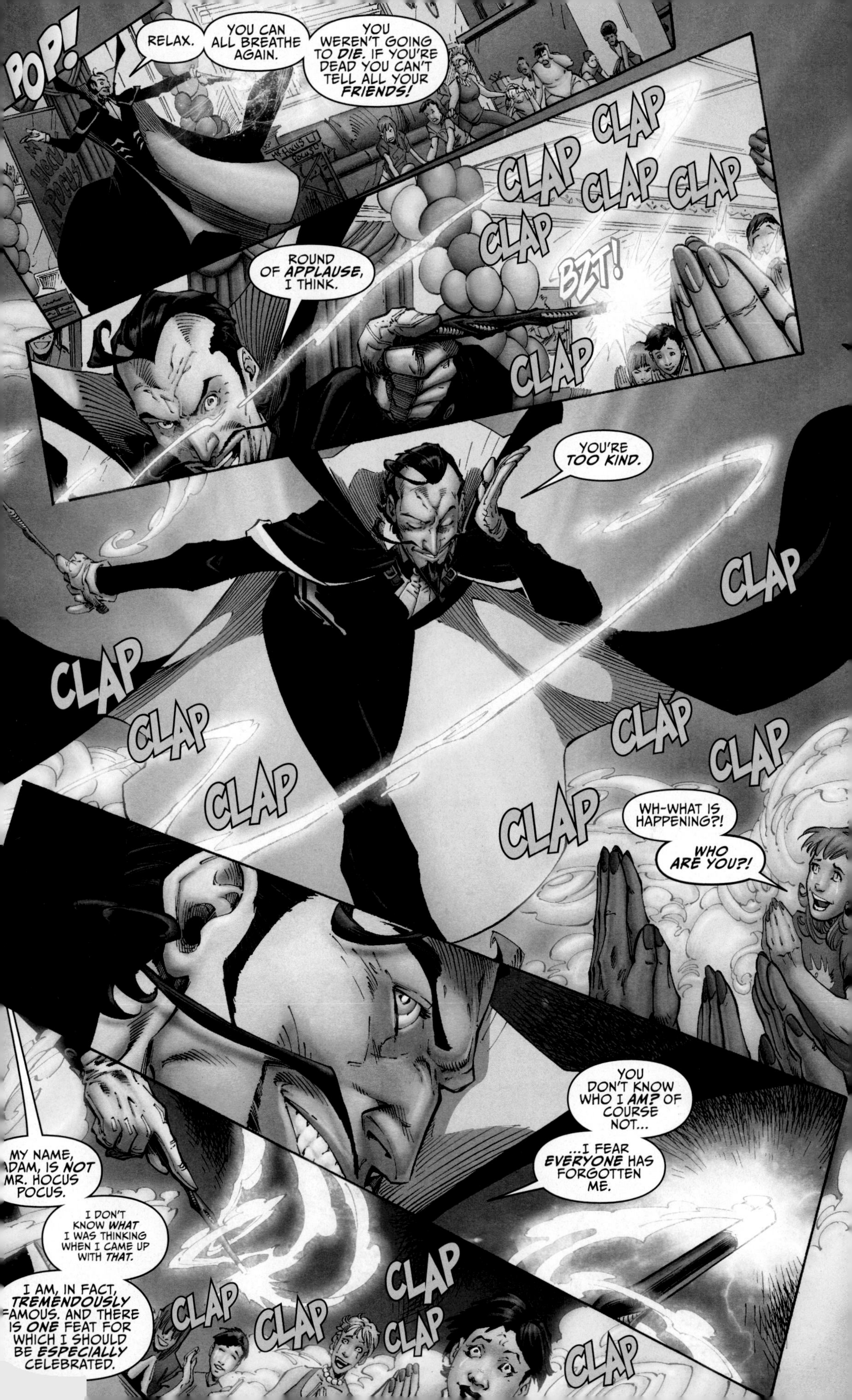

POP!
RELAX.
YOU CAN ALL BREATHE AGAIN.
YOU WEREN'T GOING TO DIE. IF YOU'RE DEAD YOU CAN'T TELL ALL YOUR FRIENDS!
CLAP CLAP CLAP CLAP CLAP
ROUND OF APPLAUSE, I THINK.
BZT!
CLAP
YOU'RE TOO KIND.
CLAP
CLAP
CLAP
CLAP
CLAP
CLAP
CLAP
WH-WHAT IS HAPPENING?!
WHO ARE YOU?!
YOU DON'T KNOW WHO I AM? OF COURSE NOT...
...I FEAR EVERYONE HAS FORGOTTEN ME.
MY NAME, ADAM, IS NOT MR. HOCUS POCUS.
I DON'T KNOW WHAT I WAS THINKING WHEN I CAME UP WITH THAT.
I AM, IN FACT, TREMENDOUSLY FAMOUS. AND THERE IS ONE FEAT FOR WHICH I SHOULD BE ESPECIALLY CELEBRATED.
CLAP CLAP CLAP CLAP CLAP

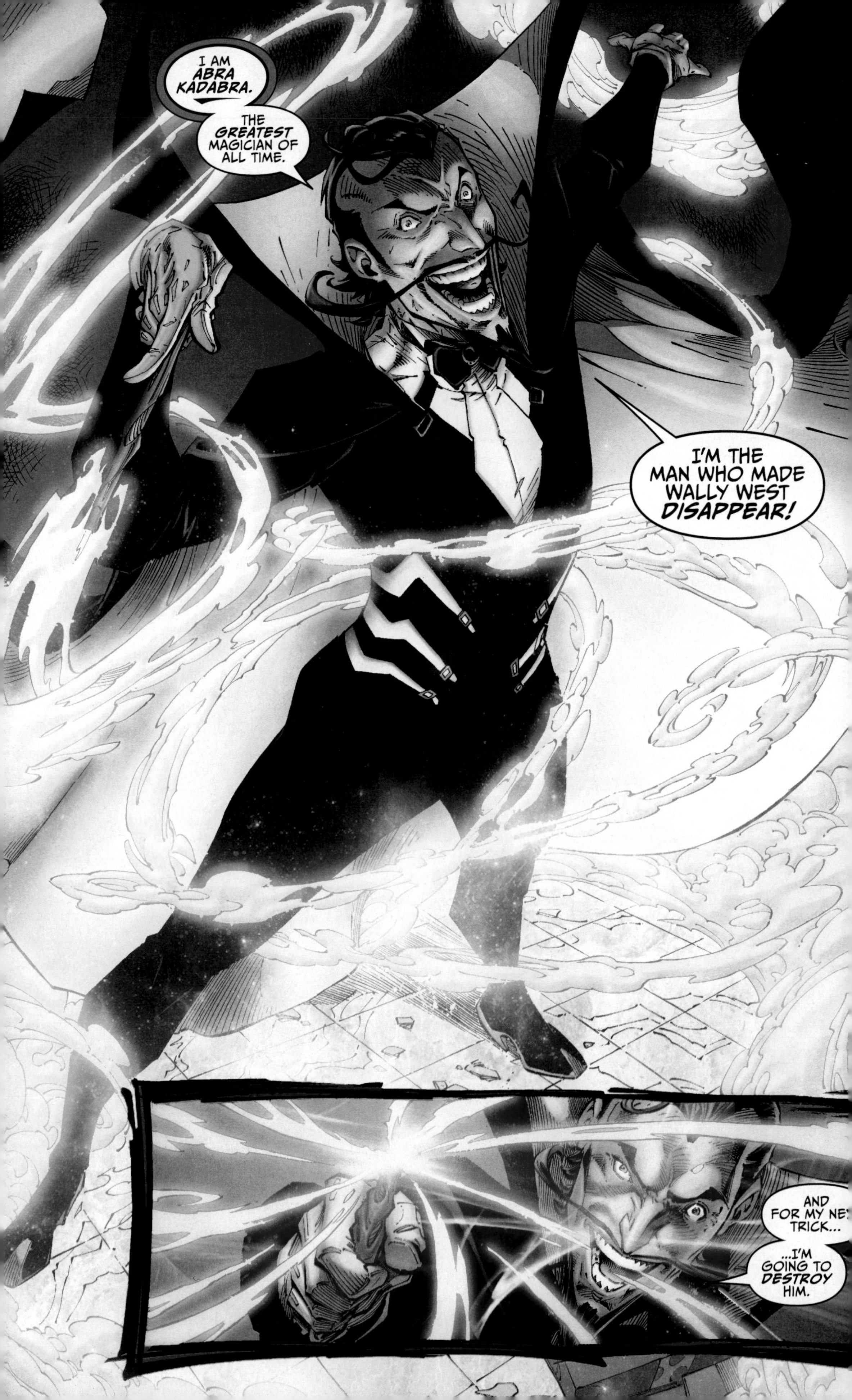
I AM ABRA KADABRA.
THE GREATEST MAGICIAN OF ALL TIME.
I'M THE MAN WHO MADE WALLY WEST DISAPPEAR!
AND FOR MY NE TRICK...
...I'M GOING TO DESTROY HIM.

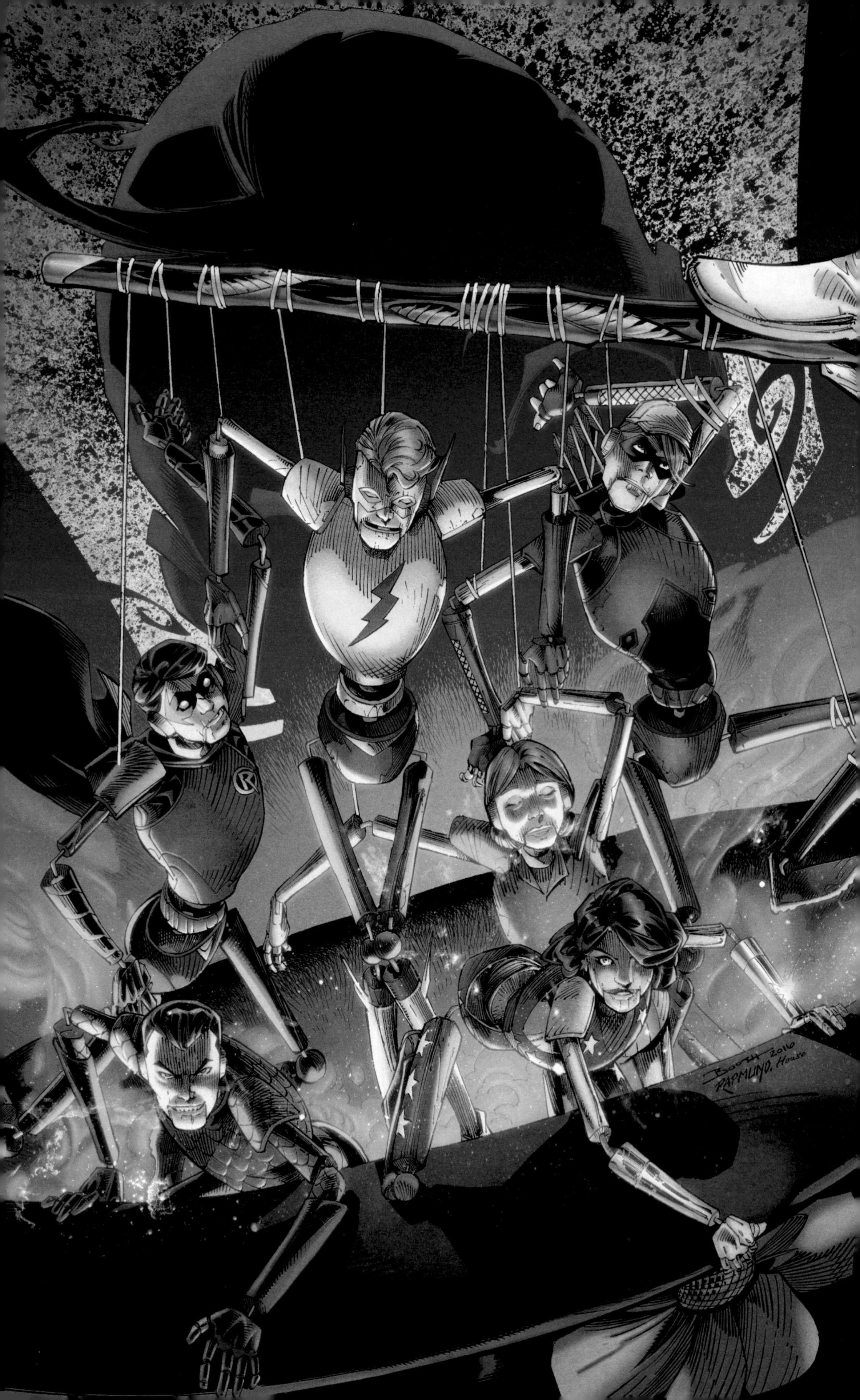
BOOTH 2016
RAPMUND. House

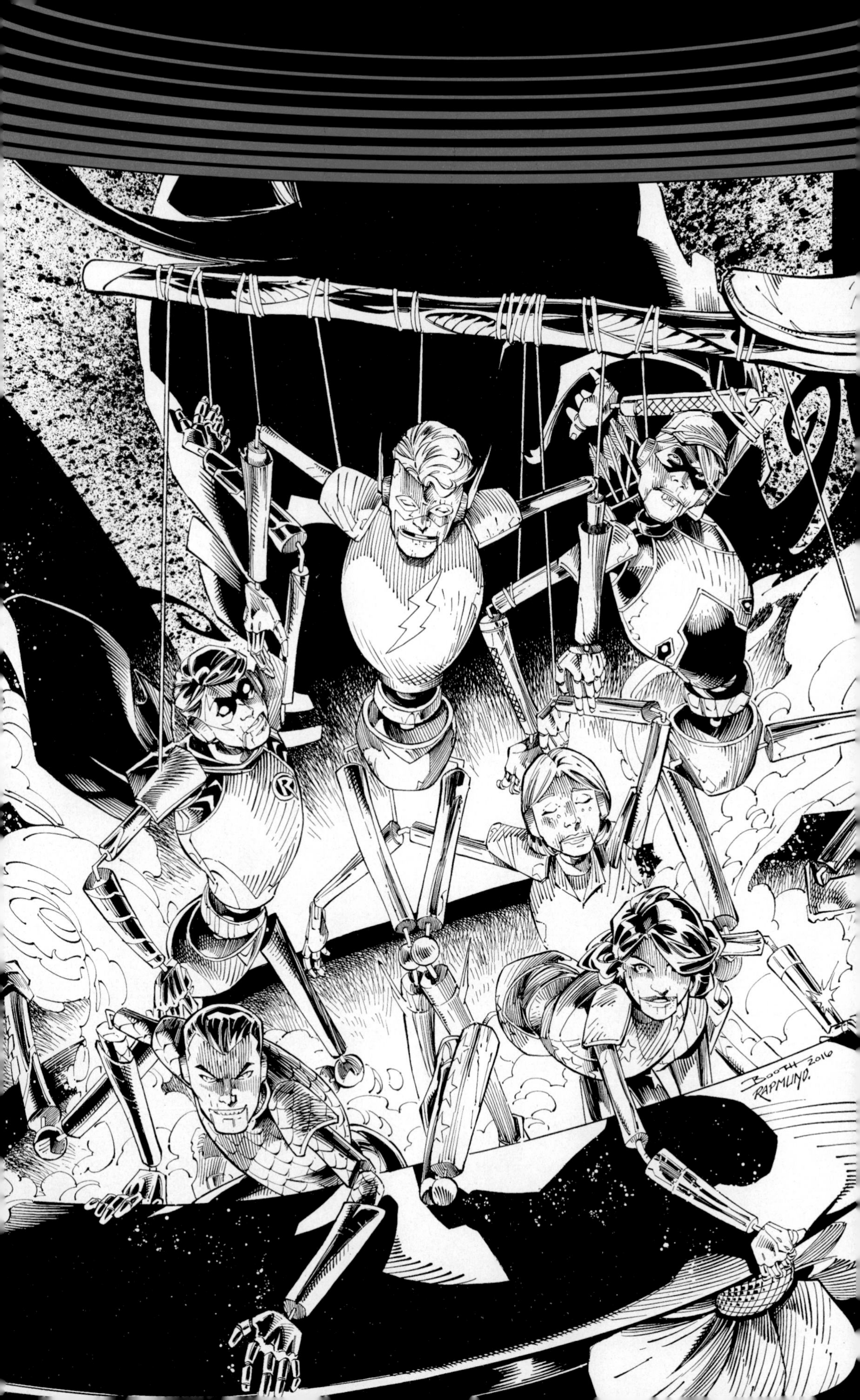
BOOTH 2016
RAPMUND.

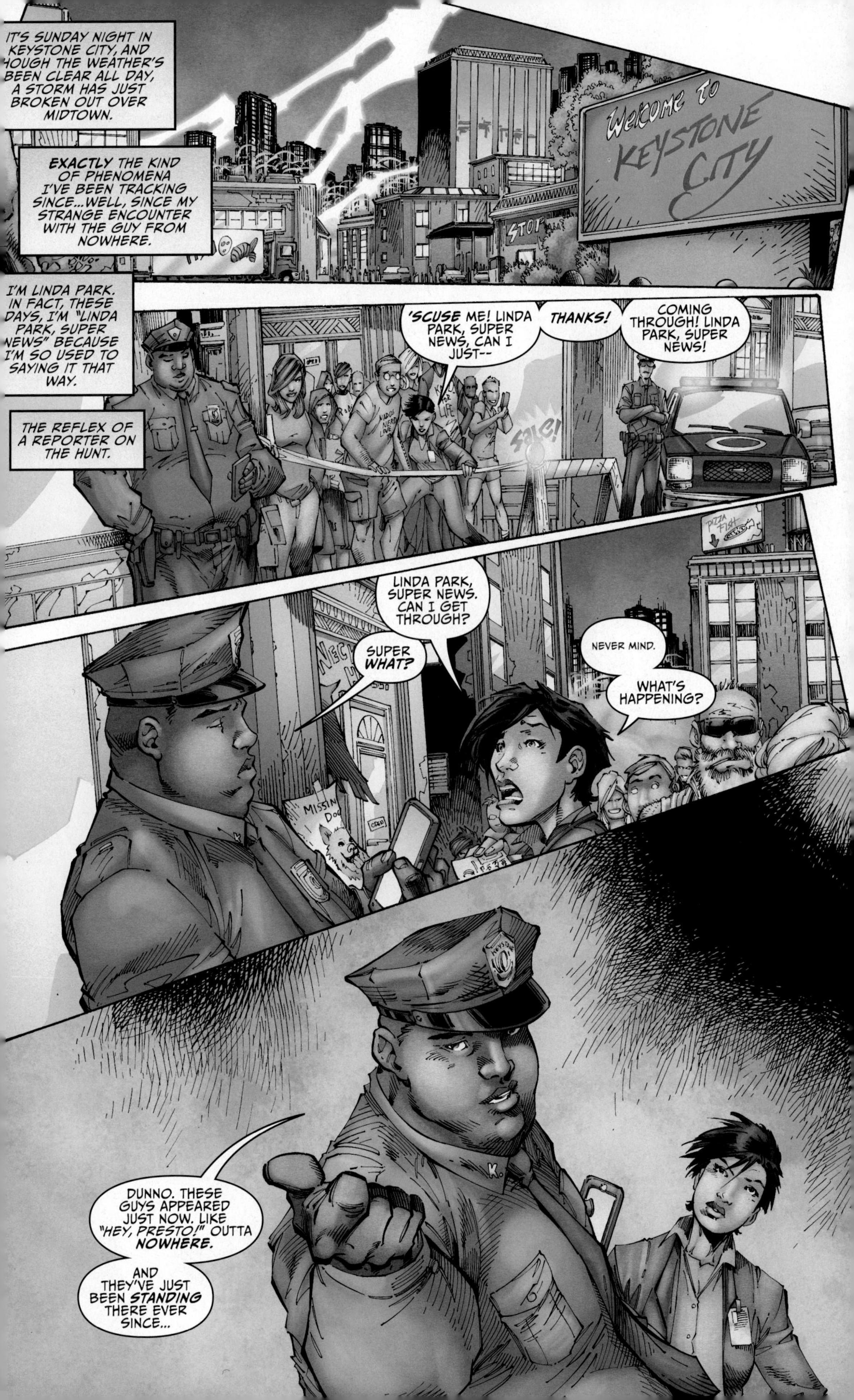
IT'S SUNDAY NIGHT IN KEYSTONE CITY, AND THOUGH THE WEATHER'S BEEN CLEAR ALL DAY, A STORM HAS JUST BROKEN OUT OVER MIDTOWN.
EXACTLY THE KIND OF PHENOMENA I'VE BEEN TRACKING SINCE...WELL, SINCE MY STRANGE ENCOUNTER WITH THE GUY FROM NOWHERE.
Welcome to KEYSTONE CITY
STOP
I'M LINDA PARK. IN FACT, THESE DAYS, I'M "LINDA PARK, SUPER NEWS" BECAUSE I'M SO USED TO SAYING IT THAT WAY.
THE REFLEX OF A REPORTER ON THE HUNT.
'SCUSE ME! LINDA PARK, SUPER NEWS, CAN I JUST--
THANKS!
COMING THROUGH! LINDA PARK, SUPER NEWS!
SALE!
PIZZA FISH
LINDA PARK, SUPER NEWS. CAN I GET THROUGH?
SUPER WHAT?
NEVER MIND.
WHAT'S HAPPENING?
MISSING DOG
DUNNO. THESE GUYS APPEARED JUST NOW. LIKE "HEY, PRESTO!" OUTTA NOWHERE.
AND THEY'VE JUST BEEN STANDING THERE EVER SINCE...

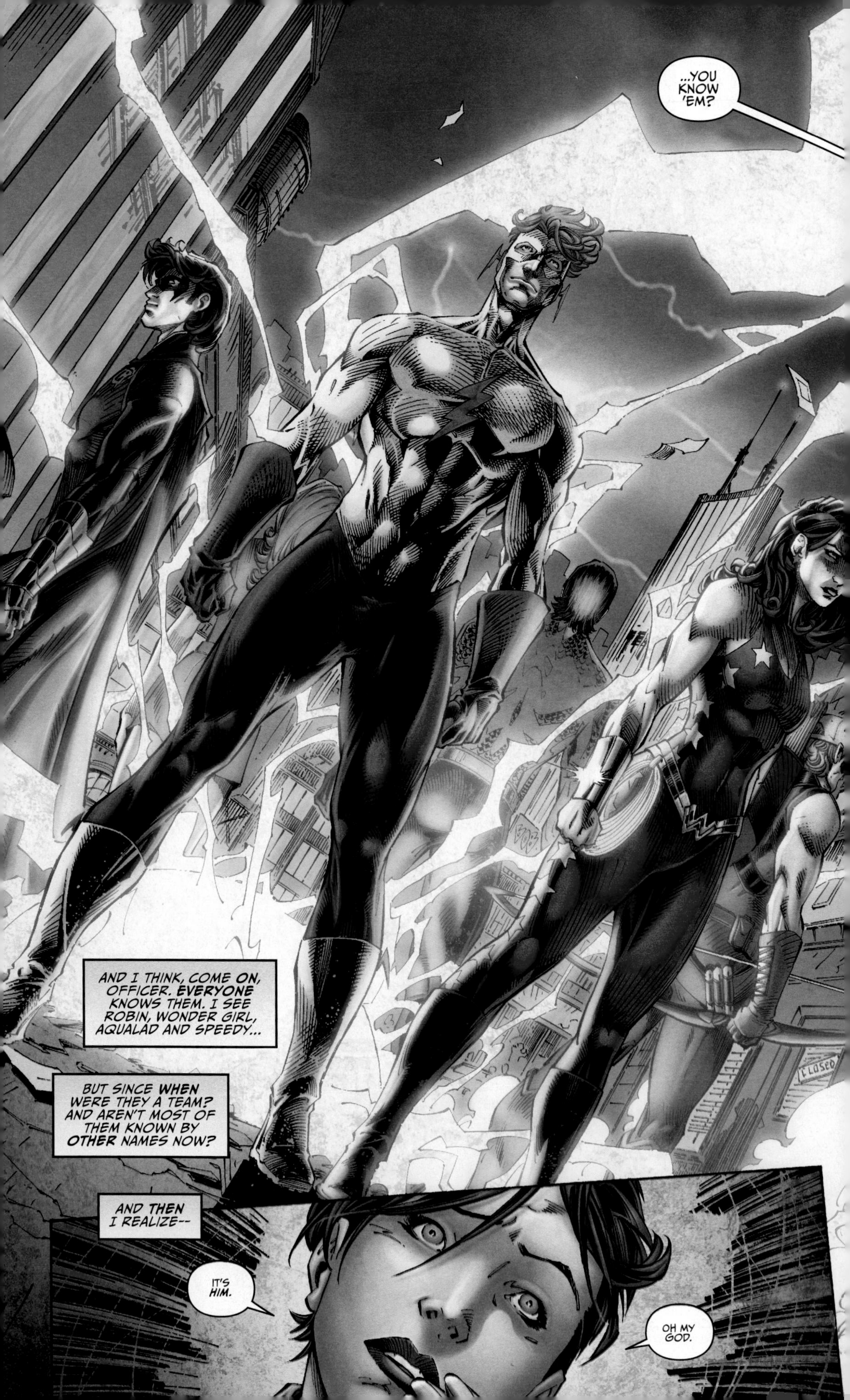
...YOU KNOW 'EM?
AND I THINK, COME ON, OFFICER. EVERYONE KNOWS THEM. I SEE ROBIN, WONDER GIRL, AQUALAD AND SPEEDY...
BUT SINCE WHEN WERE THEY A TEAM? AND AREN'T MOST OF THEM KNOWN BY OTHER NAMES NOW?
CLOSED
AND THEN I REALIZE--
IT'S HIM.
OH MY GOD.

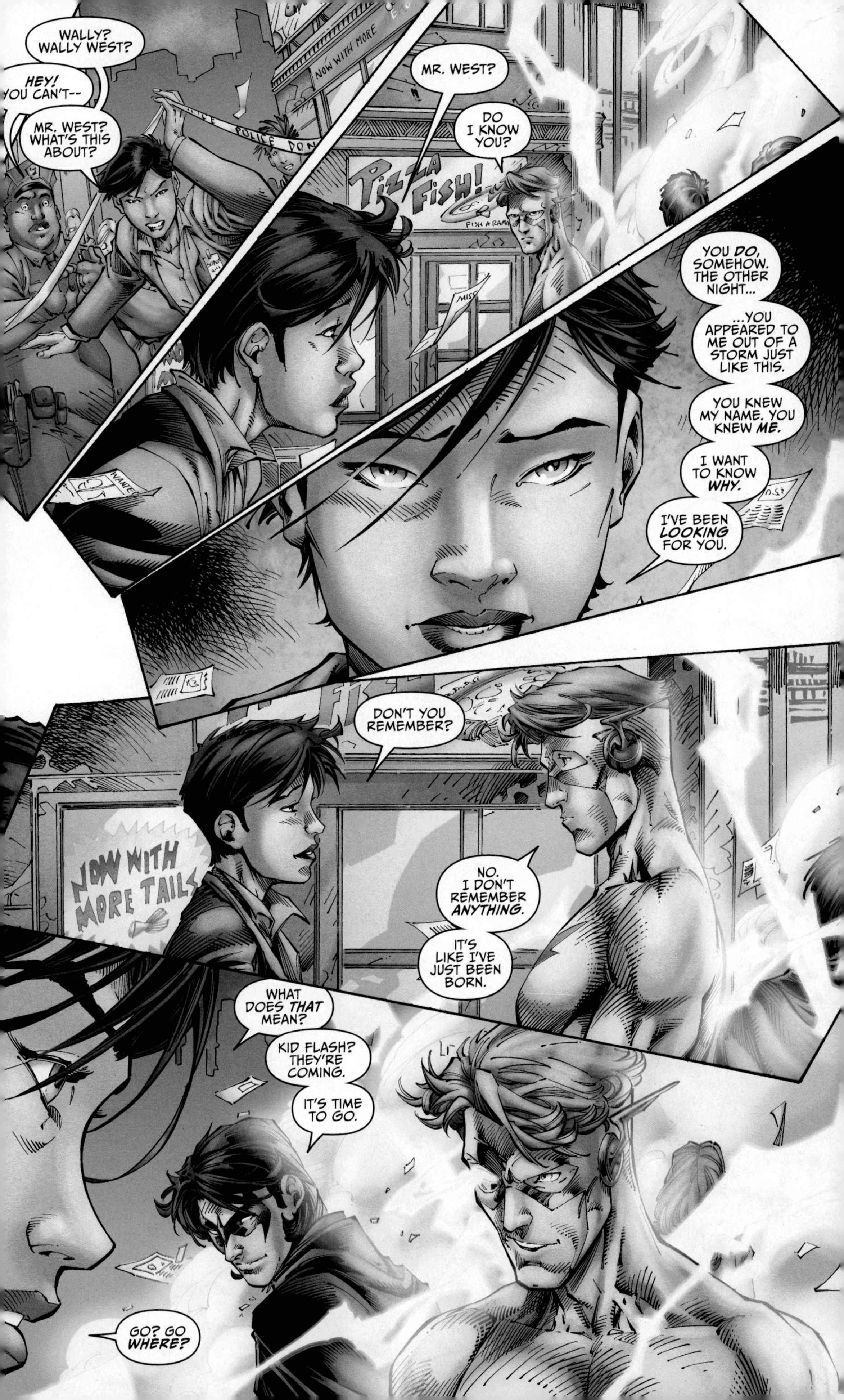

WALLY? WALLY WEST?
HEY! YOU CAN'T--
MR. WEST? WHAT'S THIS ABOUT?
POLICE
NOW WITH MORE
MR. WEST?
DO I KNOW YOU?
PIZZA FISH!
FISH A RAMA
YOU DO, SOMEHOW. THE OTHER NIGHT...
...YOU APPEARED TO ME OUT OF A STORM JUST LIKE THIS.
YOU KNEW MY NAME. YOU KNEW ME.
I WANT TO KNOW WHY.
I'VE BEEN LOOKING FOR YOU.
DON'T YOU REMEMBER?
NOW WITH MORE TAILS
NO. I DON'T REMEMBER ANYTHING.
IT'S LIKE I'VE JUST BEEN BORN.
WHAT DOES THAT MEAN?
KID FLASH? THEY'RE COMING.
IT'S TIME TO GO.
GO? GO WHERE?

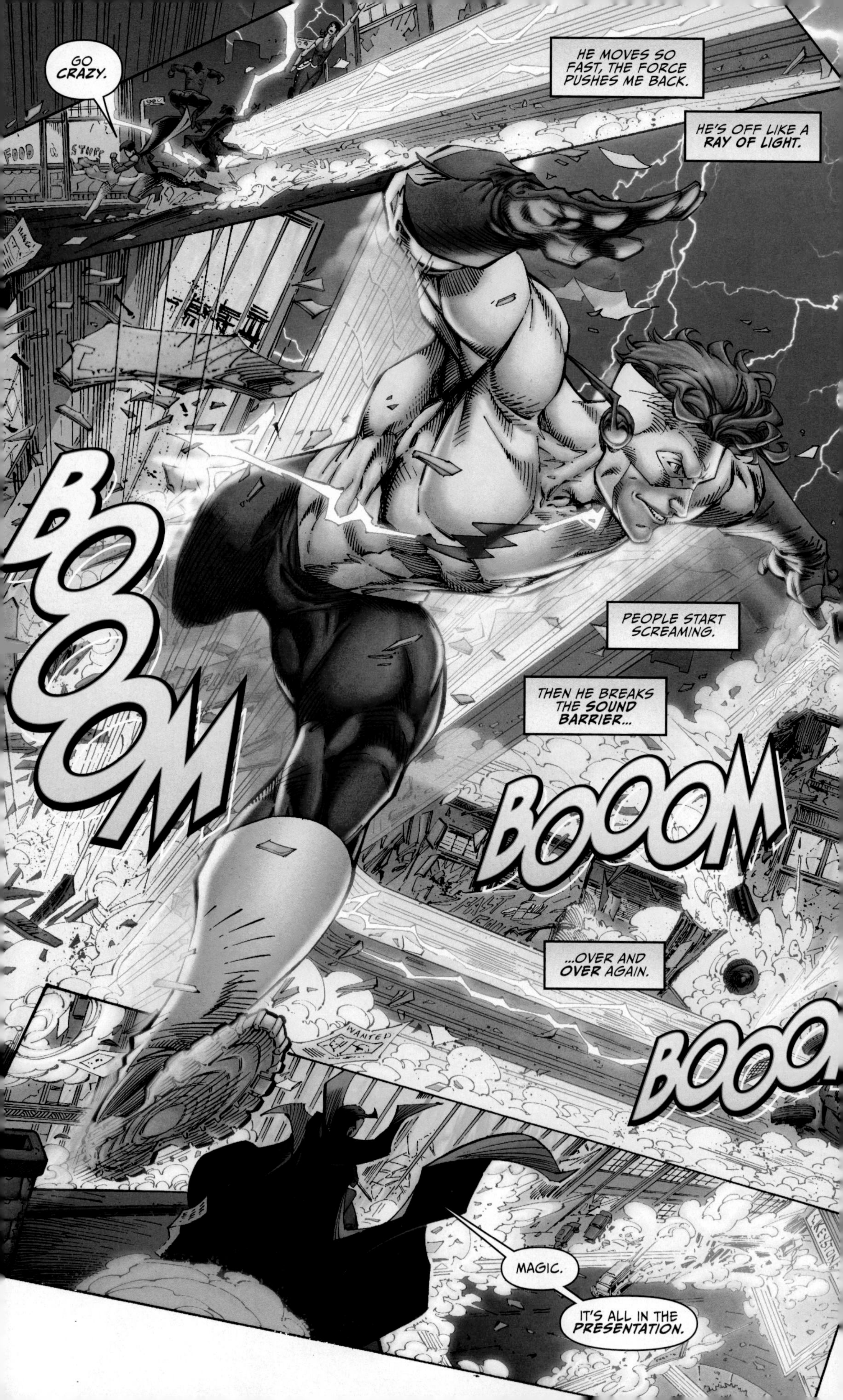
GO CRAZY.
HE MOVES SO FAST, THE FORCE PUSHES ME BACK.
HE'S OFF LIKE A RAY OF LIGHT.
PEOPLE START SCREAMING.
THEN HE BREAKS THE SOUND BARRIER...
BOOOM
BOOOM
...OVER AND OVER AGAIN.
BOOO
MAGIC.
IT'S ALL IN THE PRESENTATION.

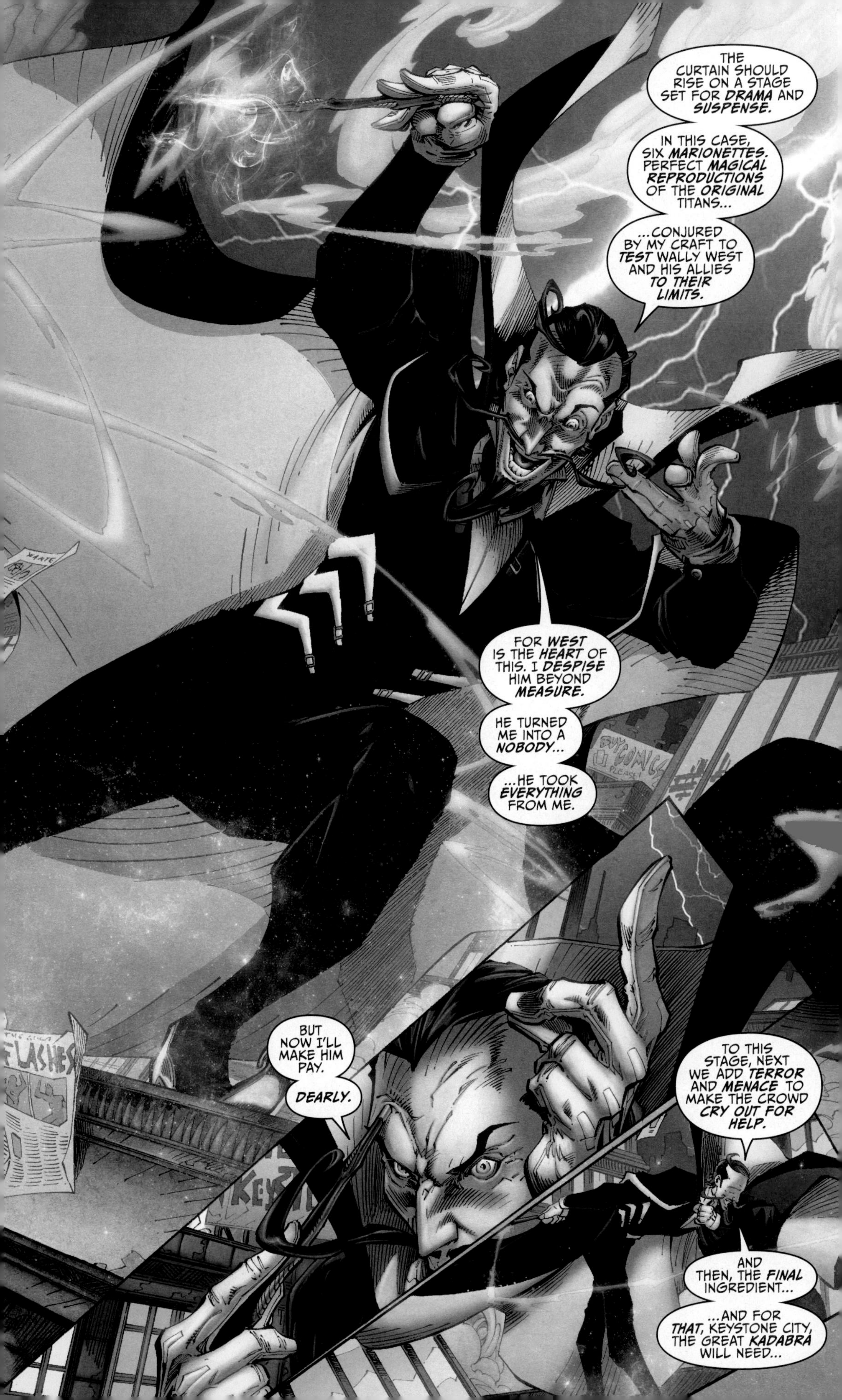
THE CURTAIN SHOULD RISE ON A STAGE SET FOR DRAMA AND SUSPENSE.
IN THIS CASE, SIX MARIONETTES. PERFECT MAGICAL REPRODUCTIONS OF THE ORIGINAL TITANS...
...CONJURED BY MY CRAFT TO TEST WALLY WEST AND HIS ALLIES TO THEIR LIMITS.
FOR WEST IS THE HEART OF THIS. I DESPISE HIM BEYOND MEASURE.
HE TURNED ME INTO A NOBODY...
...HE TOOK EVERYTHING FROM ME.
BUY COMICS PLEASE!
BUT NOW I'LL MAKE HIM PAY.
DEARLY.
FLASHES
TO THIS STAGE, NEXT WE ADD TERROR AND MENACE TO MAKE THE CROWD CRY OUT FOR HELP.
AND THEN, THE FINAL INGREDIENT...
...AND FOR THAT, KEYSTONE CITY, THE GREAT KADABRA WILL NEED...

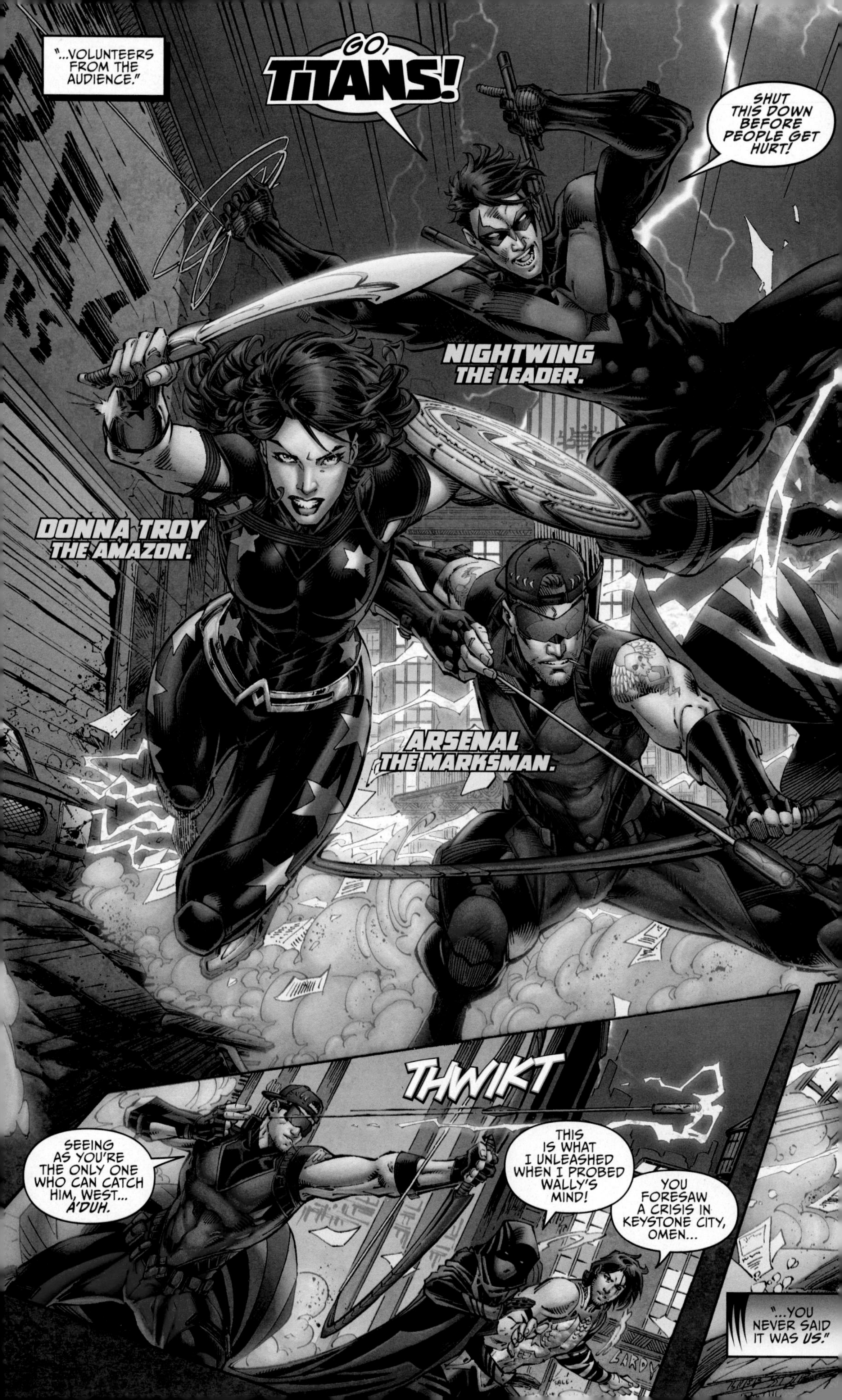
"...VOLUNTEERS FROM THE AUDIENCE."
GO, TITANS!
SHUT THIS DOWN BEFORE PEOPLE GET HURT!
NIGHTWING THE LEADER.
DONNA TROY THE AMAZON.
ARSENAL THE MARKSMAN.
THWIKT
SEEING AS YOU'RE THE ONLY ONE WHO CAN CATCH HIM, WEST... A'DUH.
THIS IS WHAT I UNLEASHED WHEN I PROBED WALLY'S MIND!
YOU FORESAW A CRISIS IN KEYSTONE CITY, OMEN...
"...YOU NEVER SAID IT WAS US."

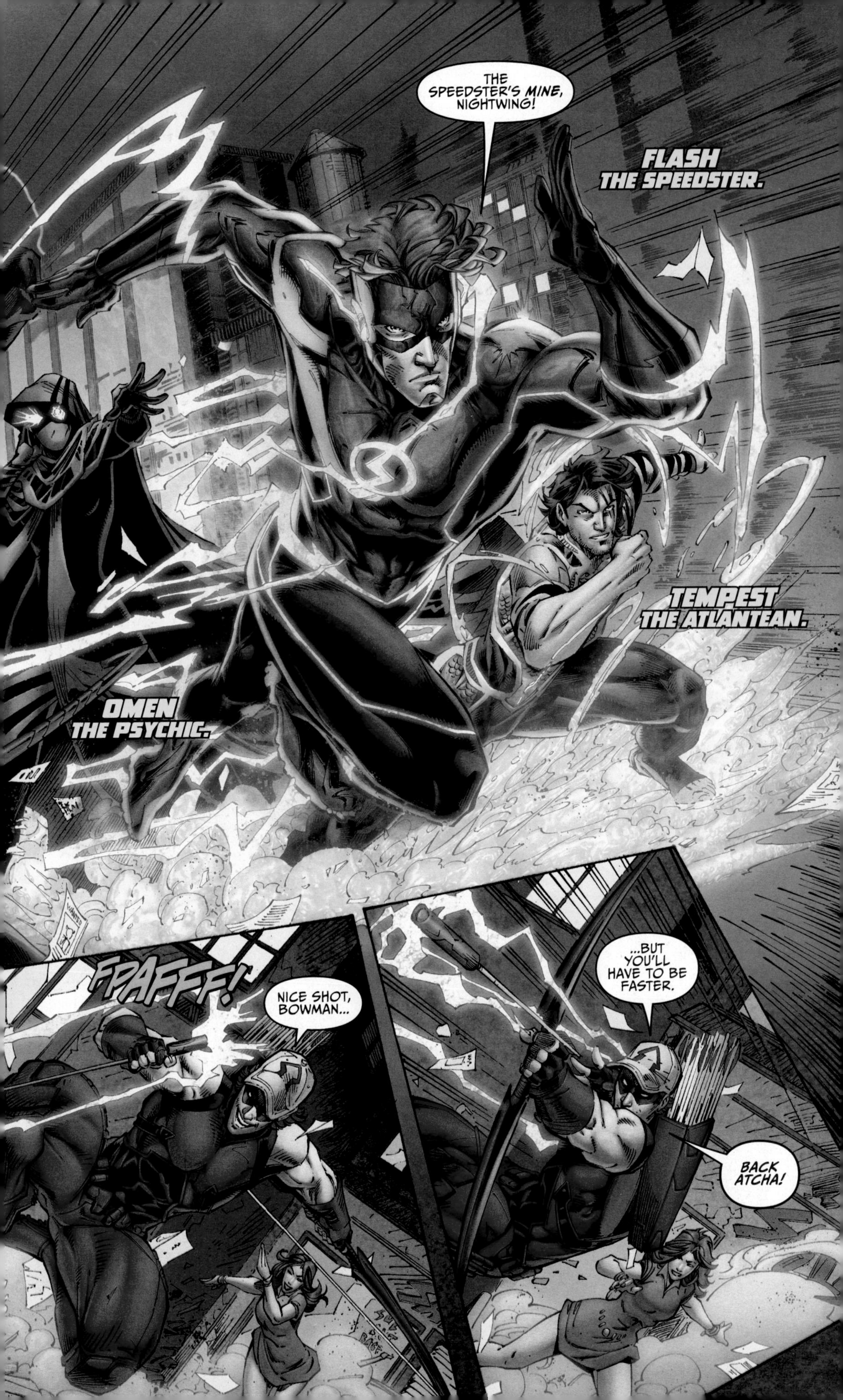
THE SPEEDSTER'S MINE, NIGHTWING!
FLASH THE SPEEDSTER.
TEMPEST THE ATLANTEAN.
OMEN THE PSYCHIC.
FPAFFFF!
NICE SHOT, BOWMAN...
...BUT YOU'LL HAVE TO BE FASTER.
BACK ATCHA!

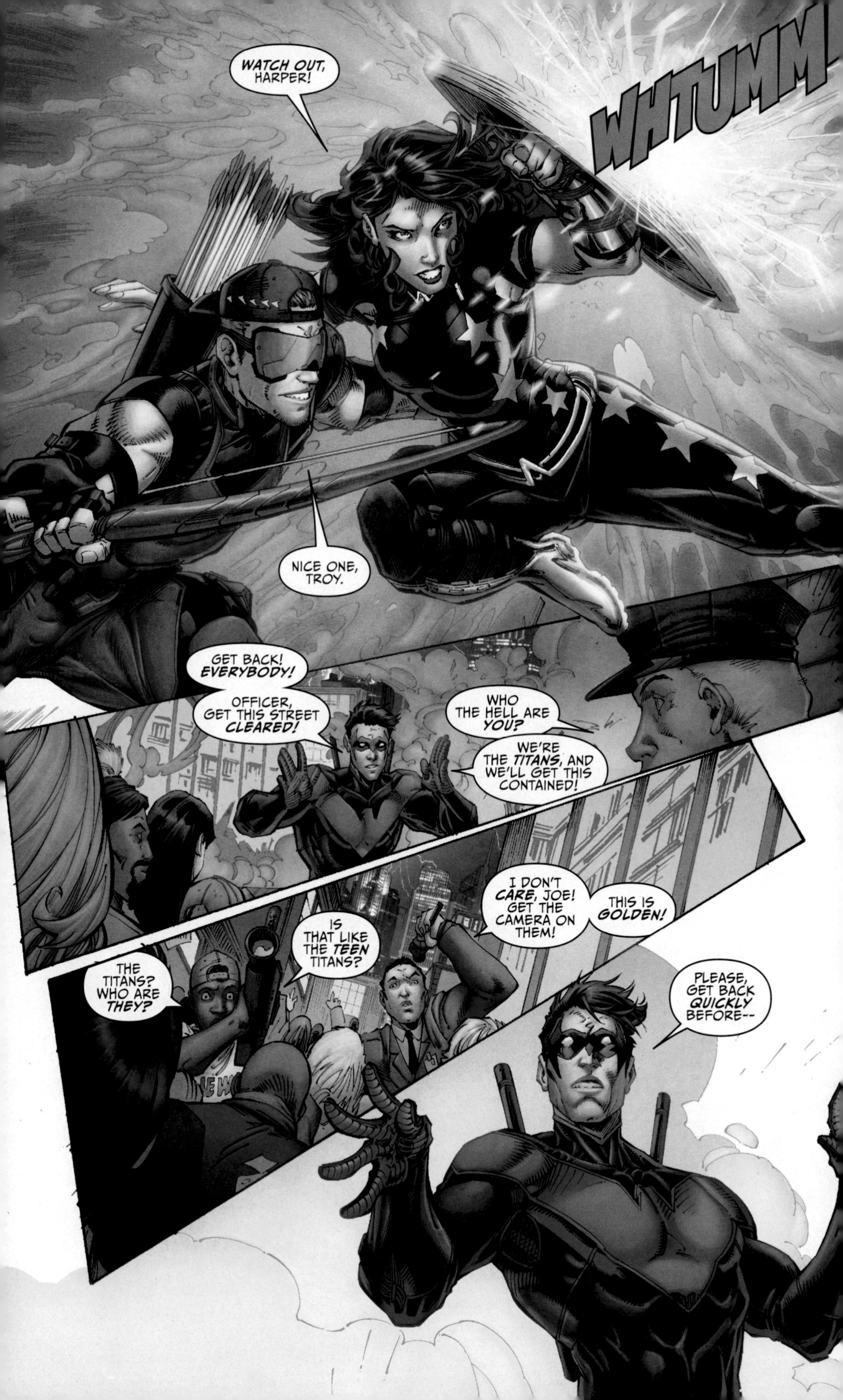
WATCH OUT, HARPER!
WHTUMM
NICE ONE, TROY.
GET BACK! EVERYBODY!
OFFICER, GET THIS STREET CLEARED!
WHO THE HELL ARE YOU?
WE'RE THE TITANS, AND WE'LL GET THIS CONTAINED!
I DON'T CARE, JOE! GET THE CAMERA ON THEM!
THIS IS GOLDEN!
IS THAT LIKE THE TEEN TITANS?
THE TITANS? WHO ARE THEY?
PLEASE, GET BACK QUICKLY BEFORE--

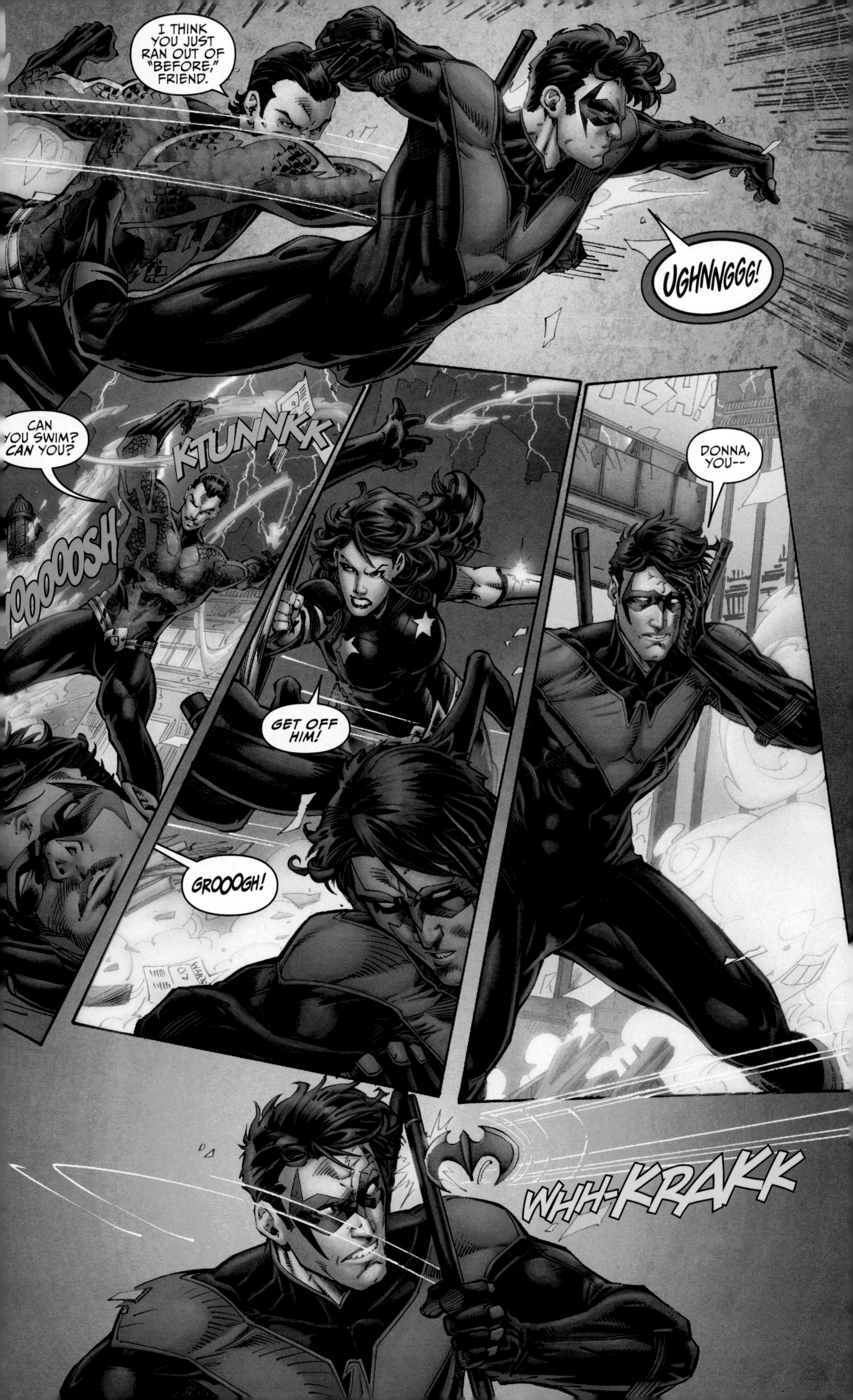

I THINK YOU JUST RAN OUT OF "BEFORE," FRIEND.
UGHNNGGG!
CAN YOU SWIM? CAN YOU?
KTUNNKK
WOOOOOSH
GET OFF HIM!
GROOOGH!
DONNA, YOU--
WHH-KRAKK

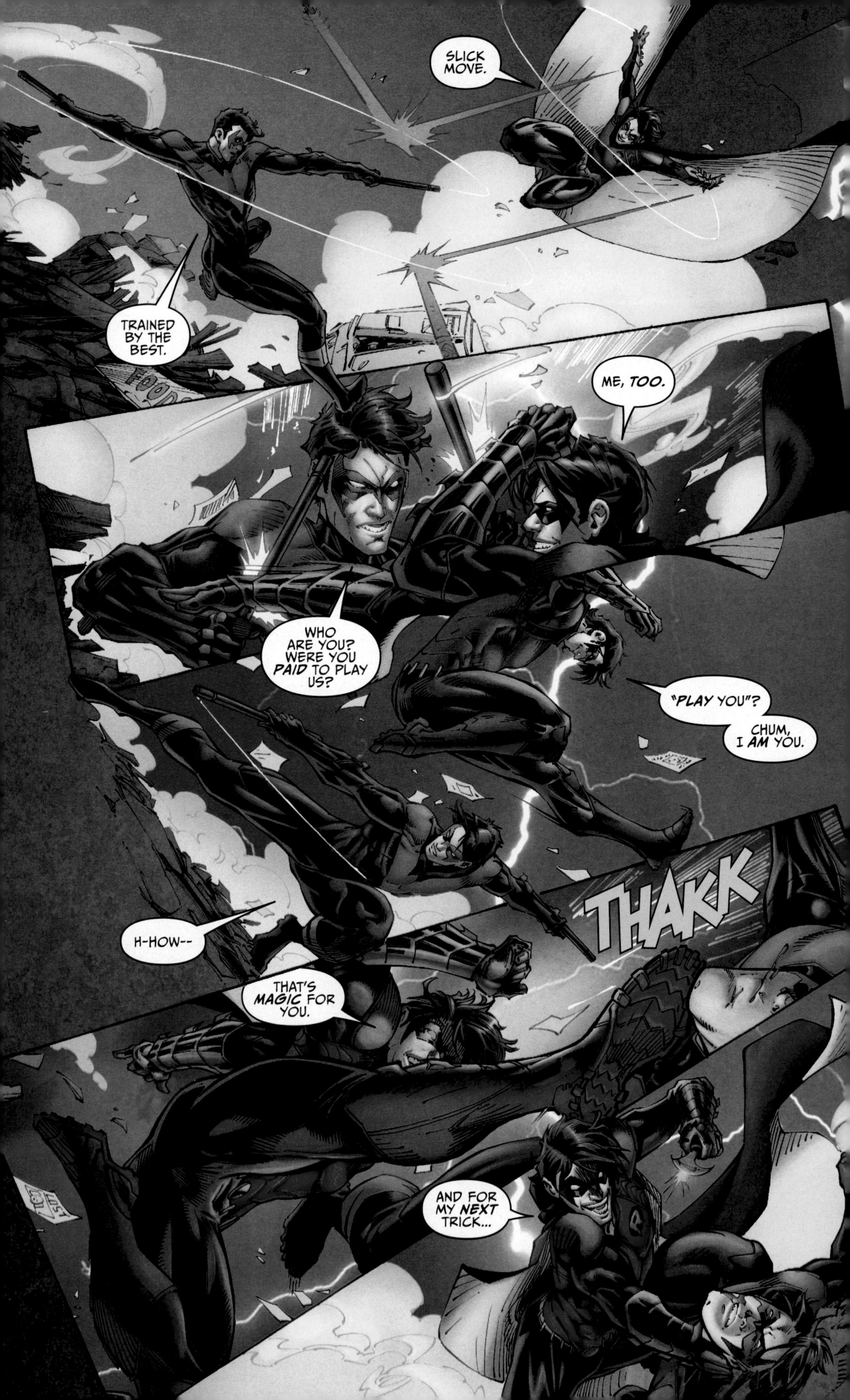
SLICK MOVE.
TRAINED BY THE BEST.
ME, TOO.
WHO ARE YOU? WERE YOU PAID TO PLAY US?
"PLAY YOU"?
CHUM, I AM YOU.
THAKK
H-HOW--
THAT'S MAGIC FOR YOU.
AND FOR MY NEXT TRICK...

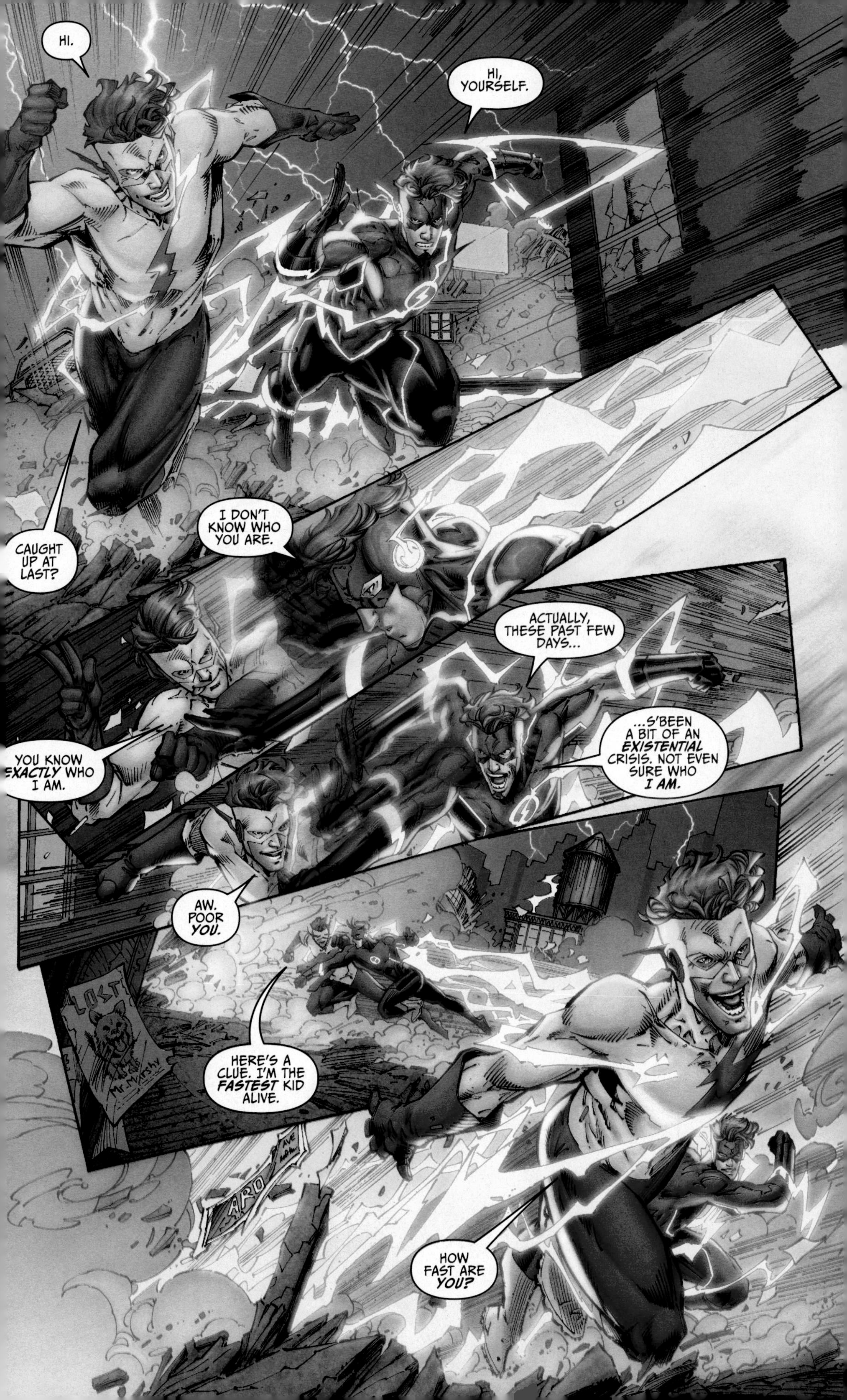
HI.
HI, YOURSELF.
CAUGHT UP AT LAST?
I DON'T KNOW WHO YOU ARE.
YOU KNOW EXACTLY WHO I AM.
ACTUALLY, THESE PAST FEW DAYS...
...S'BEEN A BIT OF AN EXISTENTIAL CRISIS. NOT EVEN SURE WHO I AM.
AW. POOR YOU.
HERE'S A CLUE. I'M THE FASTEST KID ALIVE.
HOW FAST ARE YOU?
LOST!
Mr. Marshy

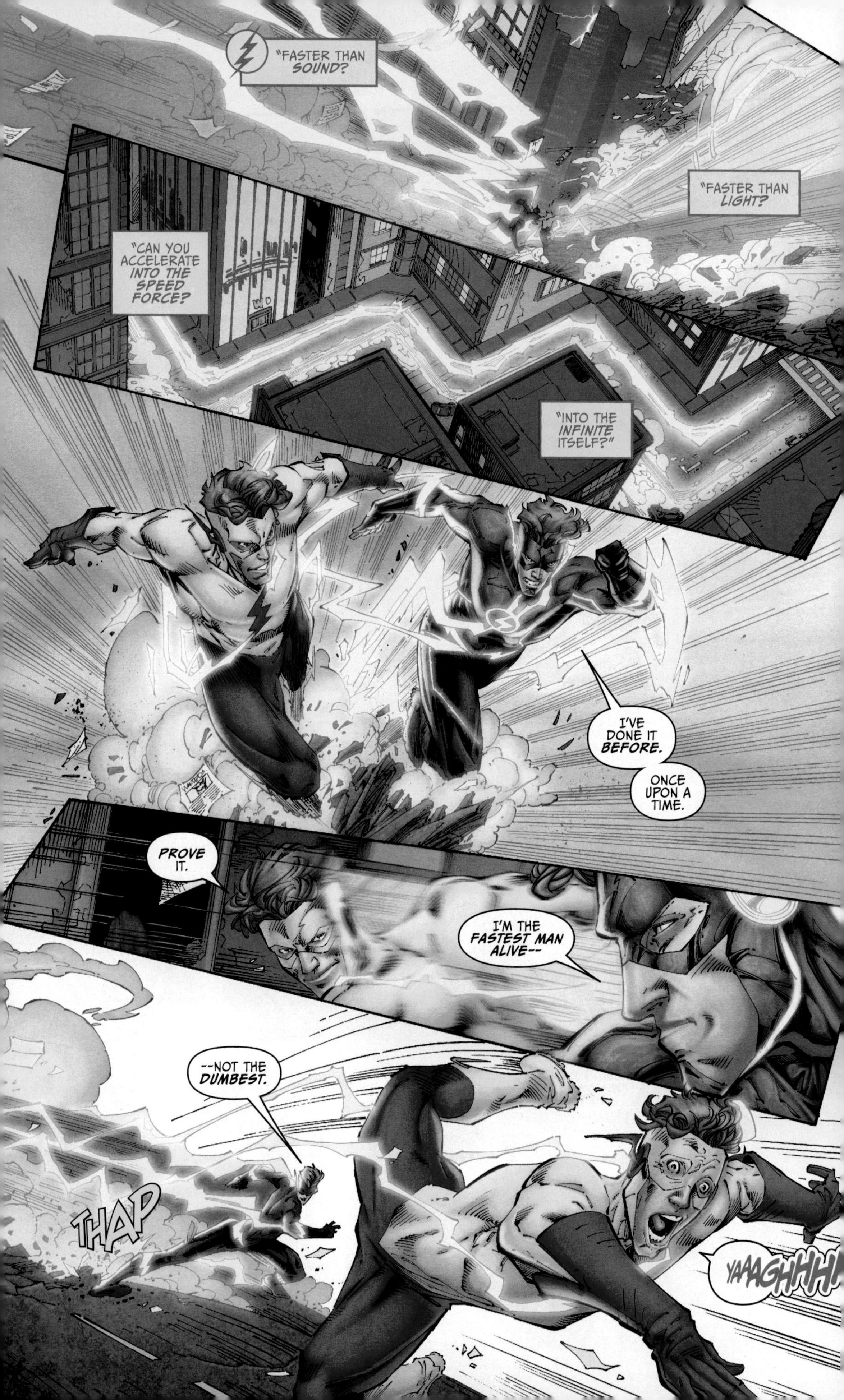
"FASTER THAN SOUND?
"FASTER THAN LIGHT?
"CAN YOU ACCELERATE INTO THE SPEED FORCE?
"INTO THE INFINITE ITSELF?"
I'VE DONE IT BEFORE.
ONCE UPON A TIME.
PROVE IT.
I'M THE FASTEST MAN ALIVE--
--NOT THE DUMBEST.
THAP
YAAAGHHHH

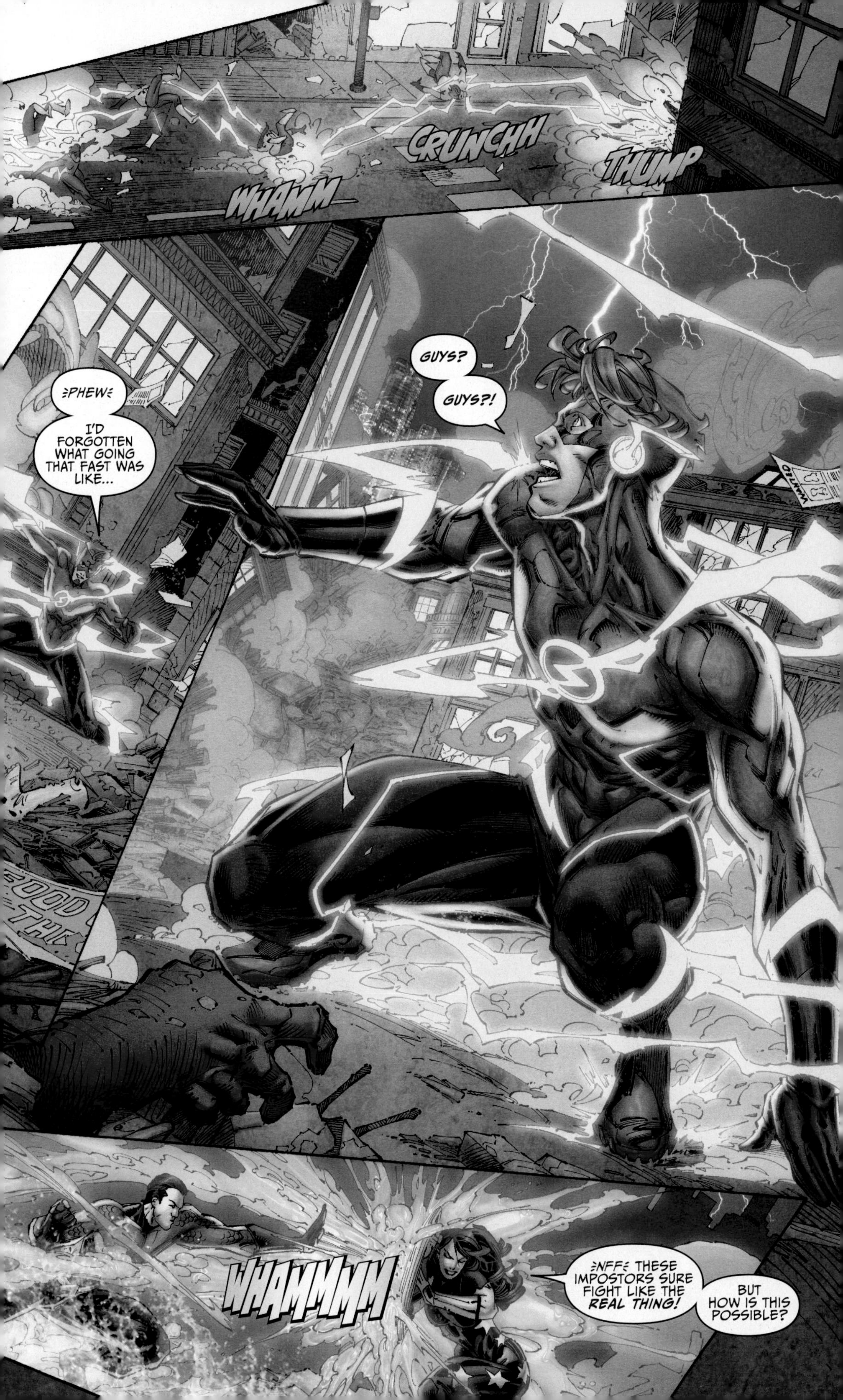
CRUNCHH
THUMP
WHAMM
GUYS?
GUYS?!
PHEW
I'D FORGOTTEN WHAT GOING THAT FAST WAS LIKE...
WHAMMMM
NFF THESE IMPOSTORS SURE FIGHT LIKE THE REAL THING!
BUT HOW IS THIS POSSIBLE?

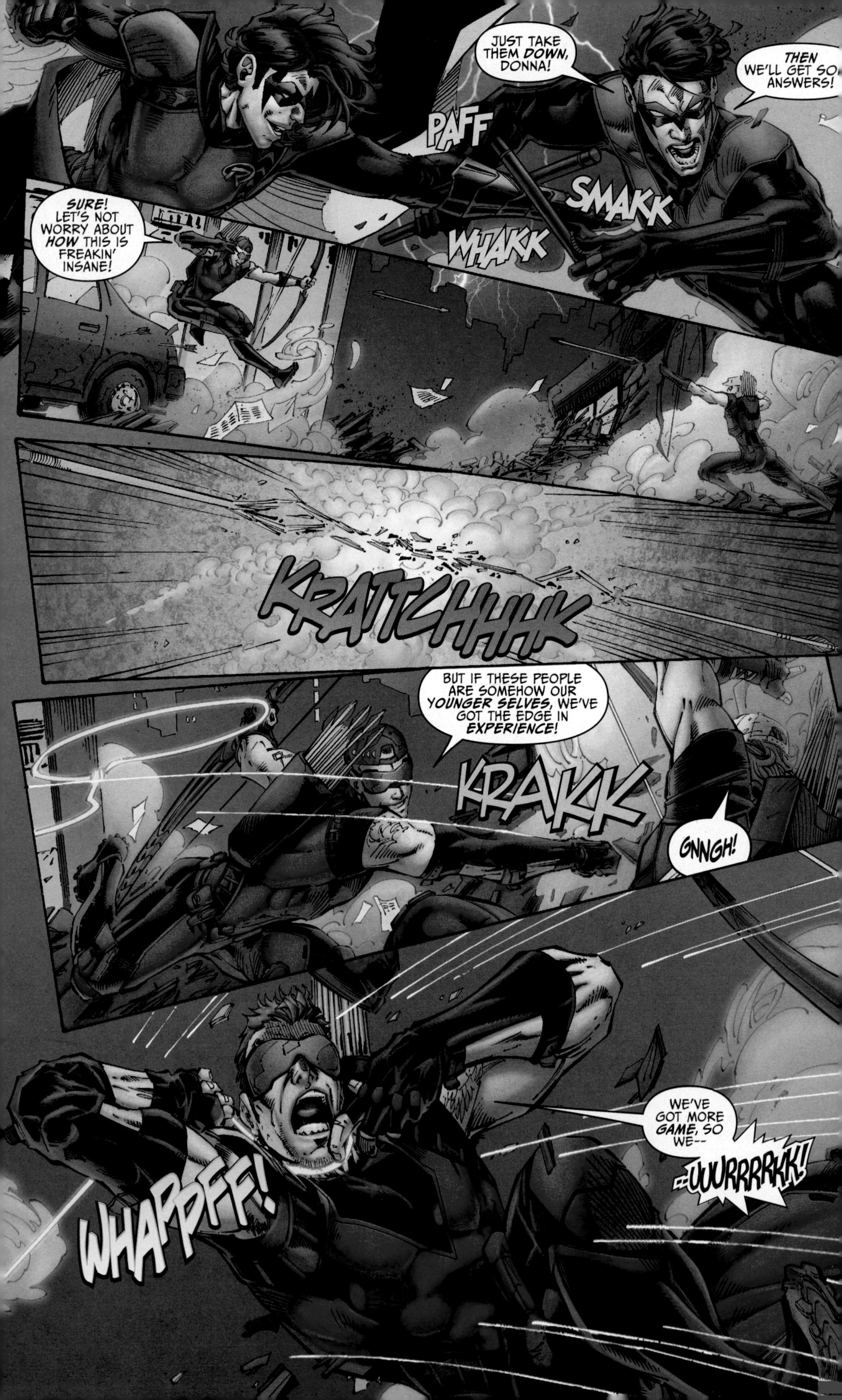

JUST TAKE THEM DOWN, DONNA!
THEN WE'LL GET SO ANSWERS!
PAFF
SMAKK
WHAKK
SURE! LET'S NOT WORRY ABOUT HOW THIS IS FREAKIN' INSANE!
KRATTCHHHK
BUT IF THESE PEOPLE ARE SOMEHOW OUR YOUNGER SELVES, WE'VE GOT THE EDGE IN EXPERIENCE!
KRAKK
GNNGH!
WE'VE GOT MORE GAME, SO WE--
--UUURRRRKK!
WHAPFF!

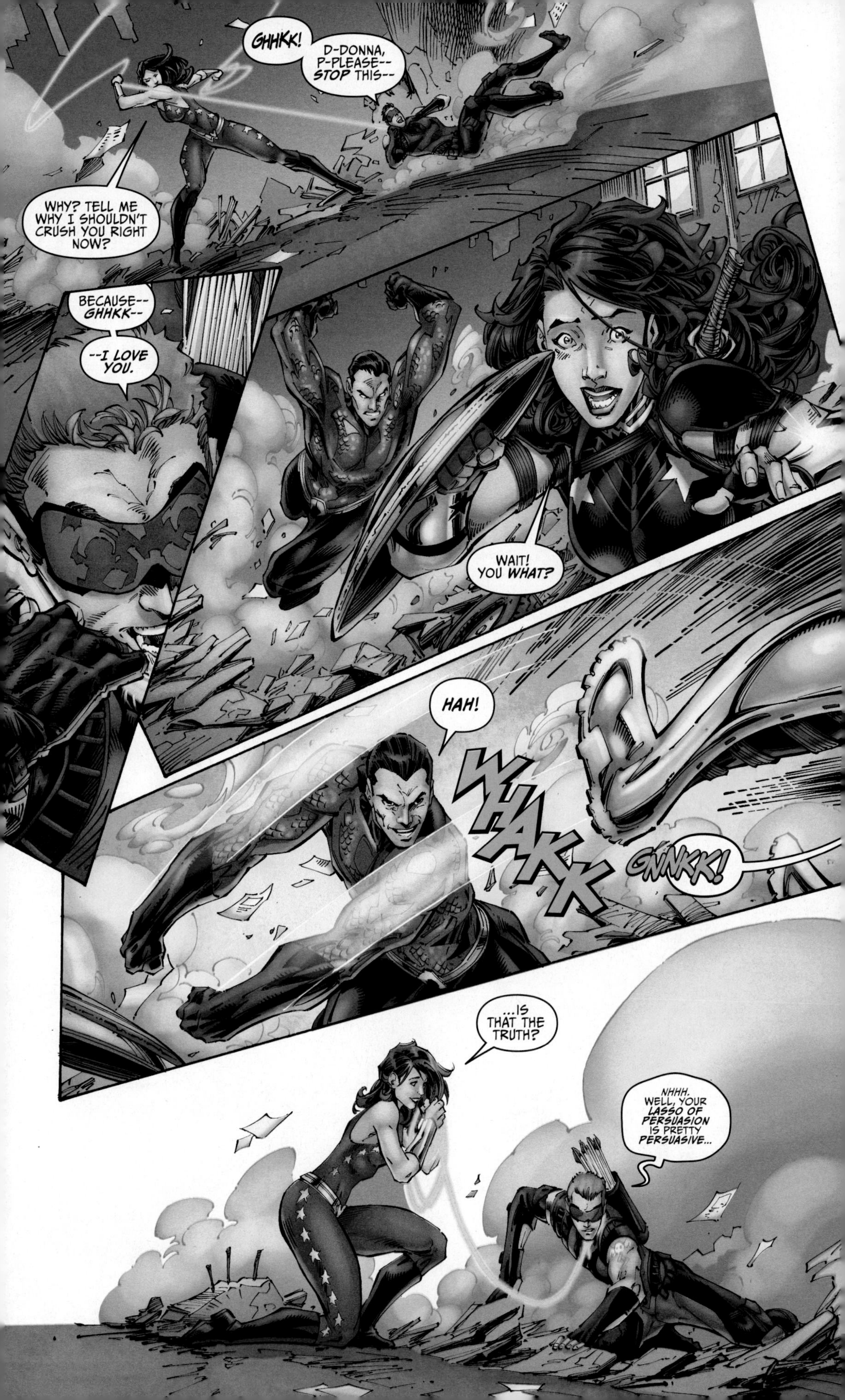
GHHKK!
D-DONNA, P-PLEASE-- STOP THIS--
WHY? TELL ME WHY I SHOULDN'T CRUSH YOU RIGHT NOW?
BECAUSE-- GHHKK--
--I LOVE YOU.
WAIT! YOU WHAT?
HAH!
WHAKK
GNNKK!
...IS THAT THE TRUTH?
NHHH. WELL, YOUR LASSO OF PERSUASION IS PRETTY PERSUASIVE...

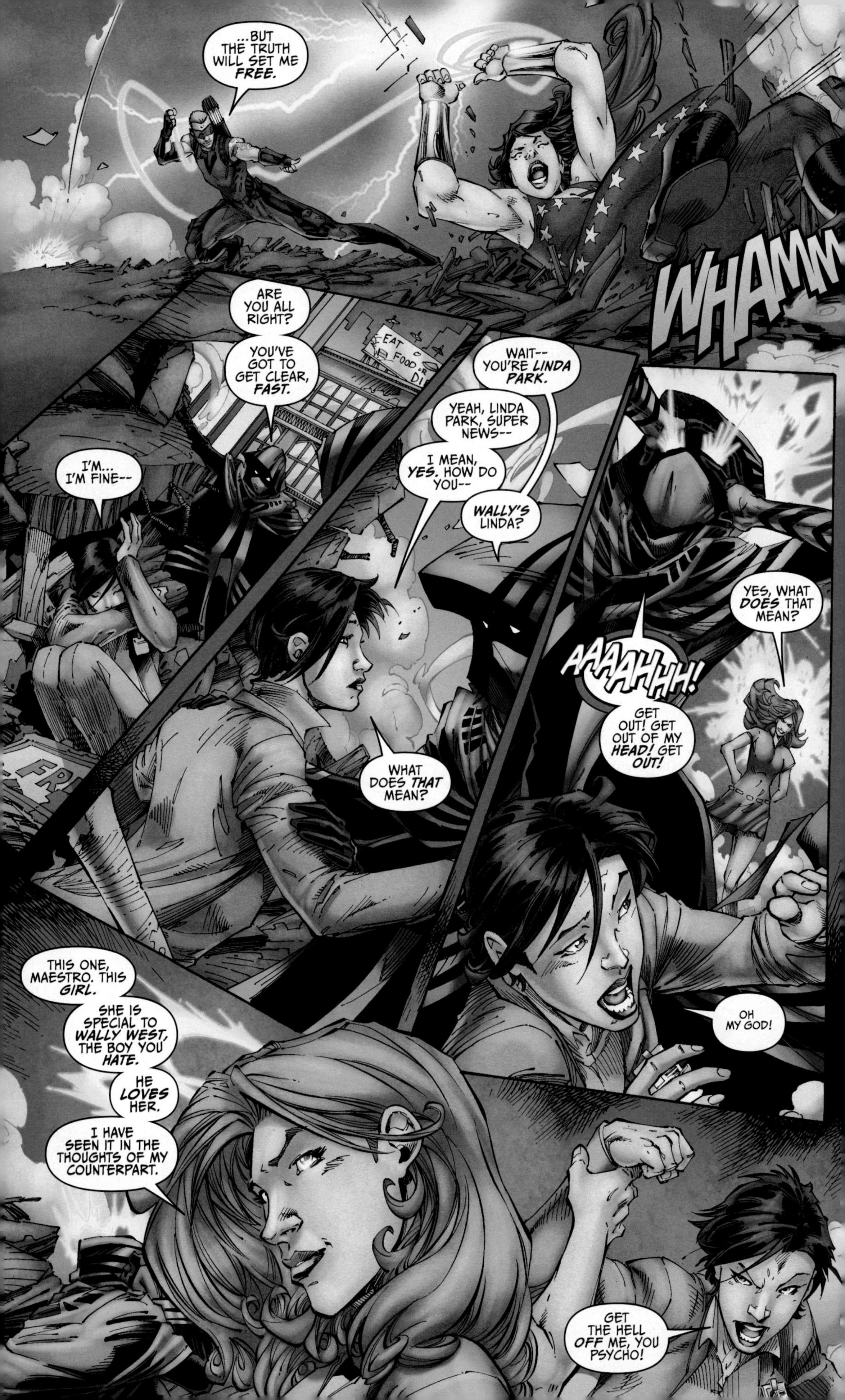

...BUT THE TRUTH WILL SET ME FREE.
WHAMM
ARE YOU ALL RIGHT?
YOU'VE GOT TO GET CLEAR, FAST.
I'M... I'M FINE--
EAT FOOD
WAIT-- YOU'RE LINDA PARK.
YEAH, LINDA PARK, SUPER NEWS--
I MEAN, YES. HOW DO YOU--
WALLY'S LINDA?
WHAT DOES THAT MEAN?
AAAAHHH!
GET OUT! GET OUT OF MY HEAD! GET OUT!
YES, WHAT DOES THAT MEAN?
OH MY GOD!
THIS ONE, MAESTRO. THIS GIRL.
SHE IS SPECIAL TO WALLY WEST, THE BOY YOU HATE.
HE LOVES HER.
I HAVE SEEN IT IN THE THOUGHTS OF MY COUNTERPART.
GET THE HELL OFF ME, YOU PSYCHO!

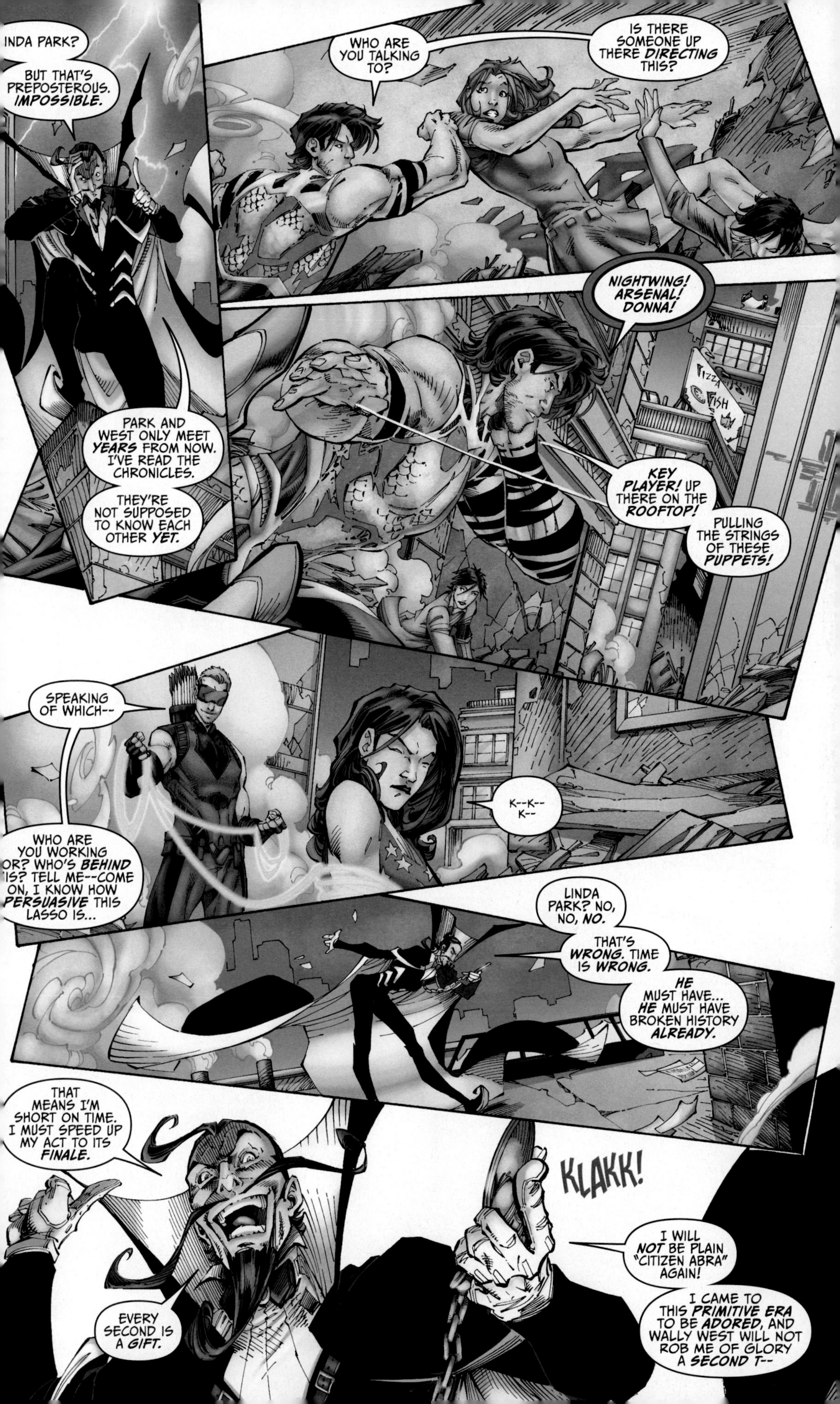

INDA PARK?
BUT THAT'S PREPOSTEROUS. IMPOSSIBLE.
WHO ARE YOU TALKING TO?
IS THERE SOMEONE UP THERE DIRECTING THIS?
PARK AND WEST ONLY MEET YEARS FROM NOW. I'VE READ THE CHRONICLES.
THEY'RE NOT SUPPOSED TO KNOW EACH OTHER YET.
NIGHTWING! ARSENAL! DONNA!
KEY PLAYER! UP THERE ON THE ROOFTOP!
PULLING THE STRINGS OF THESE PUPPETS!
PIZZA
FISH
SPEAKING OF WHICH--
WHO ARE YOU WORKING OR? WHO'S BEHIND IS? TELL ME--COME ON, I KNOW HOW PERSUASIVE THIS LASSO IS...
K--K-- K--
LINDA PARK? NO, NO, NO.
THAT'S WRONG. TIME IS WRONG.
HE MUST HAVE... HE MUST HAVE BROKEN HISTORY ALREADY.
THAT MEANS I'M SHORT ON TIME. I MUST SPEED UP MY ACT TO ITS FINALE.
KLAKK!
I WILL NOT BE PLAIN "CITIZEN ABRA" AGAIN!
I CAME TO THIS PRIMITIVE ERA TO BE ADORED, AND WALLY WEST WILL NOT ROB ME OF GLORY A SECOND T--
EVERY SECOND IS A GIFT.

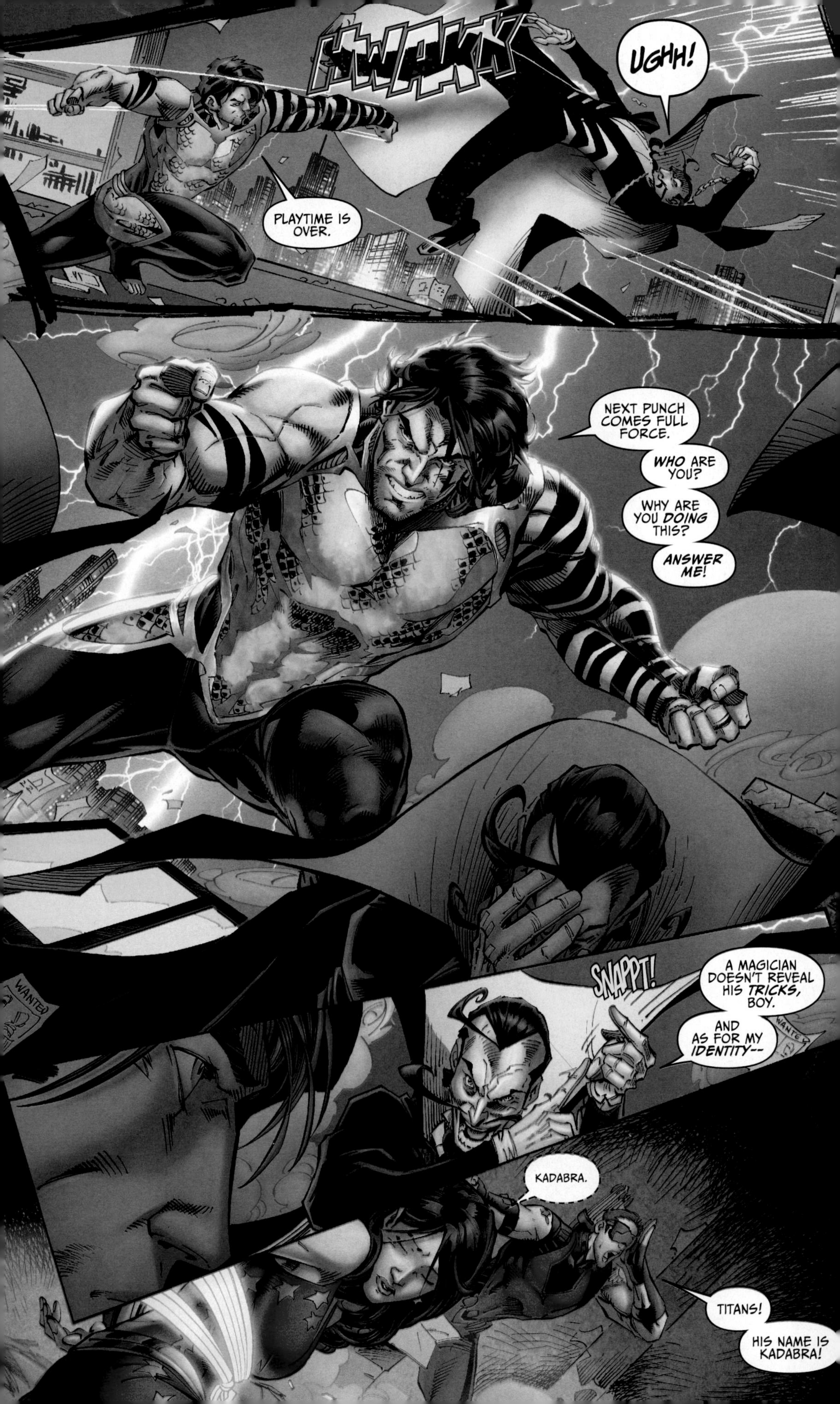

HWAKK
UGHH!
PLAYTIME IS OVER.
NEXT PUNCH COMES FULL FORCE.
WHO ARE YOU?
WHY ARE YOU DOING THIS?
ANSWER ME!
SNAPPT!
A MAGICIAN DOESN'T REVEAL HIS TRICKS, BOY.
AND AS FOR MY IDENTITY--
KADABRA.
TITANS!
HIS NAME IS KADABRA!

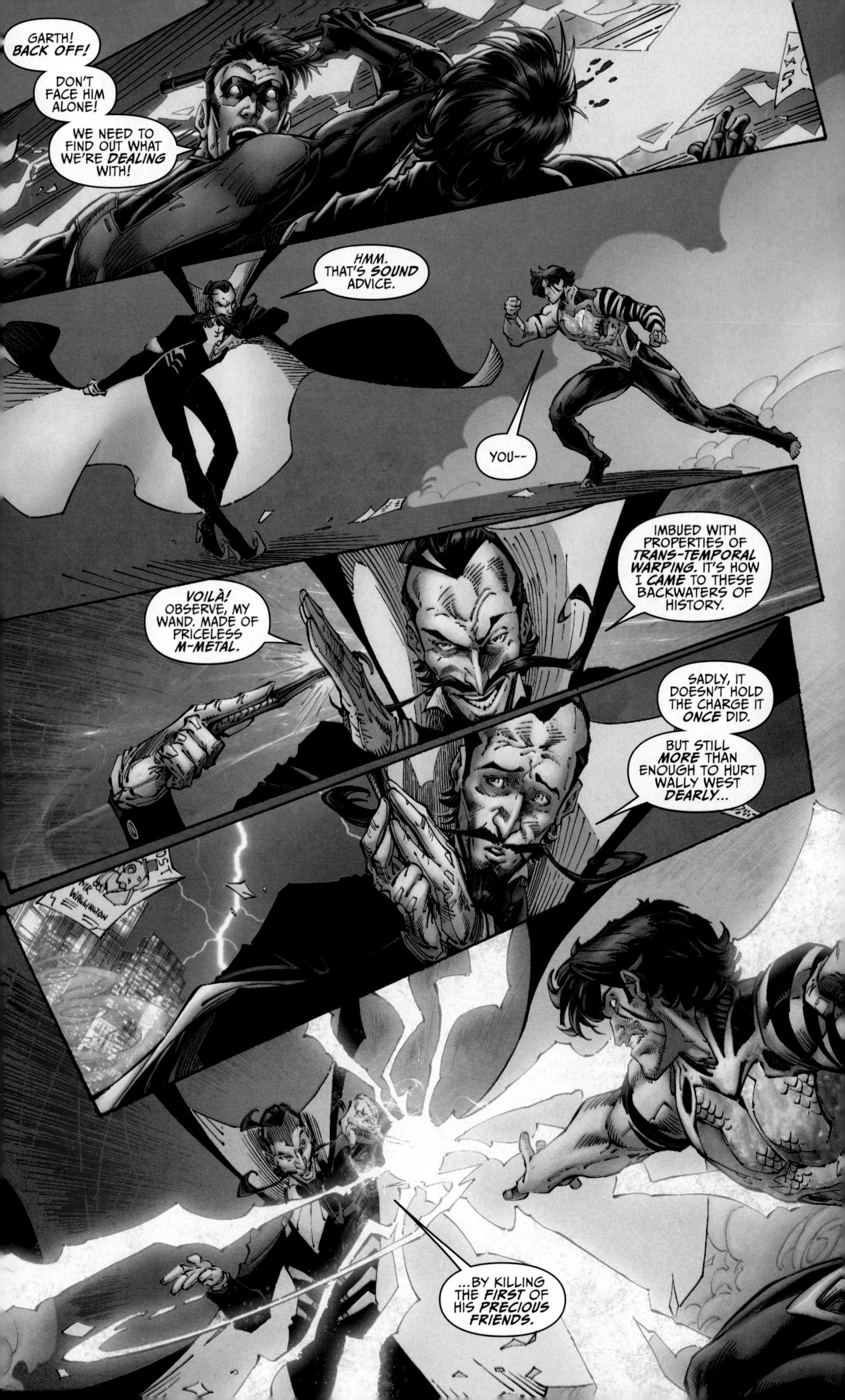
GARTH! BACK OFF!
DON'T FACE HIM ALONE!
WE NEED TO FIND OUT WHAT WE'RE DEALING WITH!
HMM. THAT'S SOUND ADVICE.
YOU--
VOILÀ! OBSERVE, MY WAND. MADE OF PRICELESS M-METAL.
IMBUED WITH PROPERTIES OF TRANS-TEMPORAL WARPING. IT'S HOW I CAME TO THESE BACKWATERS OF HISTORY.
SADLY, IT DOESN'T HOLD THE CHARGE IT ONCE DID.
BUT STILL MORE THAN ENOUGH TO HURT WALLY WEST DEARLY...
...BY KILLING THE FIRST OF HIS PRECIOUS FRIENDS.

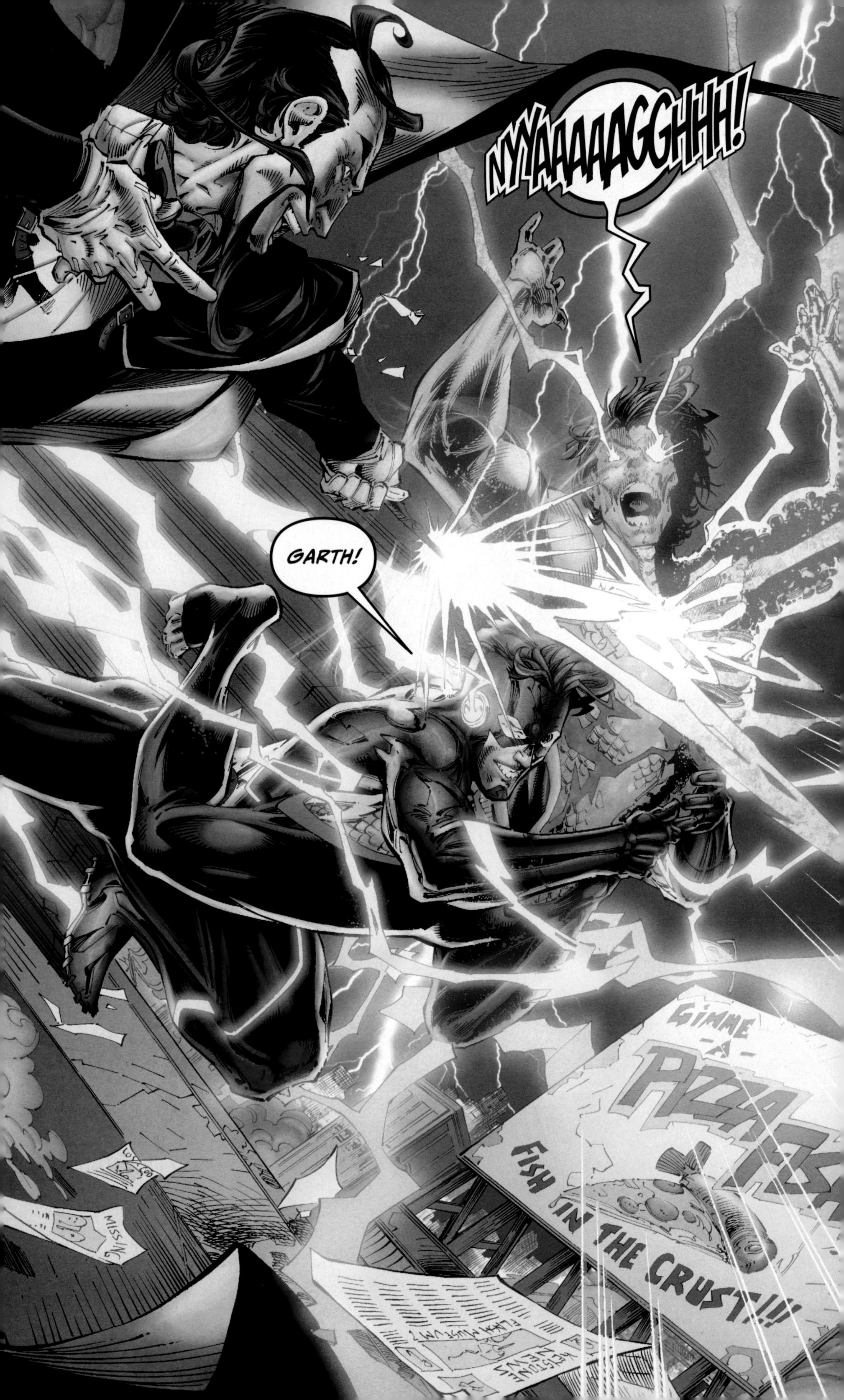

NYYAAAAAGGHHH!
GARTH!
GIMME
-A-
FISH IN THE CRUST!!!

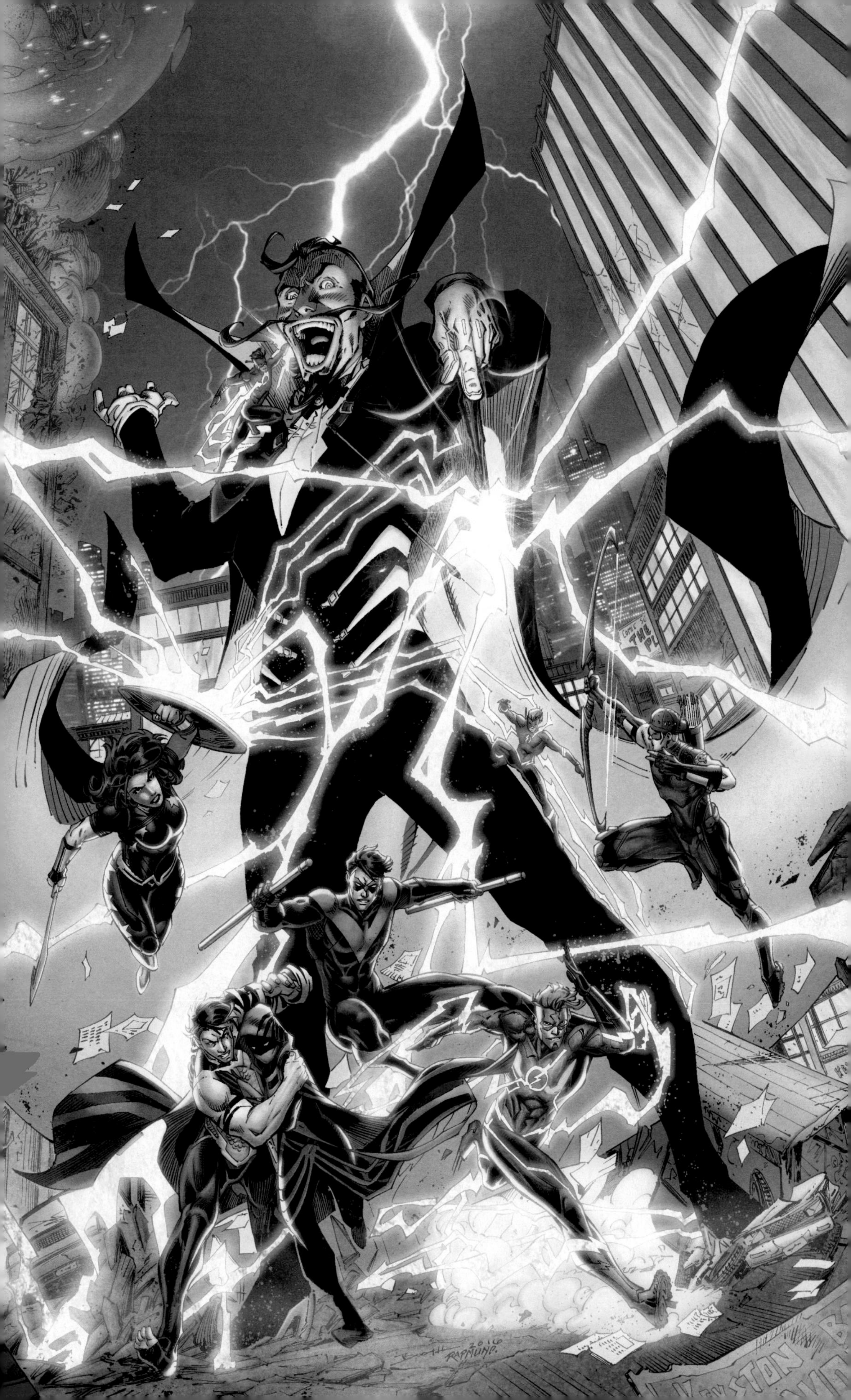

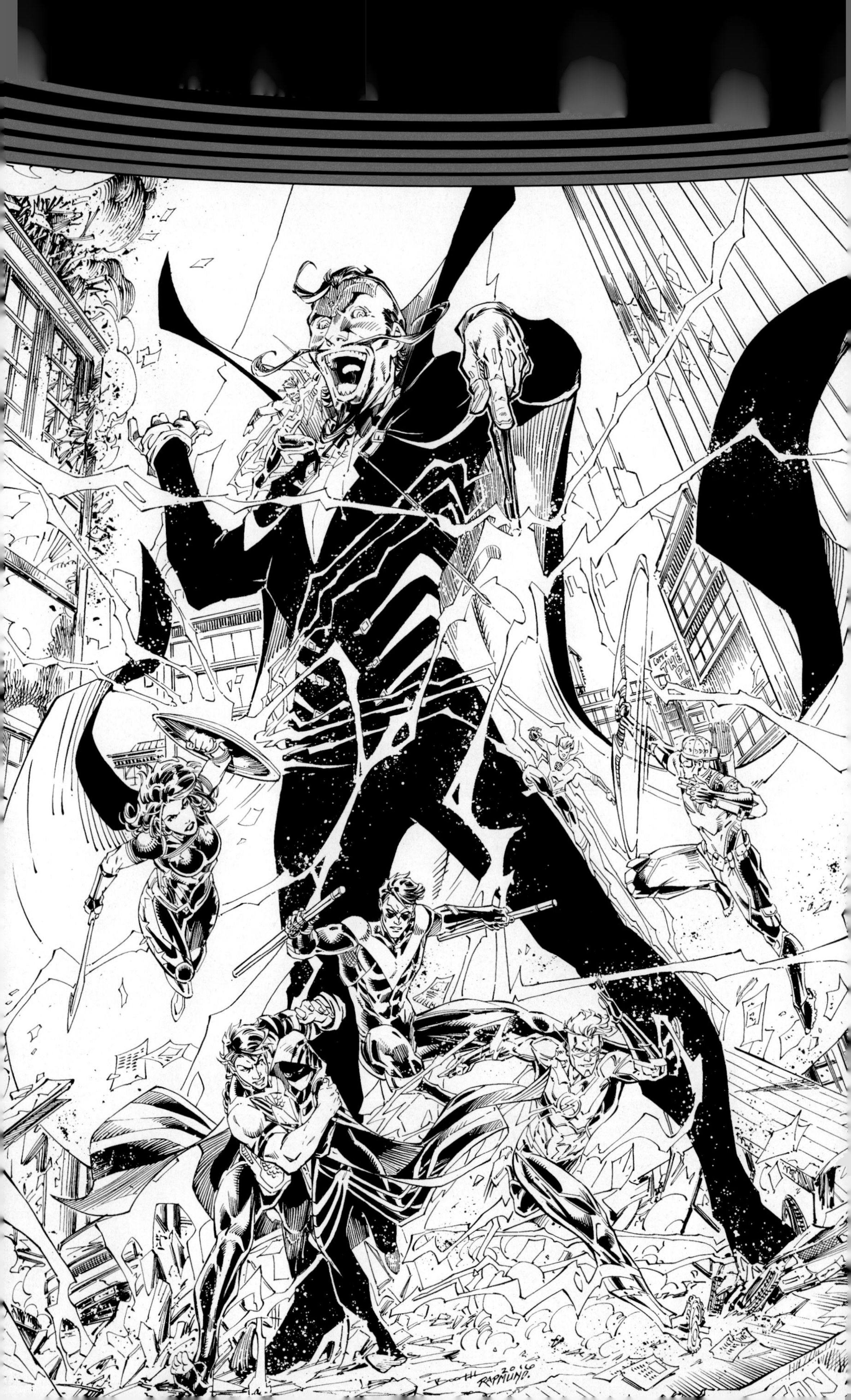
Booth
2016
RAPMUND.

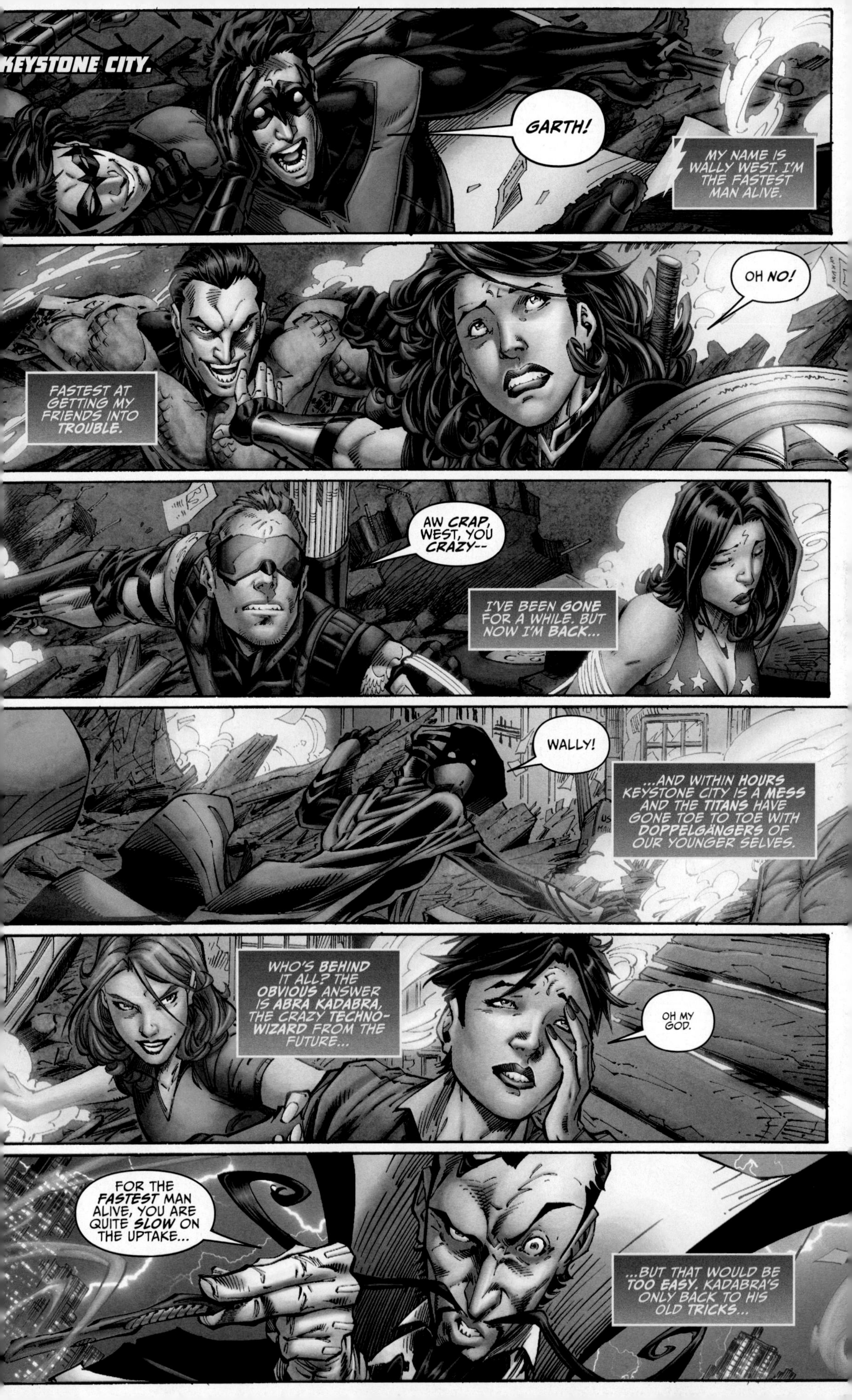
KEYSTONE CITY.
GARTH!
MY NAME IS WALLY WEST. I'M THE FASTEST MAN ALIVE.
OH NO!
FASTEST AT GETTING MY FRIENDS INTO TROUBLE.
AW CRAP, WEST, YOU CRAZY--
I'VE BEEN GONE FOR A WHILE. BUT NOW I'M BACK...
WALLY!
...AND WITHIN HOURS KEYSTONE CITY IS A MESS AND THE TITANS HAVE GONE TOE TO TOE WITH DOPPELGÄNGERS OF OUR YOUNGER SELVES.
WHO'S BEHIND IT ALL? THE OBVIOUS ANSWER IS ABRA KADABRA, THE CRAZY TECHNO-WIZARD FROM THE FUTURE...
OH MY GOD.
FOR THE FASTEST MAN ALIVE, YOU ARE QUITE SLOW ON THE UPTAKE...
...BUT THAT WOULD BE TOO EASY. KADABRA'S ONLY BACK TO HIS OLD TRICKS...

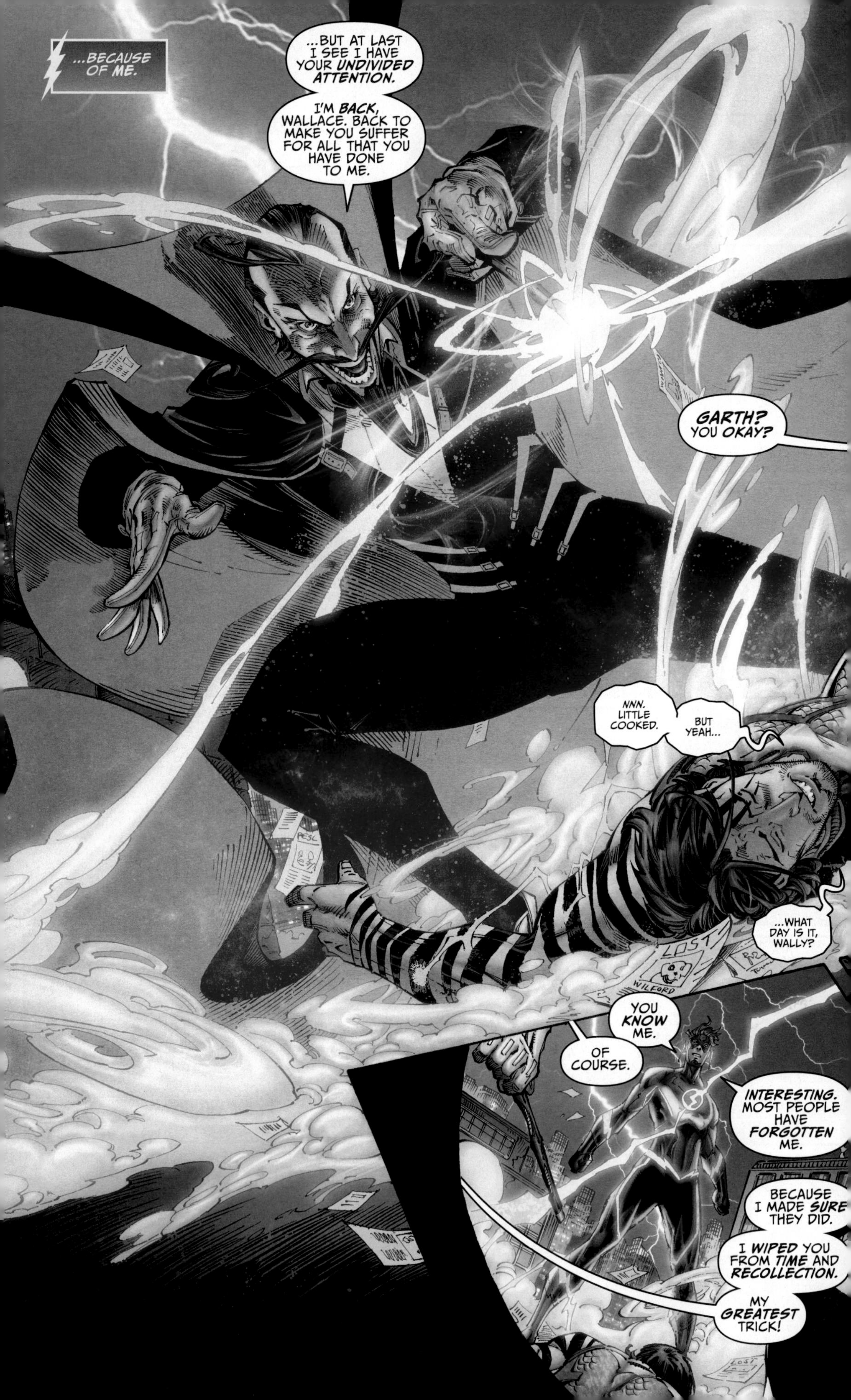
...BECAUSE OF ME.
...BUT AT LAST I SEE I HAVE YOUR UNDIVIDED ATTENTION.
I'M BACK, WALLACE. BACK TO MAKE YOU SUFFER FOR ALL THAT YOU HAVE DONE TO ME.
GARTH? YOU OKAY?
NNN. LITTLE COOKED.
BUT YEAH...
...WHAT DAY IS IT, WALLY?
YOU KNOW ME.
OF COURSE.
INTERESTING. MOST PEOPLE HAVE FORGOTTEN ME.
BECAUSE I MADE SURE THEY DID.
I WIPED YOU FROM TIME AND RECOLLECTION.
MY GREATEST TRICK!

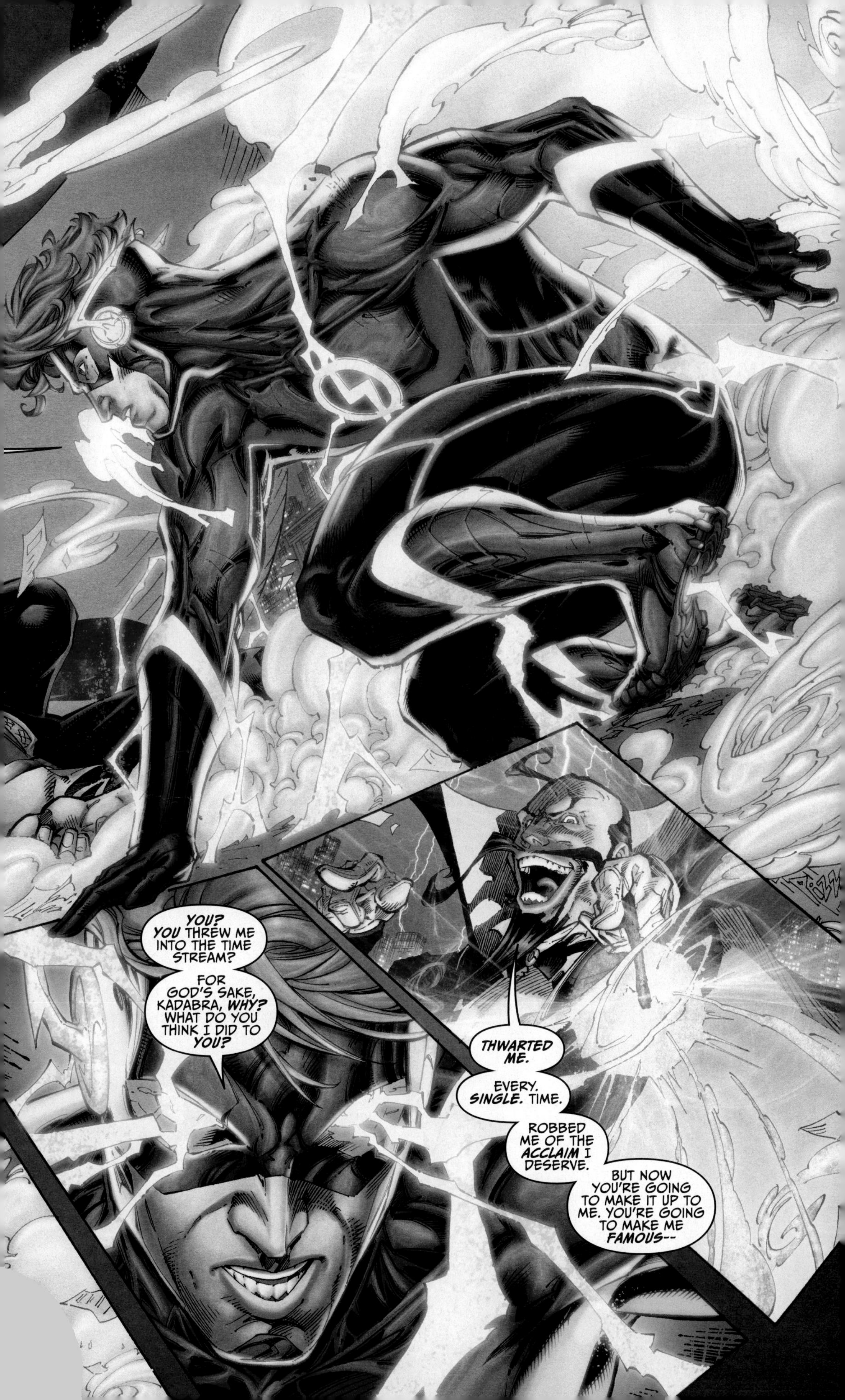
YOU? YOU THREW ME INTO THE TIME STREAM?
FOR GOD'S SAKE, KADABRA, WHY? WHAT DO YOU THINK I DID TO YOU?
THWARTED ME.
EVERY. SINGLE. TIME.
ROBBED ME OF THE ACCLAIM I DESERVE.
BUT NOW YOU'RE GOING TO MAKE IT UP TO ME. YOU'RE GOING TO MAKE ME FAMOUS--

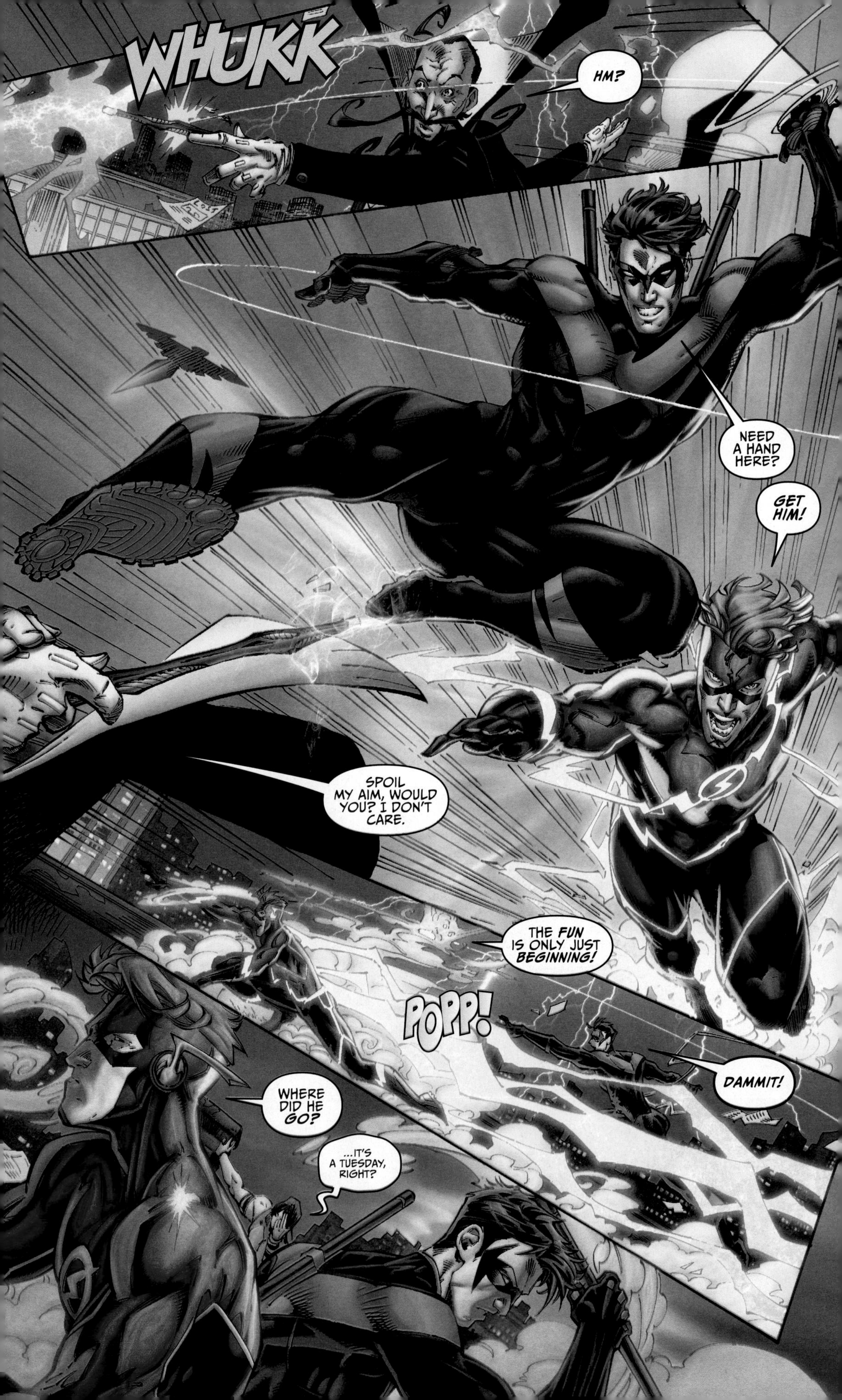
WHUKK
HM?
NEED A HAND HERE?
GET HIM!
SPOIL MY AIM, WOULD YOU? I DON'T CARE.
THE FUN IS ONLY JUST BEGINNING!
POPP!
DAMMIT!
WHERE DID HE GO?
...IT'S A TUESDAY, RIGHT?

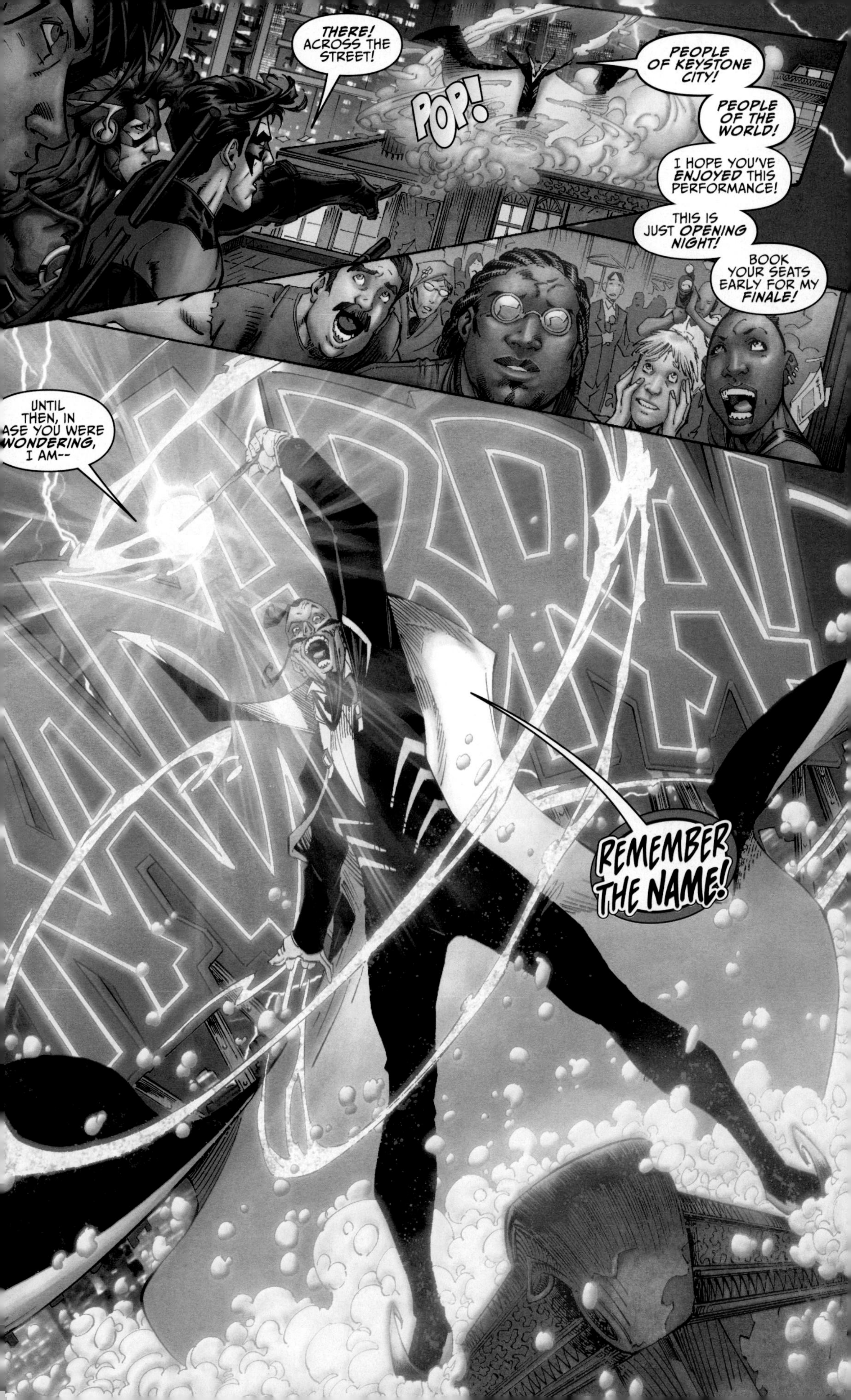
THERE! ACROSS THE STREET!
POP!
PEOPLE OF KEYSTONE CITY!
PEOPLE OF THE WORLD!
I HOPE YOU'VE ENJOYED THIS PERFORMANCE!
THIS IS JUST OPENING NIGHT!
BOOK YOUR SEATS EARLY FOR MY FINALE!
UNTIL THEN, IN ASE YOU WERE WONDERING, I AM--
REMEMBER THE NAME!

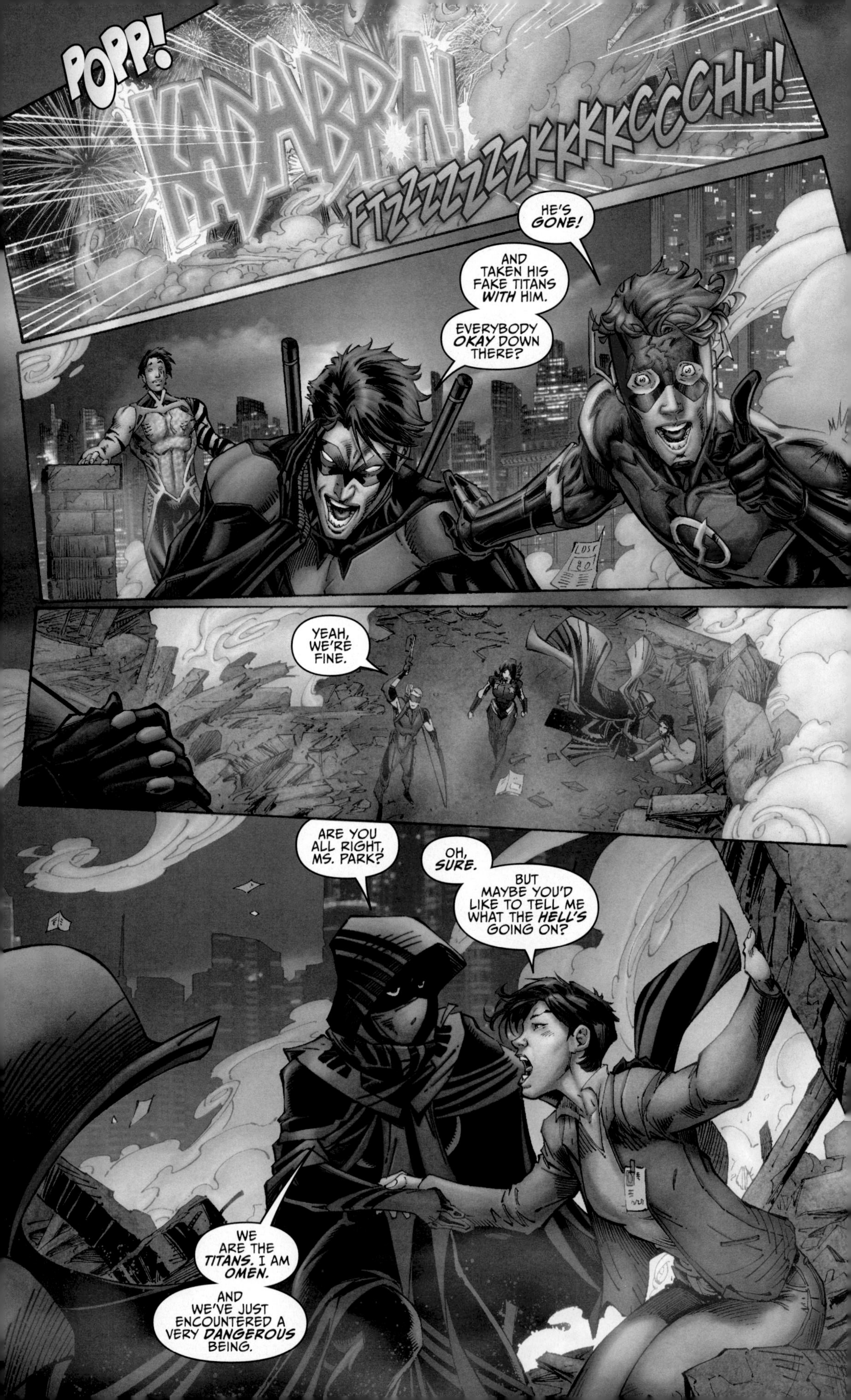
POPP!
KADABRA!
FTZZZZZZZKKKKCCCHH!
HE'S GONE!
AND TAKEN HIS FAKE TITANS WITH HIM.
EVERYBODY OKAY DOWN THERE?
YEAH, WE'RE FINE.
ARE YOU ALL RIGHT, MS. PARK?
OH, SURE.
BUT MAYBE YOU'D LIKE TO TELL ME WHAT THE HELL'S GOING ON?
WE ARE THE TITANS. I AM OMEN.
AND WE'VE JUST ENCOUNTERED A VERY DANGEROUS BEING.

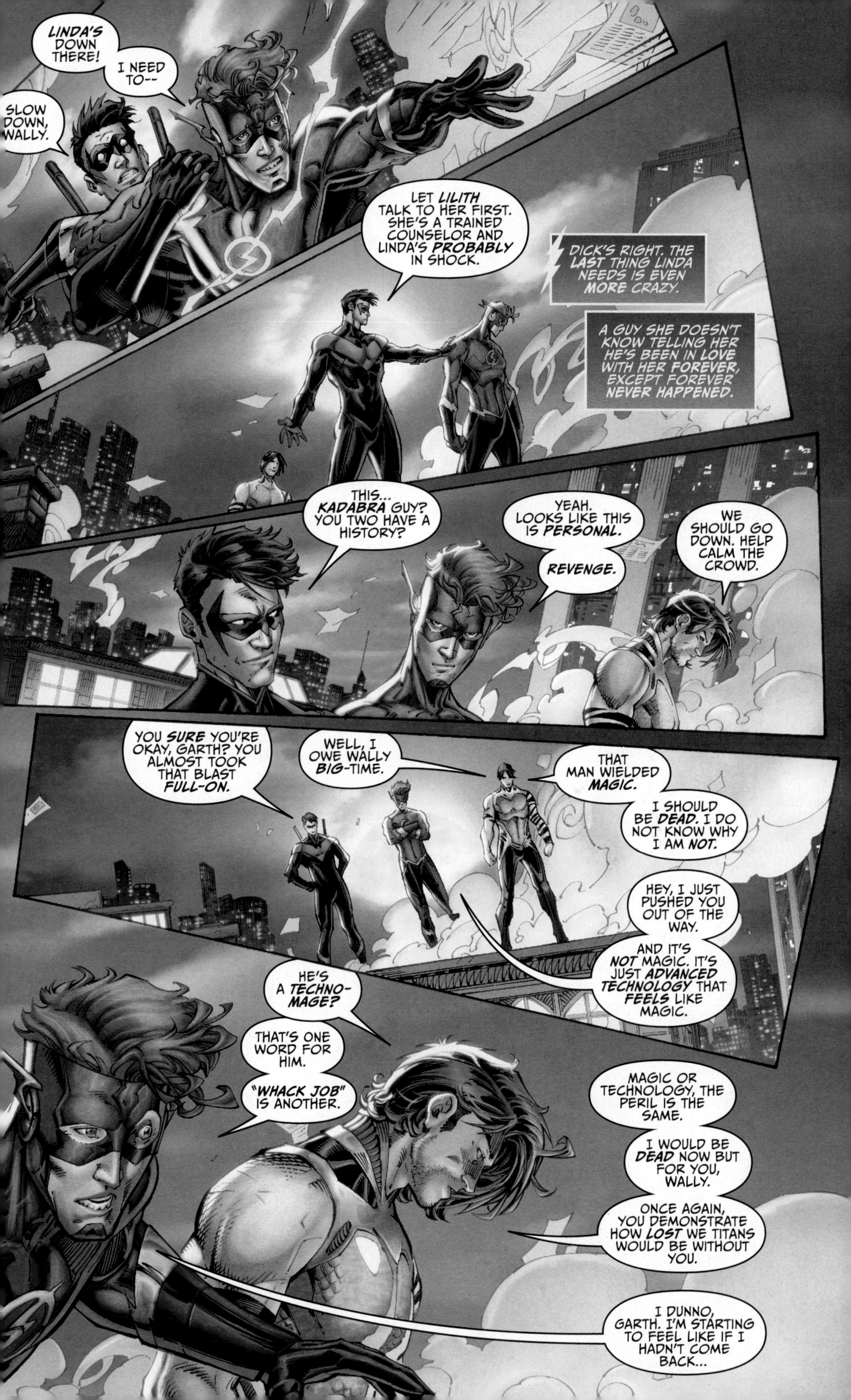
LINDA'S DOWN THERE!
I NEED TO--
SLOW DOWN, WALLY.
LET LILITH TALK TO HER FIRST. SHE'S A TRAINED COUNSELOR AND LINDA'S PROBABLY IN SHOCK.
DICK'S RIGHT. THE LAST THING LINDA NEEDS IS EVEN MORE CRAZY.
A GUY SHE DOESN'T KNOW TELLING HER HE'S BEEN IN LOVE WITH HER FOREVER, EXCEPT FOREVER NEVER HAPPENED.
THIS... KADABRA GUY? YOU TWO HAVE A HISTORY?
YEAH. LOOKS LIKE THIS IS PERSONAL.
REVENGE.
WE SHOULD GO DOWN. HELP CALM THE CROWD.
YOU SURE YOU'RE OKAY, GARTH? YOU ALMOST TOOK THAT BLAST FULL-ON.
WELL, I OWE WALLY BIG-TIME.
THAT MAN WIELDED MAGIC.
I SHOULD BE DEAD. I DO NOT KNOW WHY I AM NOT.
HEY, I JUST PUSHED YOU OUT OF THE WAY.
AND IT'S NOT MAGIC. IT'S JUST ADVANCED TECHNOLOGY THAT FEELS LIKE MAGIC.
HE'S A TECHNO-MAGE?
THAT'S ONE WORD FOR HIM.
"WHACK JOB" IS ANOTHER.
MAGIC OR TECHNOLOGY, THE PERIL IS THE SAME.
I WOULD BE DEAD NOW BUT FOR YOU, WALLY.
ONCE AGAIN, YOU DEMONSTRATE HOW LOST WE TITANS WOULD BE WITHOUT YOU.
I DUNNO, GARTH. I'M STARTING TO FEEL LIKE IF I HADN'T COME BACK...

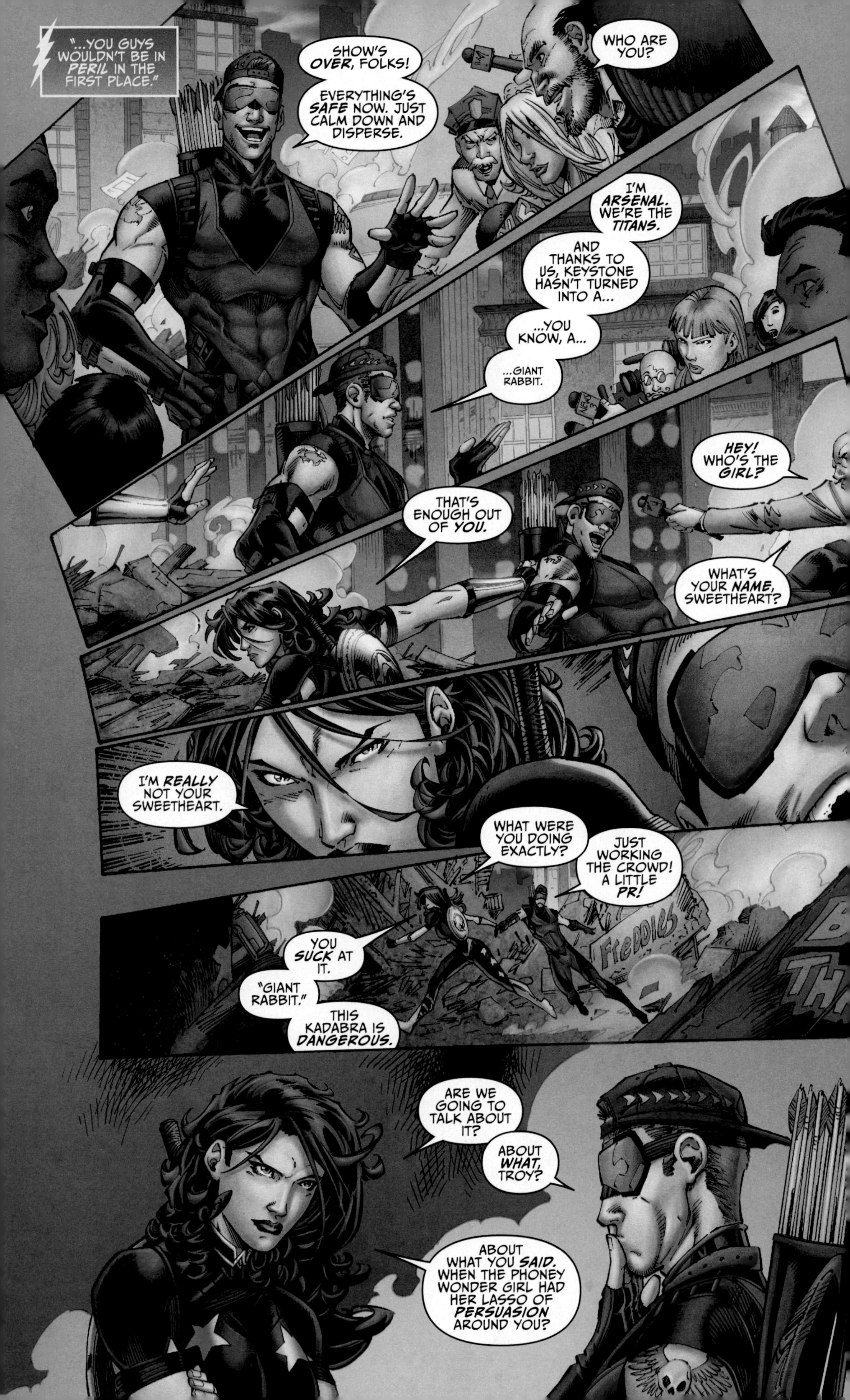
"...YOU GUYS WOULDN'T BE IN PERIL IN THE FIRST PLACE."
SHOW'S OVER, FOLKS!
EVERYTHING'S SAFE NOW. JUST CALM DOWN AND DISPERSE.
WHO ARE YOU?
I'M ARSENAL. WE'RE THE TITANS.
AND THANKS TO US, KEYSTONE HASN'T TURNED INTO A...
...YOU KNOW, A...
...GIANT RABBIT.
HEY! WHO'S THE GIRL?
THAT'S ENOUGH OUT OF YOU.
WHAT'S YOUR NAME, SWEETHEART?
I'M REALLY NOT YOUR SWEETHEART.
WHAT WERE YOU DOING EXACTLY?
JUST WORKING THE CROWD! A LITTLE PR!
YOU SUCK AT IT.
"GIANT RABBIT."
THIS KADABRA IS DANGEROUS.
ARE WE GOING TO TALK ABOUT IT?
ABOUT WHAT, TROY?
ABOUT WHAT YOU SAID. WHEN THE PHONEY WONDER GIRL HAD HER LASSO OF PERSUASION AROUND YOU?

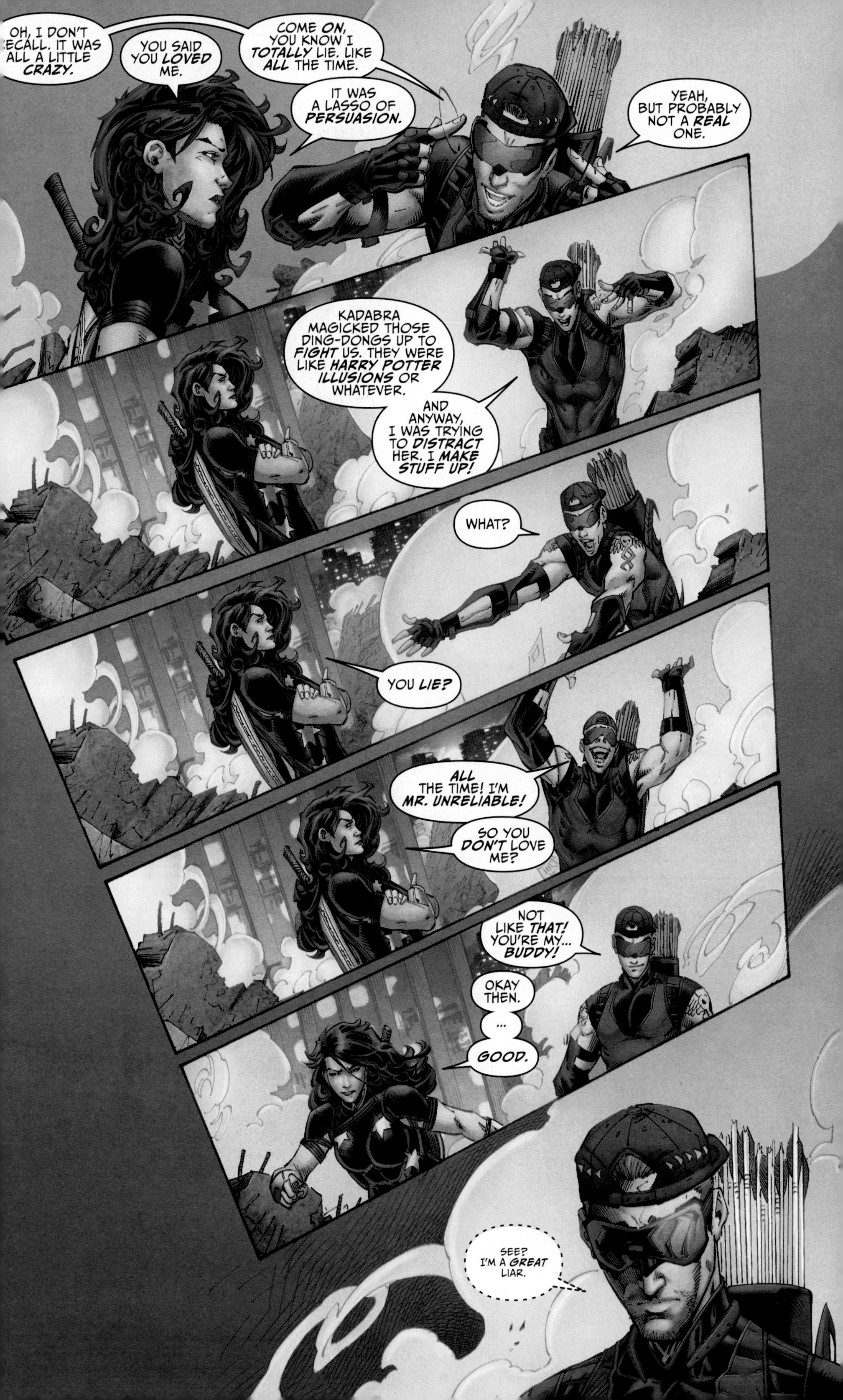
OH, I DON'T RECALL. IT WAS ALL A LITTLE CRAZY.
YOU SAID YOU LOVED ME.
COME ON, YOU KNOW I TOTALLY LIE. LIKE ALL THE TIME.
IT WAS A LASSO OF PERSUASION.
YEAH, BUT PROBABLY NOT A REAL ONE.
KADABRA MAGICKED THOSE DING-DONGS UP TO FIGHT US. THEY WERE LIKE HARRY POTTER ILLUSIONS OR WHATEVER.
AND ANYWAY, I WAS TRYING TO DISTRACT HER. I MAKE STUFF UP!
WHAT?
YOU LIE?
ALL THE TIME! I'M MR. UNRELIABLE!
SO YOU DON'T LOVE ME?
NOT LIKE THAT! YOU'RE MY... BUDDY!
OKAY THEN.
...
GOOD.
SEE? I'M A GREAT LIAR.

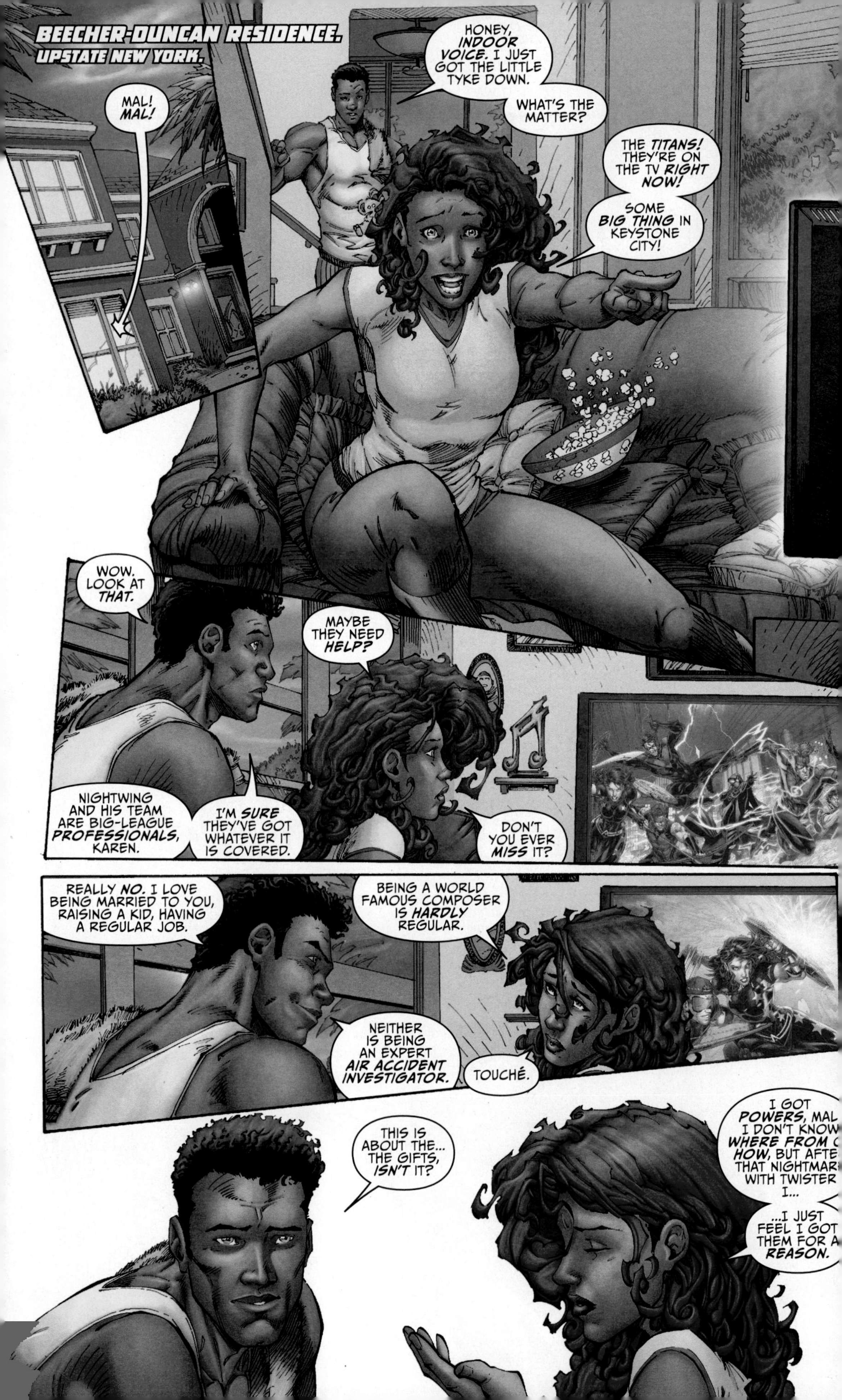
BEECHER-DUNCAN RESIDENCE.
UPSTATE NEW YORK.
MAL! MAL!
HONEY, INDOOR VOICE. I JUST GOT THE LITTLE TYKE DOWN.
WHAT'S THE MATTER?
THE TITANS! THEY'RE ON THE TV RIGHT NOW!
SOME BIG THING IN KEYSTONE CITY!
WOW. LOOK AT THAT.
MAYBE THEY NEED HELP?
NIGHTWING AND HIS TEAM ARE BIG-LEAGUE PROFESSIONALS, KAREN.
I'M SURE THEY'VE GOT WHATEVER IT IS COVERED.
DON'T YOU EVER MISS IT?
REALLY NO. I LOVE BEING MARRIED TO YOU, RAISING A KID, HAVING A REGULAR JOB.
BEING A WORLD FAMOUS COMPOSER IS HARDLY REGULAR.
NEITHER IS BEING AN EXPERT AIR ACCIDENT INVESTIGATOR.
TOUCHÉ.
THIS IS ABOUT THE... THE GIFTS, ISN'T IT?
I GOT POWERS, MAL I DON'T KNOW WHERE FROM HOW, BUT AFTE THAT NIGHTMAR WITH TWISTER I...
...I JUST FEEL I GOT THEM FOR A REASON.

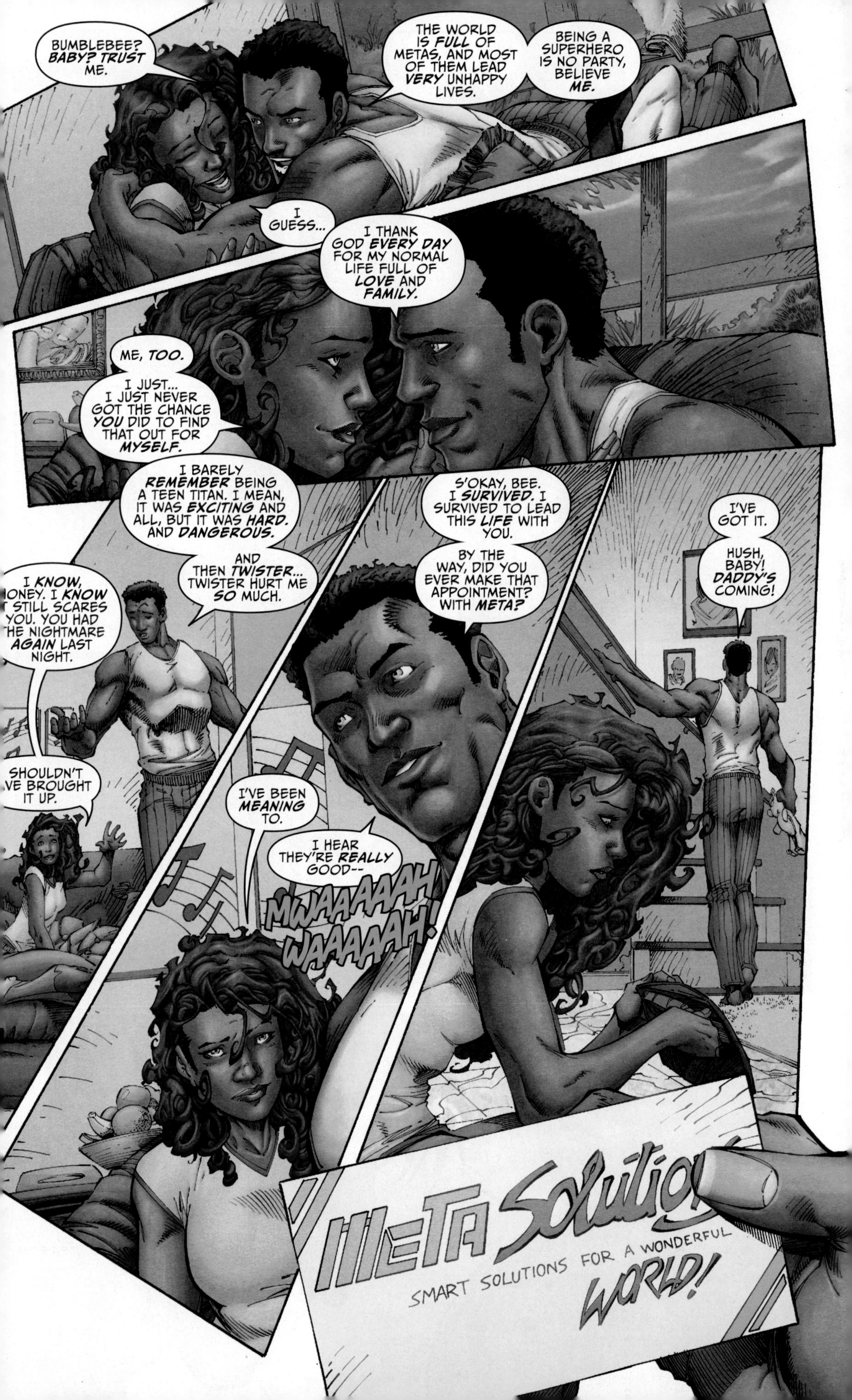
BUMBLEBEE? BABY? TRUST ME.
THE WORLD IS FULL OF METAS, AND MOST OF THEM LEAD VERY UNHAPPY LIVES.
BEING A SUPERHERO IS NO PARTY, BELIEVE ME.
I GUESS...
I THANK GOD EVERY DAY FOR MY NORMAL LIFE FULL OF LOVE AND FAMILY.
ME, TOO.
I JUST... I JUST NEVER GOT THE CHANCE YOU DID TO FIND THAT OUT FOR MYSELF.
I BARELY REMEMBER BEING A TEEN TITAN. I MEAN, IT WAS EXCITING AND ALL, BUT IT WAS HARD. AND DANGEROUS.
AND THEN TWISTER... TWISTER HURT ME SO MUCH.
I KNOW, HONEY. I KNOW IT STILL SCARES YOU. YOU HAD THE NIGHTMARE AGAIN LAST NIGHT.
SHOULDN'T HAVE BROUGHT IT UP.
S'OKAY, BEE. I SURVIVED. I SURVIVED TO LEAD THIS LIFE WITH YOU.
BY THE WAY, DID YOU EVER MAKE THAT APPOINTMENT? WITH META?
I'VE BEEN MEANING TO.
I HEAR THEY'RE REALLY GOOD--
MWAAAAAH! WAAAAAH!
I'VE GOT IT.
HUSH, BABY! DADDY'S COMING!
META Solutions
SMART SOLUTIONS FOR A WONDERFUL WORLD!

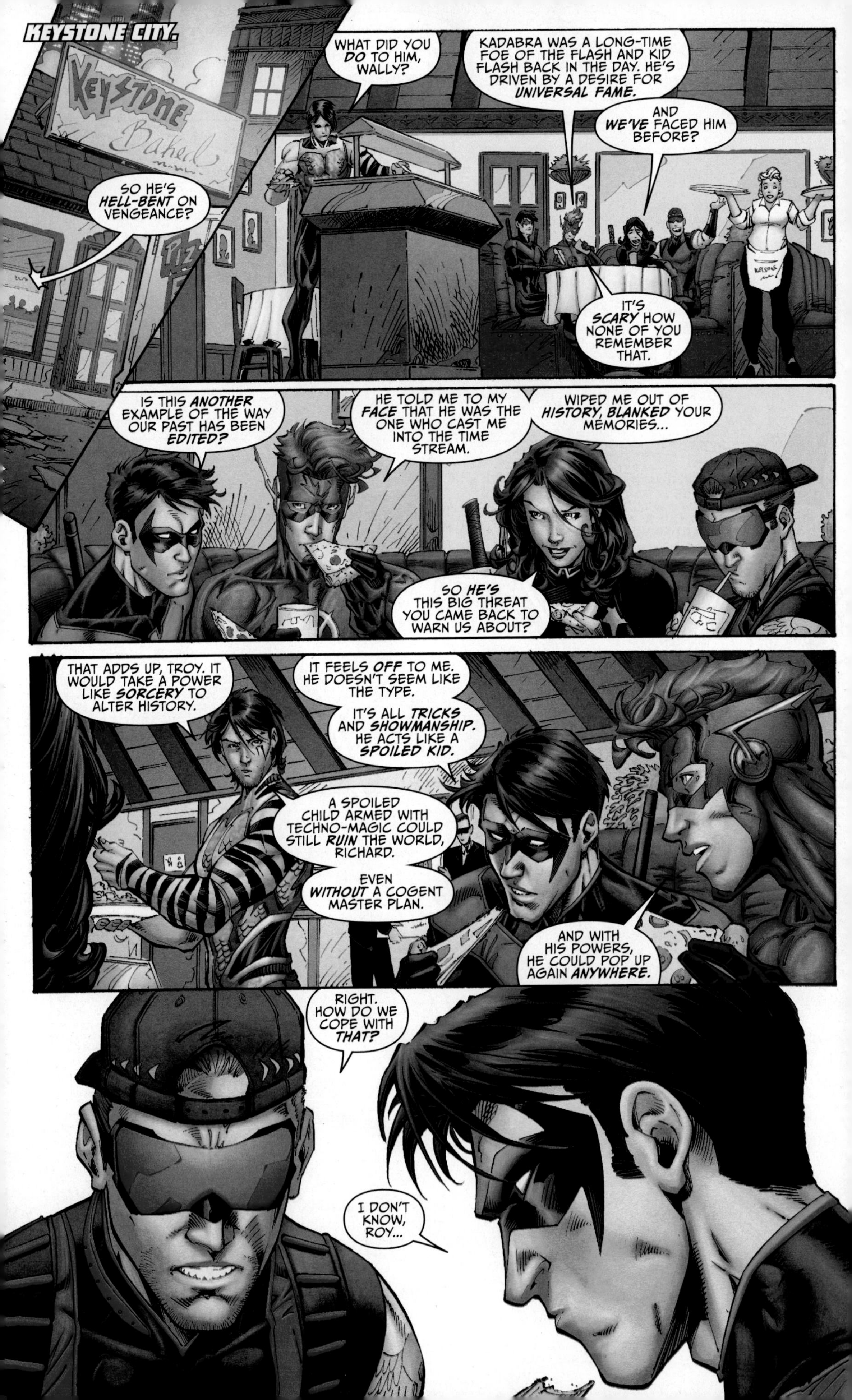
KEYSTONE CITY.
KEYSTONE Baked
WHAT DID YOU DO TO HIM, WALLY?
KADABRA WAS A LONG-TIME FOE OF THE FLASH AND KID FLASH BACK IN THE DAY. HE'S DRIVEN BY A DESIRE FOR UNIVERSAL FAME.
AND WE'VE FACED HIM BEFORE?
SO HE'S HELL-BENT ON VENGEANCE?
IT'S SCARY HOW NONE OF YOU REMEMBER THAT.
IS THIS ANOTHER EXAMPLE OF THE WAY OUR PAST HAS BEEN EDITED?
HE TOLD ME TO MY FACE THAT HE WAS THE ONE WHO CAST ME INTO THE TIME STREAM.
WIPED ME OUT OF HISTORY, BLANKED YOUR MEMORIES...
SO HE'S THIS BIG THREAT YOU CAME BACK TO WARN US ABOUT?
THAT ADDS UP, TROY. IT WOULD TAKE A POWER LIKE SORCERY TO ALTER HISTORY.
IT FEELS OFF TO ME. HE DOESN'T SEEM LIKE THE TYPE.
IT'S ALL TRICKS AND SHOWMANSHIP. HE ACTS LIKE A SPOILED KID.
A SPOILED CHILD ARMED WITH TECHNO-MAGIC COULD STILL RUIN THE WORLD, RICHARD.
EVEN WITHOUT A COGENT MASTER PLAN.
AND WITH HIS POWERS, HE COULD POP UP AGAIN ANYWHERE.
RIGHT. HOW DO WE COPE WITH THAT?
I DON'T KNOW, ROY...

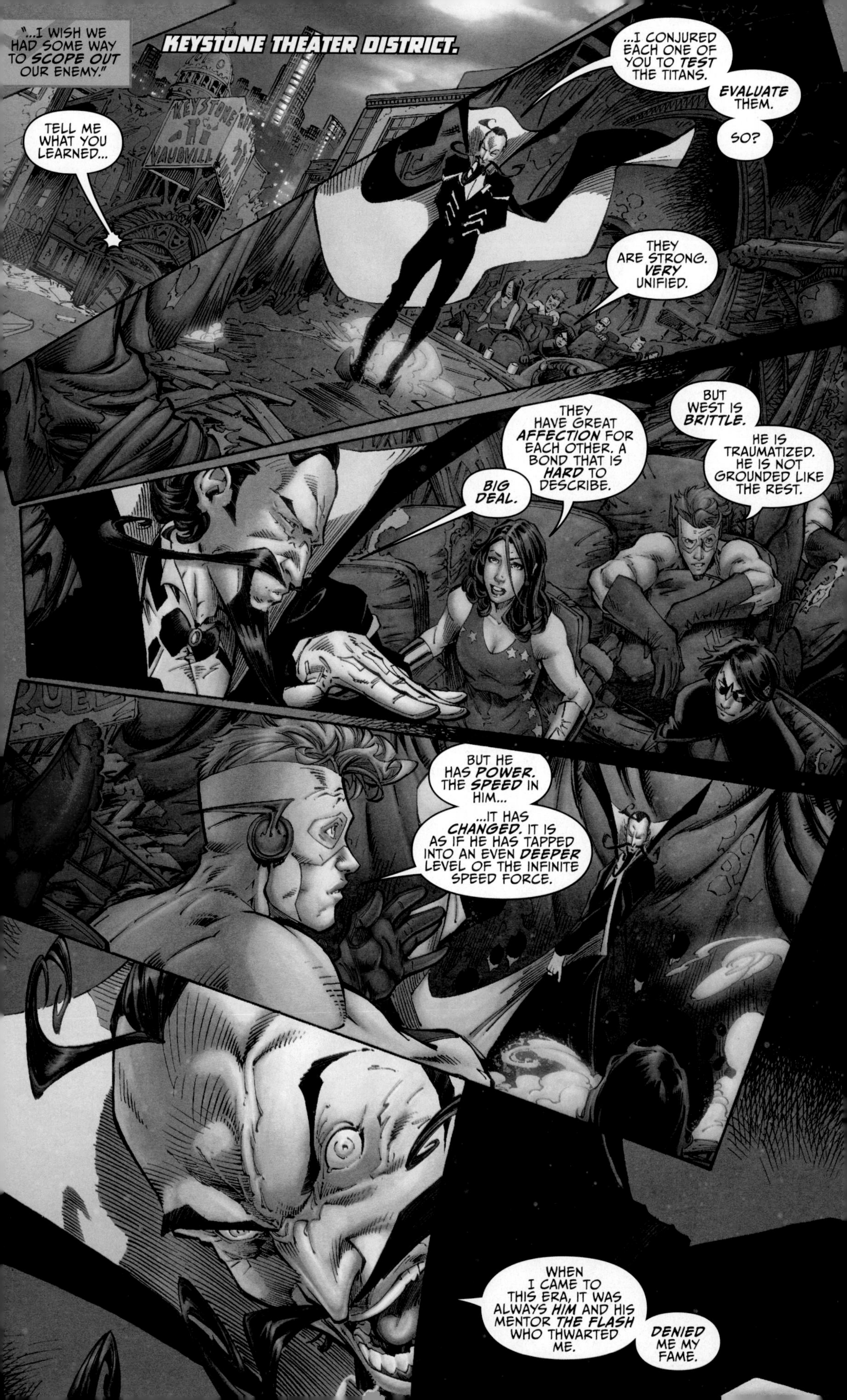

"...I WISH WE HAD SOME WAY TO SCOPE OUT OUR ENEMY."
KEYSTONE THEATER DISTRICT.
TELL ME WHAT YOU LEARNED...
...I CONJURED EACH ONE OF YOU TO TEST THE TITANS.
EVALUATE THEM.
SO?
THEY ARE STRONG. VERY UNIFIED.
THEY HAVE GREAT AFFECTION FOR EACH OTHER. A BOND THAT IS HARD TO DESCRIBE.
BIG DEAL.
BUT WEST IS BRITTLE.
HE IS TRAUMATIZED. HE IS NOT GROUNDED LIKE THE REST.
BUT HE HAS POWER. THE SPEED IN HIM...
...IT HAS CHANGED. IT IS AS IF HE HAS TAPPED INTO AN EVEN DEEPER LEVEL OF THE INFINITE SPEED FORCE.
WHEN I CAME TO THIS ERA, IT WAS ALWAYS HIM AND HIS MENTOR THE FLASH WHO THWARTED ME.
DENIED ME MY FAME.

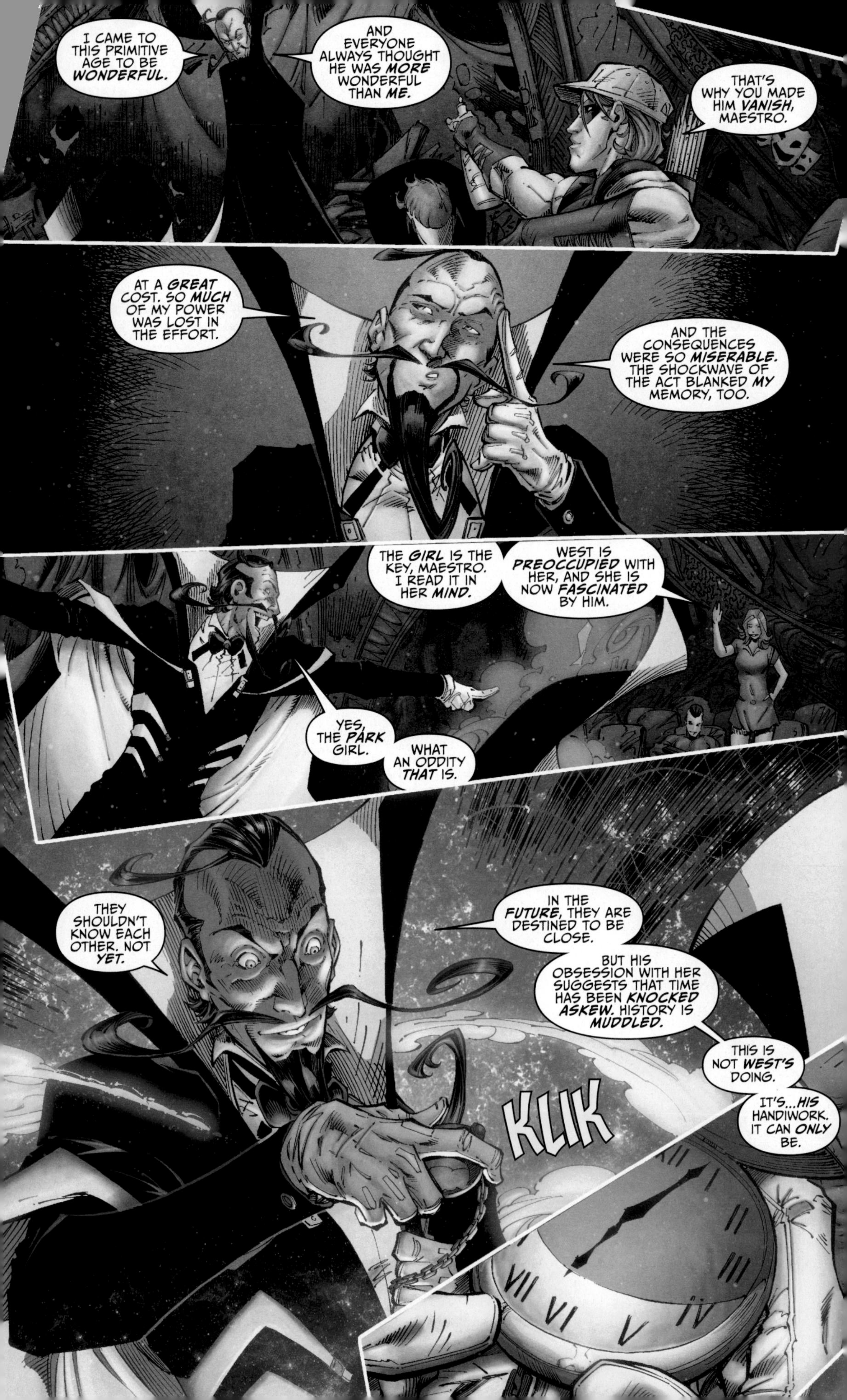
I CAME TO THIS PRIMITIVE AGE TO BE WONDERFUL.
AND EVERYONE ALWAYS THOUGHT HE WAS MORE WONDERFUL THAN ME.
THAT'S WHY YOU MADE HIM VANISH, MAESTRO.
AT A GREAT COST. SO MUCH OF MY POWER WAS LOST IN THE EFFORT.
AND THE CONSEQUENCES WERE SO MISERABLE. THE SHOCKWAVE OF THE ACT BLANKED MY MEMORY, TOO.
THE GIRL IS THE KEY, MAESTRO. I READ IT IN HER MIND.
WEST IS PREOCCUPIED WITH HER, AND SHE IS NOW FASCINATED BY HIM.
YES, THE PARK GIRL.
WHAT AN ODDITY THAT IS.
THEY SHOULDN'T KNOW EACH OTHER. NOT YET.
IN THE FUTURE, THEY ARE DESTINED TO BE CLOSE.
BUT HIS OBSESSION WITH HER SUGGESTS THAT TIME HAS BEEN KNOCKED ASKEW. HISTORY IS MUDDLED.
THIS IS NOT WEST'S DOING.
IT'S...HIS HANDIWORK. IT CAN ONLY BE.
KLIK

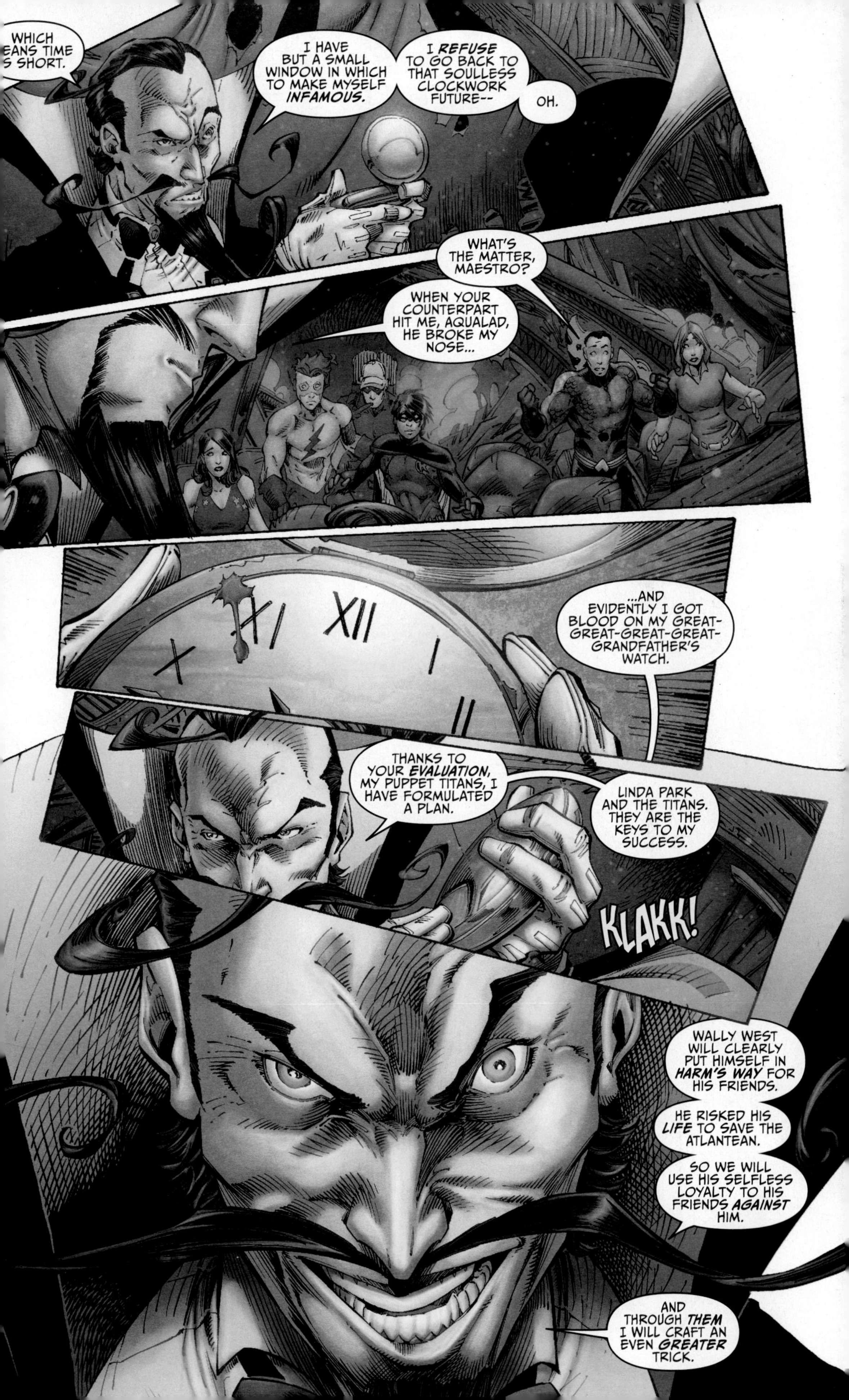
WHICH
EANS TIME
S SHORT.
I HAVE BUT A SMALL WINDOW IN WHICH TO MAKE MYSELF *INFAMOUS.*
I *REFUSE* TO GO BACK TO THAT SOULLESS CLOCKWORK FUTURE--
OH.
WHAT'S THE MATTER, MAESTRO?
WHEN YOUR COUNTERPART HIT ME, AQUALAD, HE BROKE MY NOSE...
...AND EVIDENTLY I GOT BLOOD ON MY GREAT-GREAT-GREAT-GREAT-GRANDFATHER'S WATCH.
XII
THANKS TO YOUR *EVALUATION,* MY PUPPET TITANS, I HAVE FORMULATED A PLAN.
LINDA PARK AND THE TITANS. THEY ARE THE KEYS TO MY SUCCESS.
KLAKK!
WALLY WEST WILL CLEARLY PUT HIMSELF IN *HARM'S WAY* FOR HIS FRIENDS.
HE RISKED HIS *LIFE* TO SAVE THE ATLANTEAN.
SO WE WILL USE HIS SELFLESS LOYALTY TO HIS FRIENDS *AGAINST* HIM.
AND THROUGH *THEM* I WILL CRAFT AN EVEN *GREATER* TRICK.

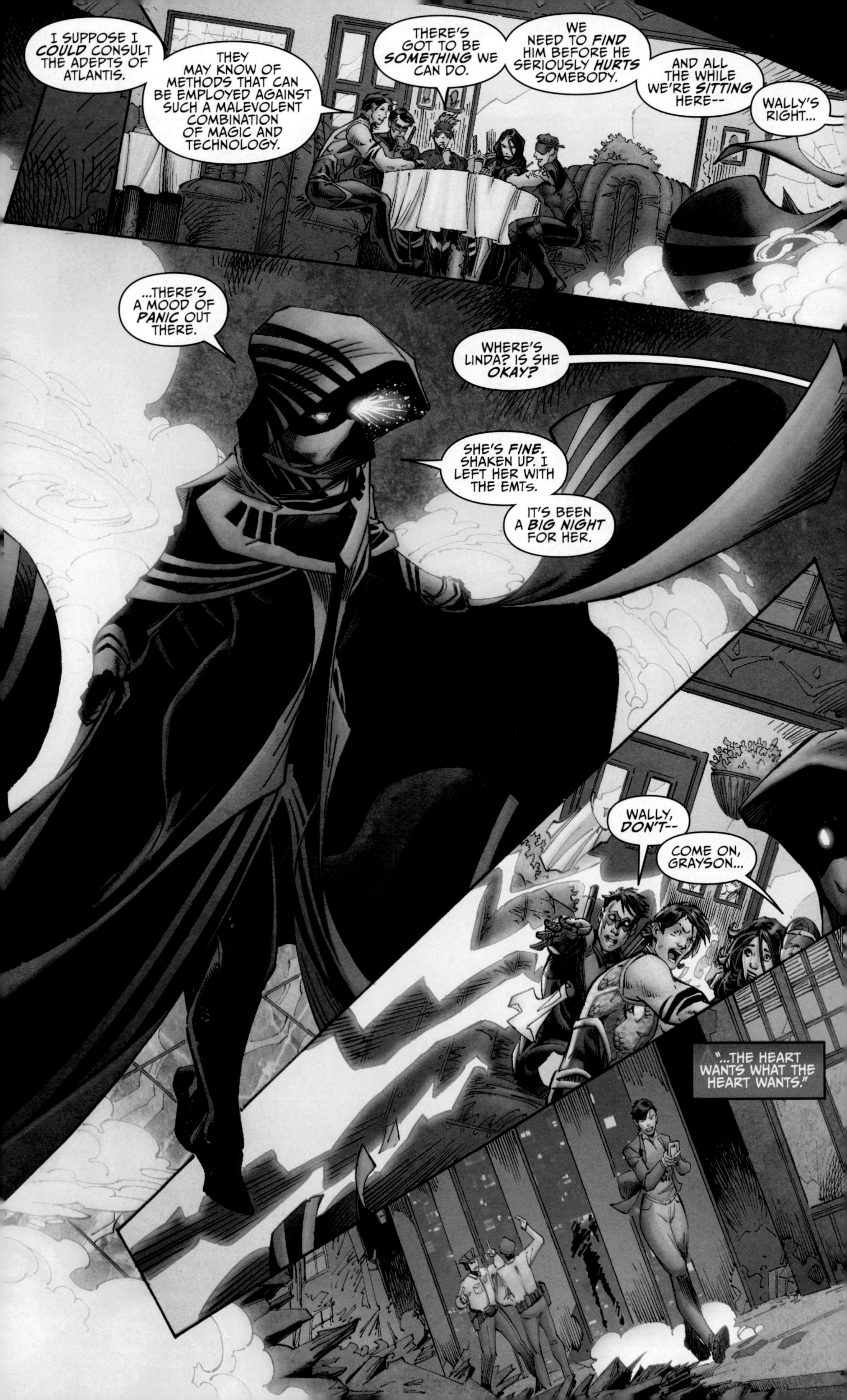
I SUPPOSE I COULD CONSULT THE ADEPTS OF ATLANTIS.
THEY MAY KNOW OF METHODS THAT CAN BE EMPLOYED AGAINST SUCH A MALEVOLENT COMBINATION OF MAGIC AND TECHNOLOGY.
THERE'S GOT TO BE SOMETHING WE CAN DO.
WE NEED TO FIND HIM BEFORE HE SERIOUSLY HURTS SOMEBODY.
AND ALL THE WHILE WE'RE SITTING HERE--
WALLY'S RIGHT...
...THERE'S A MOOD OF PANIC OUT THERE.
WHERE'S LINDA? IS SHE OKAY?
SHE'S FINE. SHAKEN UP. I LEFT HER WITH THE EMTS.
IT'S BEEN A BIG NIGHT FOR HER.
WALLY, DON'T--
COME ON, GRAYSON...
"...THE HEART WANTS WHAT THE HEART WANTS."

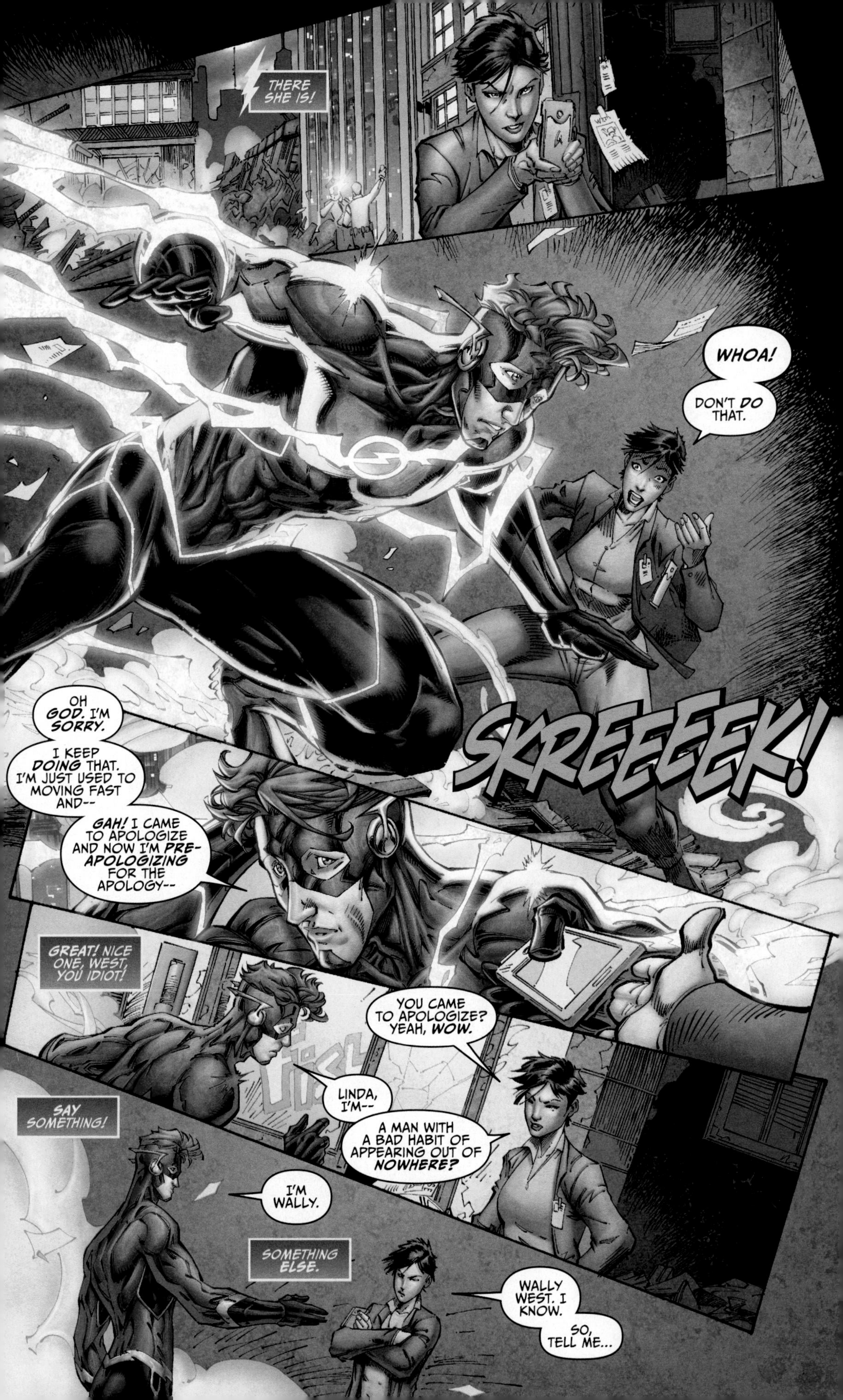

THERE SHE IS!
WHOA!
DON'T DO THAT.
SKREEEEEK!
OH GOD. I'M SORRY.
I KEEP DOING THAT. I'M JUST USED TO MOVING FAST AND--
GAH! I CAME TO APOLOGIZE AND NOW I'M PRE-APOLOGIZING FOR THE APOLOGY--
GREAT! NICE ONE, WEST, YOU IDIOT!
YOU CAME TO APOLOGIZE? YEAH, WOW.
LINDA, I'M--
A MAN WITH A BAD HABIT OF APPEARING OUT OF NOWHERE?
SAY SOMETHING!
I'M WALLY.
SOMETHING ELSE.
WALLY WEST. I KNOW.
SO, TELL ME...

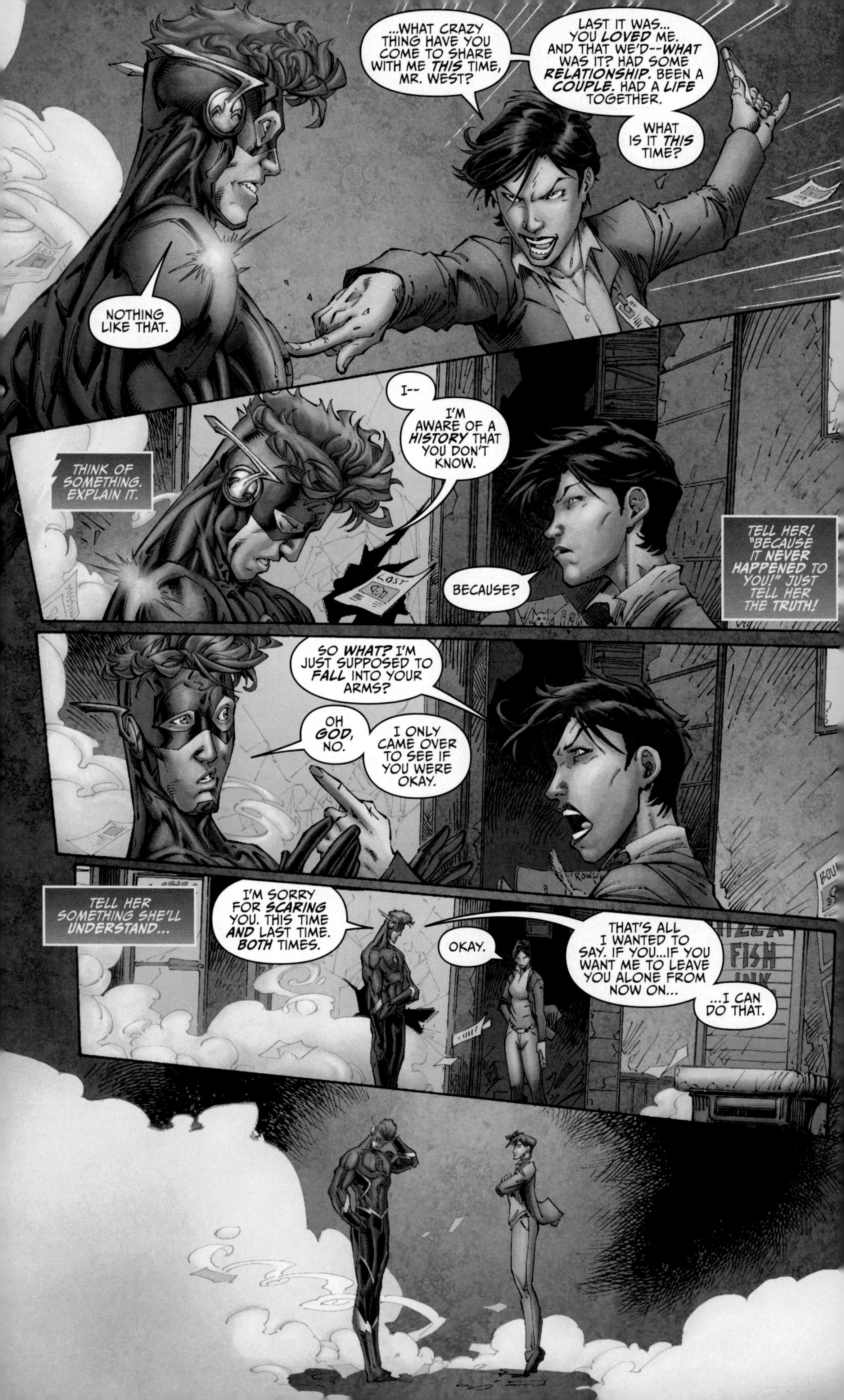
...WHAT CRAZY THING HAVE YOU COME TO SHARE WITH ME THIS TIME, MR. WEST?
LAST IT WAS... YOU LOVED ME. AND THAT WE'D--WHAT WAS IT? HAD SOME RELATIONSHIP. BEEN A COUPLE. HAD A LIFE TOGETHER.
WHAT IS IT THIS TIME?
NOTHING LIKE THAT.
I--
I'M AWARE OF A HISTORY THAT YOU DON'T KNOW.
THINK OF SOMETHING. EXPLAIN IT.
BECAUSE?
TELL HER! "BECAUSE IT NEVER HAPPENED TO YOU!" JUST TELL HER THE TRUTH!
SO WHAT? I'M JUST SUPPOSED TO FALL INTO YOUR ARMS?
OH GOD, NO.
I ONLY CAME OVER TO SEE IF YOU WERE OKAY.
TELL HER SOMETHING SHE'LL UNDERSTAND...
I'M SORRY FOR SCARING YOU. THIS TIME AND LAST TIME. BOTH TIMES.
OKAY.
THAT'S ALL I WANTED TO SAY. IF YOU...IF YOU WANT ME TO LEAVE YOU ALONE FROM NOW ON...
...I CAN DO THAT.

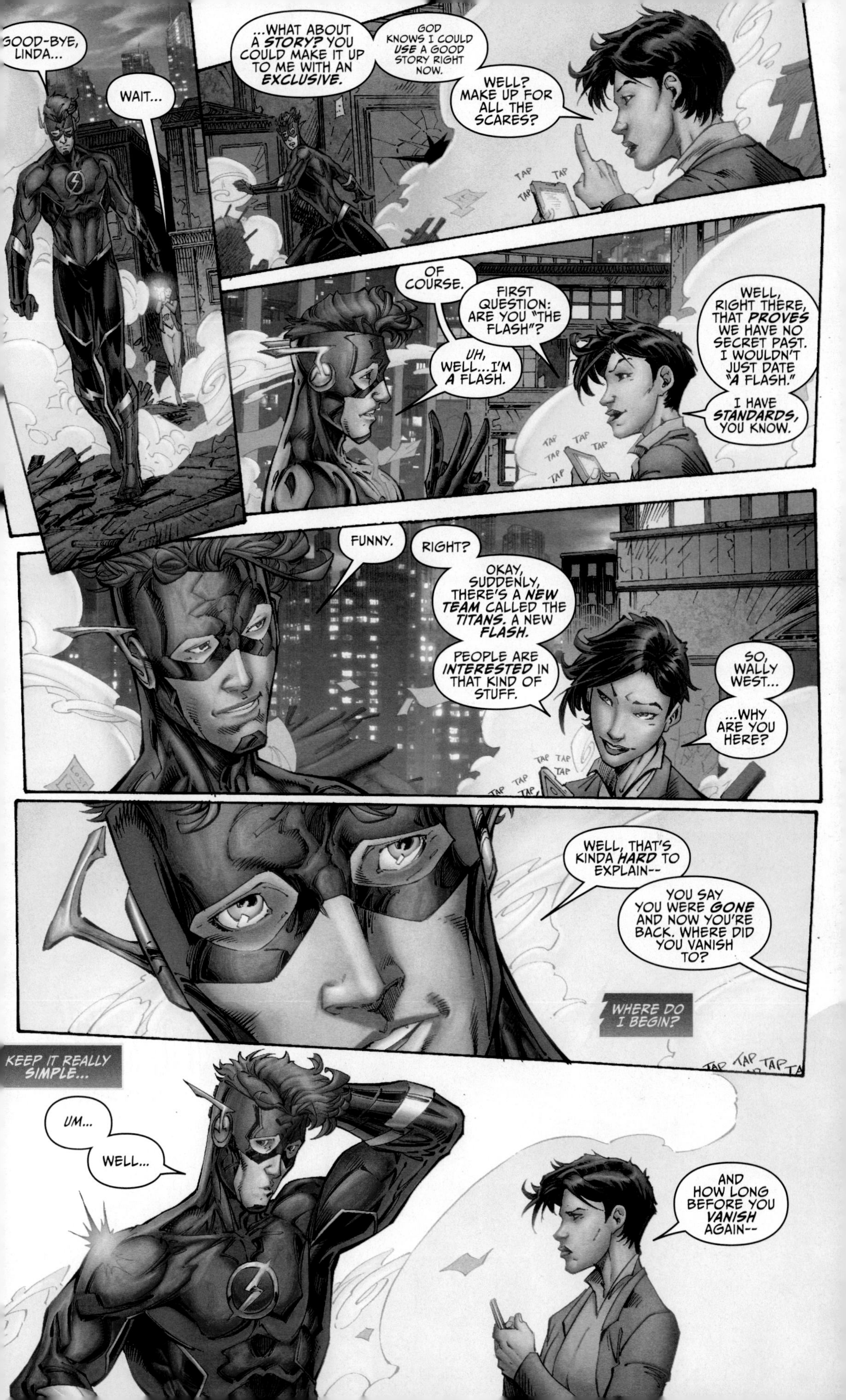
GOOD-BYE, LINDA...
WAIT...
...WHAT ABOUT A STORY? YOU COULD MAKE IT UP TO ME WITH AN EXCLUSIVE.
GOD KNOWS I COULD USE A GOOD STORY RIGHT NOW.
WELL? MAKE UP FOR ALL THE SCARES?
TAP TAP TAP
OF COURSE.
FIRST QUESTION: ARE YOU "THE FLASH"?
UH, WELL...I'M A FLASH.
WELL, RIGHT THERE, THAT PROVES WE HAVE NO SECRET PAST. I WOULDN'T JUST DATE "A FLASH."
I HAVE STANDARDS, YOU KNOW.
TAP TAP TAP TAP TAP
FUNNY.
RIGHT?
OKAY, SUDDENLY, THERE'S A NEW TEAM CALLED THE TITANS. A NEW FLASH.
PEOPLE ARE INTERESTED IN THAT KIND OF STUFF.
SO, WALLY WEST...
...WHY ARE YOU HERE?
TAP TAP TAP TAP TAP
WELL, THAT'S KINDA HARD TO EXPLAIN--
YOU SAY YOU WERE GONE AND NOW YOU'RE BACK. WHERE DID YOU VANISH TO?
WHERE DO I BEGIN?
TAP TAP TAP
KEEP IT REALLY SIMPLE...
UM...
WELL...
AND HOW LONG BEFORE YOU VANISH AGAIN--

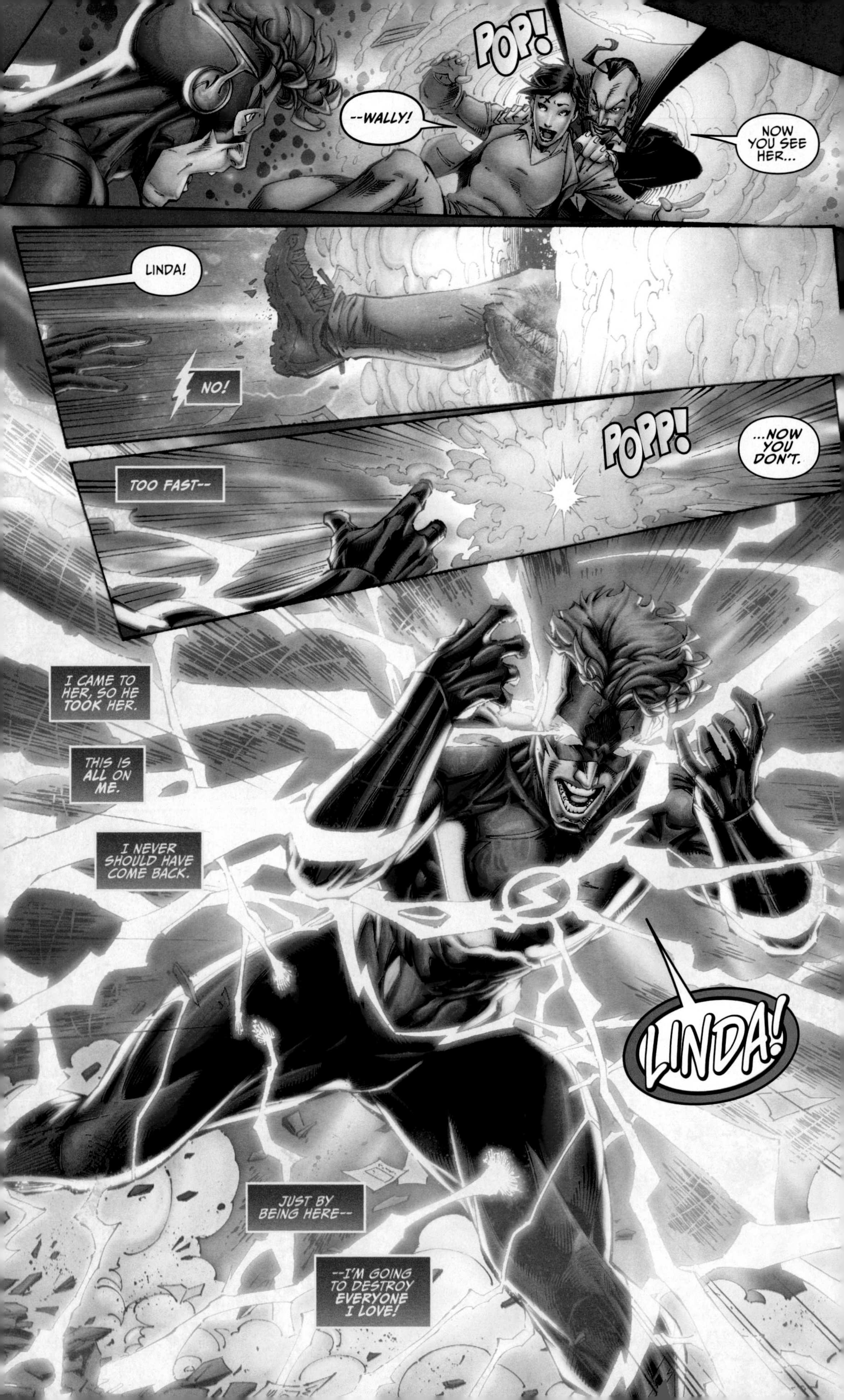
POP!
--WALLY!
NOW YOU SEE HER...
LINDA!
NO!
POPP!
...NOW YOU DON'T.
TOO FAST--
I CAME TO HER, SO HE TOOK HER.
THIS IS ALL ON ME.
I NEVER SHOULD HAVE COME BACK.
LINDA!
JUST BY BEING HERE--
--I'M GOING TO DESTROY EVERYONE I LOVE!

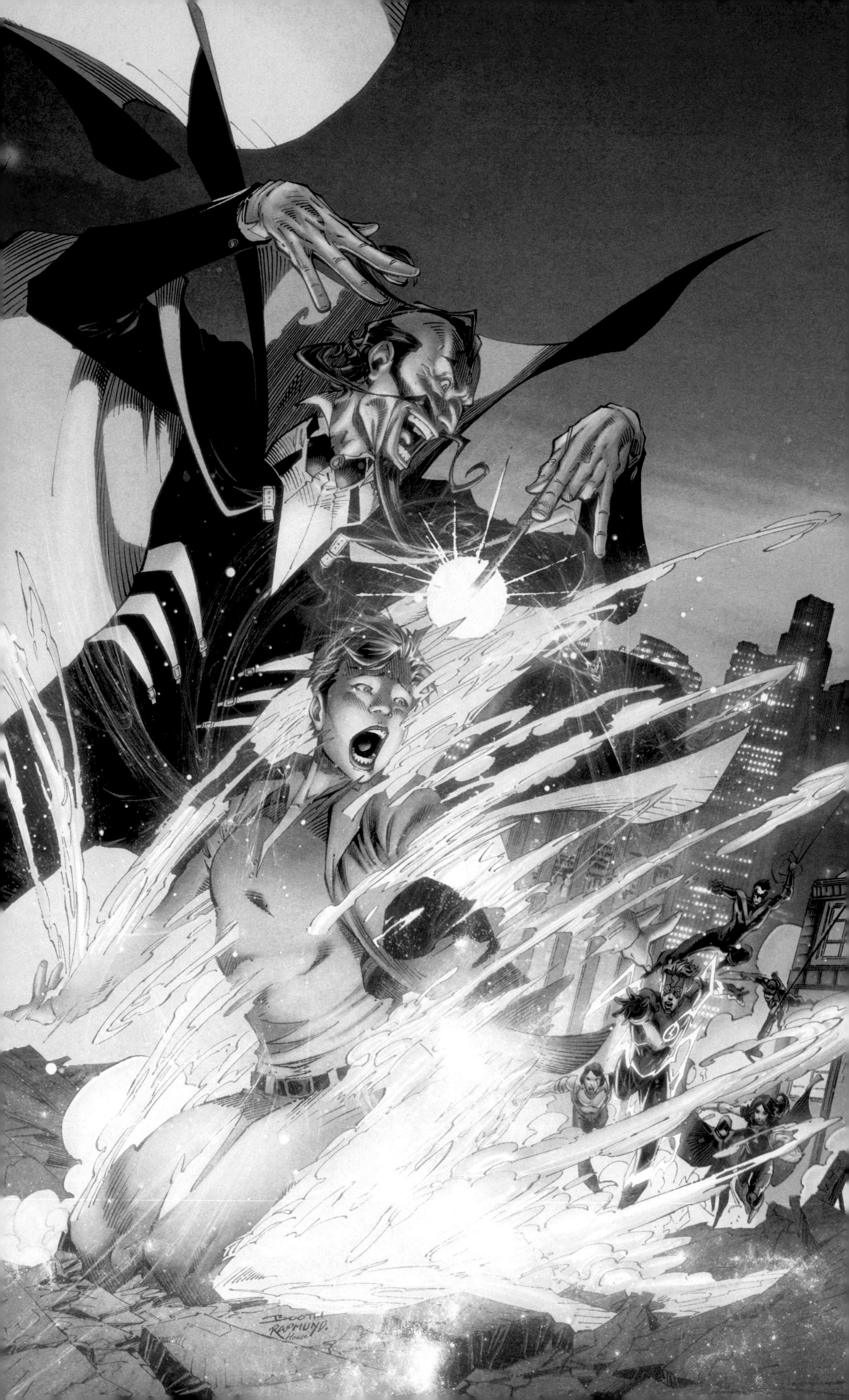
BOOTH
RAPMUND

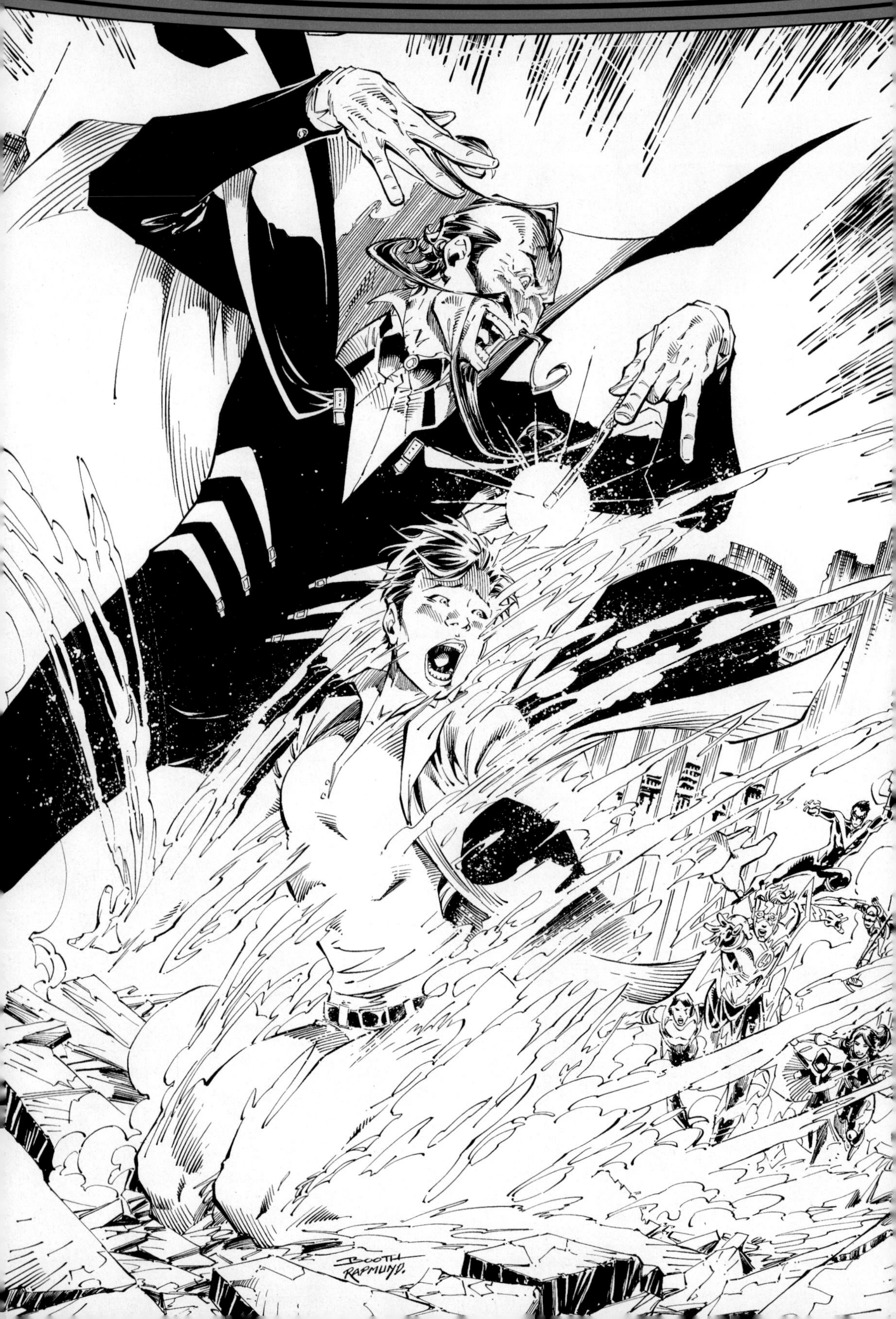
BOOTH
RAPMUND

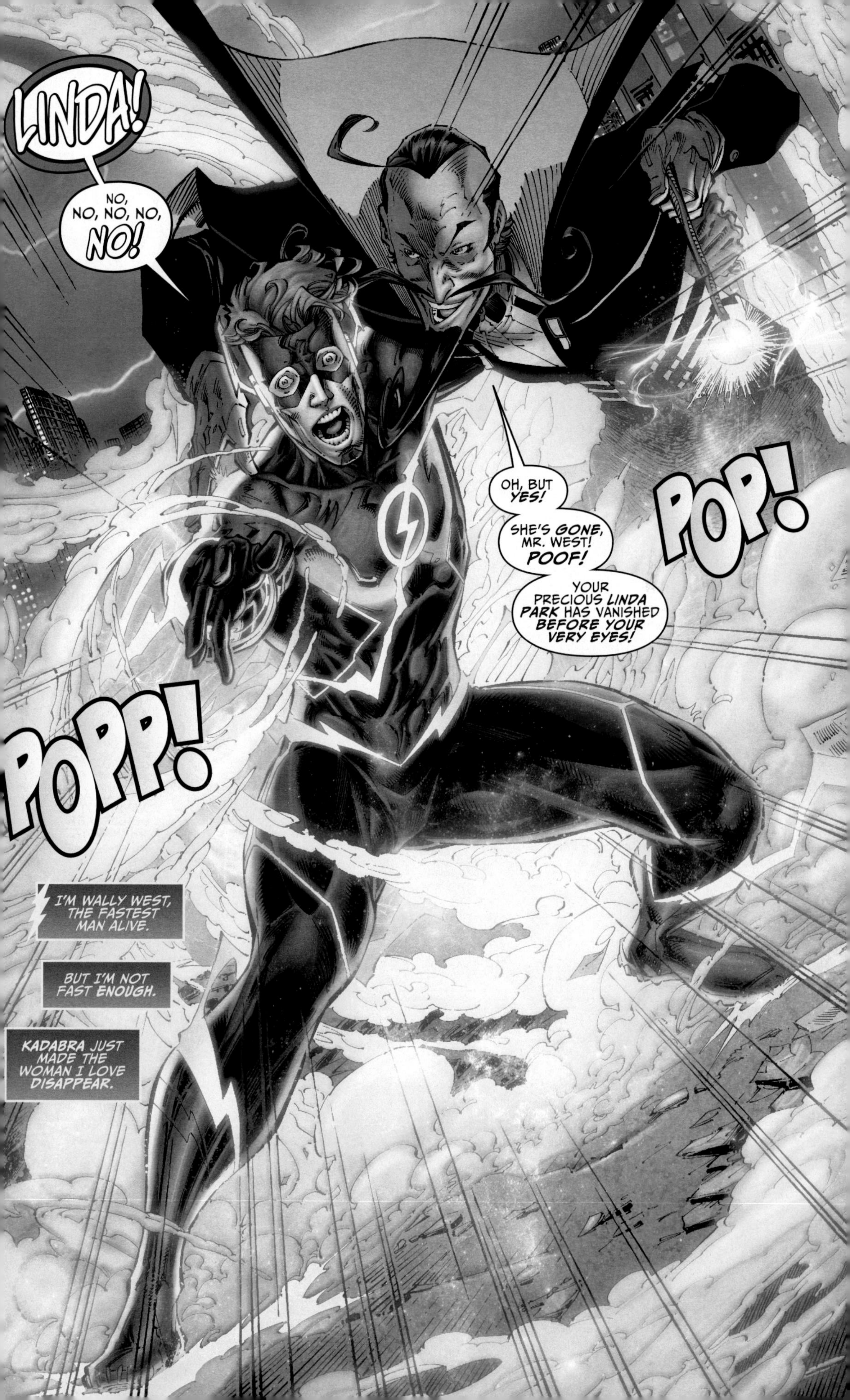

LINDA!
NO, NO, NO, NO, NO!
OH, BUT YES!
SHE'S GONE, MR. WEST! POOF!
YOUR PRECIOUS LINDA PARK HAS VANISHED BEFORE YOUR VERY EYES!
POP!
POPP!
I'M WALLY WEST, THE FASTEST MAN ALIVE.
BUT I'M NOT FAST ENOUGH.
KADABRA JUST MADE THE WOMAN I LOVE DISAPPEAR.

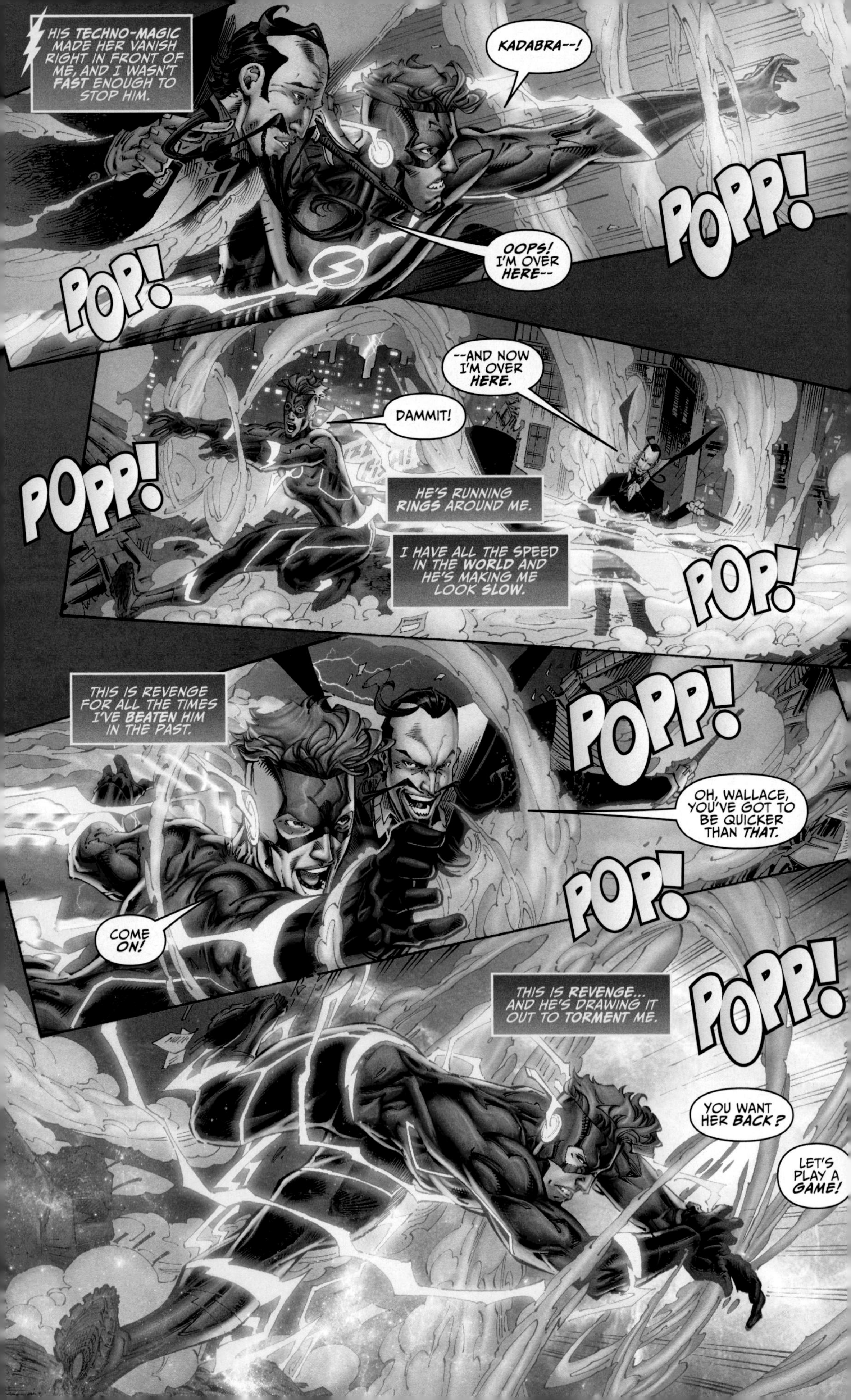
HIS TECHNO-MAGIC MADE HER VANISH RIGHT IN FRONT OF ME, AND I WASN'T FAST ENOUGH TO STOP HIM.
KADABRA--!
POPP!
OOPS! I'M OVER HERE--
POP!
--AND NOW I'M OVER HERE.
DAMMIT!
POPP!
HE'S RUNNING RINGS AROUND ME.
I HAVE ALL THE SPEED IN THE WORLD AND HE'S MAKING ME LOOK SLOW.
POP!
THIS IS REVENGE FOR ALL THE TIMES I'VE BEATEN HIM IN THE PAST.
POPP!
OH, WALLACE, YOU'VE GOT TO BE QUICKER THAN THAT.
POP!
COME ON!
THIS IS REVENGE... AND HE'S DRAWING IT OUT TO TORMENT ME.
POPP!
YOU WANT HER BACK?
LET'S PLAY A GAME!

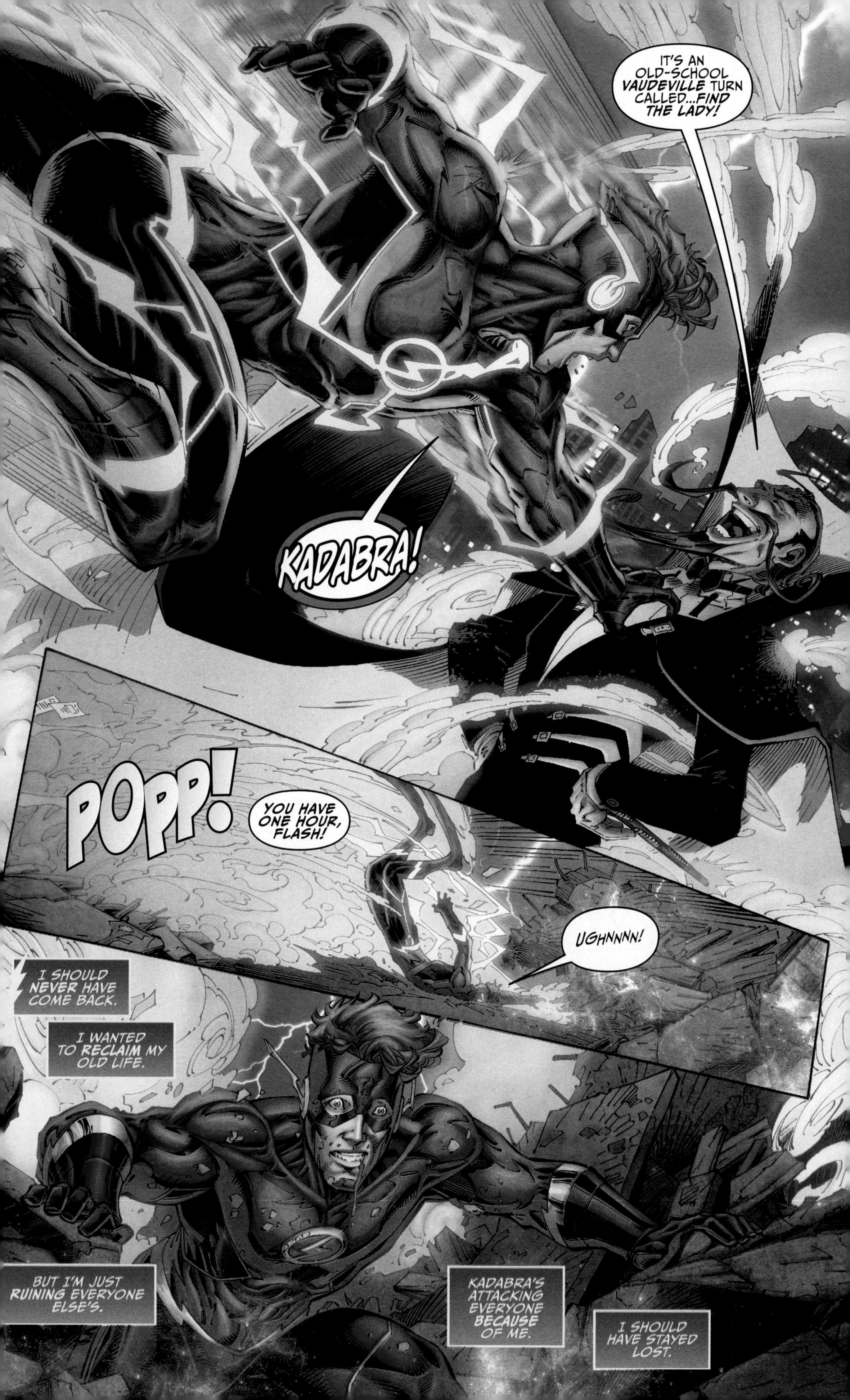
IT'S AN OLD-SCHOOL VAUDEVILLE TURN CALLED...FIND THE LADY!
KADABRA!
POPP!
YOU HAVE ONE HOUR, FLASH!
UGHNNNN!
I SHOULD NEVER HAVE COME BACK.
I WANTED TO RECLAIM MY OLD LIFE.
BUT I'M JUST RUINING EVERYONE ELSE'S.
KADABRA'S ATTACKING EVERYONE BECAUSE OF ME.
I SHOULD HAVE STAYED LOST.

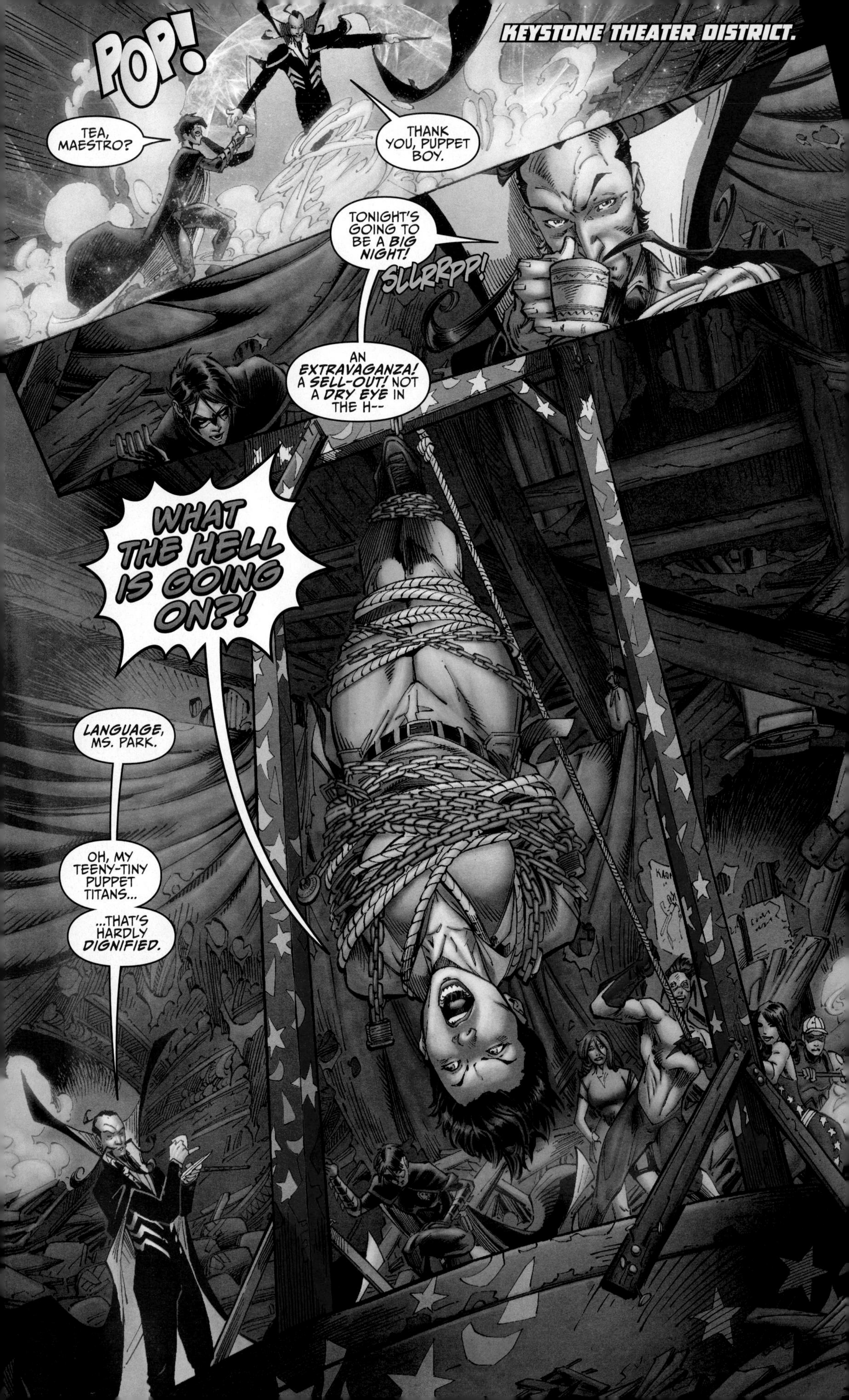
KEYSTONE THEATER DISTRICT.
POP!
TEA, MAESTRO?
THANK YOU, PUPPET BOY.
TONIGHT'S GOING TO BE A BIG NIGHT!
SLLRRPP!
AN EXTRAVAGANZA! A SELL-OUT! NOT A DRY EYE IN THE H--
WHAT THE HELL IS GOING ON?!
LANGUAGE, MS. PARK.
OH, MY TEENY-TINY PUPPET TITANS...
...THAT'S HARDLY DIGNIFIED.

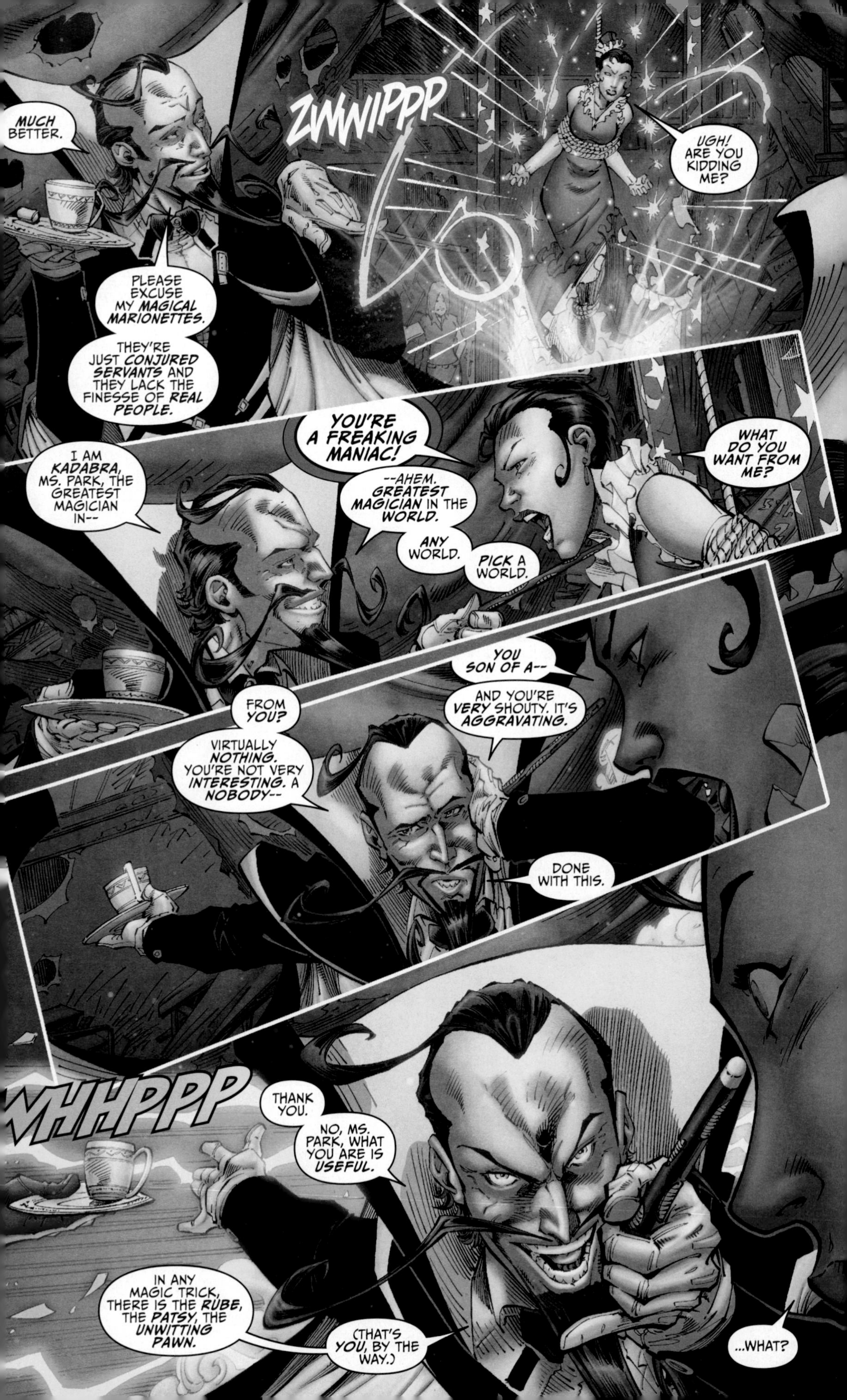
MUCH BETTER.
ZWWIPPP
UGH! ARE YOU KIDDING ME?
PLEASE EXCUSE MY MAGICAL MARIONETTES.
THEY'RE JUST CONJURED SERVANTS AND THEY LACK THE FINESSE OF REAL PEOPLE.
I AM KADABRA, MS. PARK, THE GREATEST MAGICIAN IN--
YOU'RE A FREAKING MANIAC!
--AHEM. GREATEST MAGICIAN IN THE WORLD.
ANY WORLD.
PICK A WORLD.
WHAT DO YOU WANT FROM ME?
FROM YOU?
VIRTUALLY NOTHING. YOU'RE NOT VERY INTERESTING. A NOBODY--
YOU SON OF A--
AND YOU'RE VERY SHOUTY. IT'S AGGRAVATING.
DONE WITH THIS.
WHHPPP
THANK YOU.
NO, MS. PARK, WHAT YOU ARE IS USEFUL.
IN ANY MAGIC TRICK, THERE IS THE RUBE, THE PATSY, THE UNWITTING PAWN.
(THAT'S YOU, BY THE WAY.)
...WHAT?

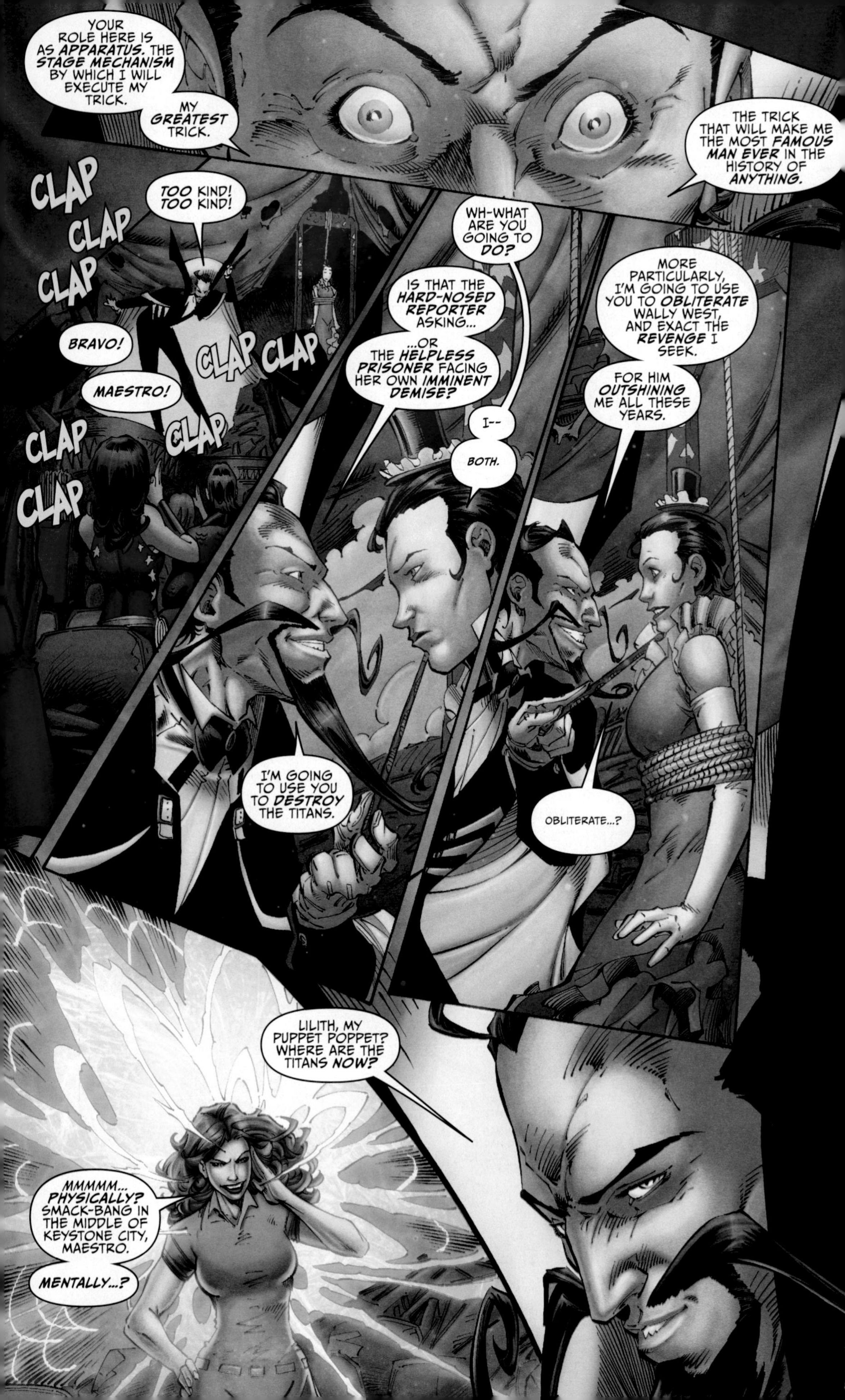
YOUR ROLE HERE IS AS APPARATUS. THE STAGE MECHANISM BY WHICH I WILL EXECUTE MY TRICK.
MY GREATEST TRICK.
THE TRICK THAT WILL MAKE ME THE MOST FAMOUS MAN EVER IN THE HISTORY OF ANYTHING.
CLAP CLAP CLAP
TOO KIND! TOO KIND!
BRAVO!
CLAP CLAP
MAESTRO!
CLAP
CLAP CLAP
WH-WHAT ARE YOU GOING TO DO?
IS THAT THE HARD-NOSED REPORTER ASKING...
...OR THE HELPLESS PRISONER FACING HER OWN IMMINENT DEMISE?
I--
BOTH.
I'M GOING TO USE YOU TO DESTROY THE TITANS.
MORE PARTICULARLY, I'M GOING TO USE YOU TO OBLITERATE WALLY WEST, AND EXACT THE REVENGE I SEEK.
FOR HIM OUTSHINING ME ALL THESE YEARS.
OBLITERATE...?
LILITH, MY PUPPET POPPET? WHERE ARE THE TITANS NOW?
MMMMM... PHYSICALLY? SMACK-BANG IN THE MIDDLE OF KEYSTONE CITY, MAESTRO.
MENTALLY...?

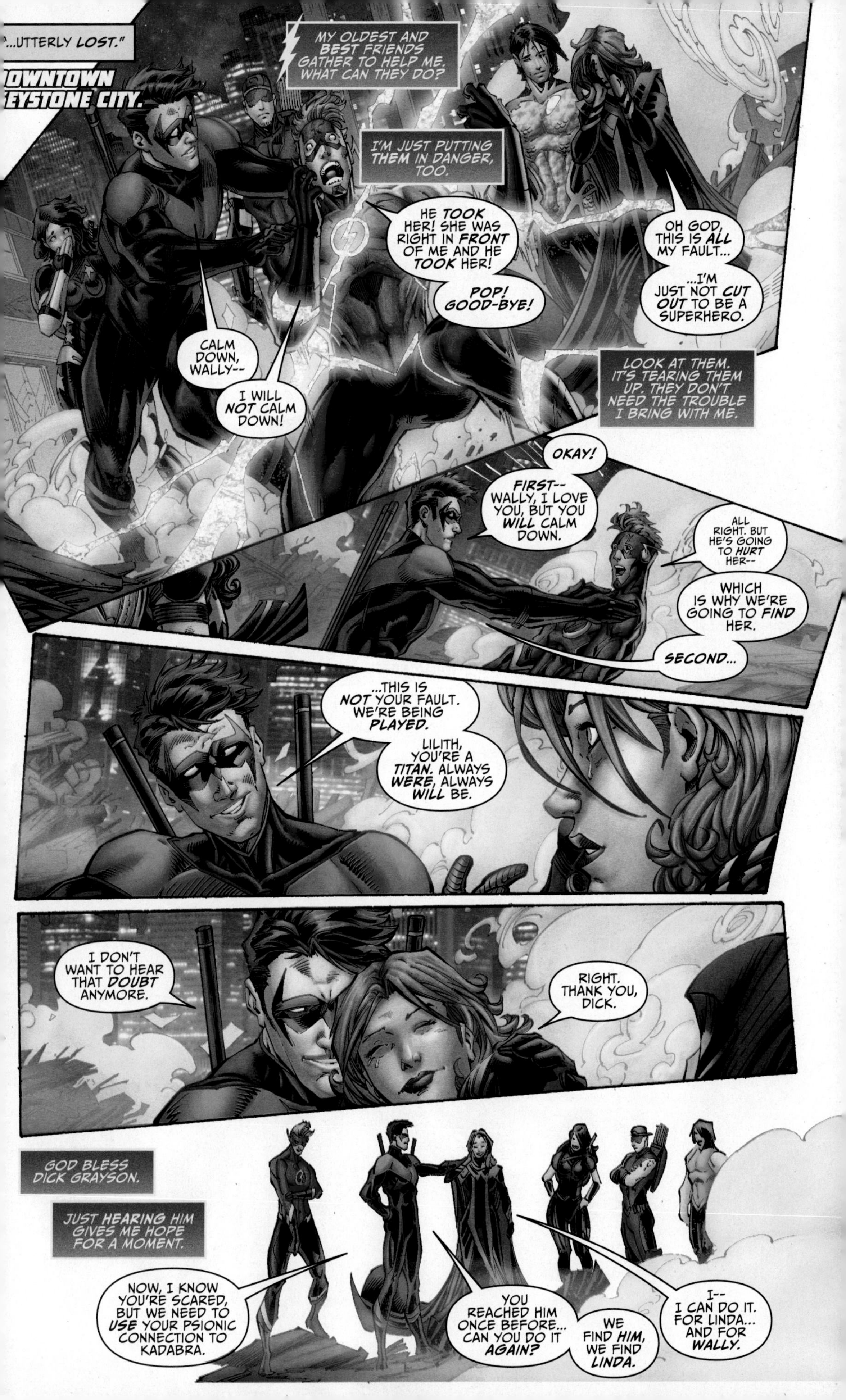

"...UTTERLY LOST."
OWNTOWN
EYSTONE CITY.
MY OLDEST AND BEST FRIENDS GATHER TO HELP ME. WHAT CAN THEY DO?
I'M JUST PUTTING THEM IN DANGER, TOO.
HE TOOK HER! SHE WAS RIGHT IN FRONT OF ME AND HE TOOK HER!
POP! GOOD-BYE!
OH GOD, THIS IS ALL MY FAULT...
...I'M JUST NOT CUT OUT TO BE A SUPERHERO.
CALM DOWN, WALLY--
I WILL NOT CALM DOWN!
LOOK AT THEM. IT'S TEARING THEM UP. THEY DON'T NEED THE TROUBLE I BRING WITH ME.
OKAY!
FIRST-- WALLY, I LOVE YOU, BUT YOU WILL CALM DOWN.
ALL RIGHT. BUT HE'S GOING TO HURT HER--
WHICH IS WHY WE'RE GOING TO FIND HER.
SECOND...
...THIS IS NOT YOUR FAULT. WE'RE BEING PLAYED.
LILITH, YOU'RE A TITAN. ALWAYS WERE, ALWAYS WILL BE.
I DON'T WANT TO HEAR THAT DOUBT ANYMORE.
RIGHT. THANK YOU, DICK.
GOD BLESS DICK GRAYSON.
JUST HEARING HIM GIVES ME HOPE FOR A MOMENT.
NOW, I KNOW YOU'RE SCARED, BUT WE NEED TO USE YOUR PSIONIC CONNECTION TO KADABRA.
YOU REACHED HIM ONCE BEFORE... CAN YOU DO IT AGAIN?
WE FIND HIM, WE FIND LINDA.
I-- I CAN DO IT. FOR LINDA... AND FOR WALLY.

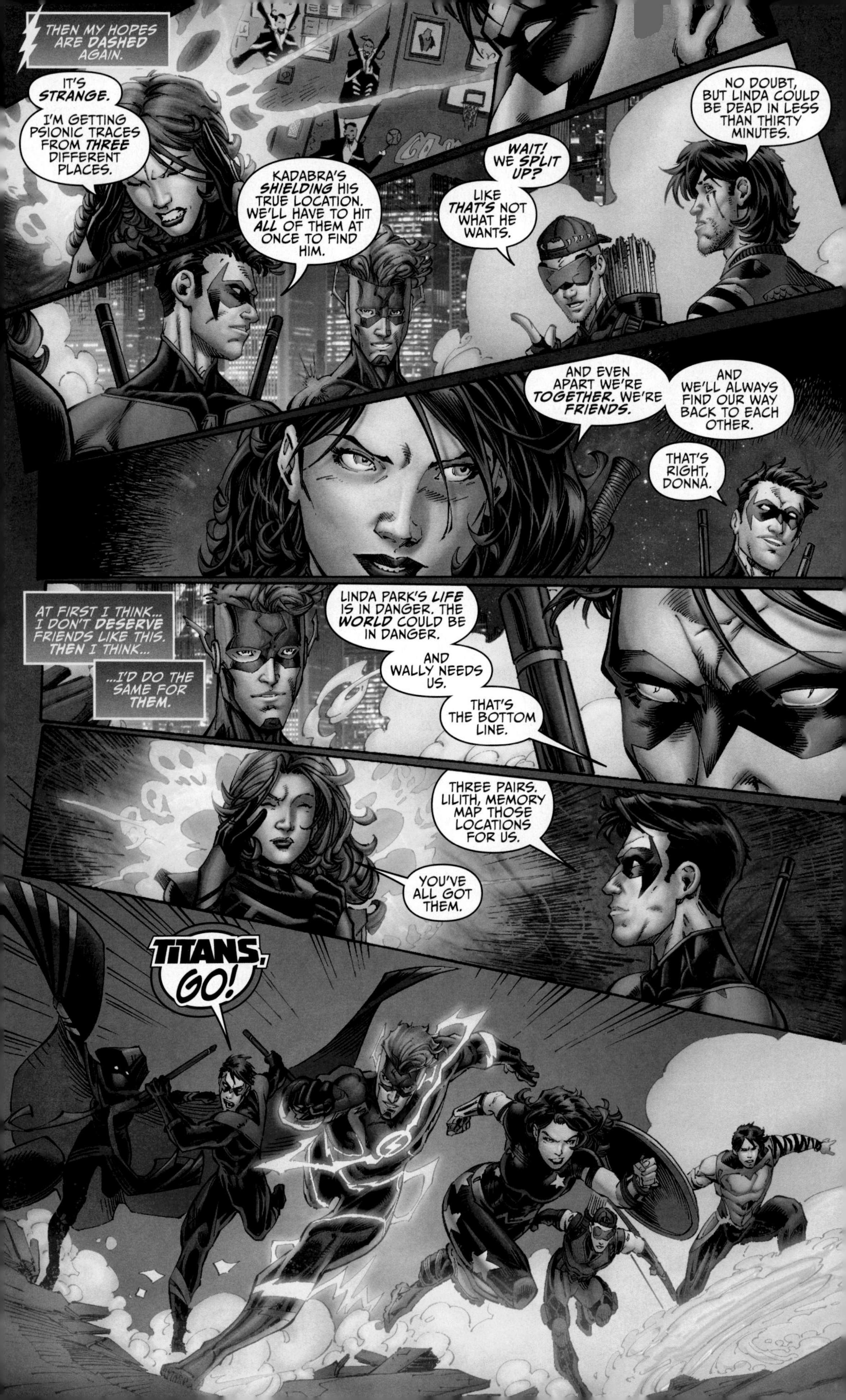
THEN MY HOPES ARE DASHED AGAIN.
IT'S STRANGE.
I'M GETTING PSIONIC TRACES FROM THREE DIFFERENT PLACES.
KADABRA'S SHIELDING HIS TRUE LOCATION. WE'LL HAVE TO HIT ALL OF THEM AT ONCE TO FIND HIM.
WAIT! WE SPLIT UP?
LIKE THAT'S NOT WHAT HE WANTS.
NO DOUBT, BUT LINDA COULD BE DEAD IN LESS THAN THIRTY MINUTES.
AND EVEN APART WE'RE TOGETHER. WE'RE FRIENDS.
AND WE'LL ALWAYS FIND OUR WAY BACK TO EACH OTHER.
THAT'S RIGHT, DONNA.
AT FIRST I THINK... I DON'T DESERVE FRIENDS LIKE THIS. THEN I THINK...
...I'D DO THE SAME FOR THEM.
LINDA PARK'S LIFE IS IN DANGER. THE WORLD COULD BE IN DANGER.
AND WALLY NEEDS US.
THAT'S THE BOTTOM LINE.
THREE PAIRS. LILITH, MEMORY MAP THOSE LOCATIONS FOR US.
YOU'VE ALL GOT THEM.
TITANS, GO!

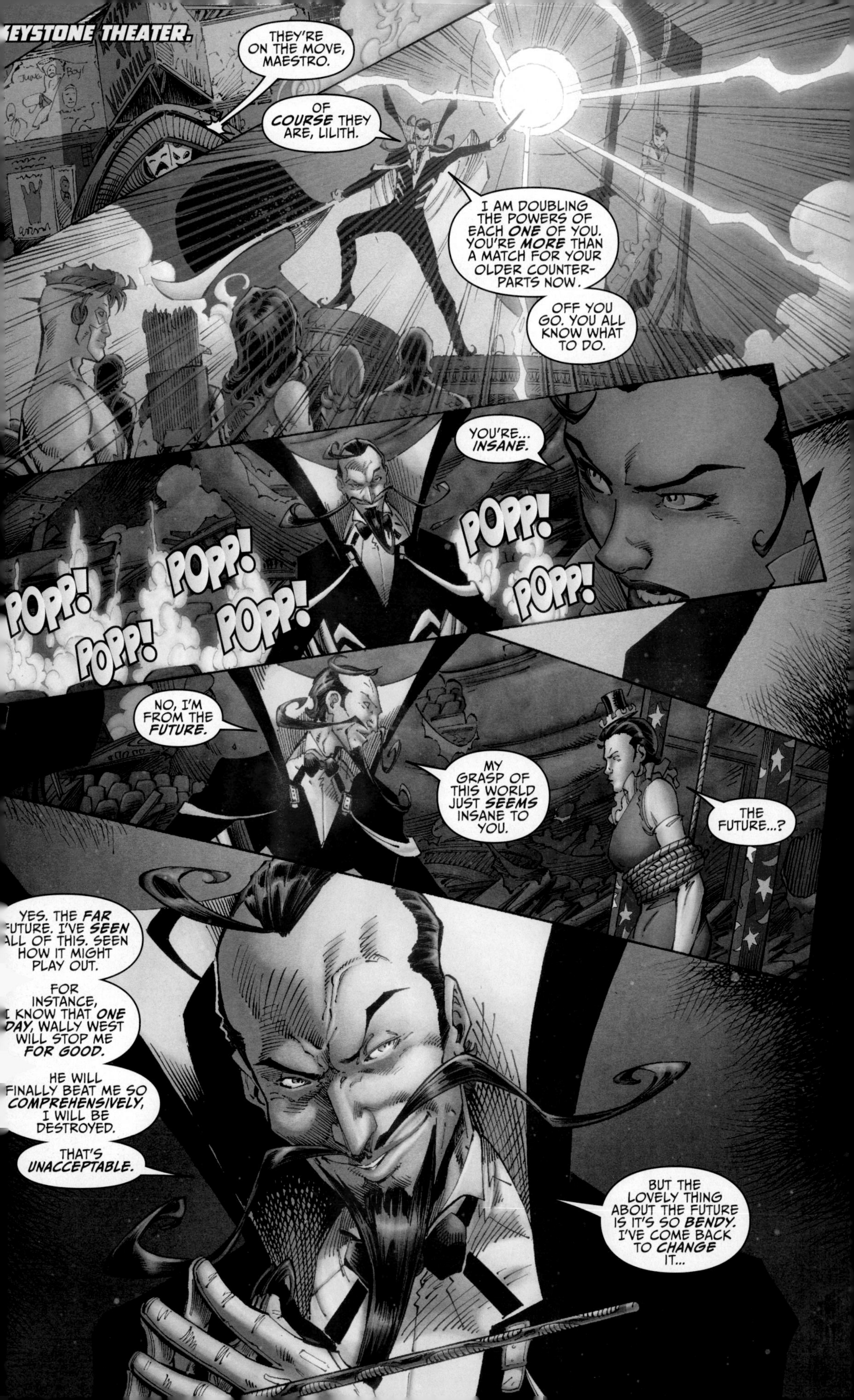
KEYSTONE THEATER.
THEY'RE ON THE MOVE, MAESTRO.
OF COURSE THEY ARE, LILITH.
I AM DOUBLING THE POWERS OF EACH ONE OF YOU. YOU'RE MORE THAN A MATCH FOR YOUR OLDER COUNTER-PARTS NOW.
OFF YOU GO. YOU ALL KNOW WHAT TO DO.
YOU'RE... INSANE.
POPP!
POPP!
POPP!
POPP!
POPP!
POPP!
NO, I'M FROM THE FUTURE.
MY GRASP OF THIS WORLD JUST SEEMS INSANE TO YOU.
THE FUTURE...?
YES. THE FAR FUTURE. I'VE SEEN ALL OF THIS. SEEN HOW IT MIGHT PLAY OUT.
FOR INSTANCE, I KNOW THAT ONE DAY, WALLY WEST WILL STOP ME FOR GOOD.
HE WILL FINALLY BEAT ME SO COMPREHENSIVELY, I WILL BE DESTROYED.
THAT'S UNACCEPTABLE.
BUT THE LOVELY THING ABOUT THE FUTURE IS IT'S SO BENDY. I'VE COME BACK TO CHANGE IT...

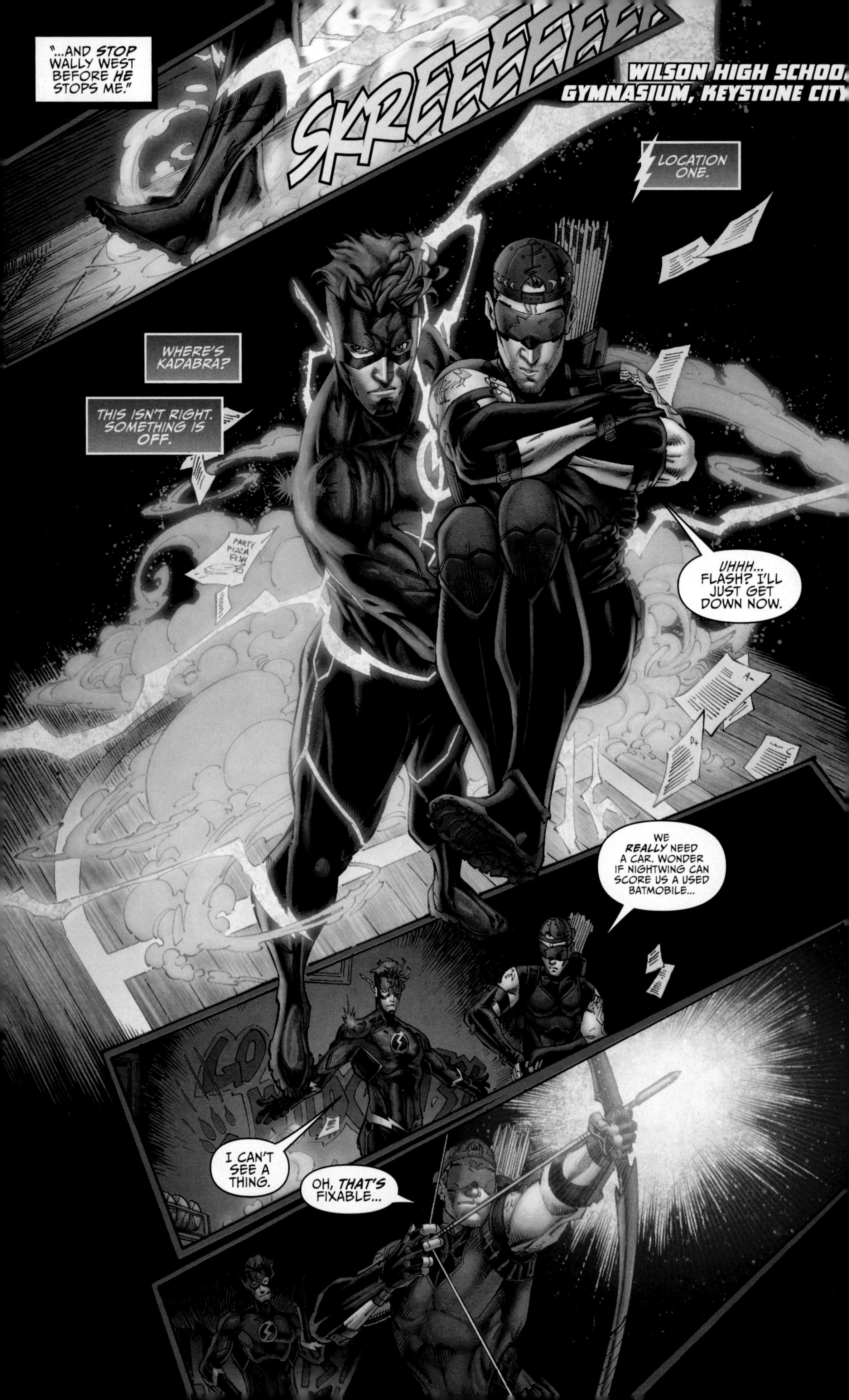
"...AND STOP WALLY WEST BEFORE HE STOPS ME."
SKREEEEEEE
WILSON HIGH SCHOO
GYMNASIUM, KEYSTONE CITY
LOCATION ONE.
WHERE'S KADABRA?
THIS ISN'T RIGHT. SOMETHING IS OFF.
PARTY PIZZA FISH
UHHH... FLASH? I'LL JUST GET DOWN NOW.
A-
D+
WE REALLY NEED A CAR. WONDER IF NIGHTWING CAN SCORE US A USED BATMOBILE...
I CAN'T SEE A THING.
OH, THAT'S FIXABLE...

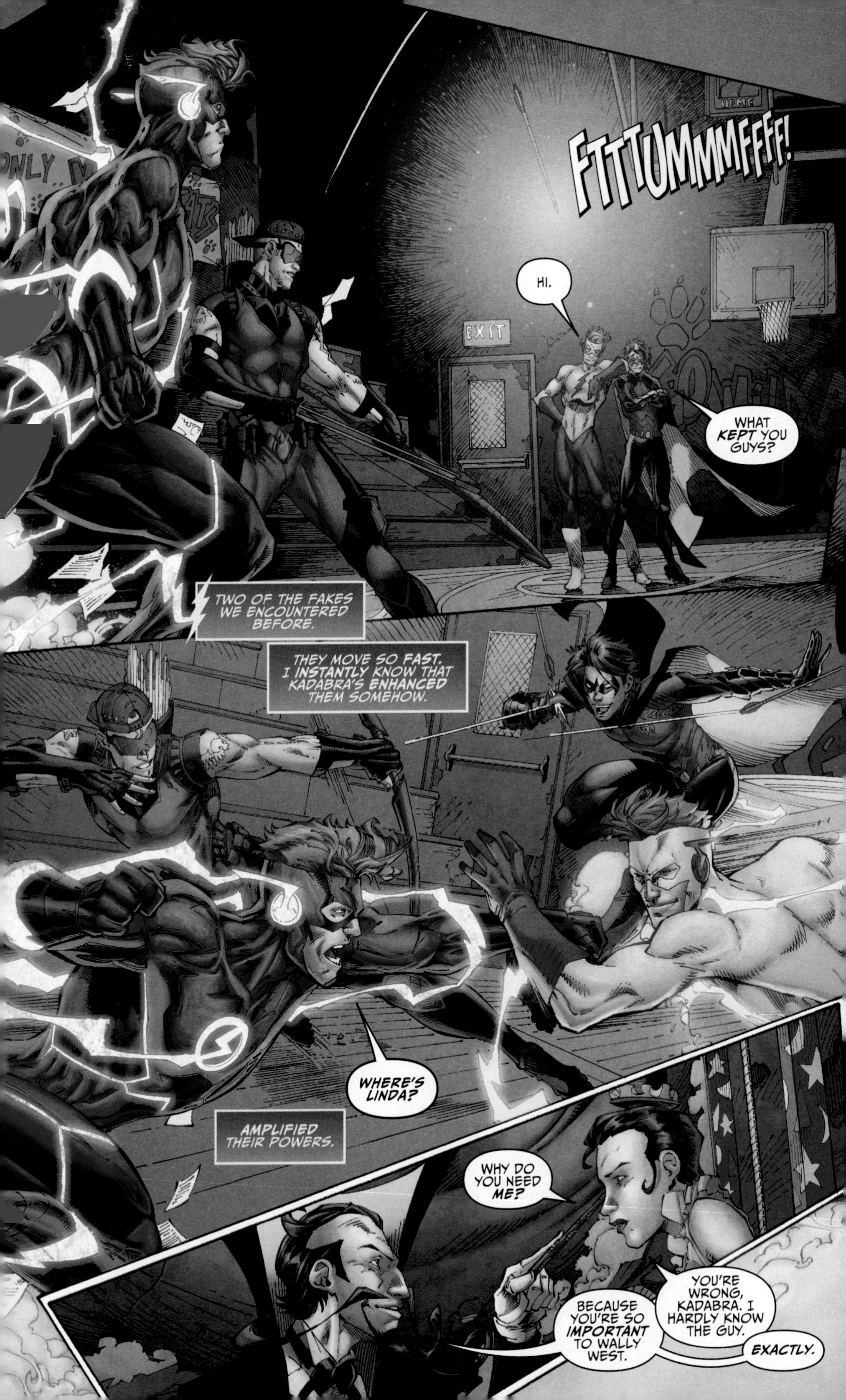
FTTTUMMMFFFF!
HI.
WHAT KEPT YOU GUYS?
TWO OF THE FAKES WE ENCOUNTERED BEFORE.
THEY MOVE SO FAST. I INSTANTLY KNOW THAT KADABRA'S ENHANCED THEM SOMEHOW.
WHERE'S LINDA?
AMPLIFIED THEIR POWERS.
WHY DO YOU NEED ME?
BECAUSE YOU'RE SO IMPORTANT TO WALLY WEST.
YOU'RE WRONG, KADABRA. I HARDLY KNOW THE GUY.
EXACTLY.

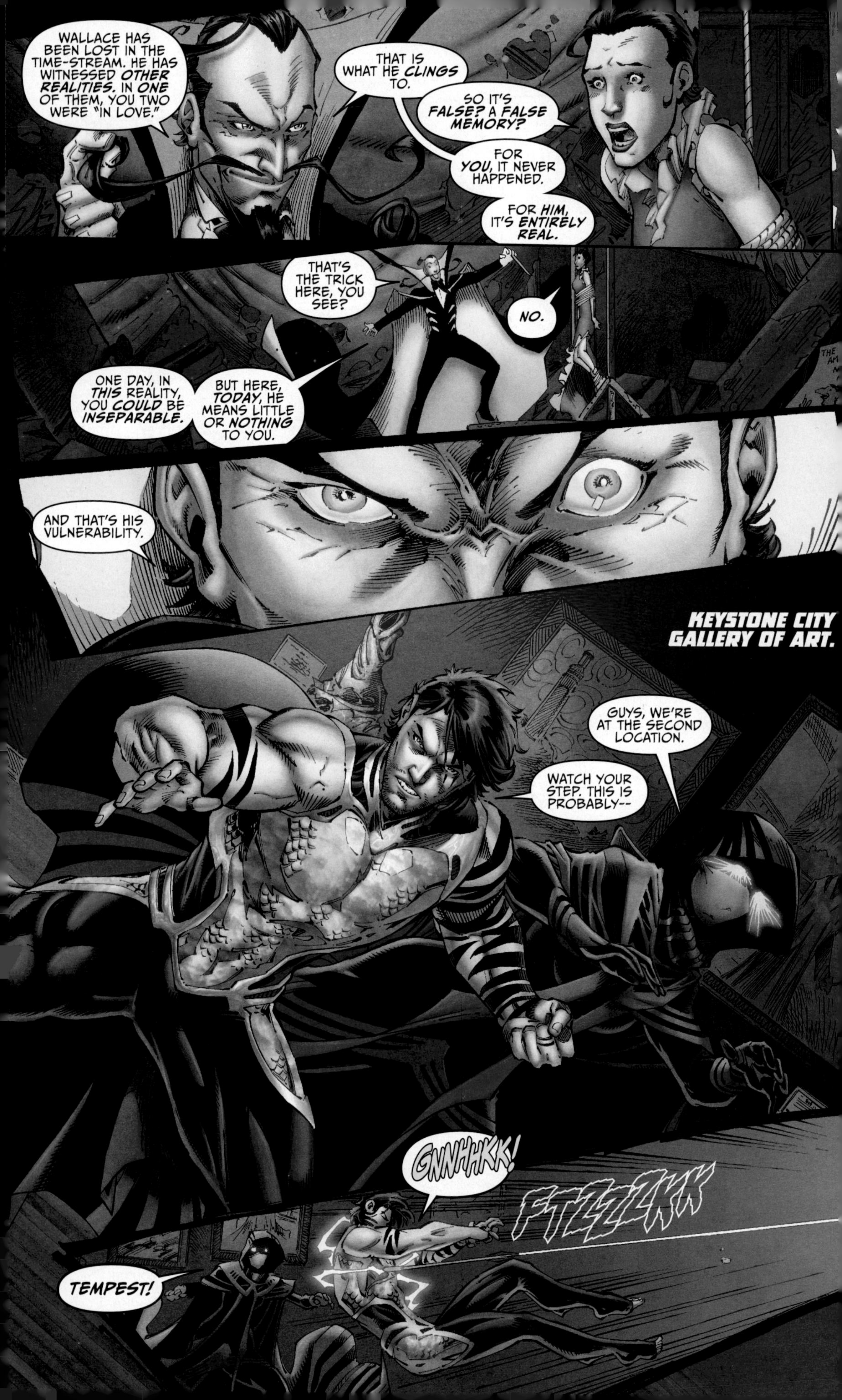
WALLACE HAS BEEN LOST IN THE TIME-STREAM. HE HAS WITNESSED OTHER REALITIES. IN ONE OF THEM, YOU TWO WERE "IN LOVE."
THAT IS WHAT HE CLINGS TO.
SO IT'S FALSE? A FALSE MEMORY?
FOR YOU, IT NEVER HAPPENED.
FOR HIM, IT'S ENTIRELY REAL.
THAT'S THE TRICK HERE, YOU SEE?
NO.
ONE DAY, IN THIS REALITY, YOU COULD BE INSEPARABLE.
BUT HERE, TODAY, HE MEANS LITTLE OR NOTHING TO YOU.
AND THAT'S HIS VULNERABILITY.
KEYSTONE CITY GALLERY OF ART.
GUYS, WE'RE AT THE SECOND LOCATION.
WATCH YOUR STEP. THIS IS PROBABLY--
GNNHHKK!
FTZZZKK
TEMPEST!

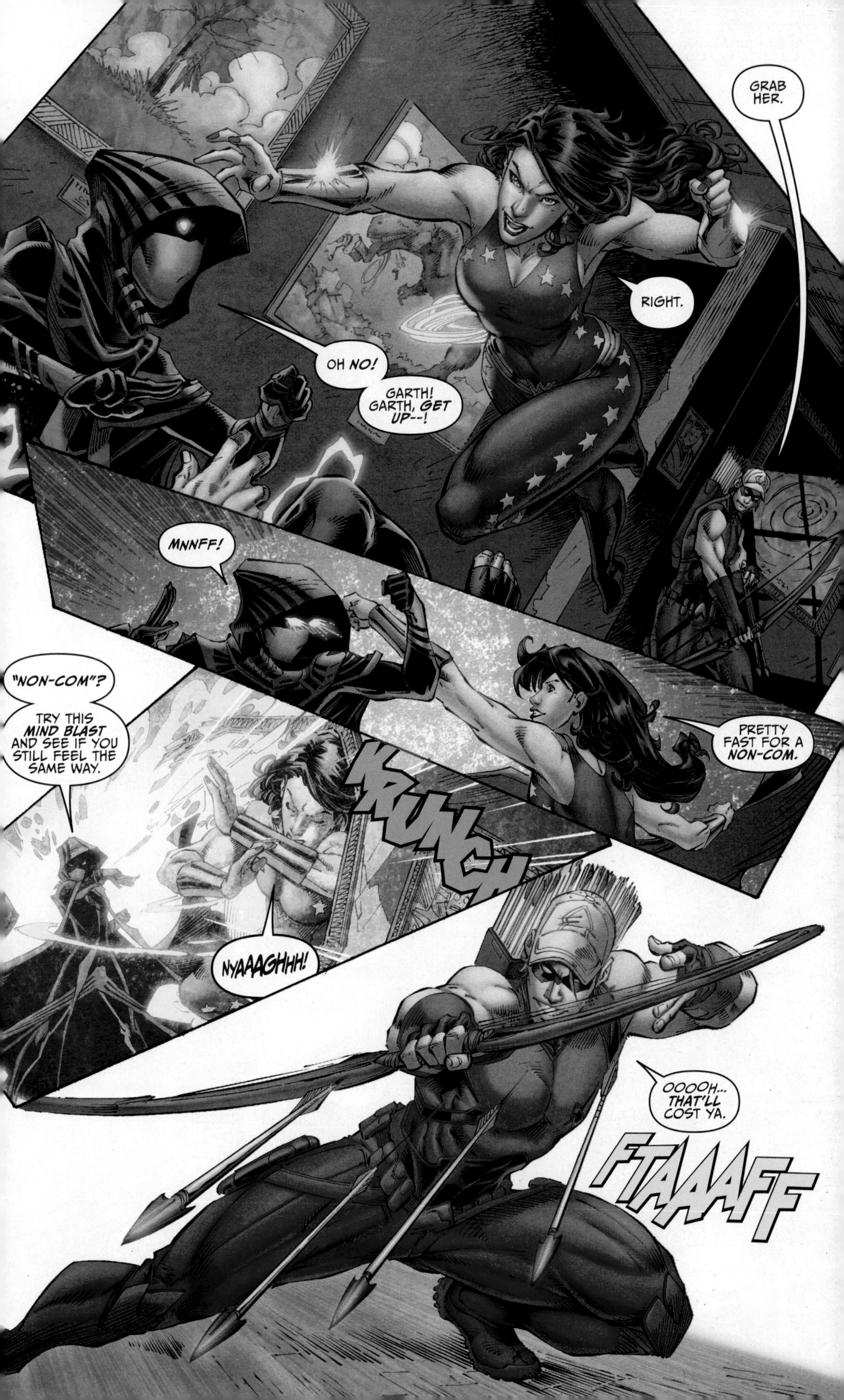
GRAB HER.
RIGHT.
OH NO!
GARTH! GARTH, GET UP--!
MNNFF!
PRETTY FAST FOR A NON-COM.
KRUNCH
"NON-COM"?
TRY THIS MIND BLAST AND SEE IF YOU STILL FEEL THE SAME WAY.
NYAAAGHHH!
OOOOH... THAT'LL COST YA.
FTAAAFF

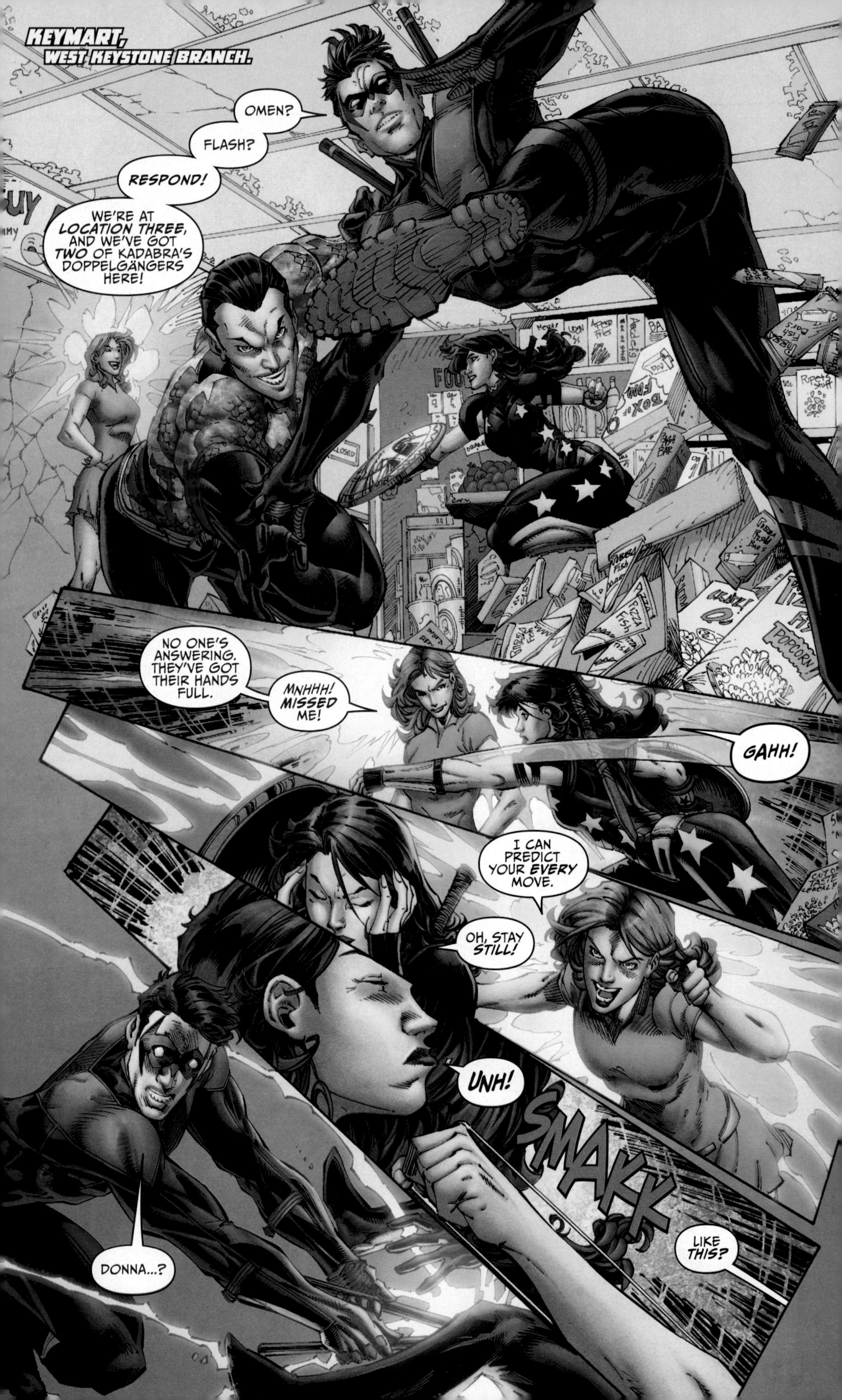
KEYMART, WEST KEYSTONE BRANCH.
OMEN?
FLASH?
RESPOND!
WE'RE AT LOCATION THREE, AND WE'VE GOT TWO OF KADABRA'S DOPPELGÄNGERS HERE!
NO ONE'S ANSWERING. THEY'VE GOT THEIR HANDS FULL.
MNHHH! MISSED ME!
GAHH!
I CAN PREDICT YOUR EVERY MOVE.
OH, STAY STILL!
UNH!
SMAKK
LIKE THIS?
DONNA...?

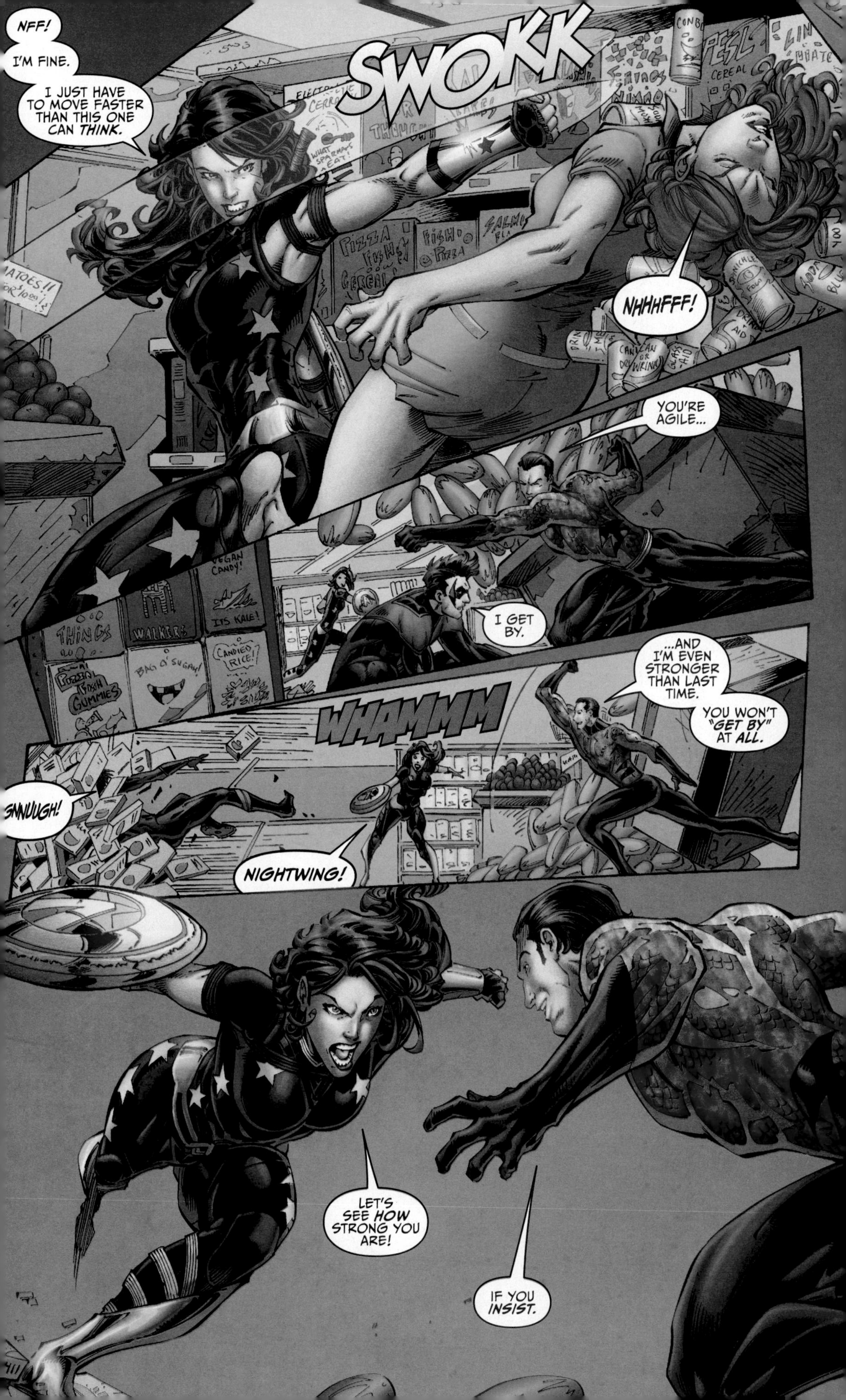
NFF!
I'M FINE.
I JUST HAVE TO MOVE FASTER THAN THIS ONE CAN THINK.
SWOKK
NHHHFFF!
YOU'RE AGILE...
I GET BY.
...AND I'M EVEN STRONGER THAN LAST TIME.
YOU WON'T "GET BY" AT ALL.
WHAMMM
SNNUUGH!
NIGHTWING!
LET'S SEE HOW STRONG YOU ARE!
IF YOU INSIST.

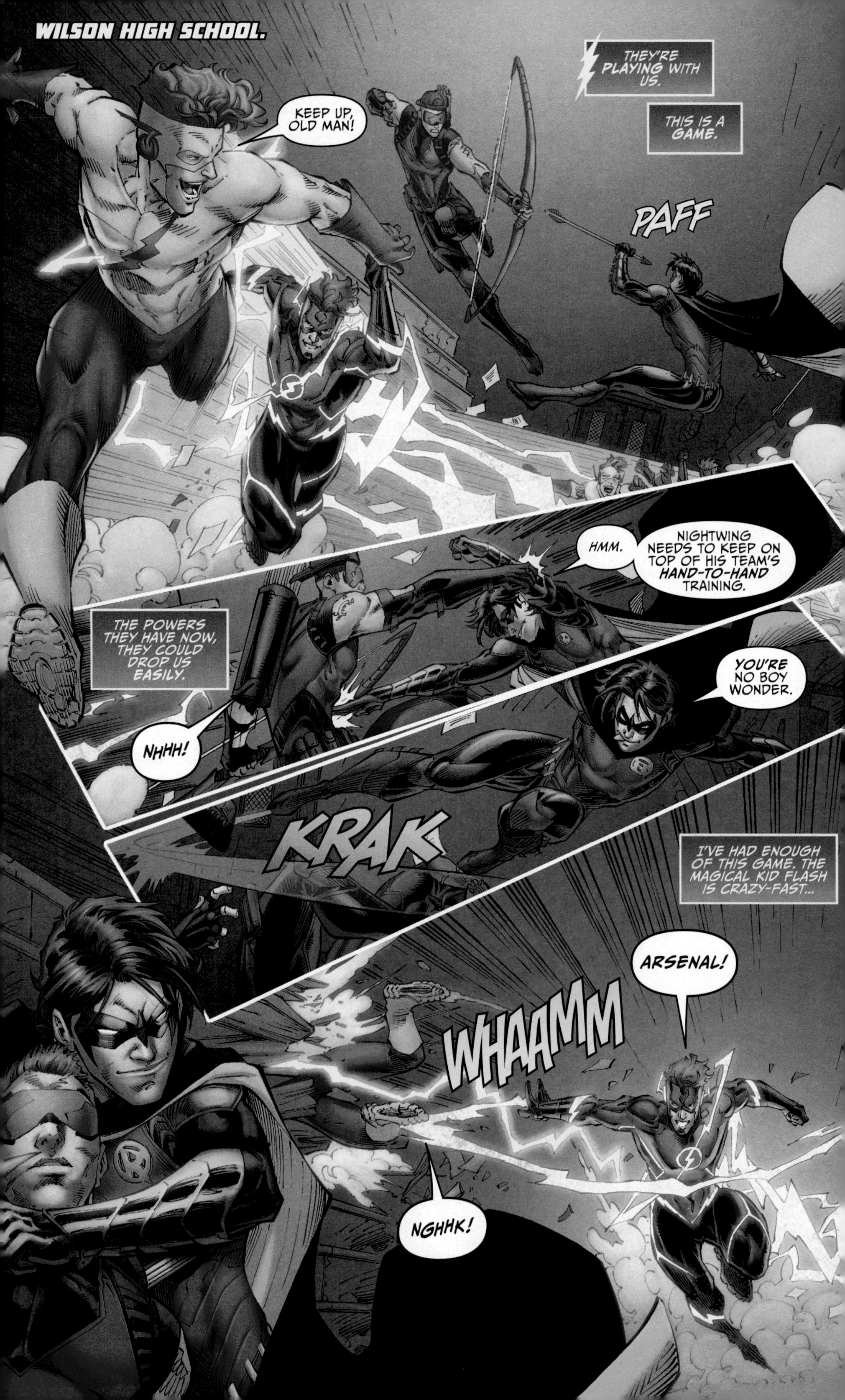
WILSON HIGH SCHOOL.
KEEP UP, OLD MAN!
THEY'RE PLAYING WITH US.
THIS IS A GAME.
PAFF
HMM.
NIGHTWING NEEDS TO KEEP ON TOP OF HIS TEAM'S HAND-TO-HAND TRAINING.
THE POWERS THEY HAVE NOW, THEY COULD DROP US EASILY.
YOU'RE NO BOY WONDER.
NHHH!
KRAK
I'VE HAD ENOUGH OF THIS GAME. THE MAGICAL KID FLASH IS CRAZY-FAST...
ARSENAL!
WHAAMM
NGHHK!

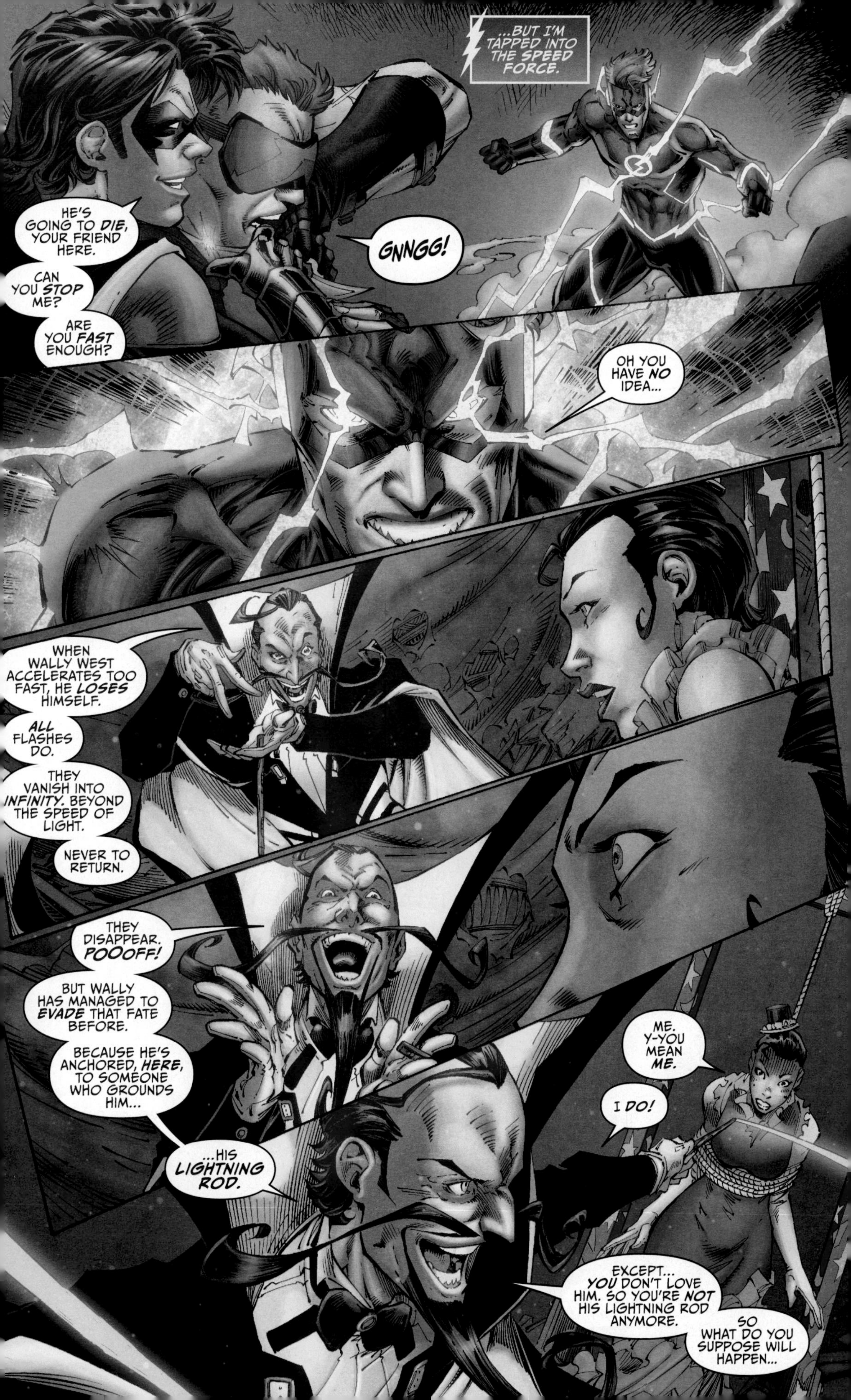
...BUT I'M TAPPED INTO THE SPEED FORCE.
HE'S GOING TO DIE, YOUR FRIEND HERE.
CAN YOU STOP ME?
ARE YOU FAST ENOUGH?
GNNGG!
OH YOU HAVE NO IDEA...
WHEN WALLY WEST ACCELERATES TOO FAST, HE LOSES HIMSELF.
ALL FLASHES DO.
THEY VANISH INTO INFINITY. BEYOND THE SPEED OF LIGHT.
NEVER TO RETURN.
THEY DISAPPEAR. POOOFF!
BUT WALLY HAS MANAGED TO EVADE THAT FATE BEFORE.
BECAUSE HE'S ANCHORED, HERE, TO SOMEONE WHO GROUNDS HIM...
...HIS LIGHTNING ROD.
ME. Y-YOU MEAN ME.
I DO!
EXCEPT... YOU DON'T LOVE HIM. SO YOU'RE NOT HIS LIGHTNING ROD ANYMORE.
SO WHAT DO YOU SUPPOSE WILL HAPPEN...

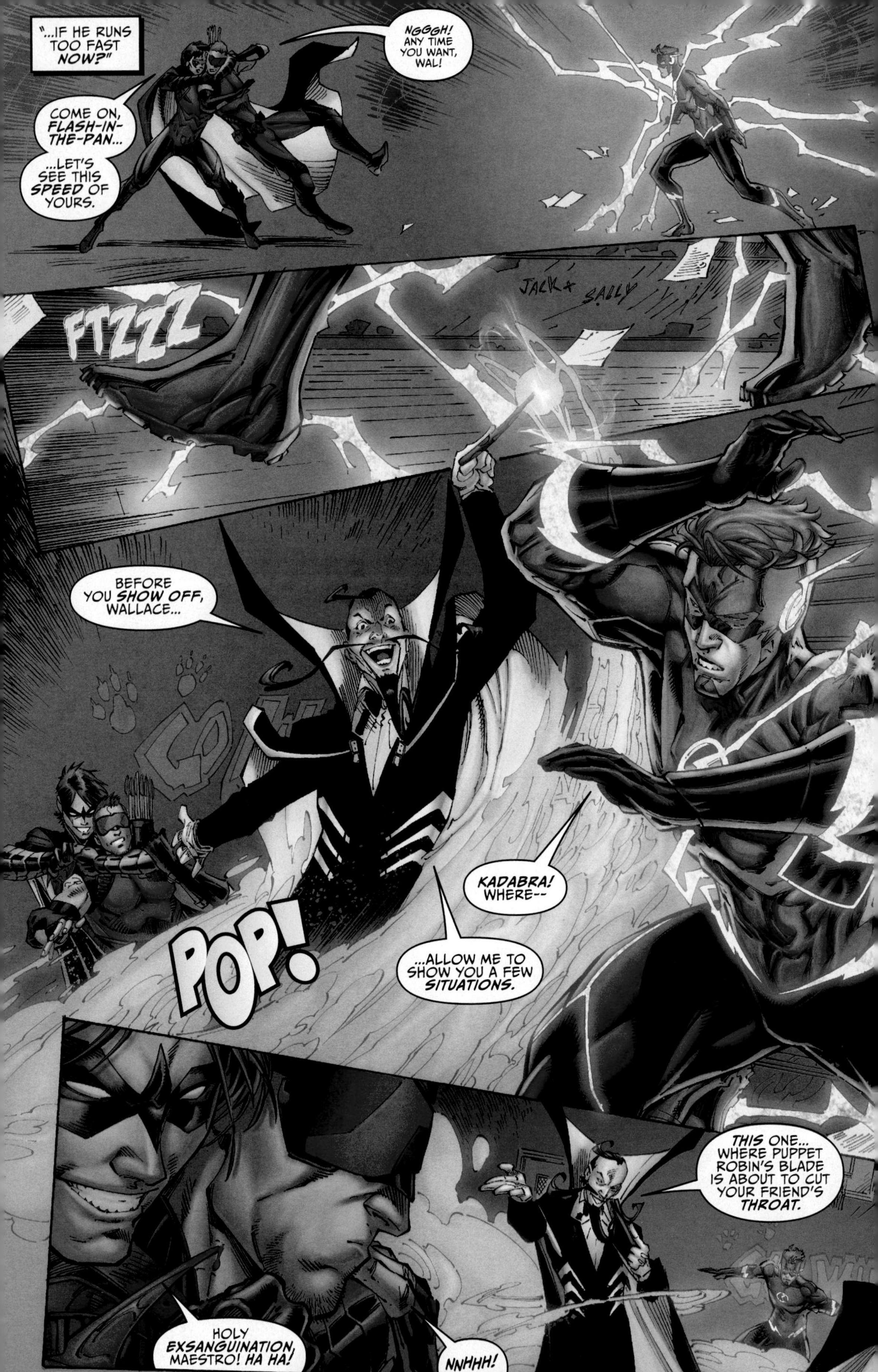

"...IF HE RUNS TOO FAST NOW?"
NGGGH! ANY TIME YOU WANT, WAL!
COME ON, FLASH-IN-THE-PAN...
...LET'S SEE THIS SPEED OF YOURS.
FTZZZ
JACK + SALLY
BEFORE YOU SHOW OFF, WALLACE...
KADABRA! WHERE--
POP!
...ALLOW ME TO SHOW YOU A FEW SITUATIONS.
THIS ONE... WHERE PUPPET ROBIN'S BLADE IS ABOUT TO CUT YOUR FRIEND'S THROAT.
HOLY EXSANGUINATION, MAESTRO! HA HA!
NNHHH!

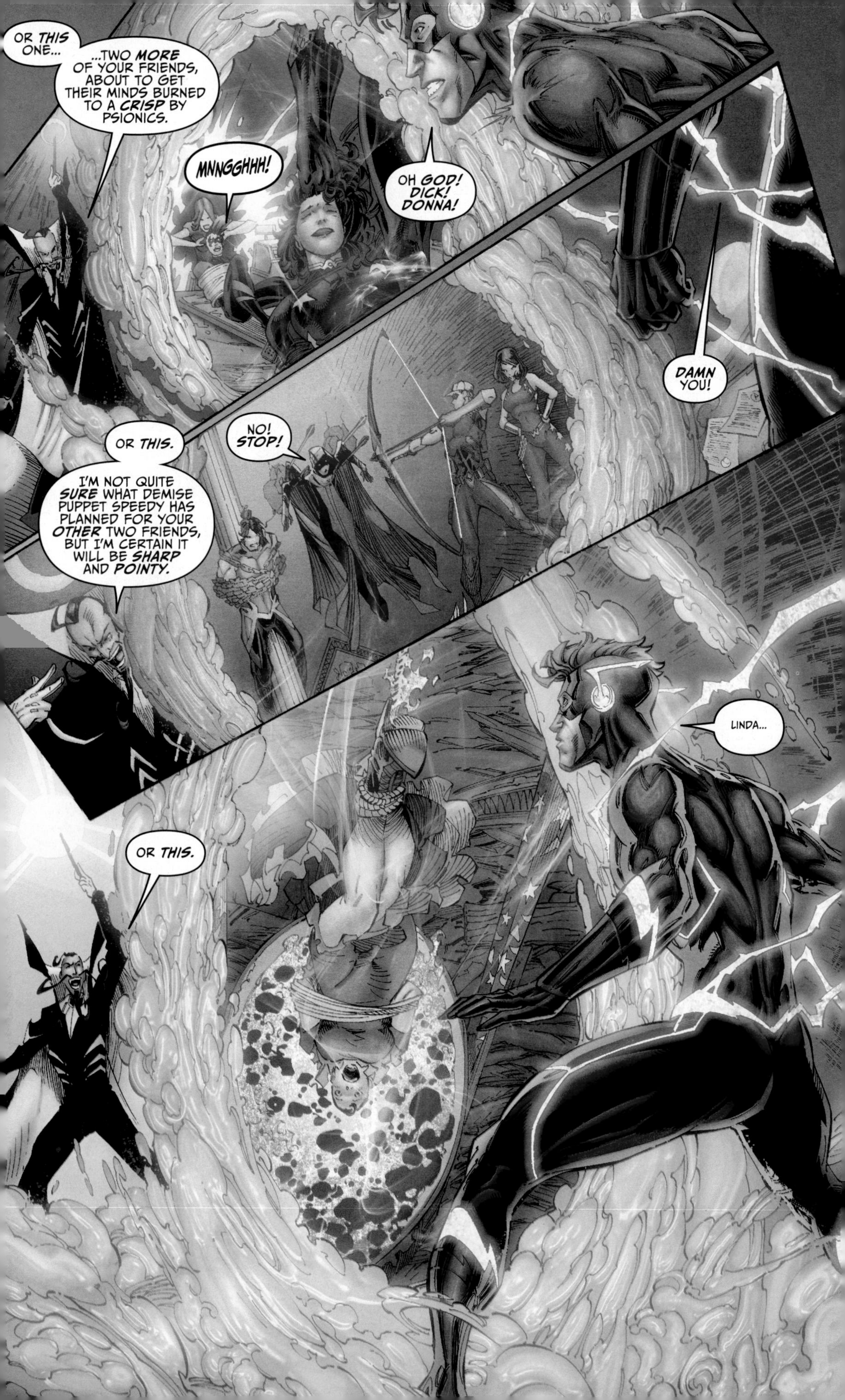
OR THIS ONE...
...TWO MORE OF YOUR FRIENDS, ABOUT TO GET THEIR MINDS BURNED TO A CRISP BY PSIONICS.
MNNGGHHH!
OH GOD! DICK! DONNA!
DAMN YOU!
OR THIS.
NO! STOP!
I'M NOT QUITE SURE WHAT DEMISE PUPPET SPEEDY HAS PLANNED FOR YOUR OTHER TWO FRIENDS, BUT I'M CERTAIN IT WILL BE SHARP AND POINTY.
LINDA...
OR THIS.

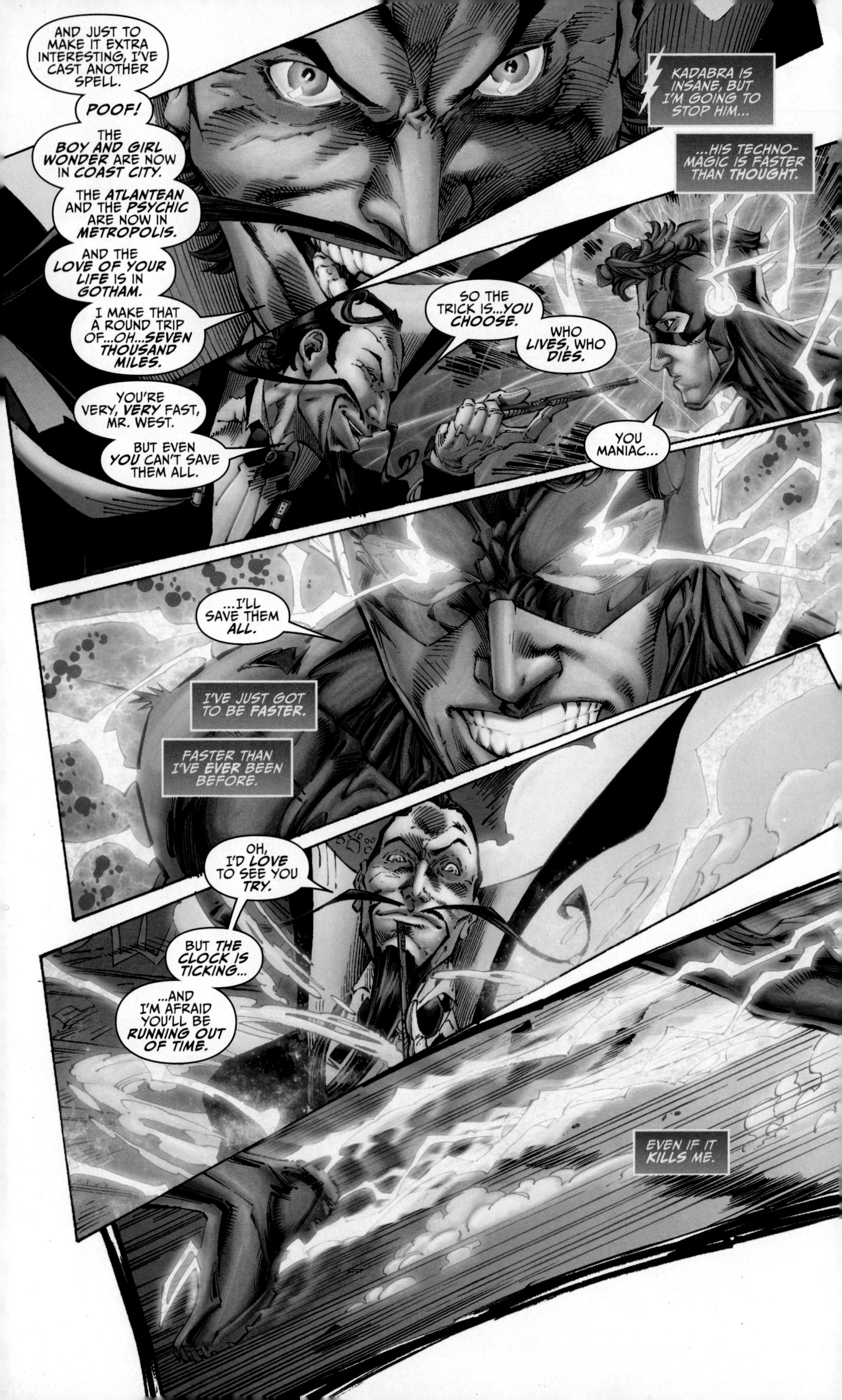
AND JUST TO MAKE IT EXTRA INTERESTING, I'VE CAST ANOTHER SPELL.
POOF!
THE BOY AND GIRL WONDER ARE NOW IN COAST CITY.
THE ATLANTEAN AND THE PSYCHIC ARE NOW IN METROPOLIS.
AND THE LOVE OF YOUR LIFE IS IN GOTHAM.
I MAKE THAT A ROUND TRIP OF...OH...SEVEN THOUSAND MILES.
KADABRA IS INSANE, BUT I'M GOING TO STOP HIM...
...HIS TECHNO-MAGIC IS FASTER THAN THOUGHT.
SO THE TRICK IS...YOU CHOOSE.
WHO LIVES, WHO DIES.
YOU'RE VERY, VERY FAST, MR. WEST.
BUT EVEN YOU CAN'T SAVE THEM ALL.
YOU MANIAC...
...I'LL SAVE THEM ALL.
I'VE JUST GOT TO BE FASTER.
FASTER THAN I'VE EVER BEEN BEFORE.
OH, I'D LOVE TO SEE YOU TRY.
BUT THE CLOCK IS TICKING...
...AND I'M AFRAID YOU'LL BE RUNNING OUT OF TIME.
EVEN IF IT KILLS ME.

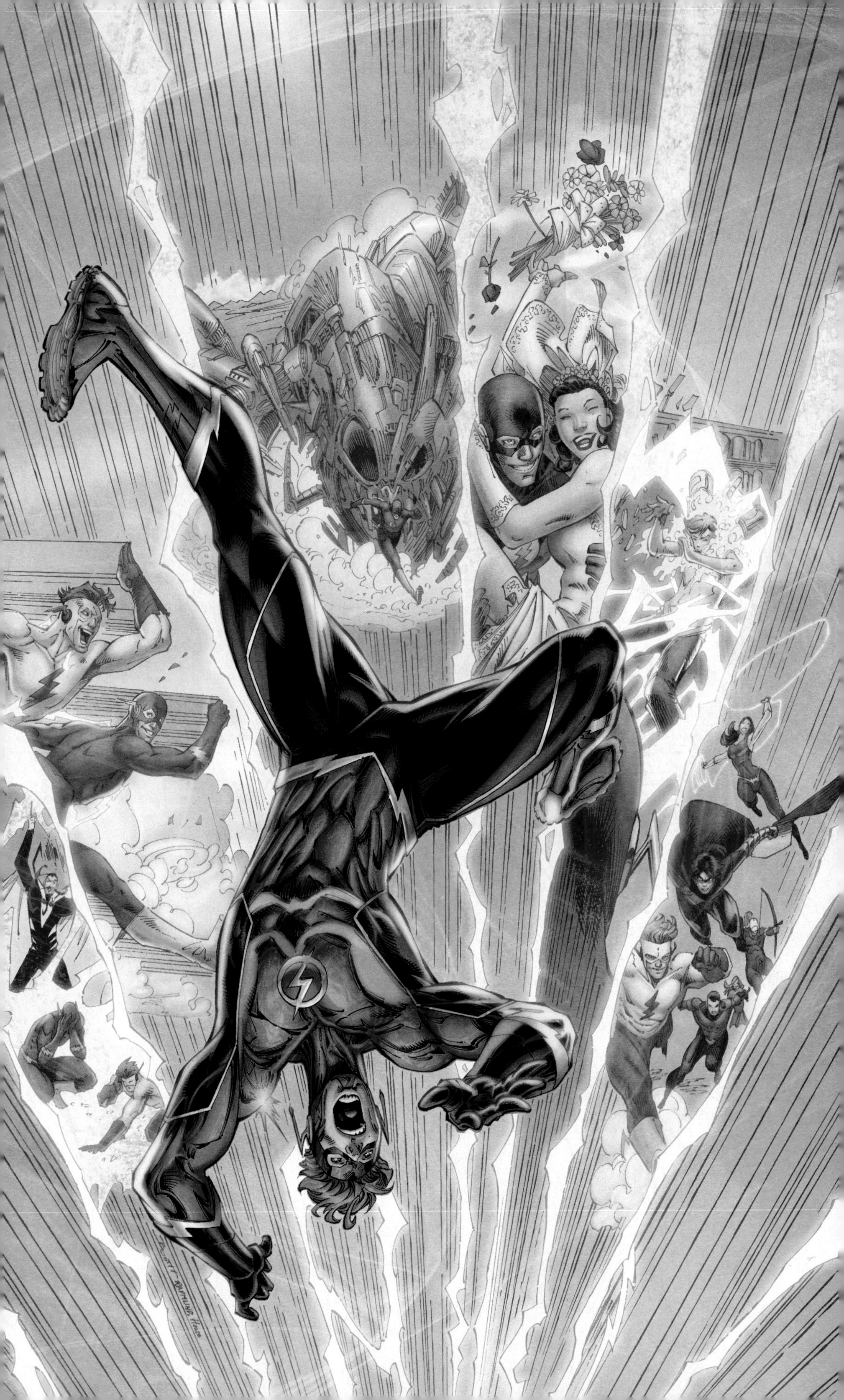

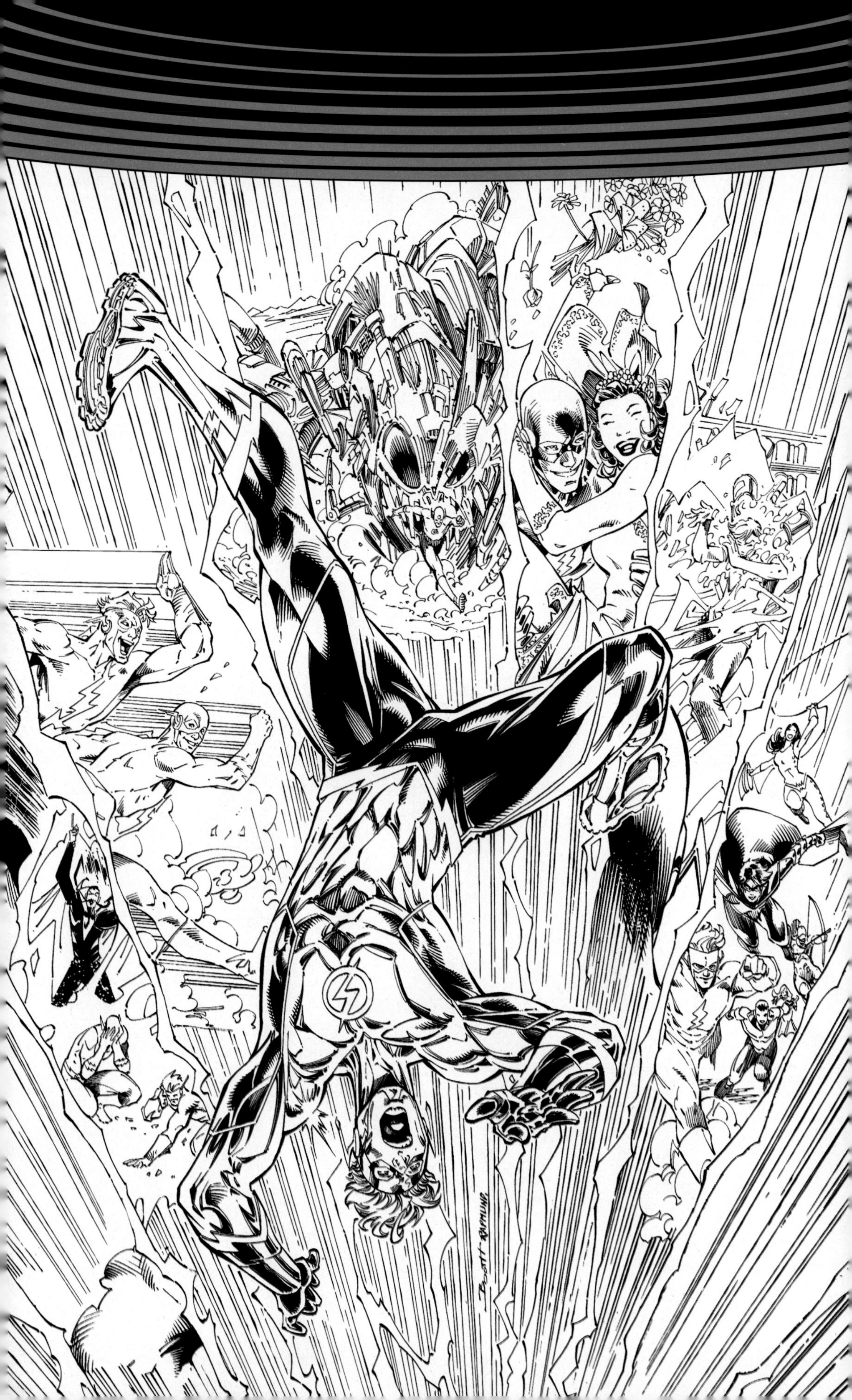

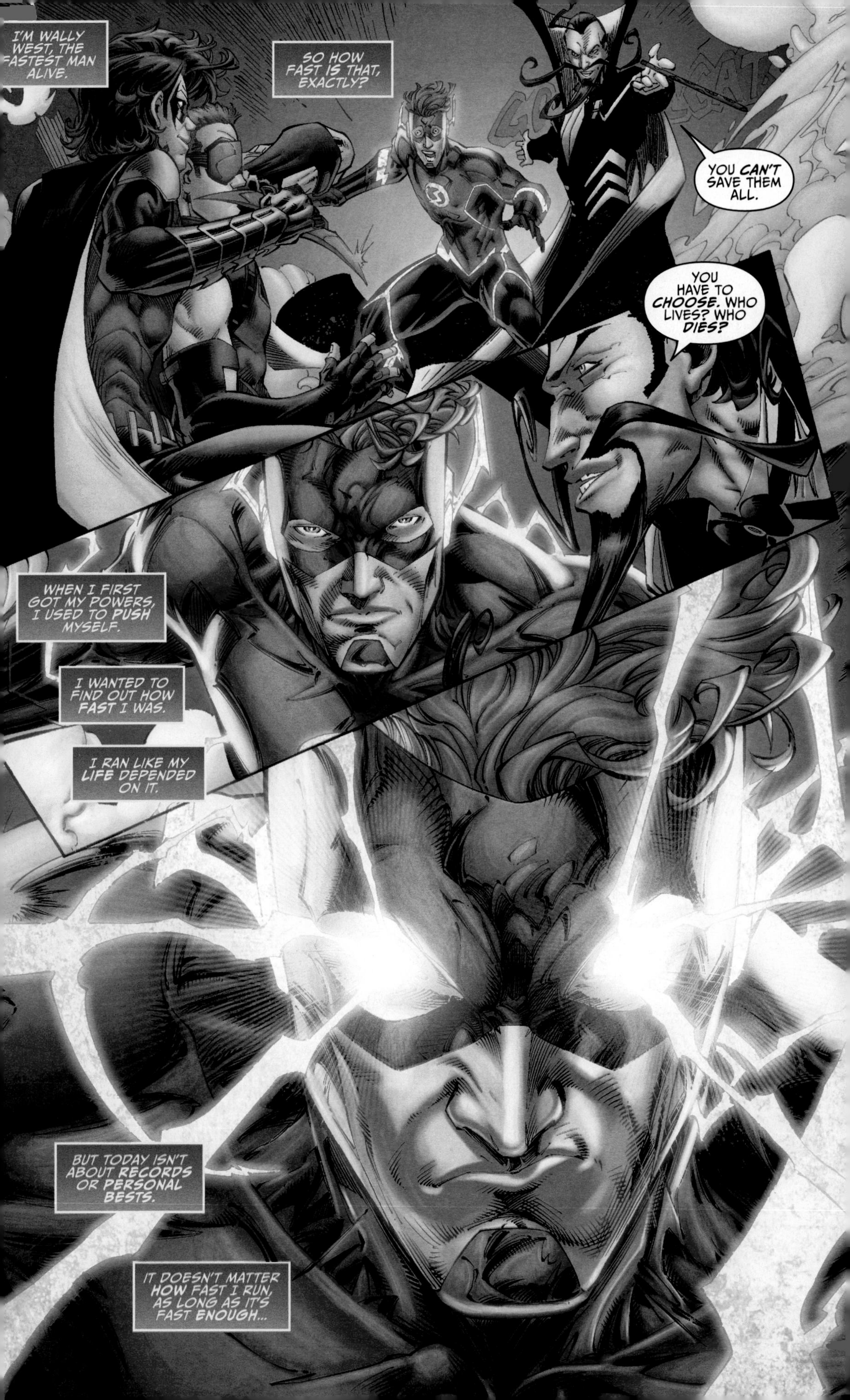
I'M WALLY WEST, THE FASTEST MAN ALIVE.
SO HOW FAST IS THAT, EXACTLY?
YOU CAN'T SAVE THEM ALL.
YOU HAVE TO CHOOSE. WHO LIVES? WHO DIES?
WHEN I FIRST GOT MY POWERS, I USED TO PUSH MYSELF.
I WANTED TO FIND OUT HOW FAST I WAS.
I RAN LIKE MY LIFE DEPENDED ON IT.
BUT TODAY ISN'T ABOUT RECORDS OR PERSONAL BESTS.
IT DOESN'T MATTER HOW FAST I RUN, AS LONG AS IT'S FAST ENOUGH...

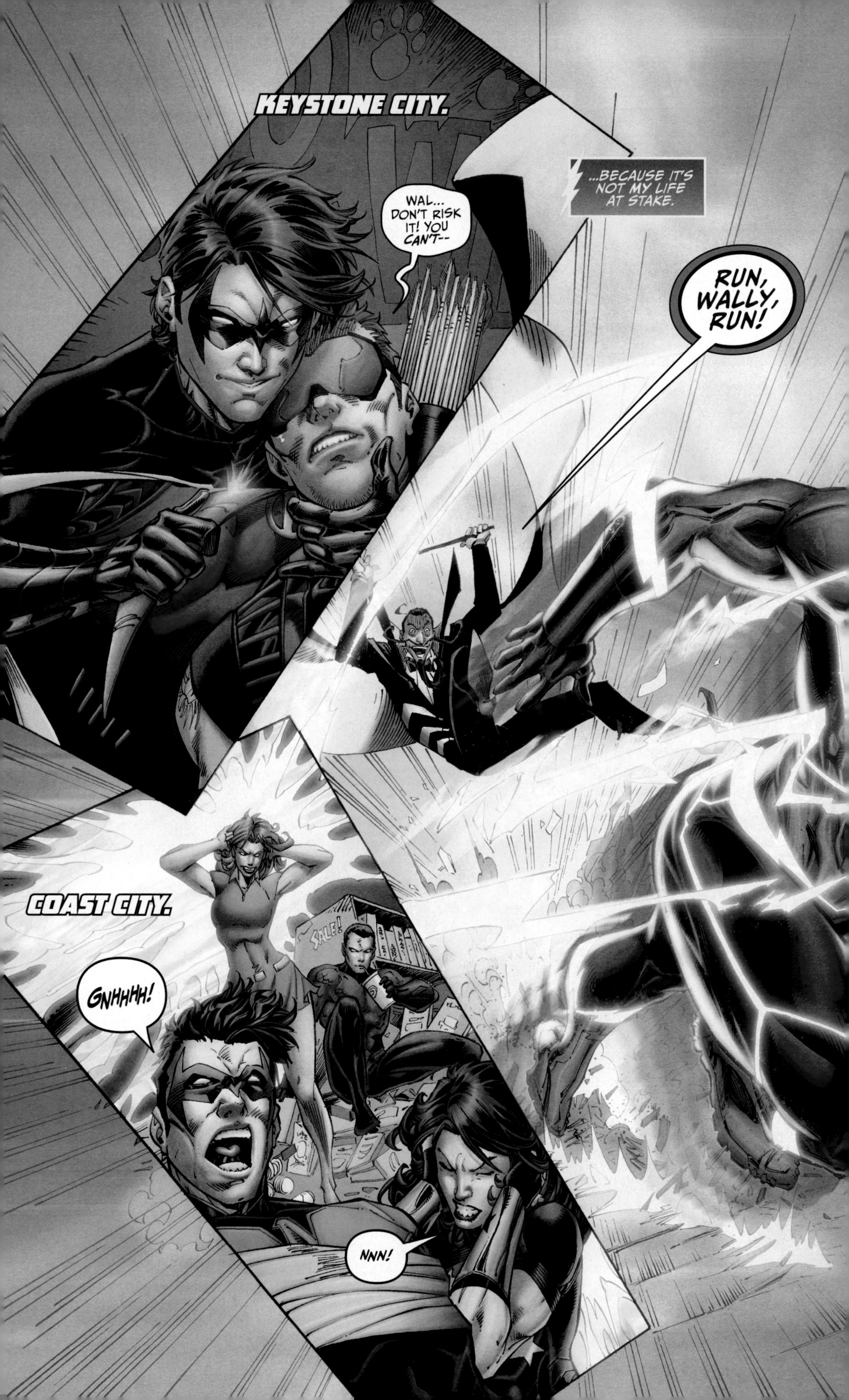
KEYSTONE CITY.
WAL... DON'T RISK IT! YOU CAN'T--
...BECAUSE IT'S NOT MY LIFE AT STAKE.
RUN, WALLY, RUN!
COAST CITY.
GNHHHH!
SALE!
NNN!

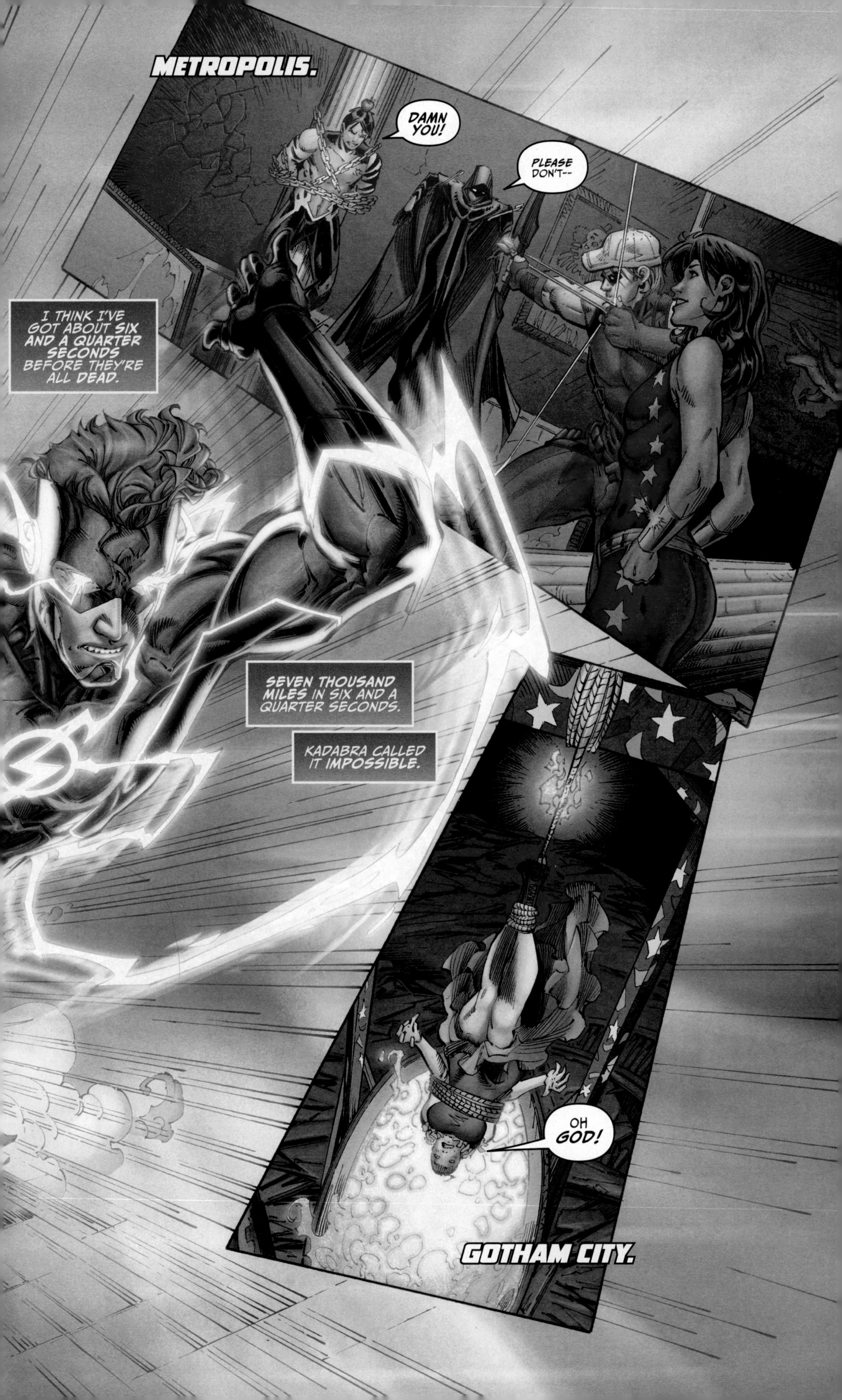
METROPOLIS.
DAMN YOU!
PLEASE DON'T--
I THINK I'VE GOT ABOUT SIX AND A QUARTER SECONDS BEFORE THEY'RE ALL DEAD.
SEVEN THOUSAND MILES IN SIX AND A QUARTER SECONDS.
KADABRA CALLED IT IMPOSSIBLE.
OH GOD!
GOTHAM CITY.

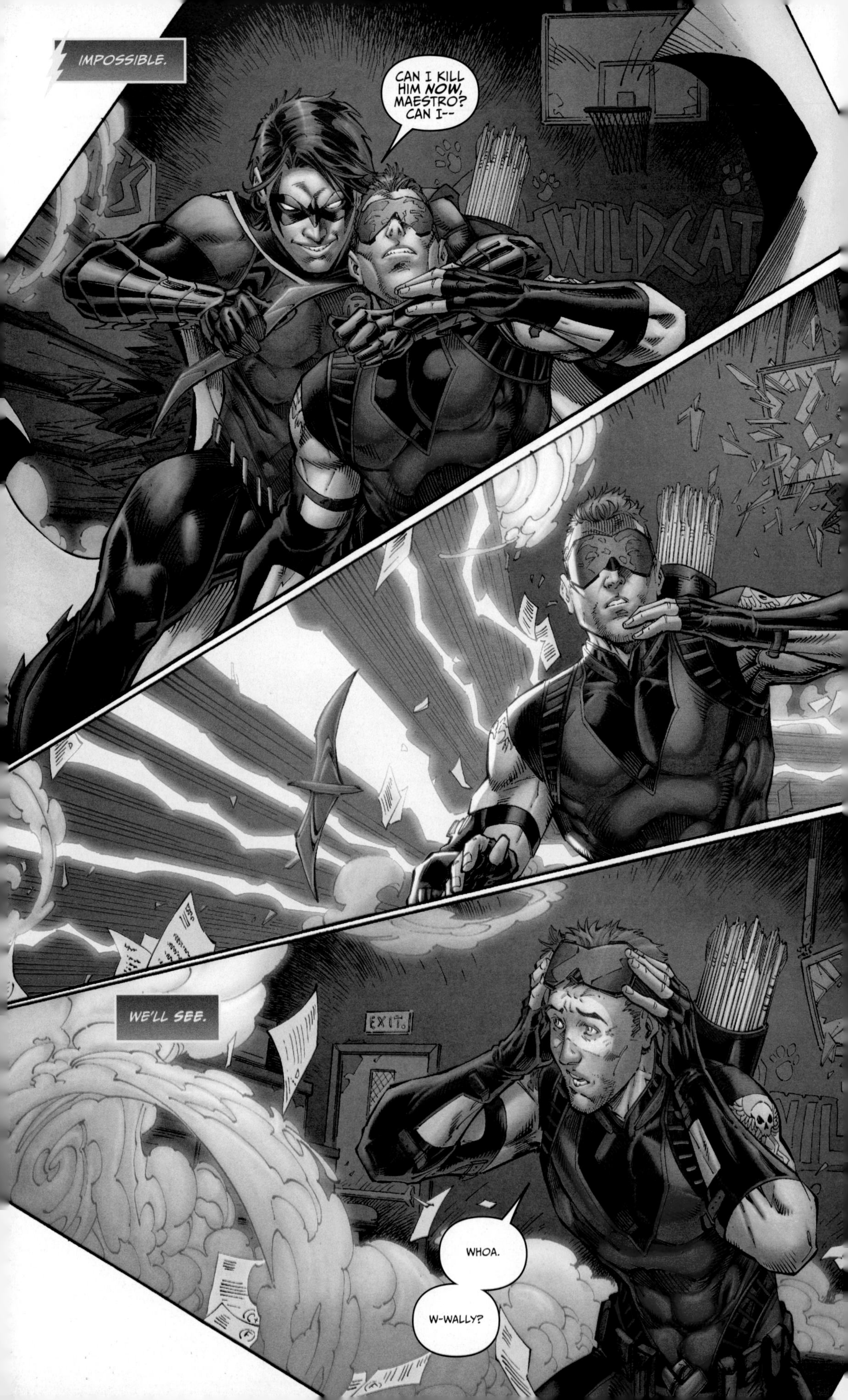
IMPOSSIBLE.
CAN I KILL HIM NOW, MAESTRO? CAN I--
WILDCAT
WE'LL SEE.
EXIT.
WHOA.
W-WALLY?

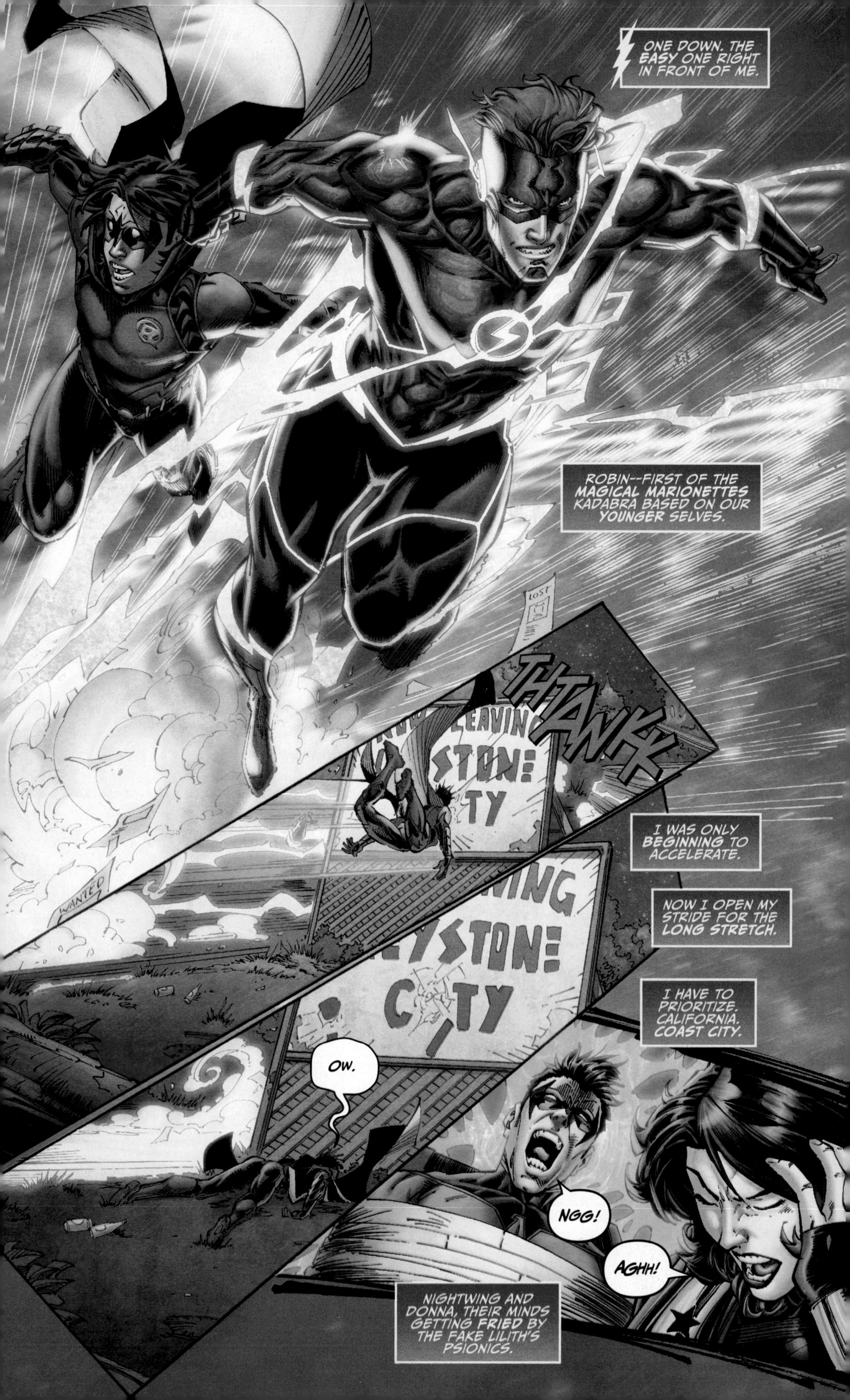

ONE DOWN. THE EASY ONE RIGHT IN FRONT OF ME.
ROBIN--FIRST OF THE MAGICAL MARIONETTES KADABRA BASED ON OUR YOUNGER SELVES.
LOST
THANKK
I WAS ONLY BEGINNING TO ACCELERATE.
NOW I OPEN MY STRIDE FOR THE LONG STRETCH.
I HAVE TO PRIORITIZE. CALIFORNIA. COAST CITY.
WANTED
OW.
NGG!
AGHH!
NIGHTWING AND DONNA, THEIR MINDS GETTING FRIED BY THE FAKE LILITH'S PSIONICS.

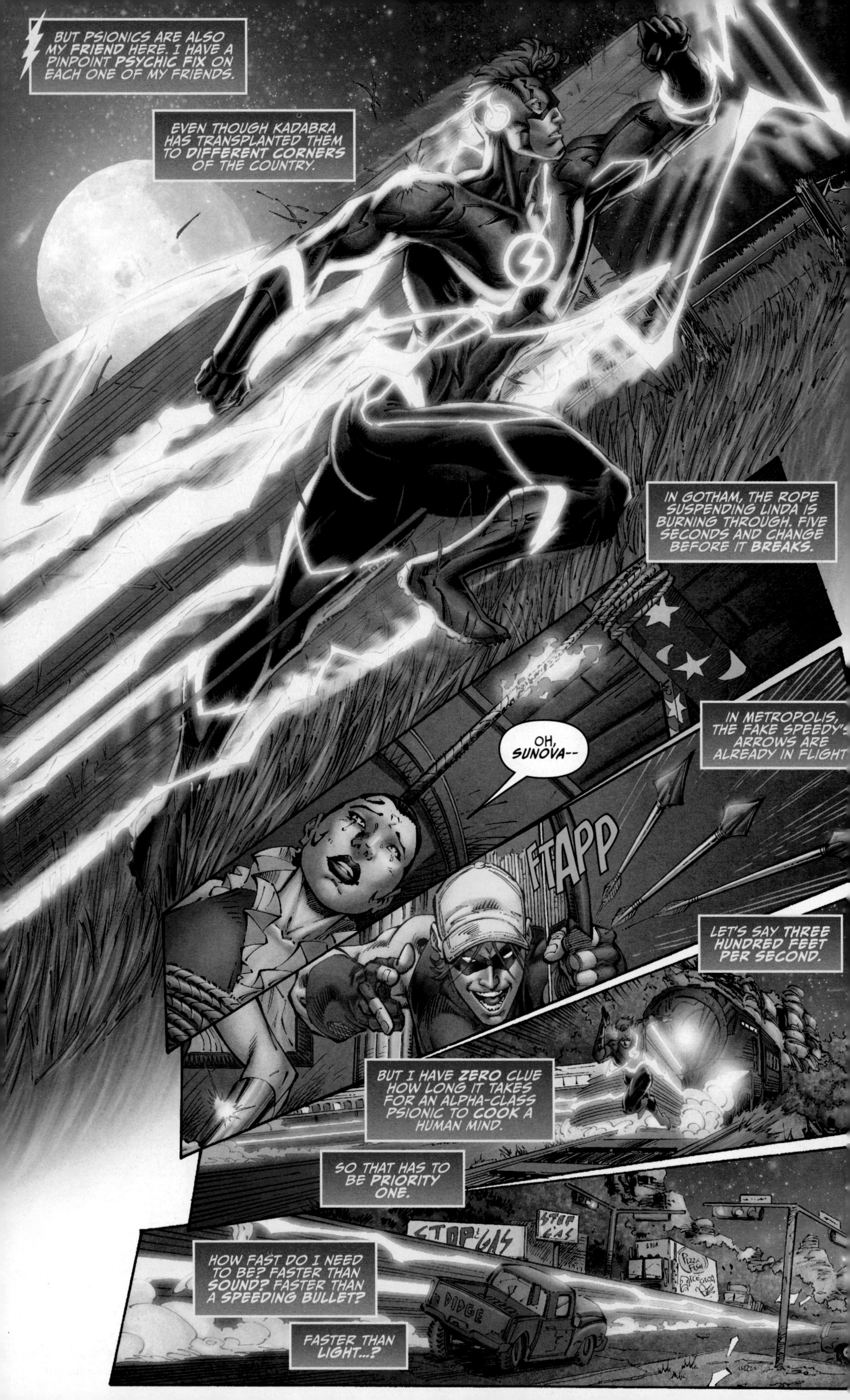

BUT PSIONICS ARE ALSO MY FRIEND HERE. I HAVE A PINPOINT PSYCHIC FIX ON EACH ONE OF MY FRIENDS.
EVEN THOUGH KADABRA HAS TRANSPLANTED THEM TO DIFFERENT CORNERS OF THE COUNTRY.
IN GOTHAM, THE ROPE SUSPENDING LINDA IS BURNING THROUGH. FIVE SECONDS AND CHANGE BEFORE IT BREAKS.
IN METROPOLIS, THE FAKE SPEEDY'S ARROWS ARE ALREADY IN FLIGHT
OH, SUNOVA--
FTAPP
LET'S SAY THREE HUNDRED FEET PER SECOND.
BUT I HAVE ZERO CLUE HOW LONG IT TAKES FOR AN ALPHA-CLASS PSIONIC TO COOK A HUMAN MIND.
SO THAT HAS TO BE PRIORITY ONE.
STOP GAS
HOW FAST DO I NEED TO BE? FASTER THAN SOUND? FASTER THAN A SPEEDING BULLET?
DIDGE
FASTER THAN LIGHT...?

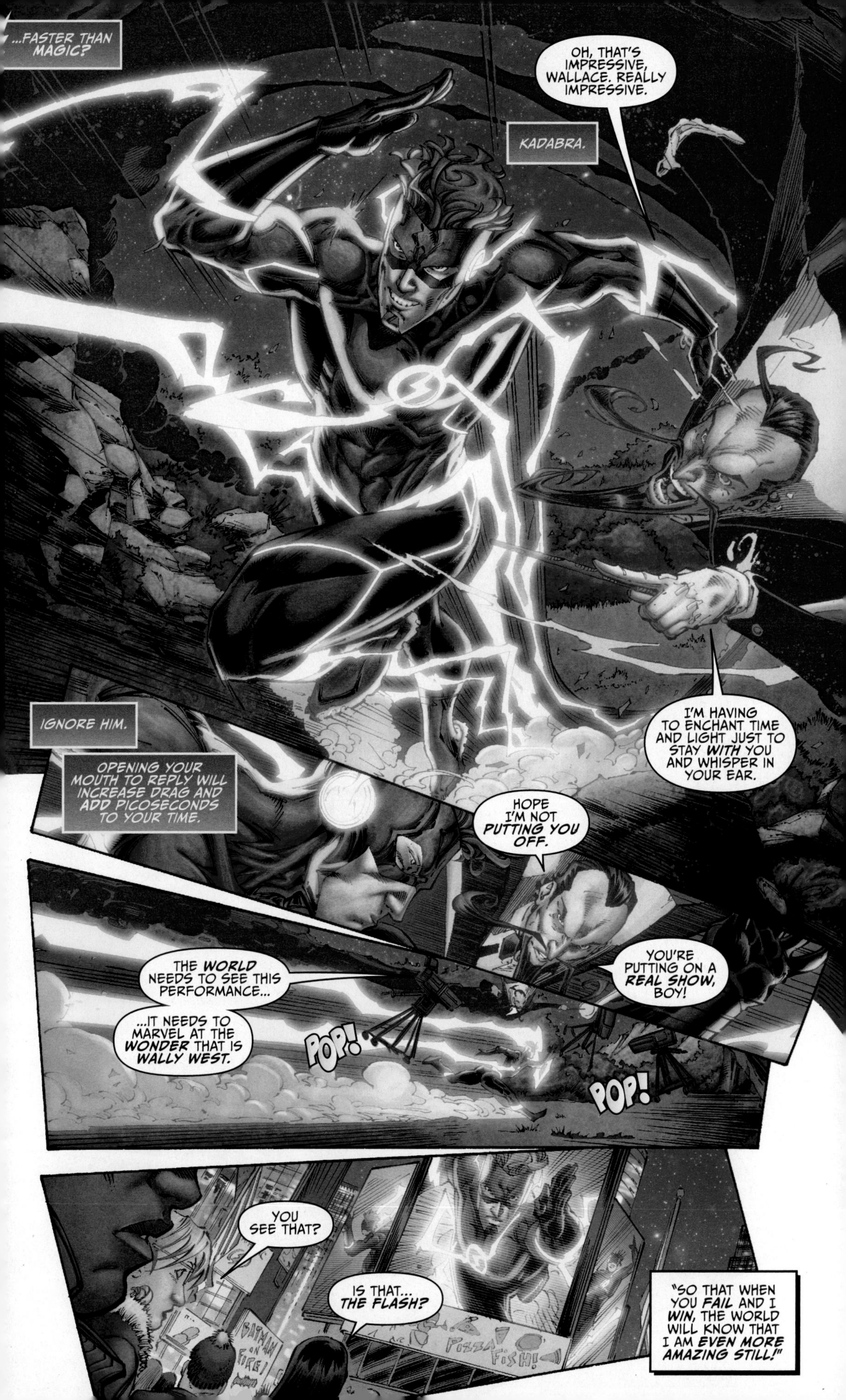

...FASTER THAN MAGIC?
OH, THAT'S IMPRESSIVE, WALLACE. REALLY IMPRESSIVE.
KADABRA.
IGNORE HIM.
OPENING YOUR MOUTH TO REPLY WILL INCREASE DRAG AND ADD PICOSECONDS TO YOUR TIME.
I'M HAVING TO ENCHANT TIME AND LIGHT JUST TO STAY WITH YOU AND WHISPER IN YOUR EAR.
HOPE I'M NOT PUTTING YOU OFF.
YOU'RE PUTTING ON A REAL SHOW, BOY!
THE WORLD NEEDS TO SEE THIS PERFORMANCE...
...IT NEEDS TO MARVEL AT THE WONDER THAT IS WALLY WEST.
POP!
POP!
YOU SEE THAT?
IS THAT... THE FLASH?
BATMAN ON FIRE!
PIZZA
FISH!
"SO THAT WHEN YOU FAIL AND I WIN, THE WORLD WILL KNOW THAT I AM EVEN MORE AMAZING STILL!"

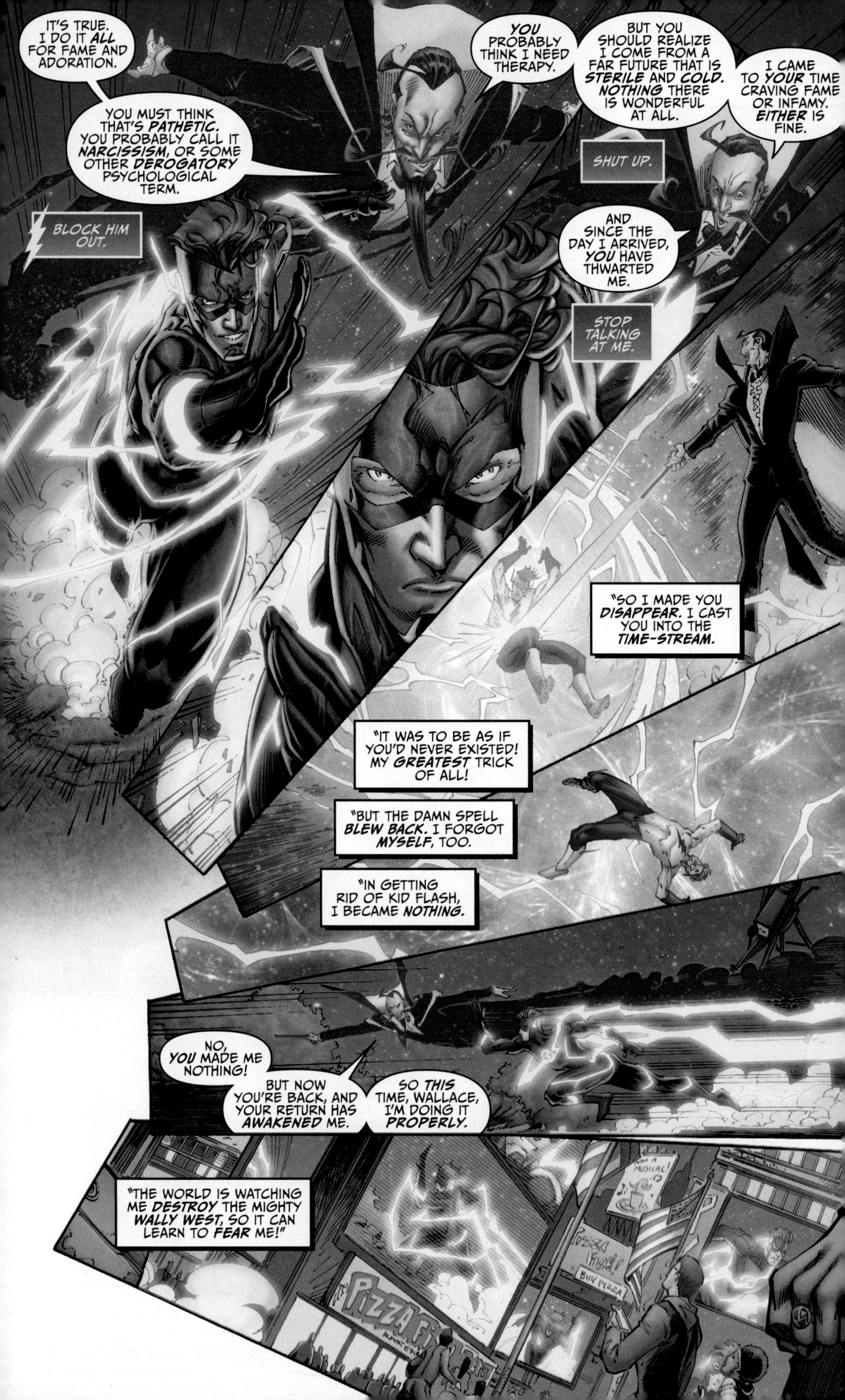
IT'S TRUE. I DO IT ALL FOR FAME AND ADORATION.
YOU MUST THINK THAT'S PATHETIC. YOU PROBABLY CALL IT NARCISSISM, OR SOME OTHER DEROGATORY PSYCHOLOGICAL TERM.
BLOCK HIM OUT.
YOU PROBABLY THINK I NEED THERAPY.
BUT YOU SHOULD REALIZE I COME FROM A FAR FUTURE THAT IS STERILE AND COLD. NOTHING THERE IS WONDERFUL AT ALL.
I CAME TO YOUR TIME CRAVING FAME OR INFAMY. EITHER IS FINE.
SHUT UP.
AND SINCE THE DAY I ARRIVED, YOU HAVE THWARTED ME.
STOP TALKING AT ME.
"SO I MADE YOU DISAPPEAR. I CAST YOU INTO THE TIME-STREAM.
"IT WAS TO BE AS IF YOU'D NEVER EXISTED! MY GREATEST TRICK OF ALL!
"BUT THE DAMN SPELL BLEW BACK. I FORGOT MYSELF, TOO.
"IN GETTING RID OF KID FLASH, I BECAME NOTHING.
NO, YOU MADE ME NOTHING!
BUT NOW YOU'RE BACK, AND YOUR RETURN HAS AWAKENED ME.
SO THIS TIME, WALLACE, I'M DOING IT PROPERLY.
"THE WORLD IS WATCHING ME DESTROY THE MIGHTY WALLY WEST, SO IT CAN LEARN TO FEAR ME!"
PIZZA
BUY PIZZA

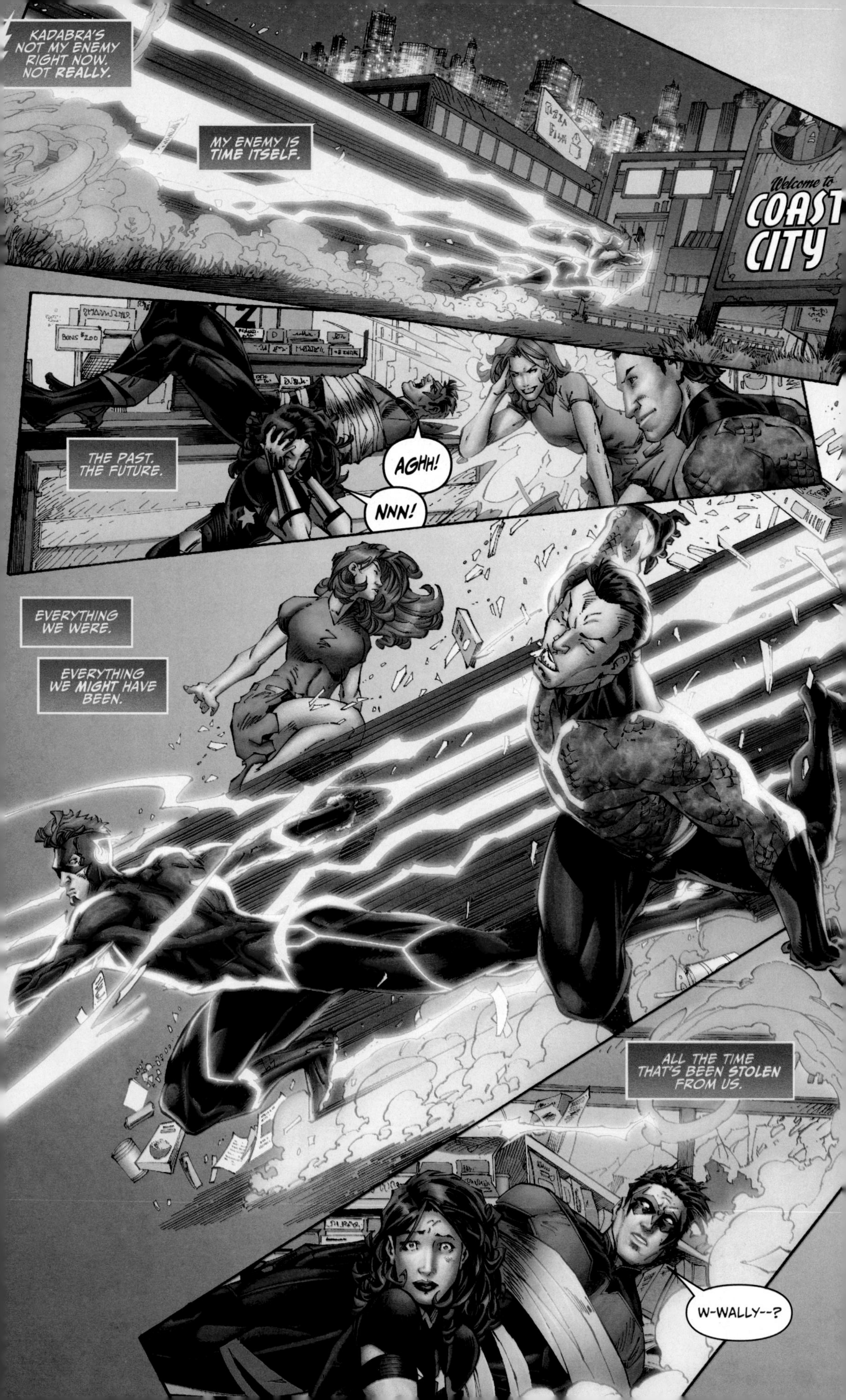
KADABRA'S NOT MY ENEMY RIGHT NOW. NOT REALLY.
MY ENEMY IS TIME ITSELF.
Welcome to COAST CITY
THE PAST. THE FUTURE.
AGHH!
NNN!
EVERYTHING WE WERE.
EVERYTHING WE MIGHT HAVE BEEN.
ALL THE TIME THAT'S BEEN STOLEN FROM US.
W-WALLY--?

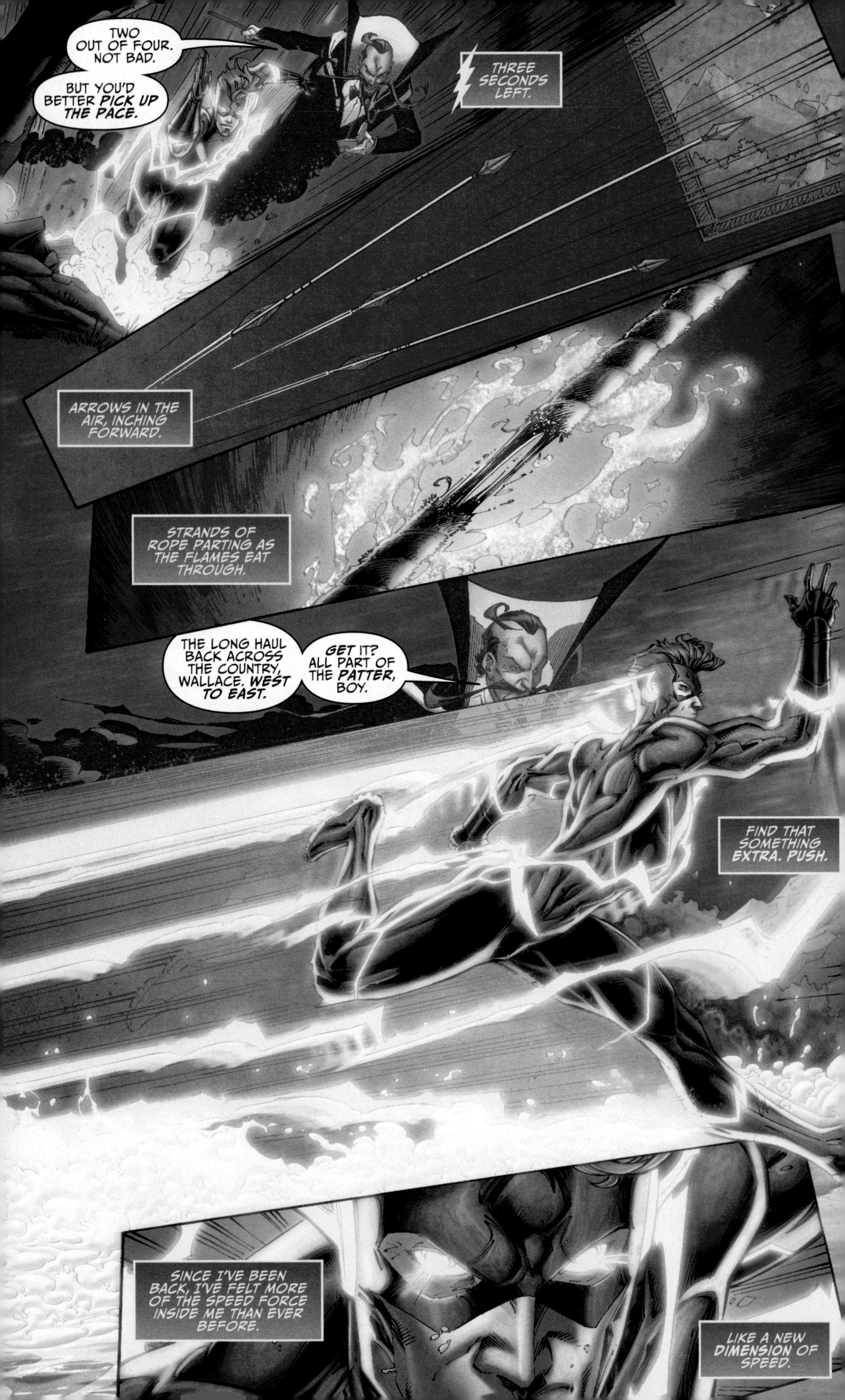
TWO OUT OF FOUR. NOT BAD.
BUT YOU'D BETTER **PICK UP THE PACE.**
THREE SECONDS LEFT.
ARROWS IN THE AIR, INCHING FORWARD.
STRANDS OF ROPE PARTING AS THE FLAMES EAT THROUGH.
THE LONG HAUL BACK ACROSS THE COUNTRY, WALLACE. **WEST TO EAST.**
GET IT? ALL PART OF THE **PATTER,** BOY.
FIND THAT SOMETHING **EXTRA. PUSH.**
SINCE I'VE BEEN BACK, I'VE FELT MORE OF THE SPEED FORCE INSIDE ME THAN EVER BEFORE.
LIKE A NEW **DIMENSION** OF SPEED.

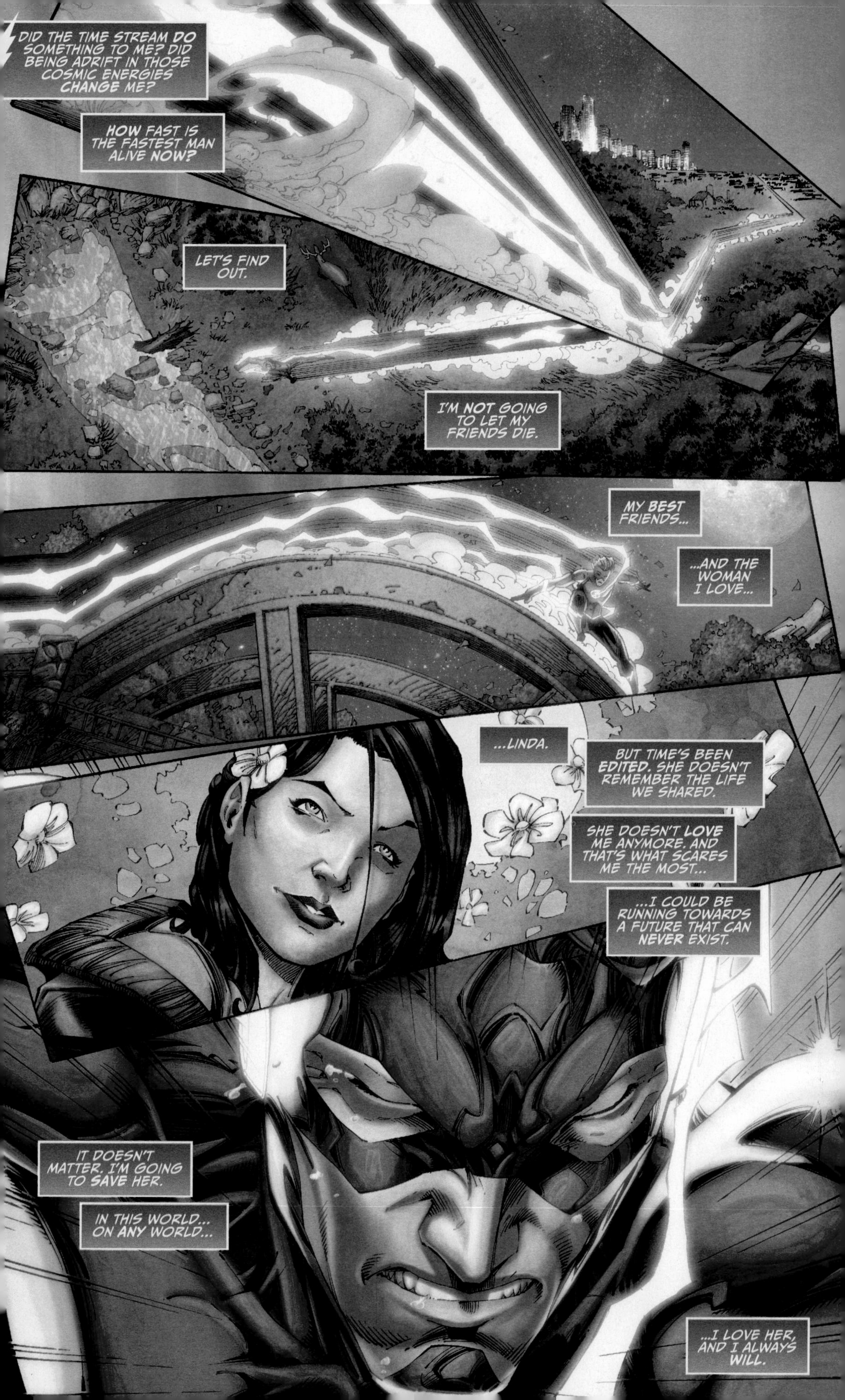
DID THE TIME STREAM DO SOMETHING TO ME? DID BEING ADRIFT IN THOSE COSMIC ENERGIES CHANGE ME?
HOW FAST IS THE FASTEST MAN ALIVE NOW?
LET'S FIND OUT.
I'M NOT GOING TO LET MY FRIENDS DIE.
MY BEST FRIENDS...
...AND THE WOMAN I LOVE...
...LINDA.
BUT TIME'S BEEN EDITED. SHE DOESN'T REMEMBER THE LIFE WE SHARED.
SHE DOESN'T LOVE ME ANYMORE. AND THAT'S WHAT SCARES ME THE MOST...
...I COULD BE RUNNING TOWARDS A FUTURE THAT CAN NEVER EXIST.
IT DOESN'T MATTER. I'M GOING TO SAVE HER.
IN THIS WORLD... ON ANY WORLD...
...I LOVE HER, AND I ALWAYS WILL.

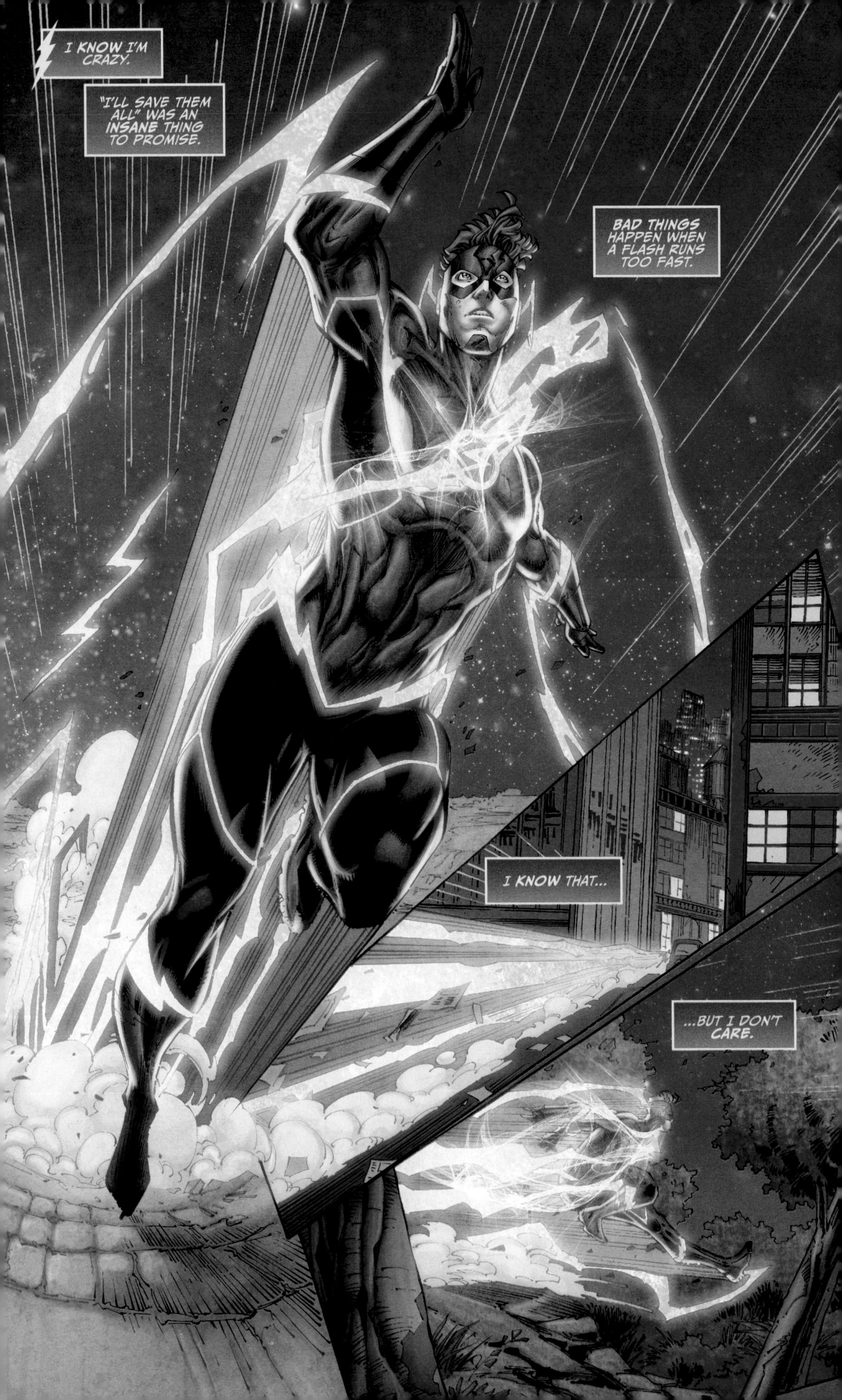

I KNOW I'M CRAZY.
"I'LL SAVE THEM ALL" WAS AN INSANE THING TO PROMISE.
BAD THINGS HAPPEN WHEN A FLASH RUNS TOO FAST.
I KNOW THAT...
...BUT I DON'T CARE.

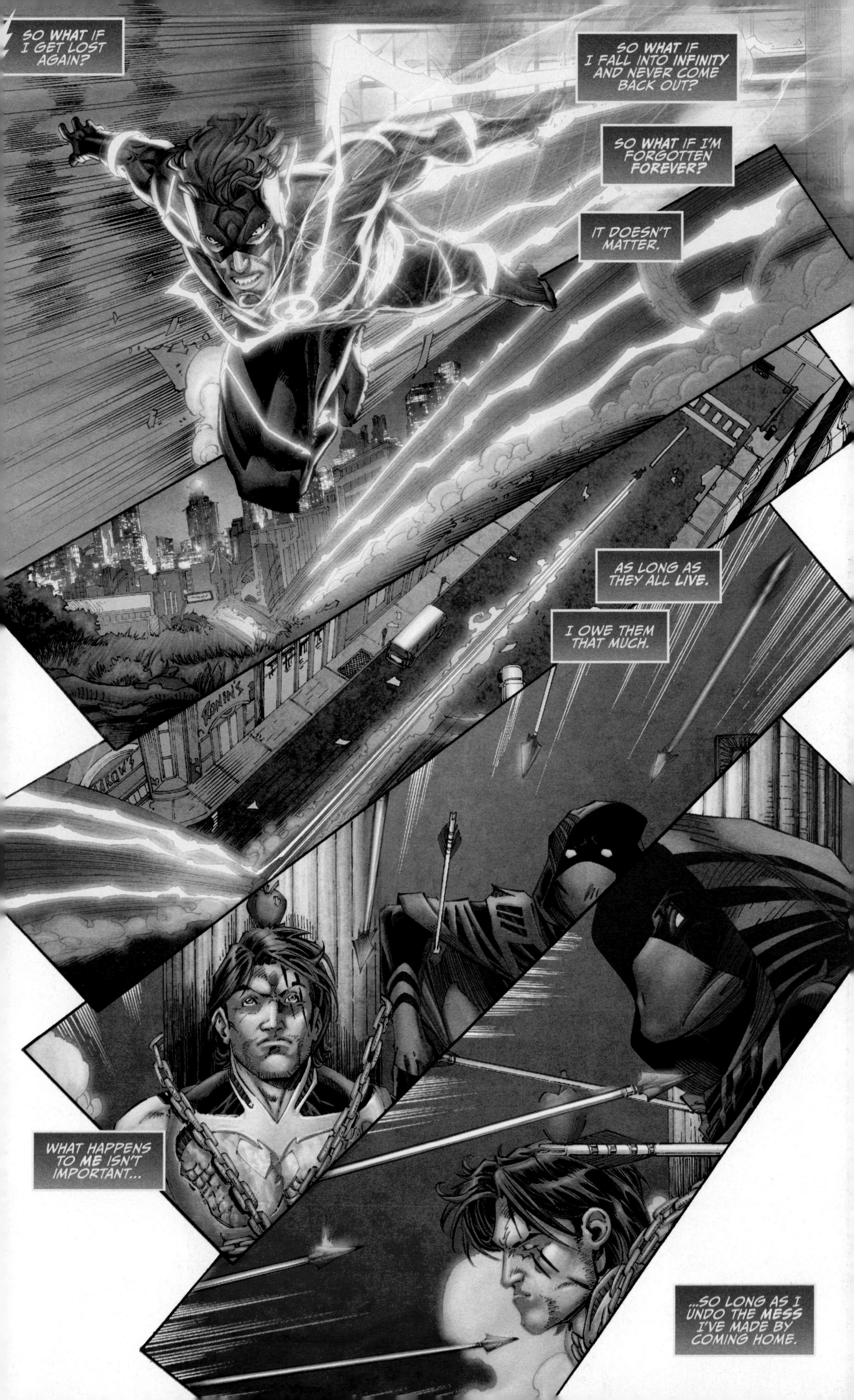
SO WHAT IF I GET LOST AGAIN?
SO WHAT IF I FALL INTO INFINITY AND NEVER COME BACK OUT?
SO WHAT IF I'M FORGOTTEN FOREVER?
IT DOESN'T MATTER.
AS LONG AS THEY ALL LIVE.
I OWE THEM THAT MUCH.
WHAT HAPPENS TO ME ISN'T IMPORTANT...
...SO LONG AS I UNDO THE MESS I'VE MADE BY COMING HOME.

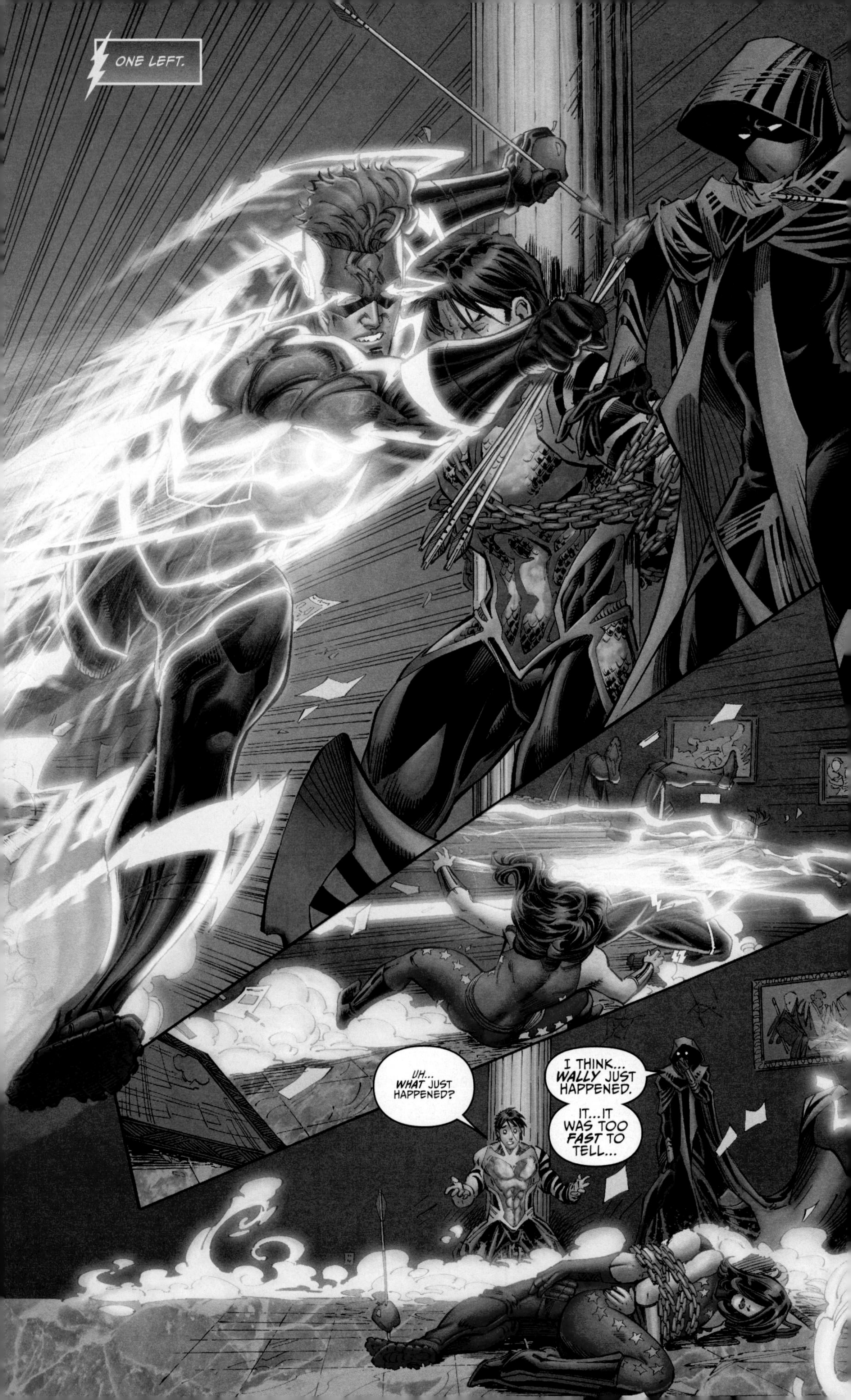
ONE LEFT.
UH... WHAT JUST HAPPENED?
I THINK... WALLY JUST HAPPENED.
IT...IT WAS TOO FAST TO TELL...

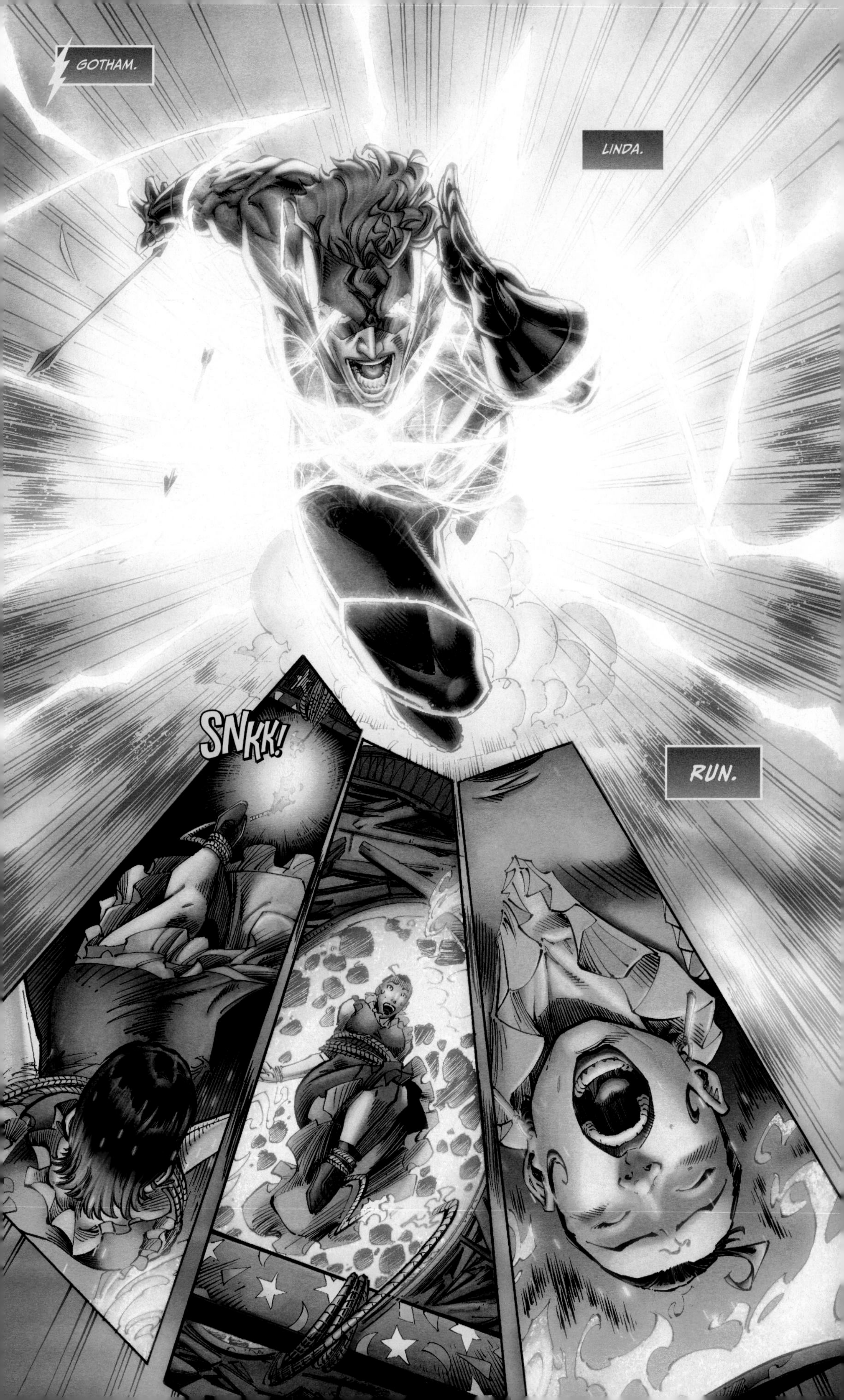
GOTHAM.
LINDA.
SNKK!
RUN.

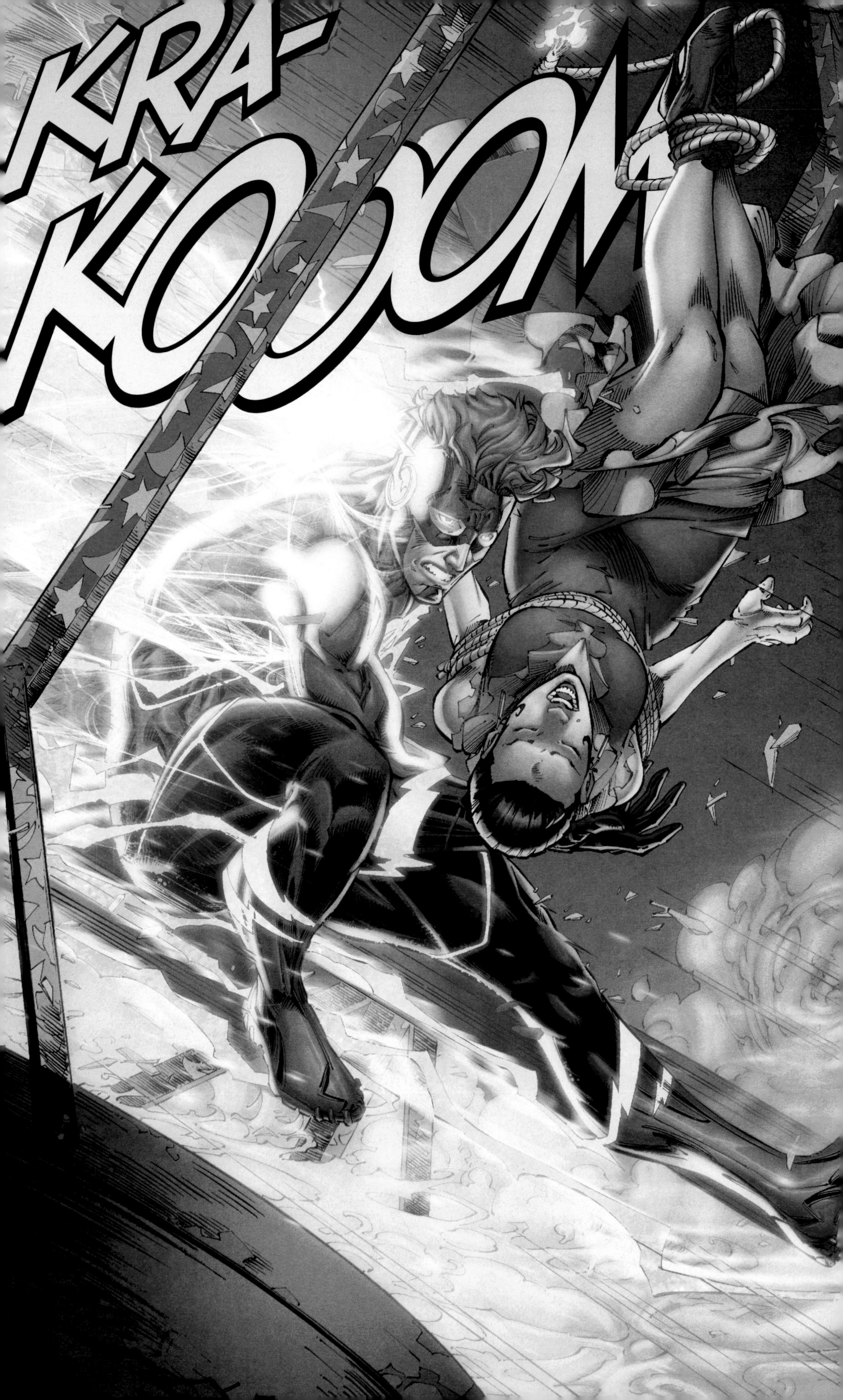
KRA-
KOOOM

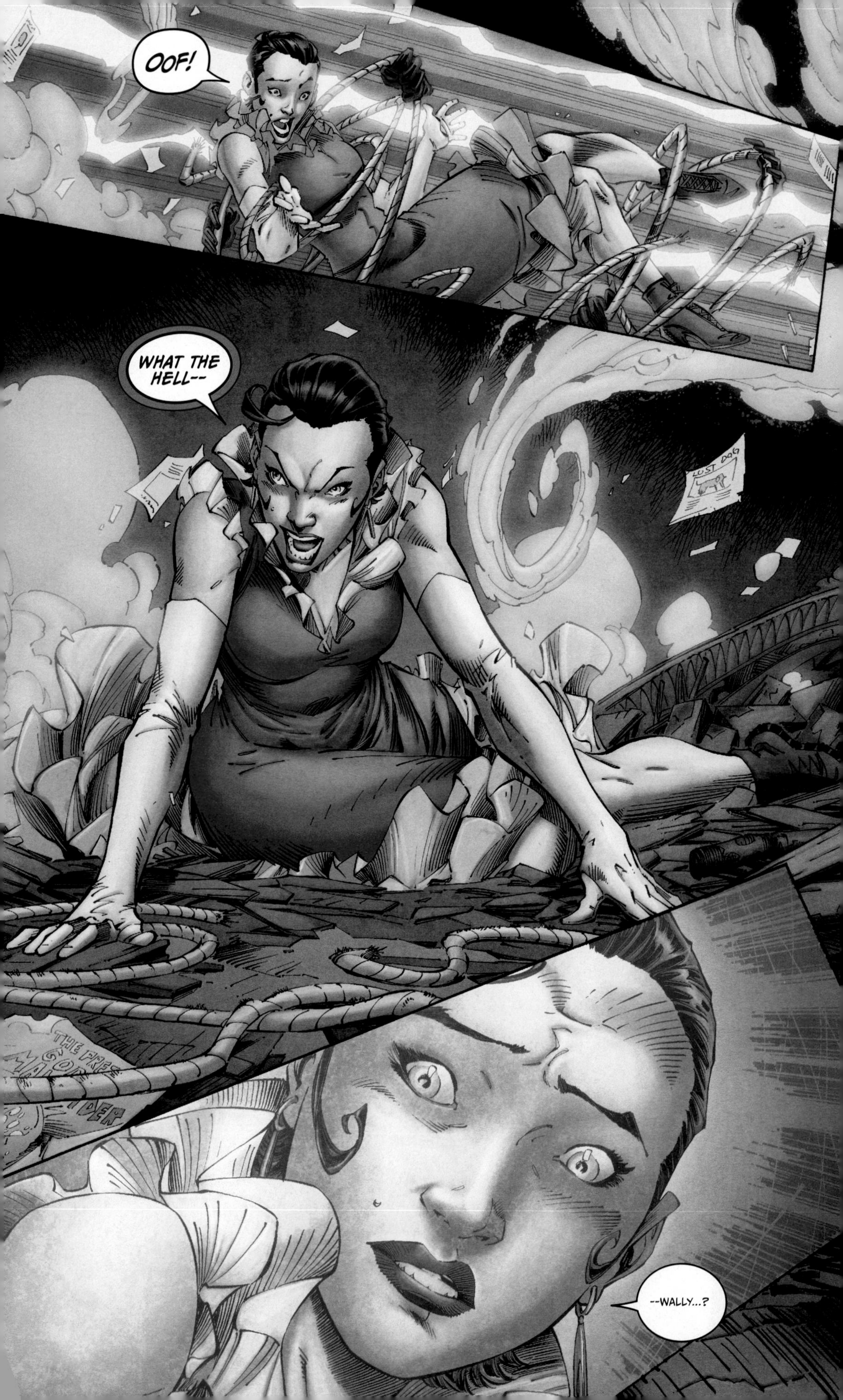
OOF!
WHAT THE HELL--
--WALLY...?

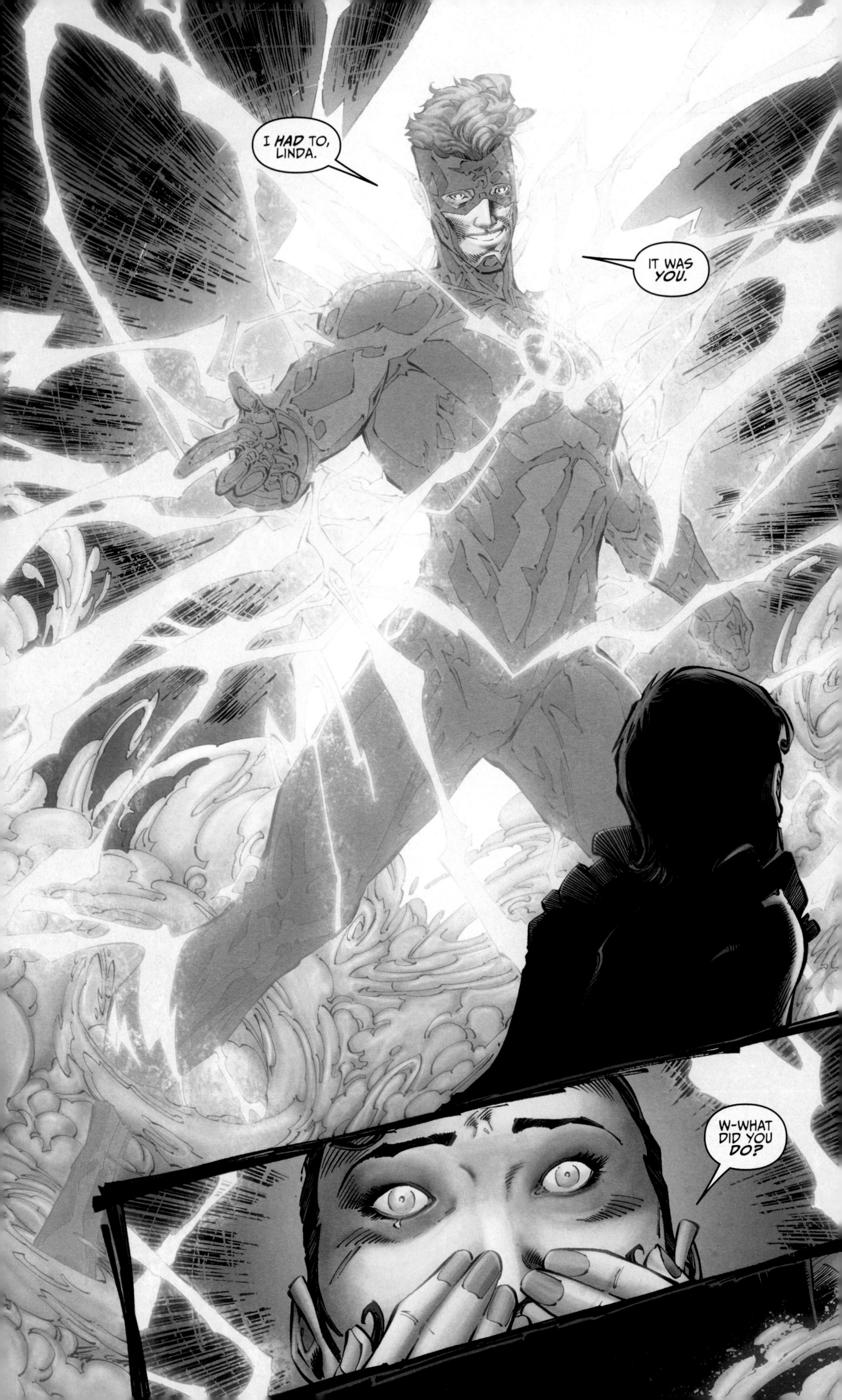
I HAD TO, LINDA.
IT WAS YOU.
W-WHAT DID YOU DO?

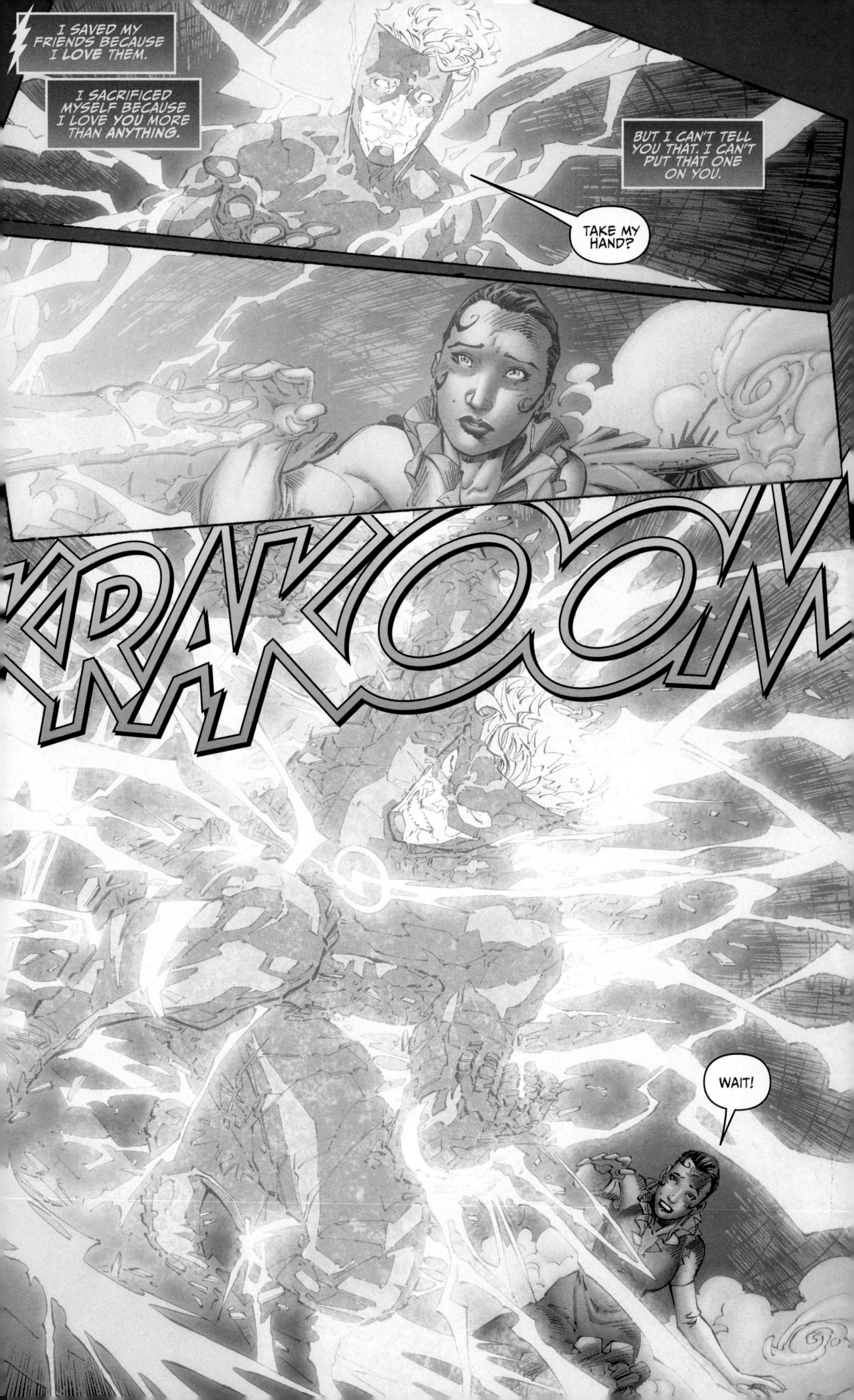
I SAVED MY FRIENDS BECAUSE I LOVE THEM.
I SACRIFICED MYSELF BECAUSE I LOVE YOU MORE THAN ANYTHING.
BUT I CAN'T TELL YOU THAT. I CAN'T PUT THAT ONE ON YOU.
TAKE MY HAND?
KRAKOOM
WAIT!

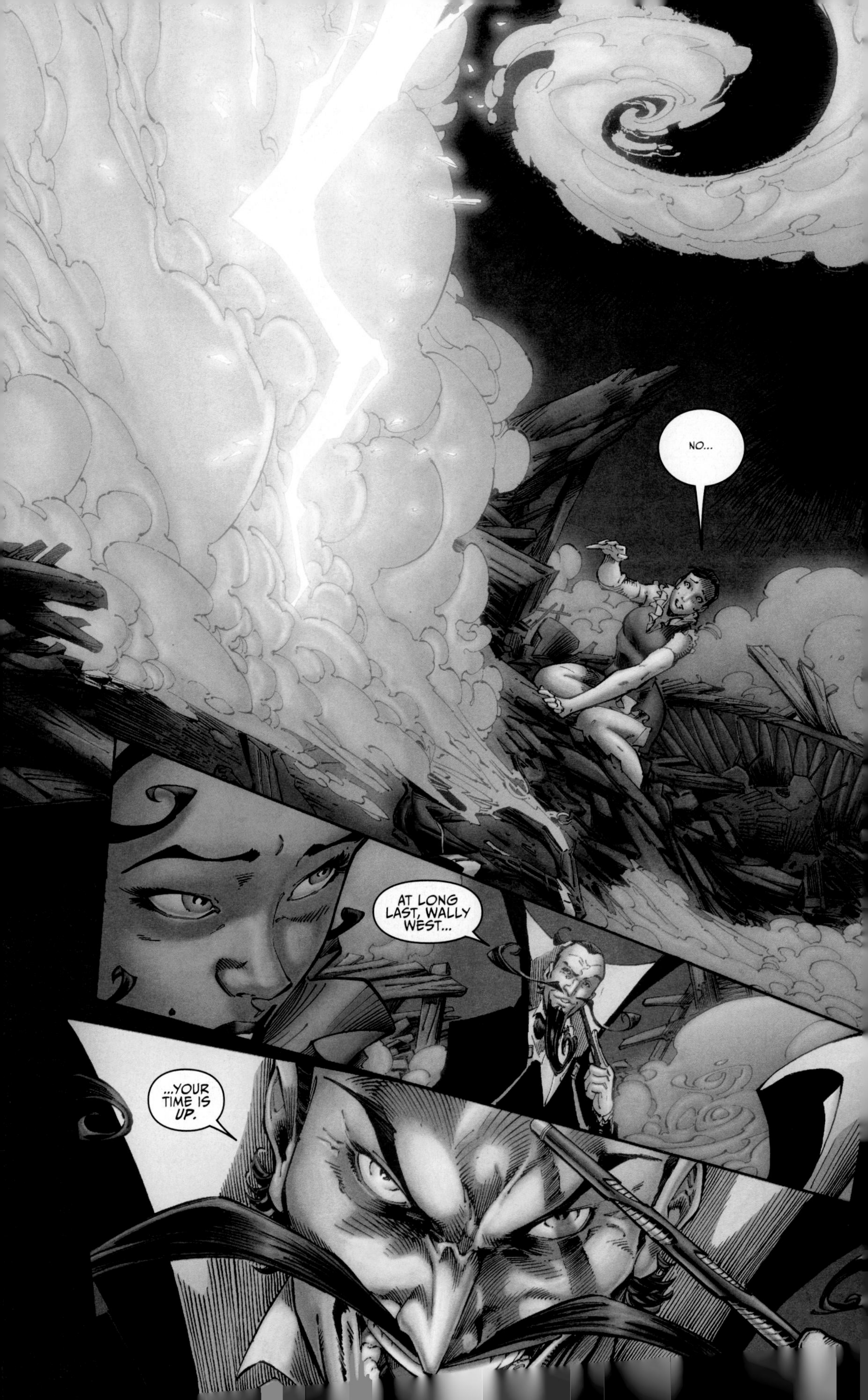
NO...
AT LONG LAST, WALLY WEST...
...YOUR TIME IS UP.

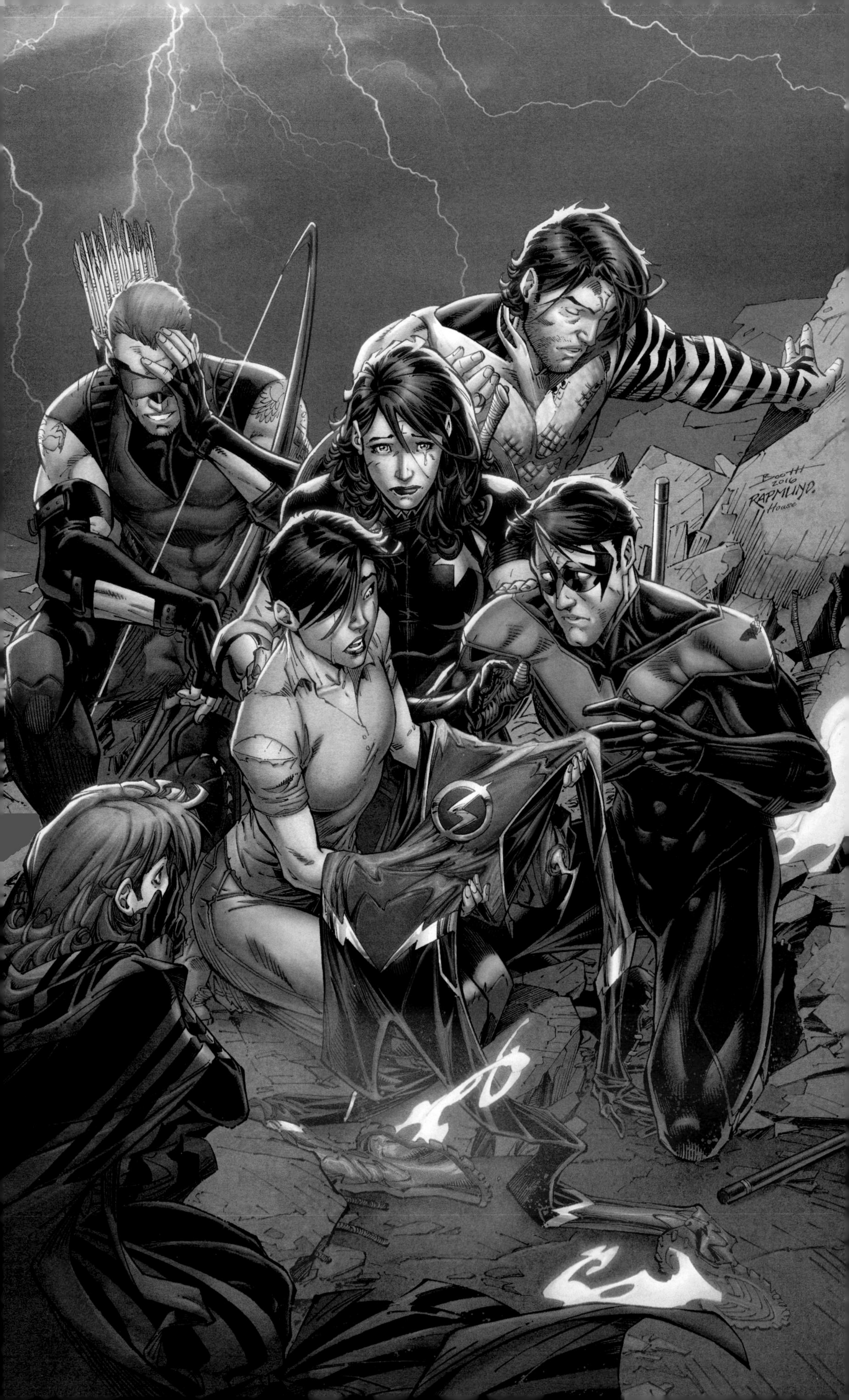
Booth
2016
RAPMUND.
House

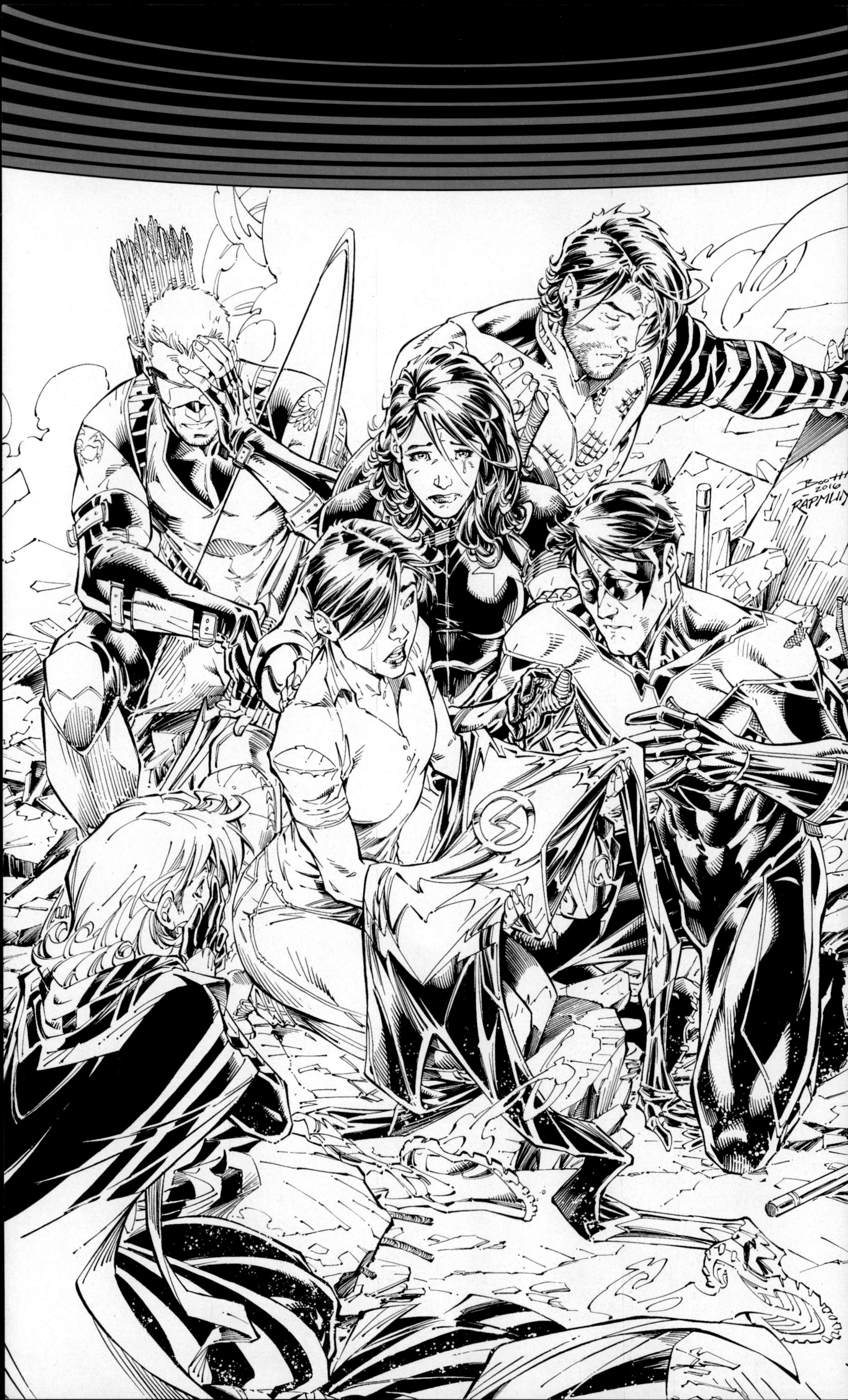

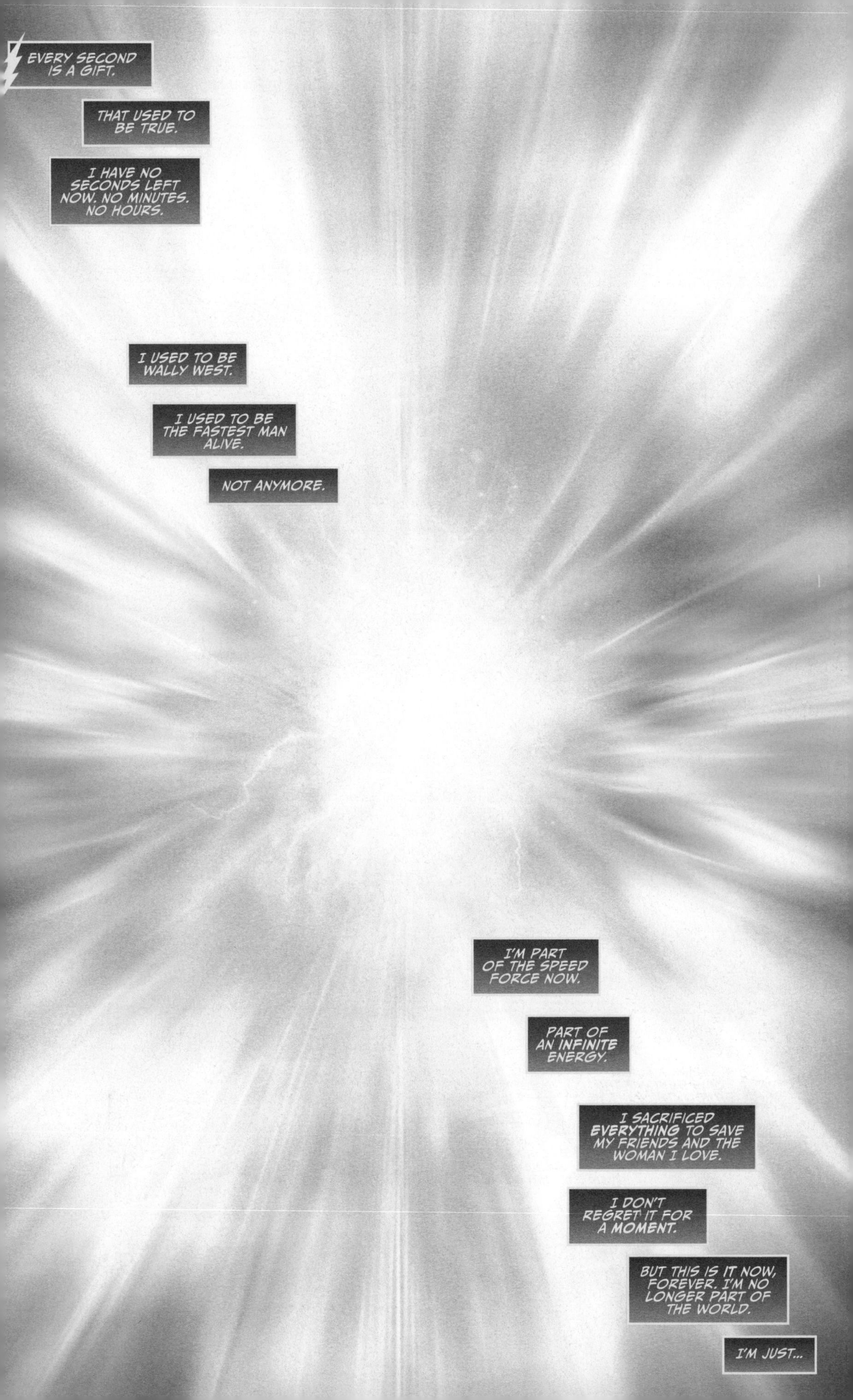
EVERY SECOND IS A GIFT.
THAT USED TO BE TRUE.
I HAVE NO SECONDS LEFT NOW. NO MINUTES. NO HOURS.
I USED TO BE WALLY WEST.
I USED TO BE THE FASTEST MAN ALIVE.
NOT ANYMORE.
I'M PART OF THE SPEED FORCE NOW.
PART OF AN INFINITE ENERGY.
I SACRIFICED EVERYTHING TO SAVE MY FRIENDS AND THE WOMAN I LOVE.
I DON'T REGRET IT FOR A MOMENT.
BUT THIS IS IT NOW, FOREVER. I'M NO LONGER PART OF THE WORLD.
I'M JUST...

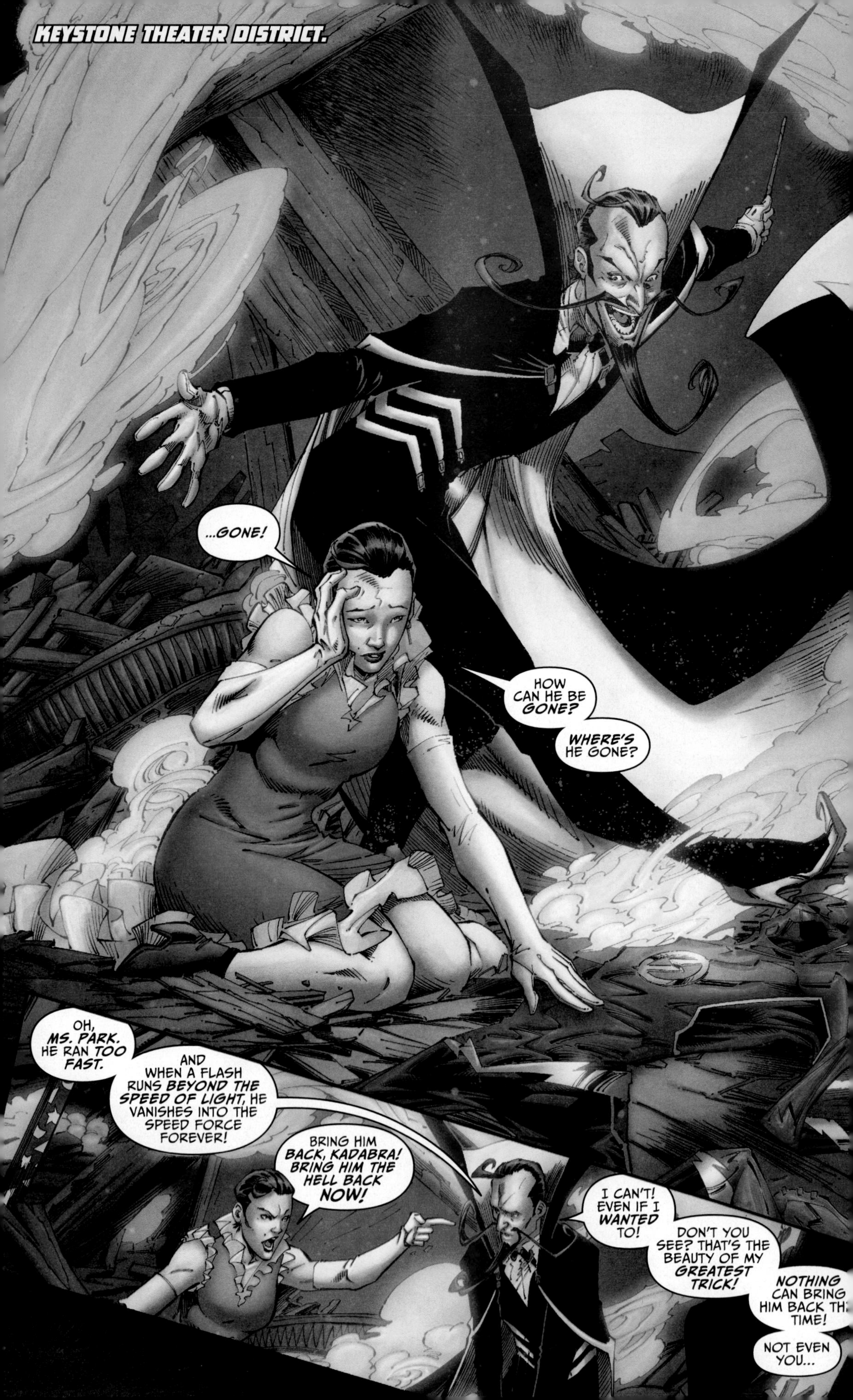
KEYSTONE THEATER DISTRICT.
...GONE!
HOW CAN HE BE GONE?
WHERE'S HE GONE?
OH, MS. PARK. HE RAN TOO FAST.
AND WHEN A FLASH RUNS BEYOND THE SPEED OF LIGHT, HE VANISHES INTO THE SPEED FORCE FOREVER!
BRING HIM BACK, KADABRA! BRING HIM THE HELL BACK NOW!
I CAN'T! EVEN IF I WANTED TO!
DON'T YOU SEE? THAT'S THE BEAUTY OF MY GREATEST TRICK!
NOTHING CAN BRING HIM BACK TH TIME!
NOT EVEN YOU...

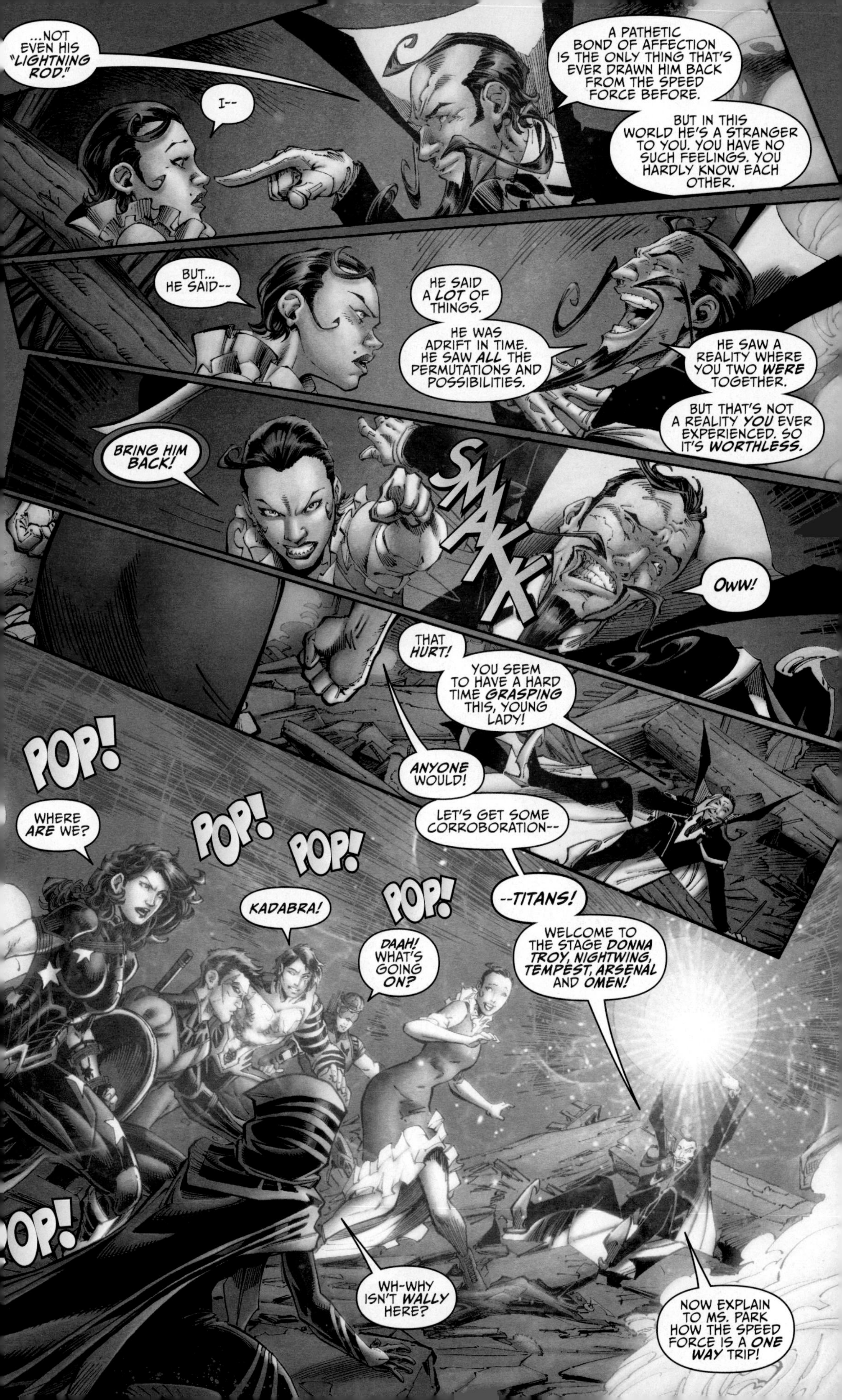

...NOT EVEN HIS "LIGHTNING ROD."
A PATHETIC BOND OF AFFECTION IS THE ONLY THING THAT'S EVER DRAWN HIM BACK FROM THE SPEED FORCE BEFORE.
I--
BUT IN THIS WORLD HE'S A STRANGER TO YOU. YOU HAVE NO SUCH FEELINGS. YOU HARDLY KNOW EACH OTHER.
BUT... HE SAID--
HE SAID A LOT OF THINGS.
HE WAS ADRIFT IN TIME. HE SAW ALL THE PERMUTATIONS AND POSSIBILITIES.
HE SAW A REALITY WHERE YOU TWO WERE TOGETHER.
BUT THAT'S NOT A REALITY YOU EVER EXPERIENCED. SO IT'S WORTHLESS.
BRING HIM BACK!
SMAKK
OWW!
THAT HURT!
YOU SEEM TO HAVE A HARD TIME GRASPING THIS, YOUNG LADY!
ANYONE WOULD!
LET'S GET SOME CORROBORATION--
--TITANS!
POP!
WHERE ARE WE?
POP!
POP!
KADABRA!
POP!
DAAH! WHAT'S GOING ON?
WELCOME TO THE STAGE DONNA TROY, NIGHTWING, TEMPEST, ARSENAL AND OMEN!
POP!
WH-WHY ISN'T WALLY HERE?
NOW EXPLAIN TO MS. PARK HOW THE SPEED FORCE IS A ONE WAY TRIP!

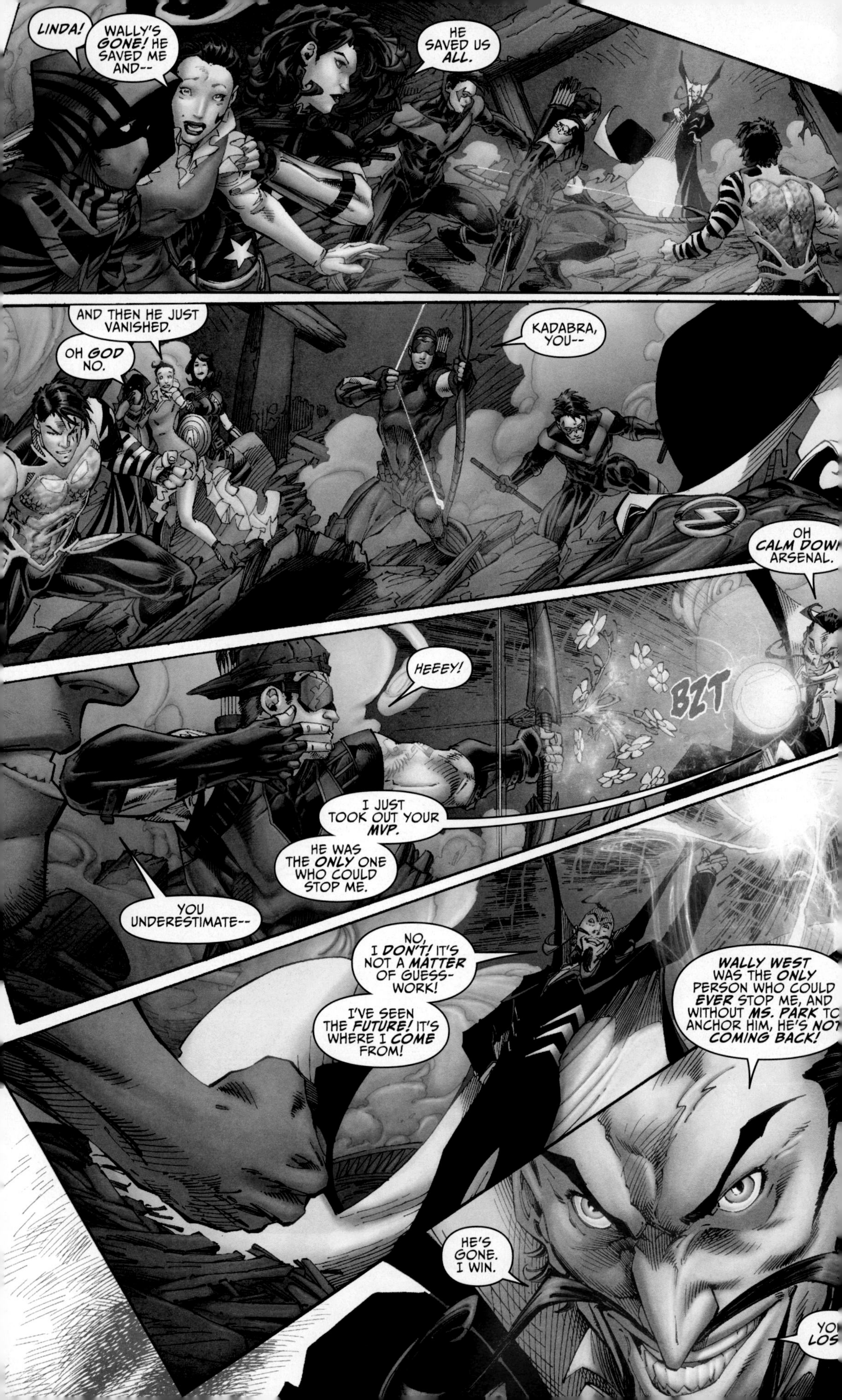
LINDA!
WALLY'S GONE! HE SAVED ME AND--
HE SAVED US ALL.
AND THEN HE JUST VANISHED.
OH GOD NO.
KADABRA, YOU--
OH CALM DOWN ARSENAL.
HEEEY!
BZT
I JUST TOOK OUT YOUR MVP.
HE WAS THE ONLY ONE WHO COULD STOP ME.
YOU UNDERESTIMATE--
NO, I DON'T! IT'S NOT A MATTER OF GUESS-WORK!
I'VE SEEN THE FUTURE! IT'S WHERE I COME FROM!
WALLY WEST WAS THE ONLY PERSON WHO COULD EVER STOP ME, AND WITHOUT MS. PARK TO ANCHOR HIM, HE'S NOT COMING BACK!
HE'S GONE. I WIN.

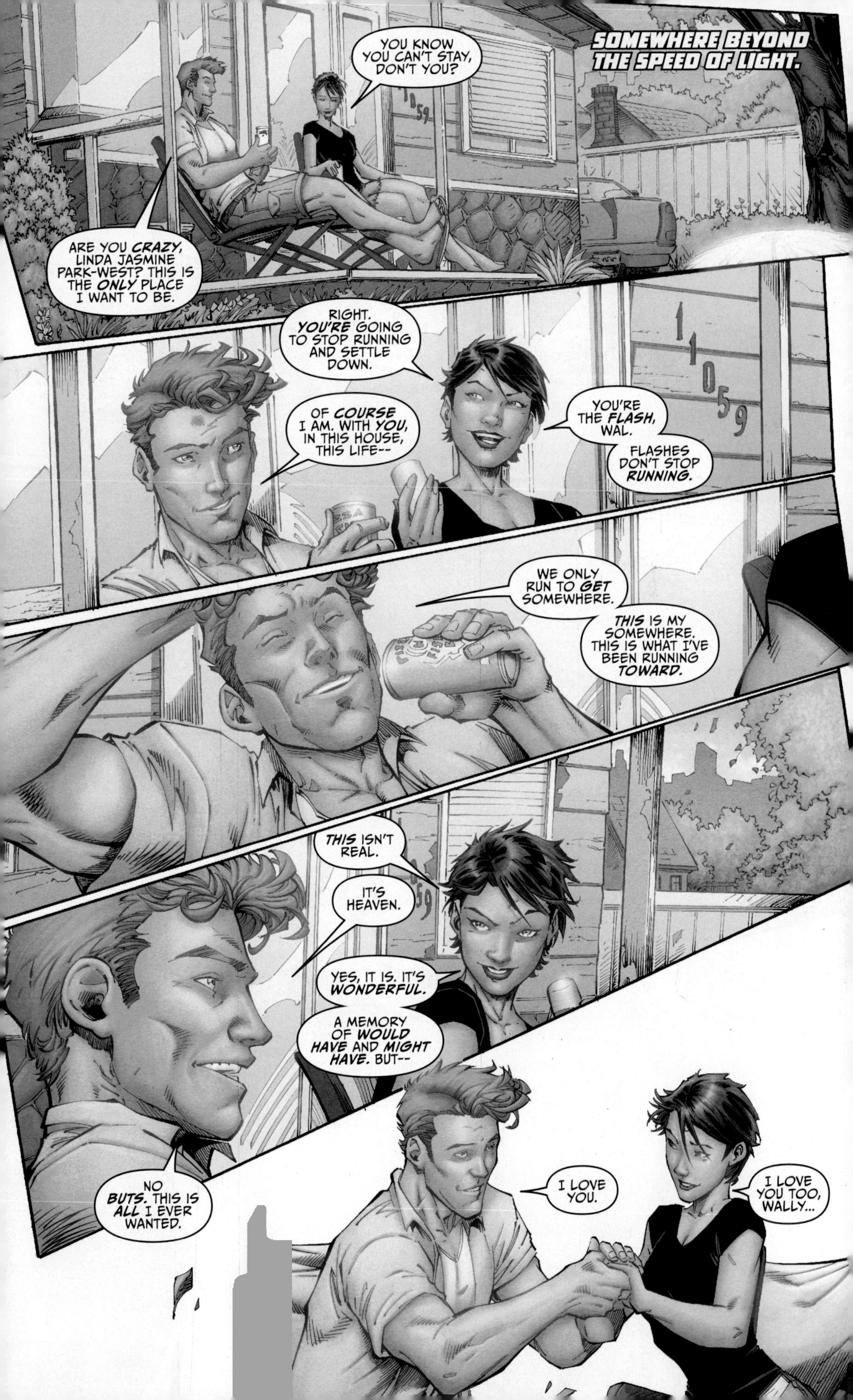
SOMEWHERE BEYOND THE SPEED OF LIGHT.
YOU KNOW YOU CAN'T STAY, DON'T YOU?
ARE YOU CRAZY, LINDA JASMINE PARK-WEST? THIS IS THE ONLY PLACE I WANT TO BE.
RIGHT. YOU'RE GOING TO STOP RUNNING AND SETTLE DOWN.
OF COURSE I AM. WITH YOU, IN THIS HOUSE, THIS LIFE--
YOU'RE THE FLASH, WAL.
FLASHES DON'T STOP RUNNING.
WE ONLY RUN TO GET SOMEWHERE.
THIS IS MY SOMEWHERE. THIS IS WHAT I'VE BEEN RUNNING TOWARD.
THIS ISN'T REAL.
IT'S HEAVEN.
YES, IT IS. IT'S WONDERFUL.
A MEMORY OF WOULD HAVE AND MIGHT HAVE. BUT--
NO BUTS. THIS IS ALL I EVER WANTED.
I LOVE YOU.
I LOVE YOU TOO, WALLY...

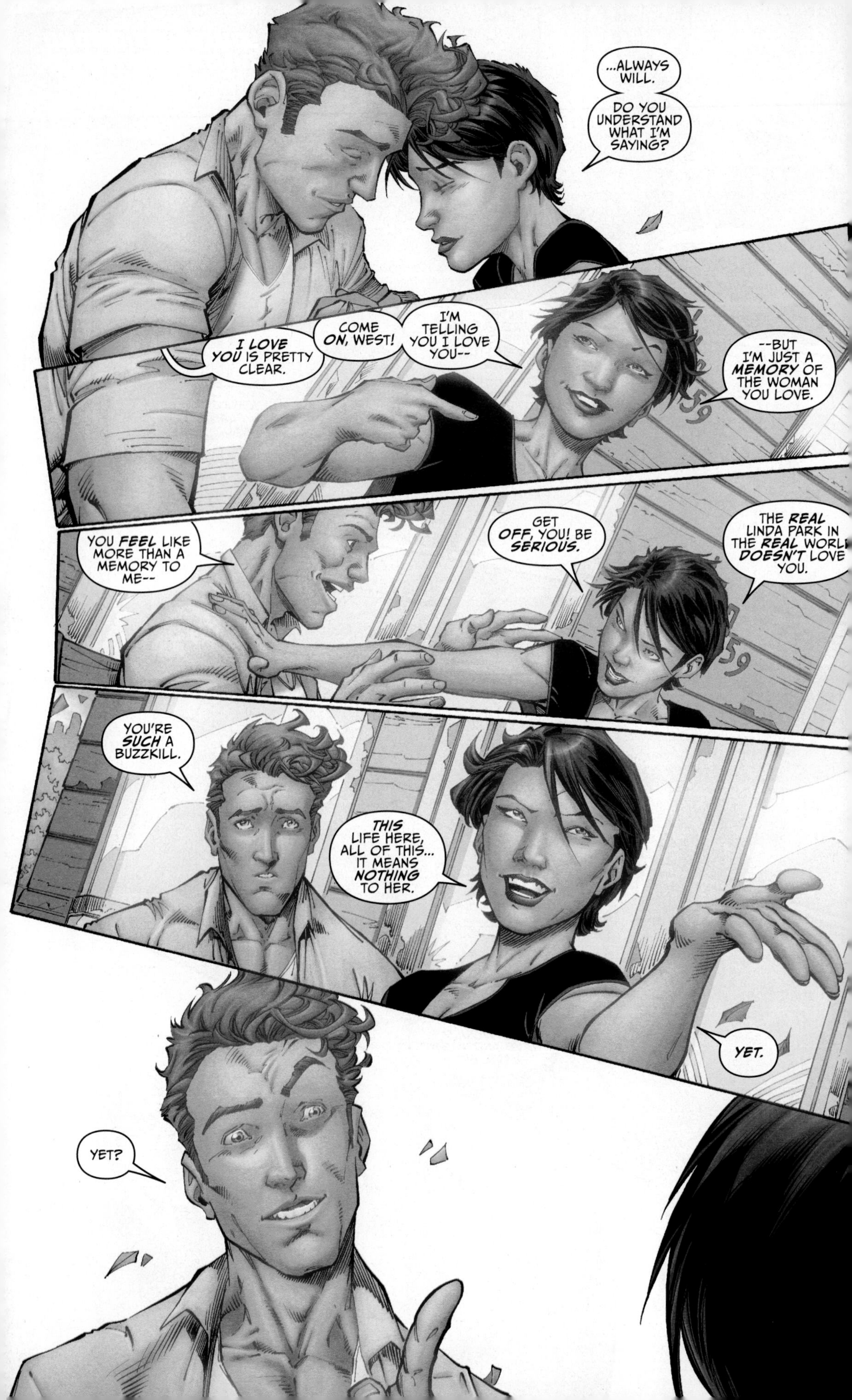

...ALWAYS WILL.
DO YOU UNDERSTAND WHAT I'M SAYING?
I LOVE YOU IS PRETTY CLEAR.
COME ON, WEST!
I'M TELLING YOU I LOVE YOU--
--BUT I'M JUST A MEMORY OF THE WOMAN YOU LOVE.
YOU FEEL LIKE MORE THAN A MEMORY TO ME--
GET OFF, YOU! BE SERIOUS.
THE REAL LINDA PARK IN THE REAL WORLD DOESN'T LOVE YOU.
YOU'RE SUCH A BUZZKILL.
THIS LIFE HERE, ALL OF THIS... IT MEANS NOTHING TO HER.
YET.
YET?

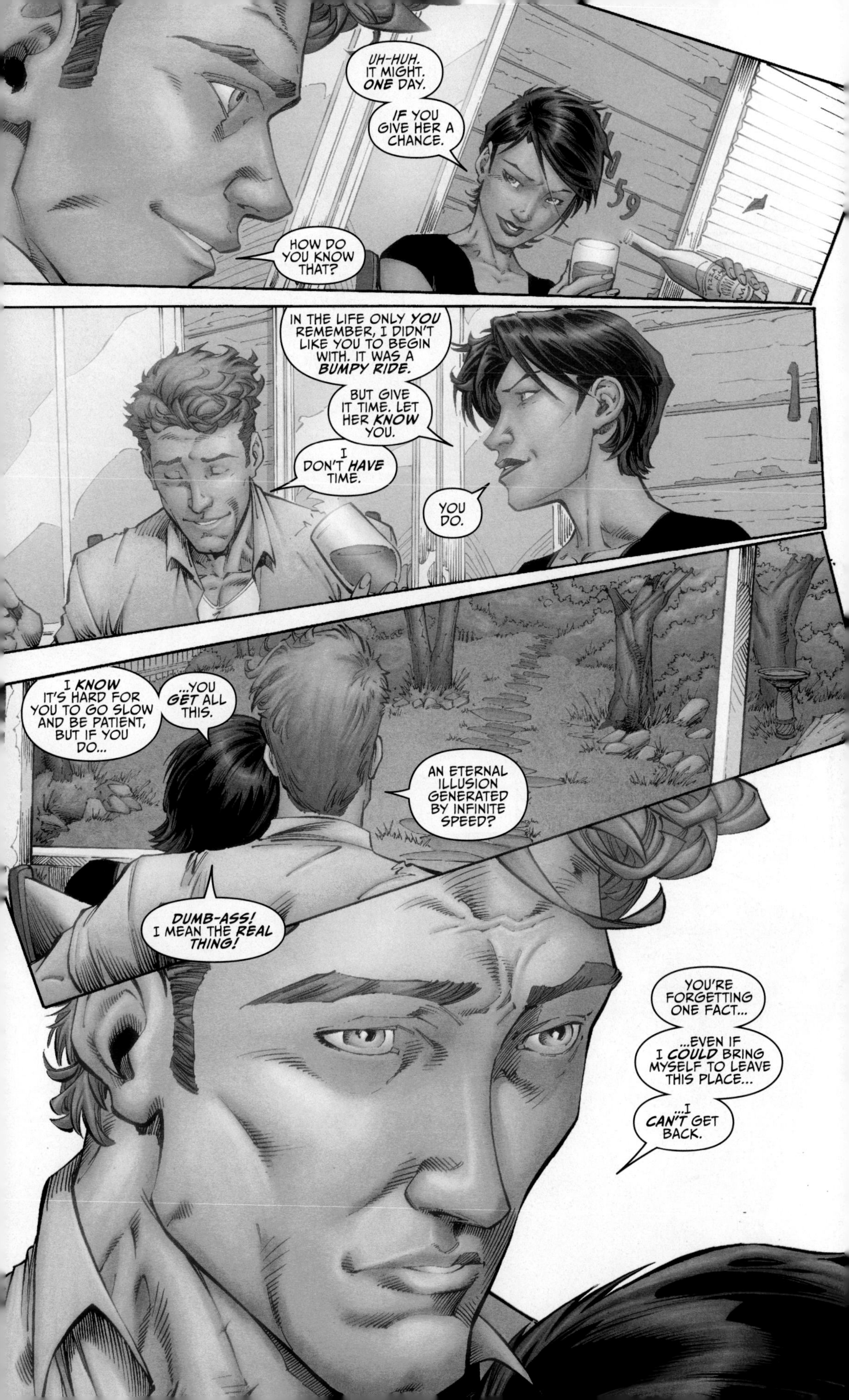
UH-HUH. IT MIGHT. ONE DAY.
IF YOU GIVE HER A CHANCE.
HOW DO YOU KNOW THAT?
IN THE LIFE ONLY YOU REMEMBER, I DIDN'T LIKE YOU TO BEGIN WITH. IT WAS A BUMPY RIDE.
BUT GIVE IT TIME. LET HER KNOW YOU.
I DON'T HAVE TIME.
YOU DO.
I KNOW IT'S HARD FOR YOU TO GO SLOW AND BE PATIENT, BUT IF YOU DO...
...YOU GET ALL THIS.
AN ETERNAL ILLUSION GENERATED BY INFINITE SPEED?
DUMB-ASS! I MEAN THE REAL THING!
YOU'RE FORGETTING ONE FACT...
...EVEN IF I COULD BRING MYSELF TO LEAVE THIS PLACE...
...I CAN'T GET BACK.

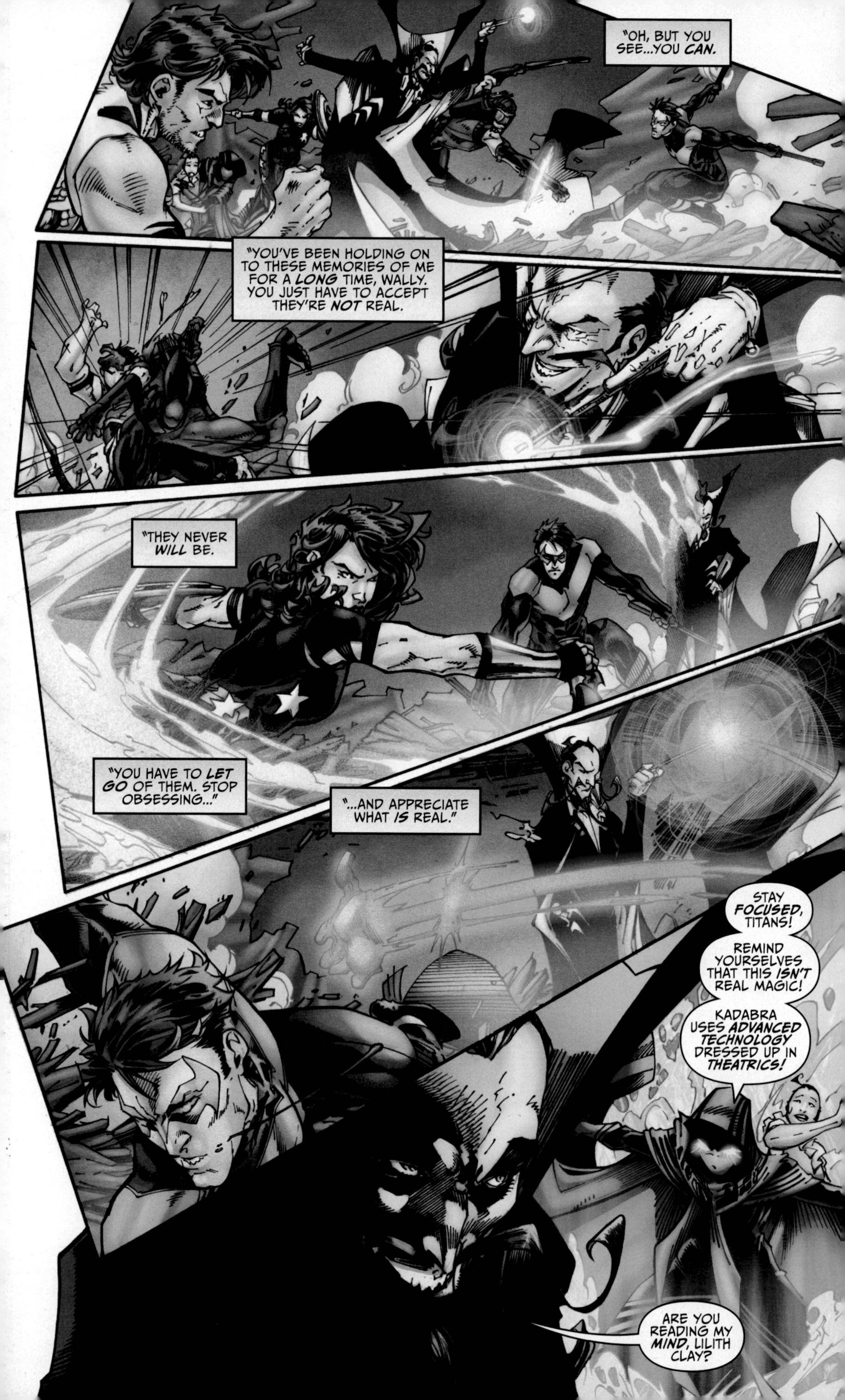
"OH, BUT YOU SEE...YOU CAN.
"YOU'VE BEEN HOLDING ON TO THESE MEMORIES OF ME FOR A LONG TIME, WALLY. YOU JUST HAVE TO ACCEPT THEY'RE NOT REAL.
"THEY NEVER WILL BE.
"YOU HAVE TO LET GO OF THEM. STOP OBSESSING..."
"...AND APPRECIATE WHAT IS REAL."
STAY FOCUSED, TITANS!
REMIND YOURSELVES THAT THIS ISN'T REAL MAGIC!
KADABRA USES ADVANCED TECHNOLOGY DRESSED UP IN THEATRICS!
ARE YOU READING MY MIND, LILITH CLAY?

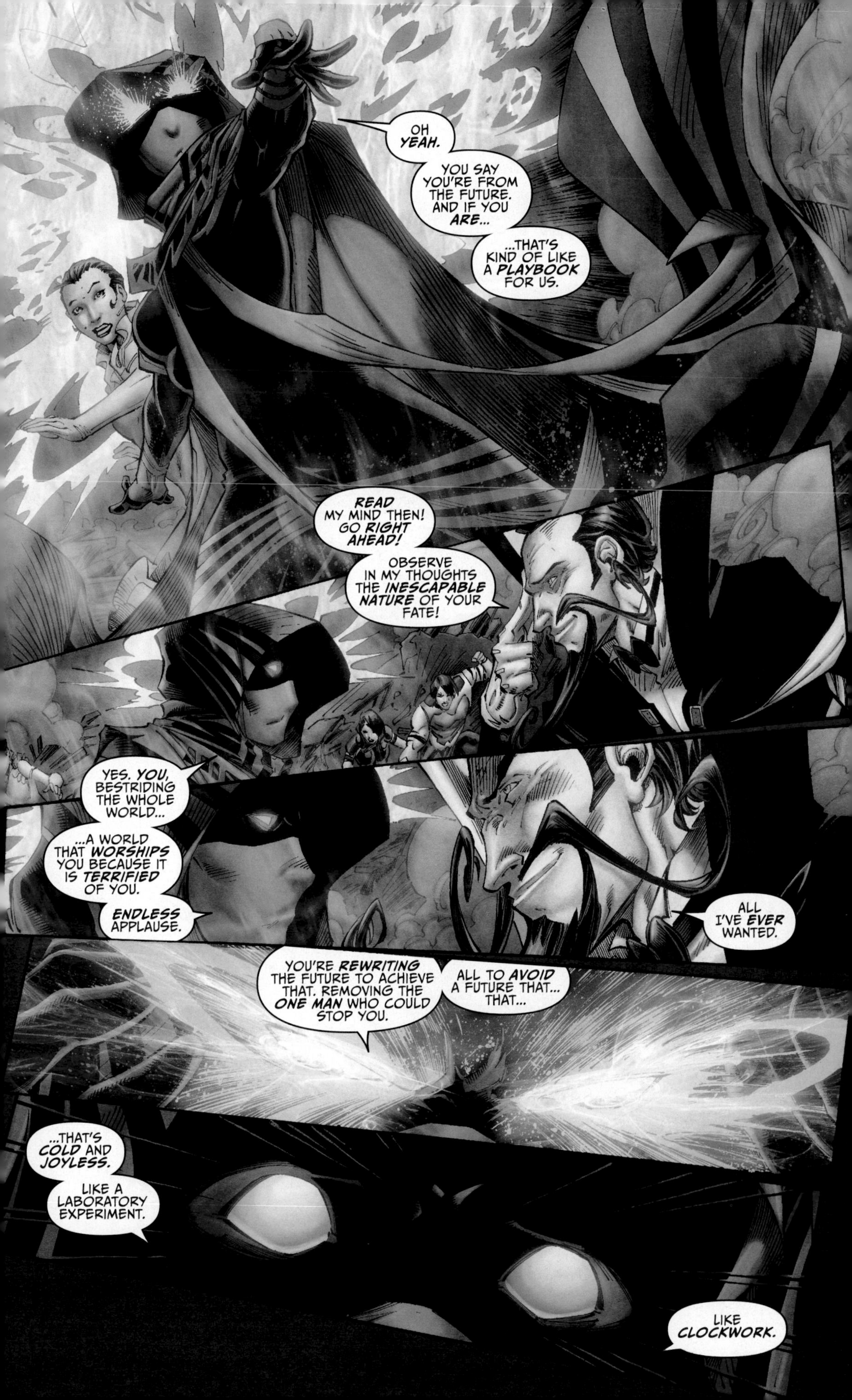
OH YEAH.
YOU SAY YOU'RE FROM THE FUTURE. AND IF YOU ARE...
...THAT'S KIND OF LIKE A PLAYBOOK FOR US.
READ MY MIND THEN! GO RIGHT AHEAD!
OBSERVE IN MY THOUGHTS THE INESCAPABLE NATURE OF YOUR FATE!
YES. YOU, BESTRIDING THE WHOLE WORLD...
...A WORLD THAT WORSHIPS YOU BECAUSE IT IS TERRIFIED OF YOU.
ENDLESS APPLAUSE.
ALL I'VE EVER WANTED.
YOU'RE REWRITING THE FUTURE TO ACHIEVE THAT. REMOVING THE ONE MAN WHO COULD STOP YOU.
ALL TO AVOID A FUTURE THAT... THAT...
...THAT'S COLD AND JOYLESS.
LIKE A LABORATORY EXPERIMENT.
LIKE CLOCKWORK.

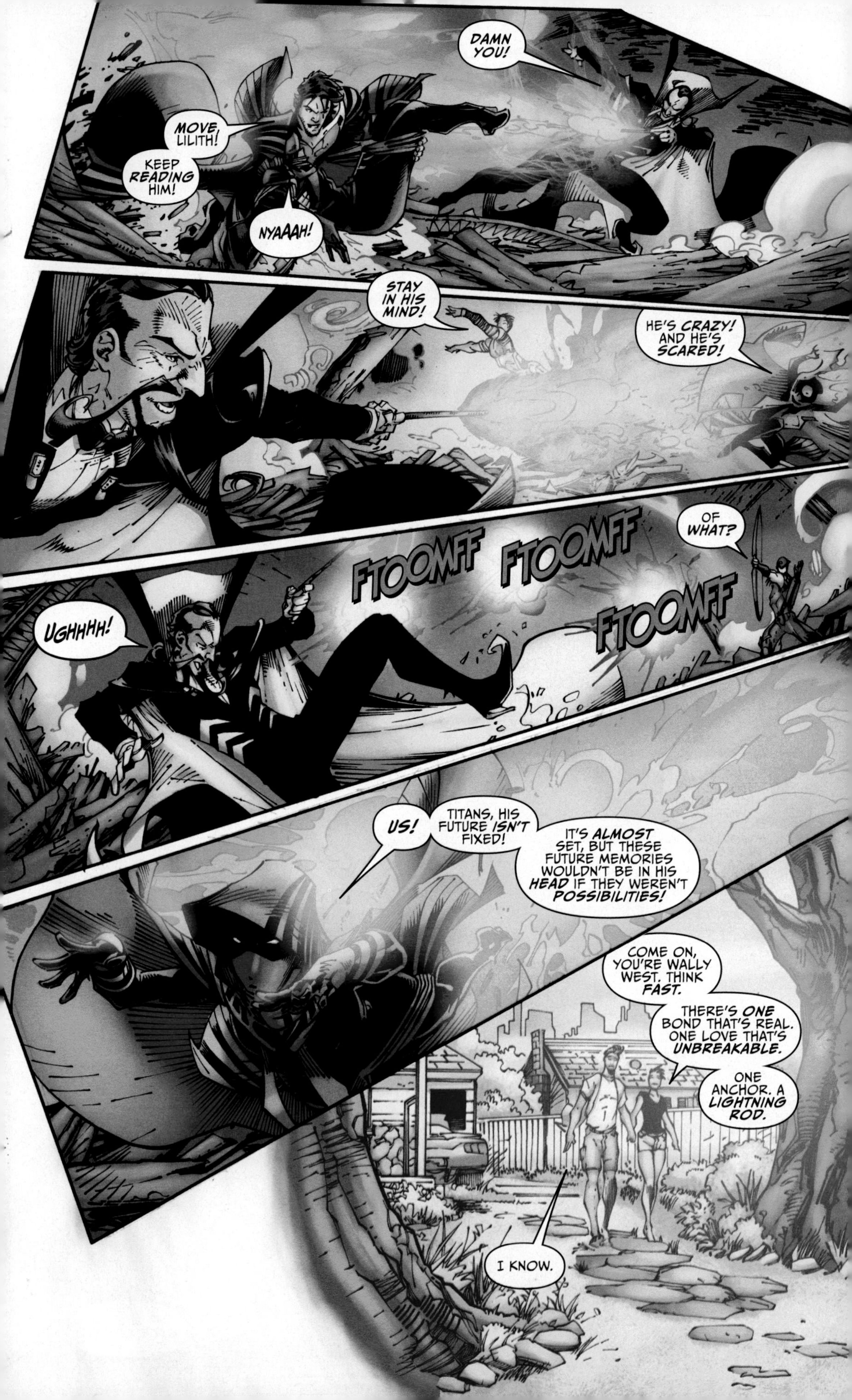
DAMN YOU!
MOVE LILITH!
KEEP READING HIM!
NYAAAH!
STAY IN HIS MIND!
HE'S CRAZY! AND HE'S SCARED!
OF WHAT?
FTOOMFF FTOOMFF
FTOOMFF
UGHHHH!
US!
TITANS, HIS FUTURE ISN'T FIXED!
IT'S ALMOST SET, BUT THESE FUTURE MEMORIES WOULDN'T BE IN HIS HEAD IF THEY WEREN'T POSSIBILITIES!
COME ON, YOU'RE WALLY WEST. THINK FAST.
THERE'S ONE BOND THAT'S REAL. ONE LOVE THAT'S UNBREAKABLE.
ONE ANCHOR. A LIGHTNING ROD.
I KNOW.

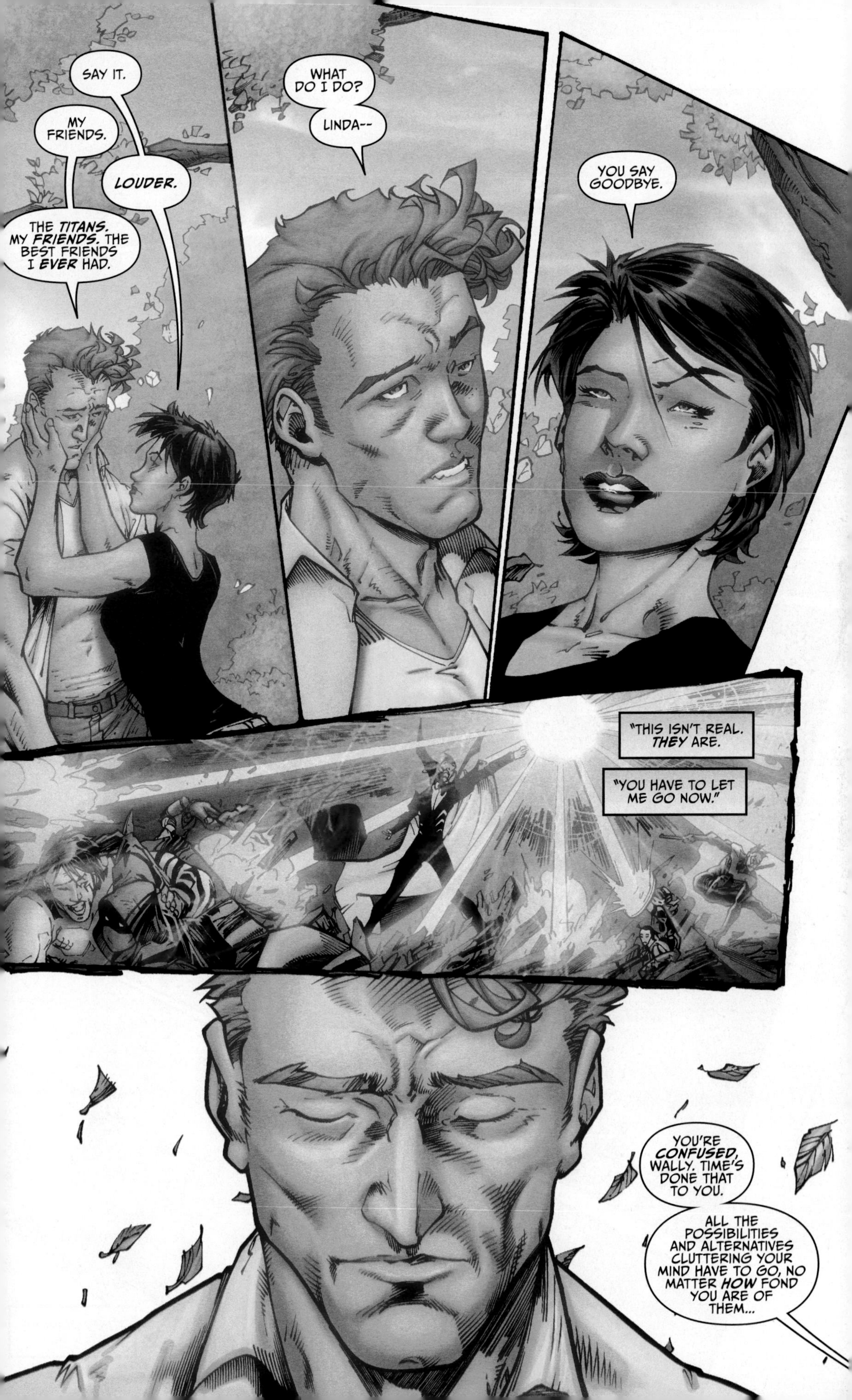
SAY IT.
MY FRIENDS.
LOUDER.
THE TITANS. MY FRIENDS. THE BEST FRIENDS I EVER HAD.
WHAT DO I DO?
LINDA--
YOU SAY GOODBYE.
"THIS ISN'T REAL. THEY ARE.
"YOU HAVE TO LET ME GO NOW."
YOU'RE CONFUSED, WALLY. TIME'S DONE THAT TO YOU.
ALL THE POSSIBILITIES AND ALTERNATIVES CLUTTERING YOUR MIND HAVE TO GO, NO MATTER HOW FOND YOU ARE OF THEM...

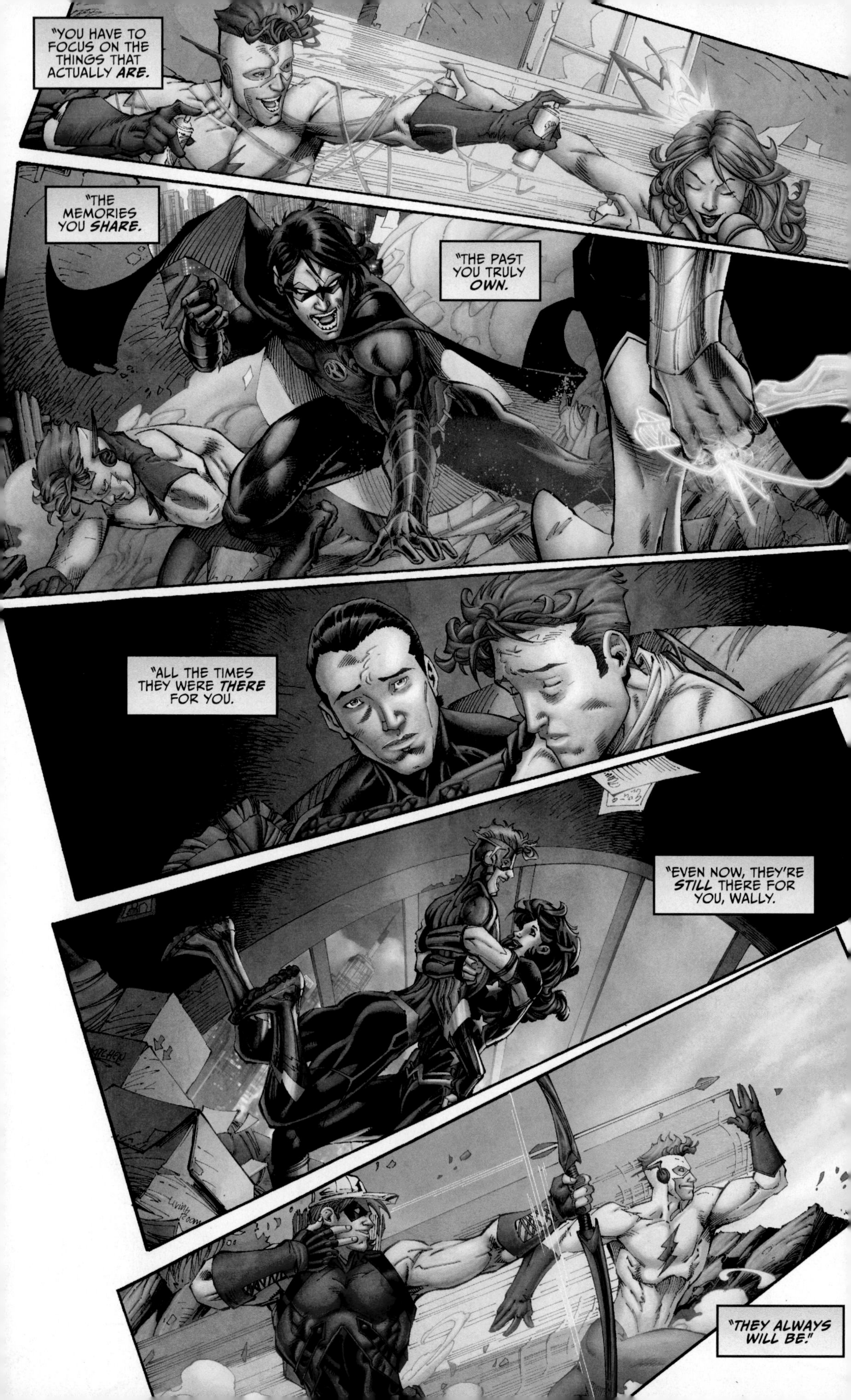
"YOU HAVE TO FOCUS ON THE THINGS THAT ACTUALLY ARE.
"THE MEMORIES YOU SHARE.
"THE PAST YOU TRULY OWN.
"ALL THE TIMES THEY WERE THERE FOR YOU.
"EVEN NOW, THEY'RE STILL THERE FOR YOU, WALLY.
"THEY ALWAYS WILL BE."

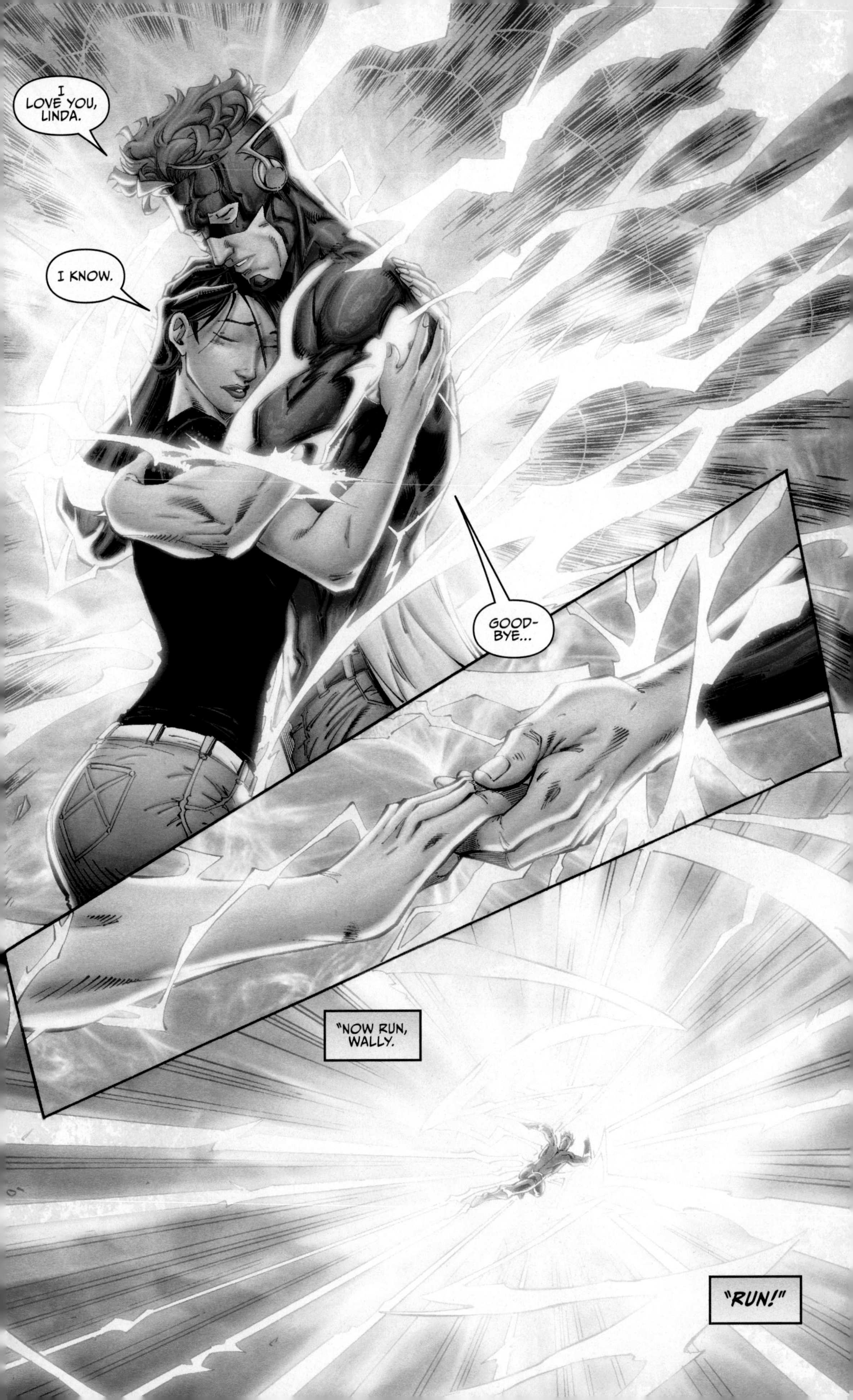
I LOVE YOU, LINDA.
I KNOW.
GOOD-BYE...
"NOW RUN, WALLY.
"RUN!"

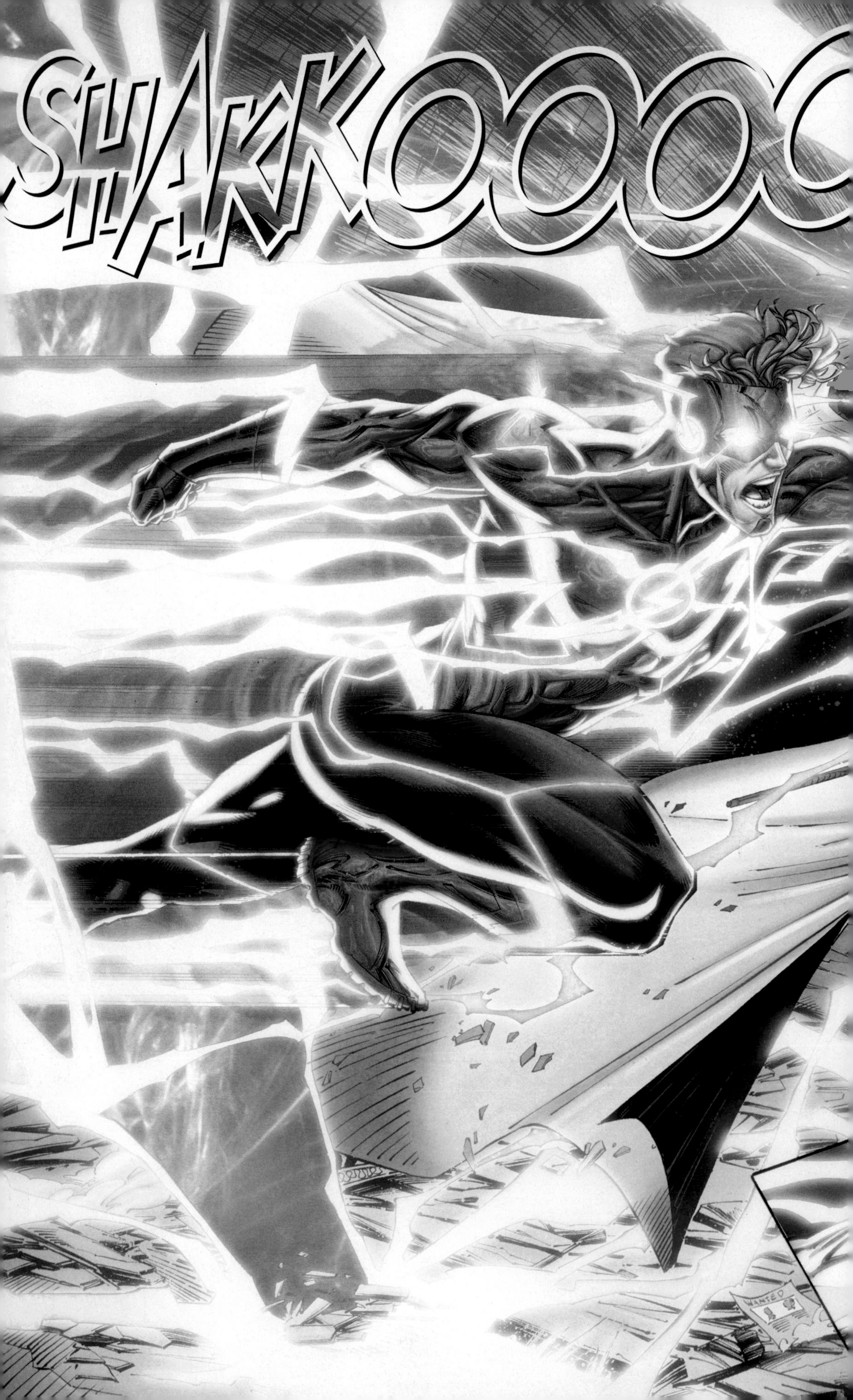
SHAKOOOO
WANTED

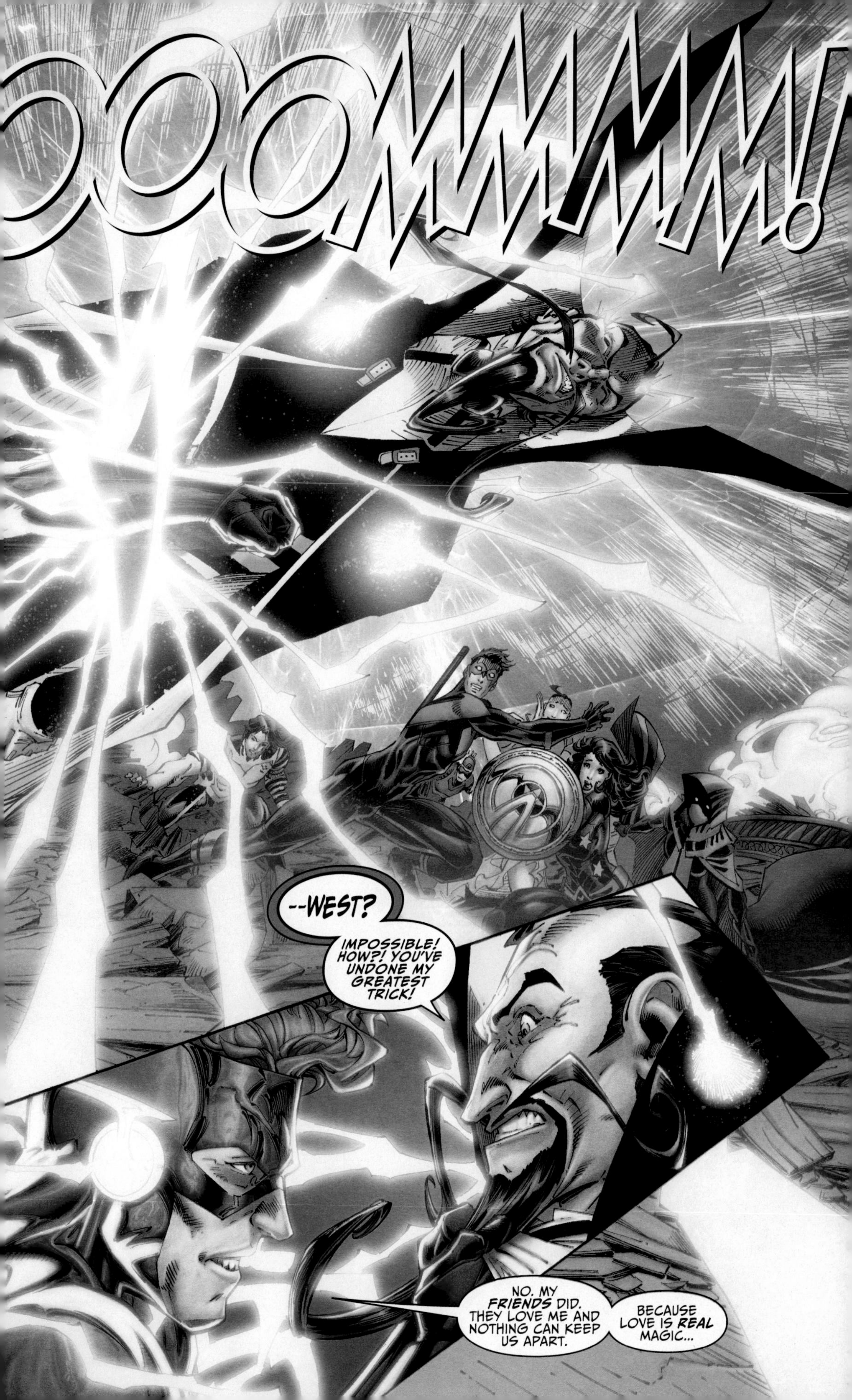
DOOOMMMM!
--WEST?
IMPOSSIBLE! HOW?! YOU'VE UNDONE MY GREATEST TRICK!
NO. MY FRIENDS DID. THEY LOVE ME AND NOTHING CAN KEEP US APART.
BECAUSE LOVE IS REAL MAGIC...

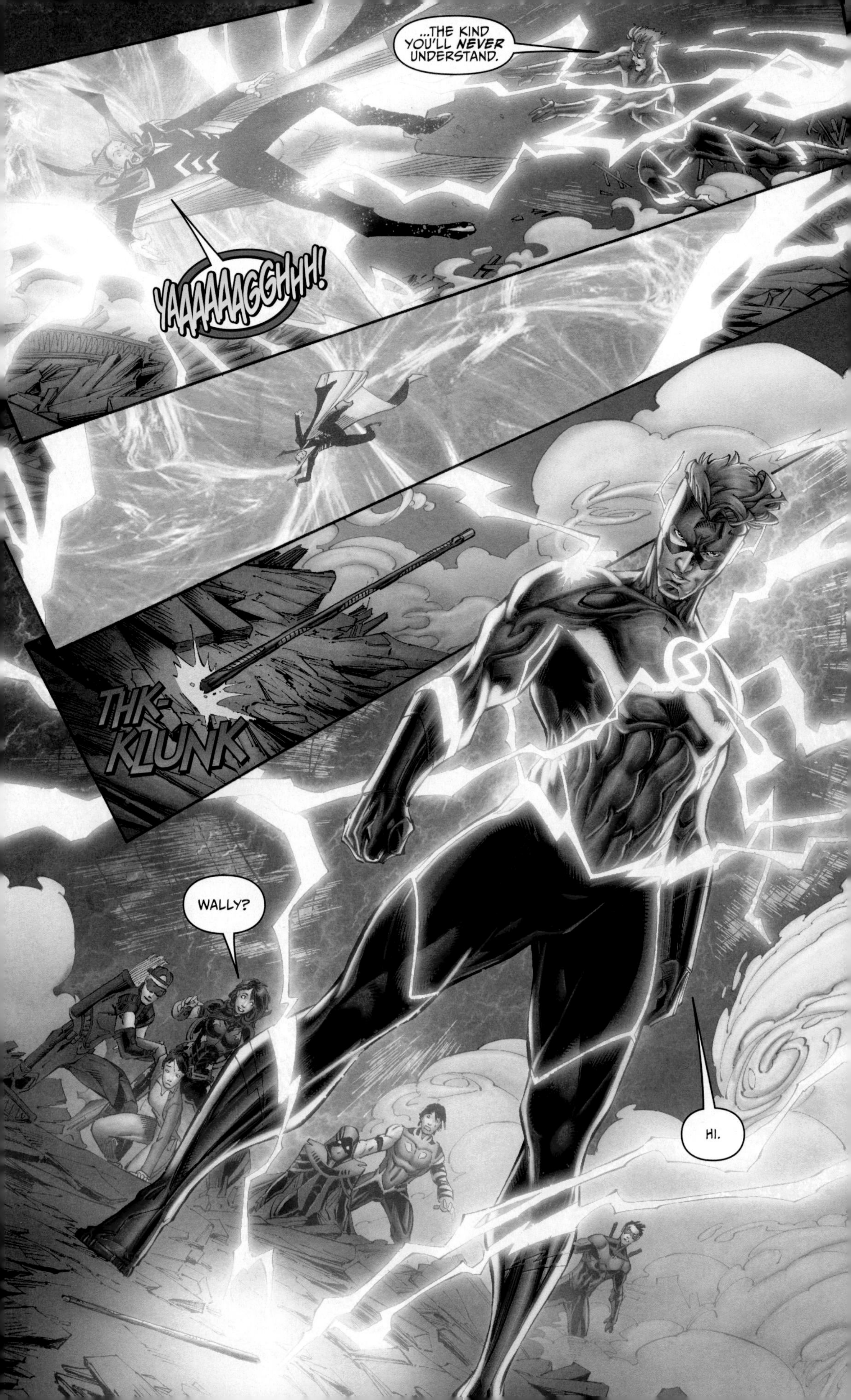
...THE KIND YOU'LL NEVER UNDERSTAND.
YAAAAAAGGHHH!
THK-KLUNK!
WALLY?
HI.

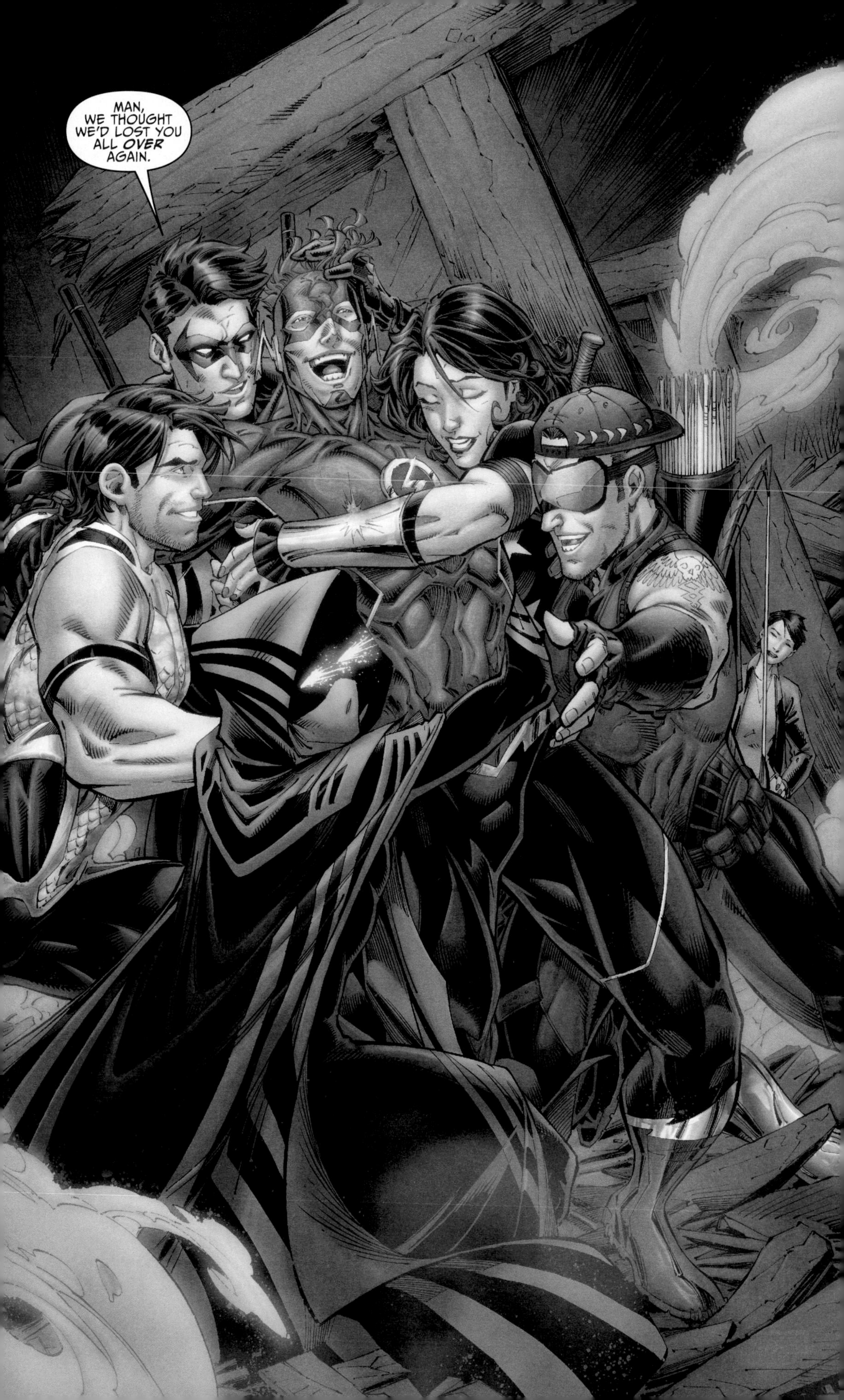
MAN, WE THOUGHT WE'D LOST YOU ALL OVER AGAIN.

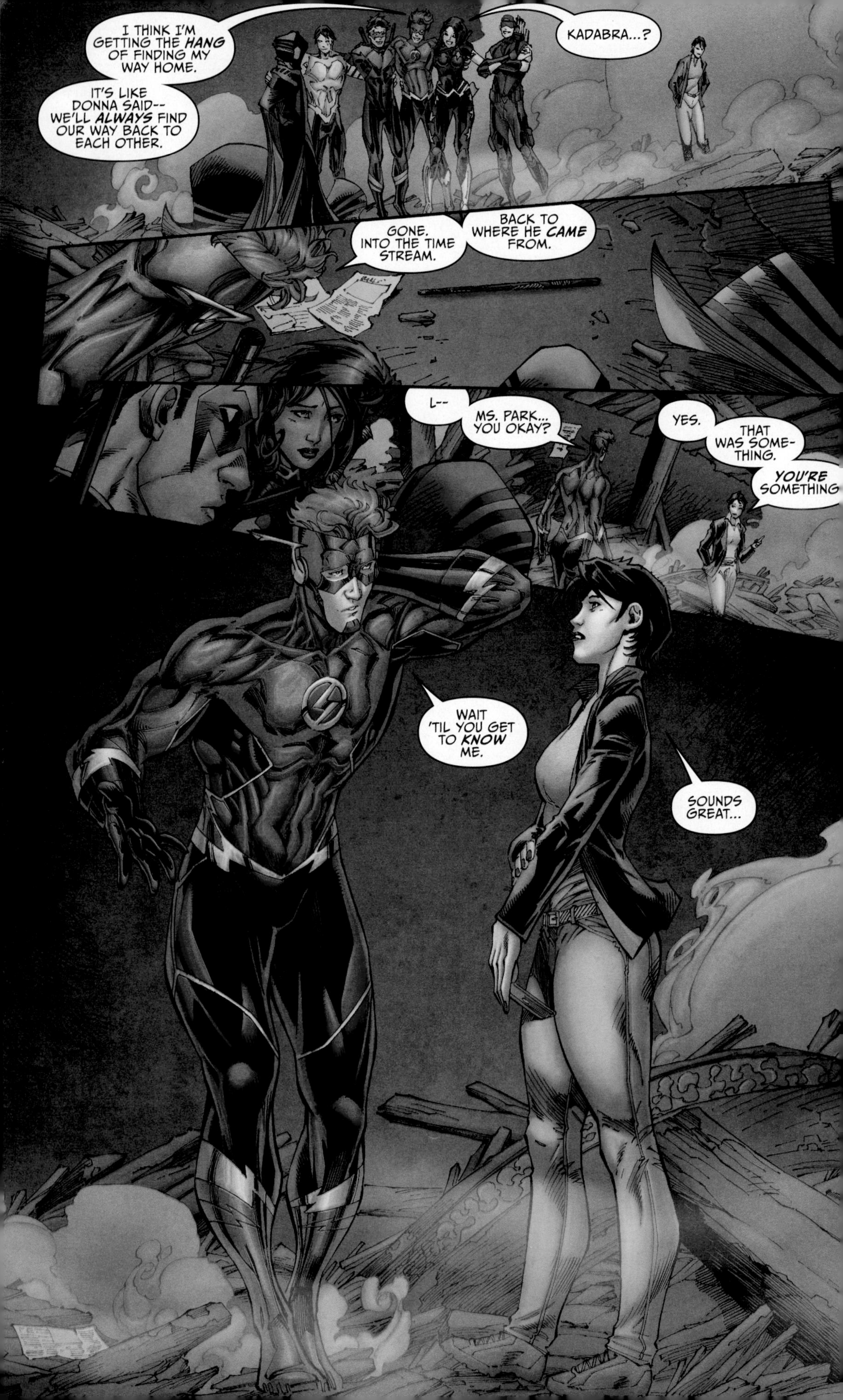

I THINK I'M GETTING THE *HANG* OF FINDING MY WAY HOME.
IT'S LIKE DONNA SAID-- WE'LL *ALWAYS* FIND OUR WAY BACK TO EACH OTHER.
KADABRA...?
GONE. INTO THE TIME STREAM.
BACK TO WHERE HE *CAME* FROM.
L--
MS. PARK... YOU OKAY?
YES.
THAT WAS SOME-THING.
YOU'RE SOMETHING
WAIT 'TIL YOU GET TO *KNOW* ME.
SOUNDS GREAT...

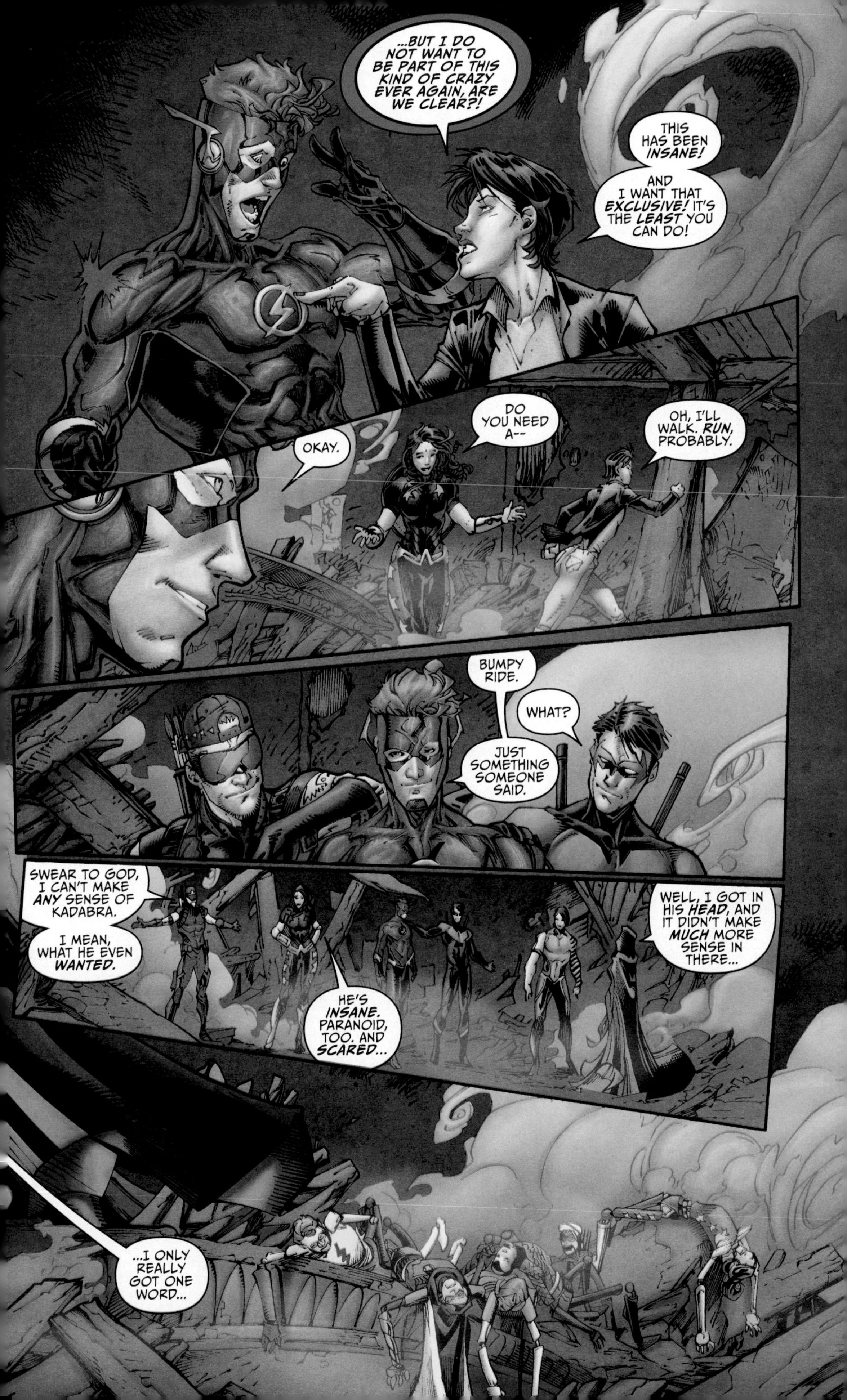
...BUT I DO NOT WANT TO BE PART OF THIS KIND OF CRAZY EVER AGAIN, ARE WE CLEAR?!
THIS HAS BEEN INSANE!
AND I WANT THAT EXCLUSIVE! IT'S THE LEAST YOU CAN DO!
OKAY.
DO YOU NEED A--
OH, I'LL WALK. RUN, PROBABLY.
BUMPY RIDE.
WHAT?
JUST SOMETHING SOMEONE SAID.
SWEAR TO GOD, I CAN'T MAKE ANY SENSE OF KADABRA.
I MEAN, WHAT HE EVEN WANTED.
HE'S INSANE. PARANOID, TOO. AND SCARED...
WELL, I GOT IN HIS HEAD, AND IT DIDN'T MAKE MUCH MORE SENSE IN THERE...
...I ONLY REALLY GOT ONE WORD...

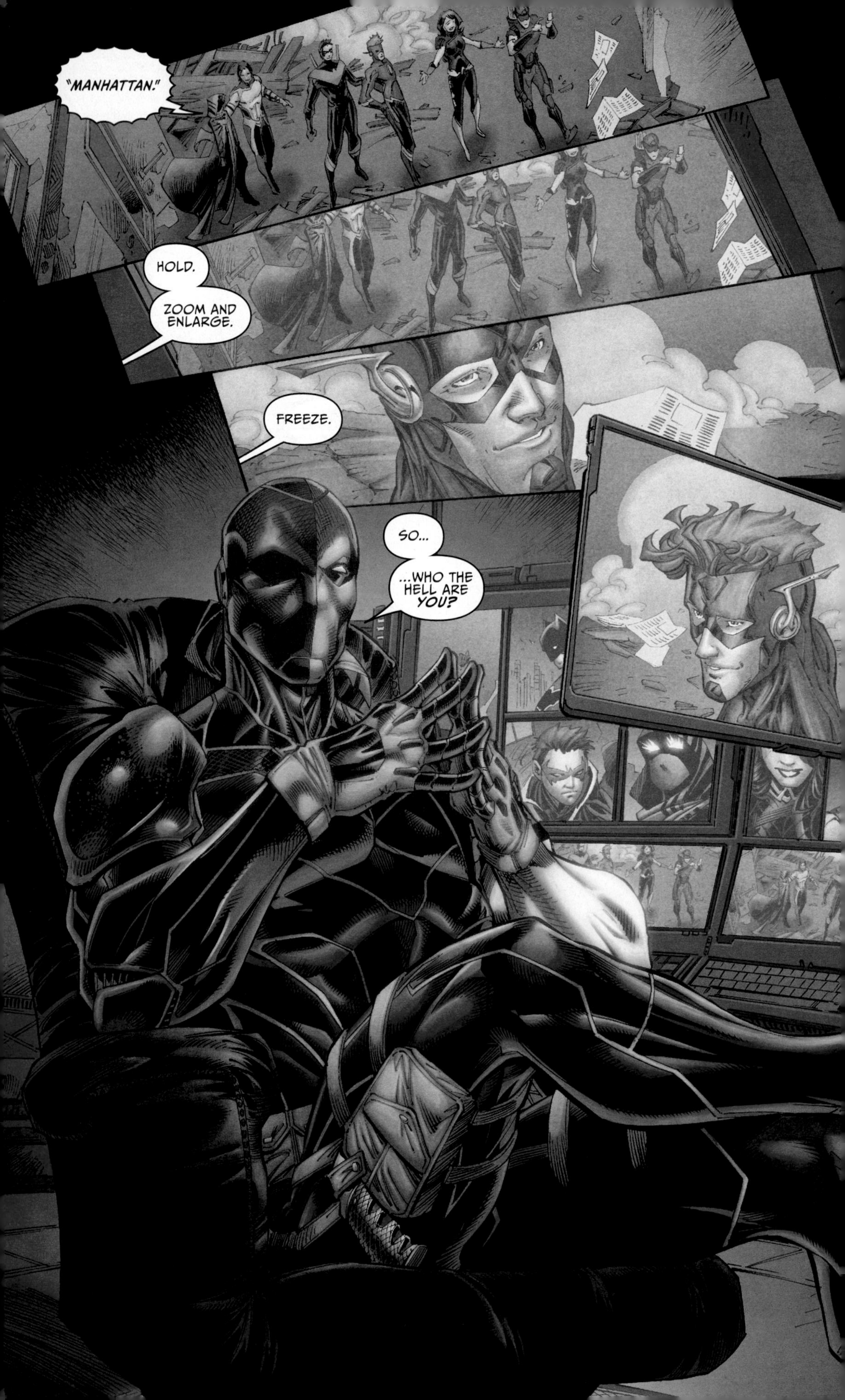
"MANHATTAN."
HOLD.
ZOOM AND ENLARGE.
FREEZE.
SO...
...WHO THE HELL ARE *YOU?*

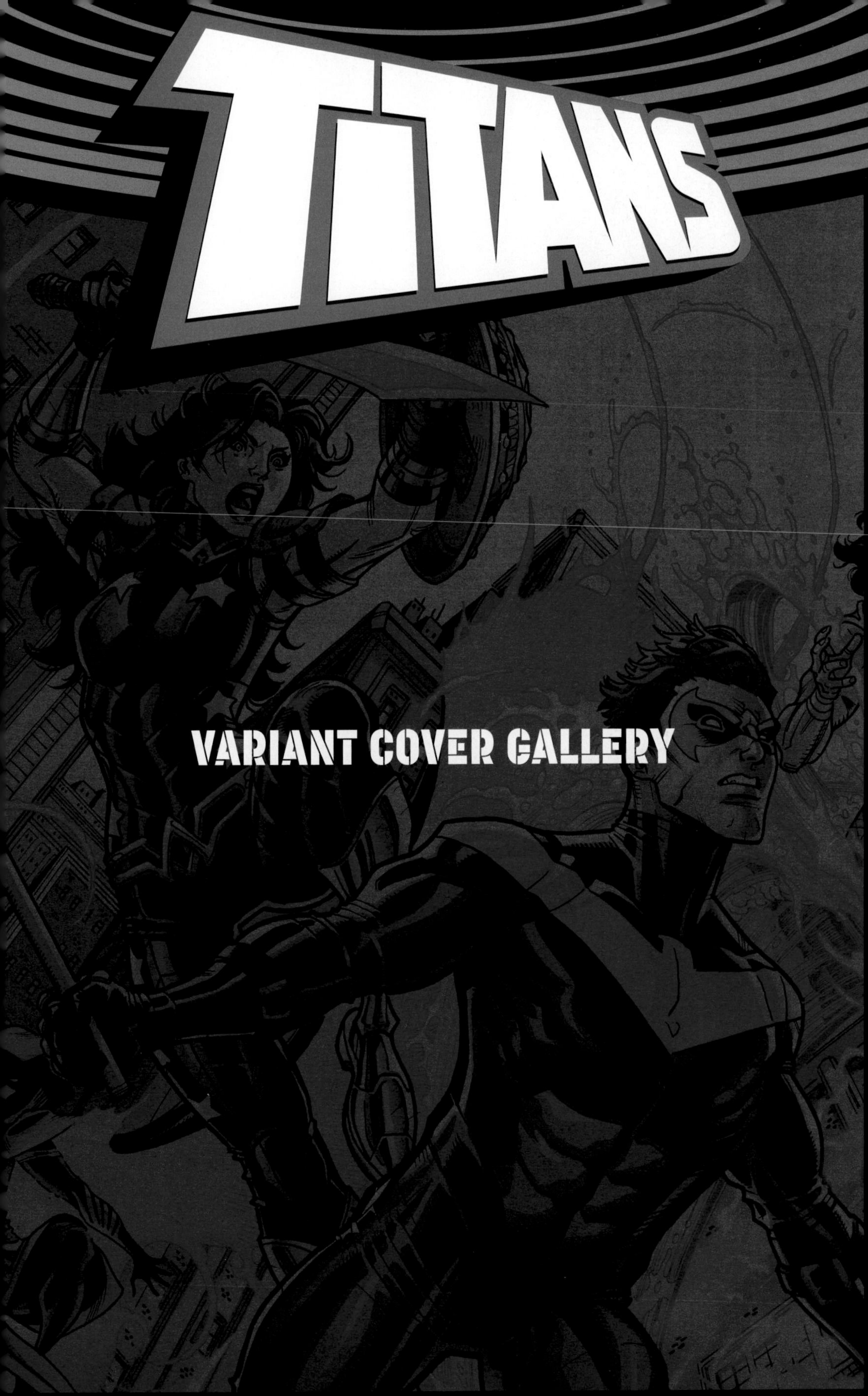
TITANS
VARIANT COVER GALLERY

TITANS: REBIRTH #1 variant cover by MIKE CHOI

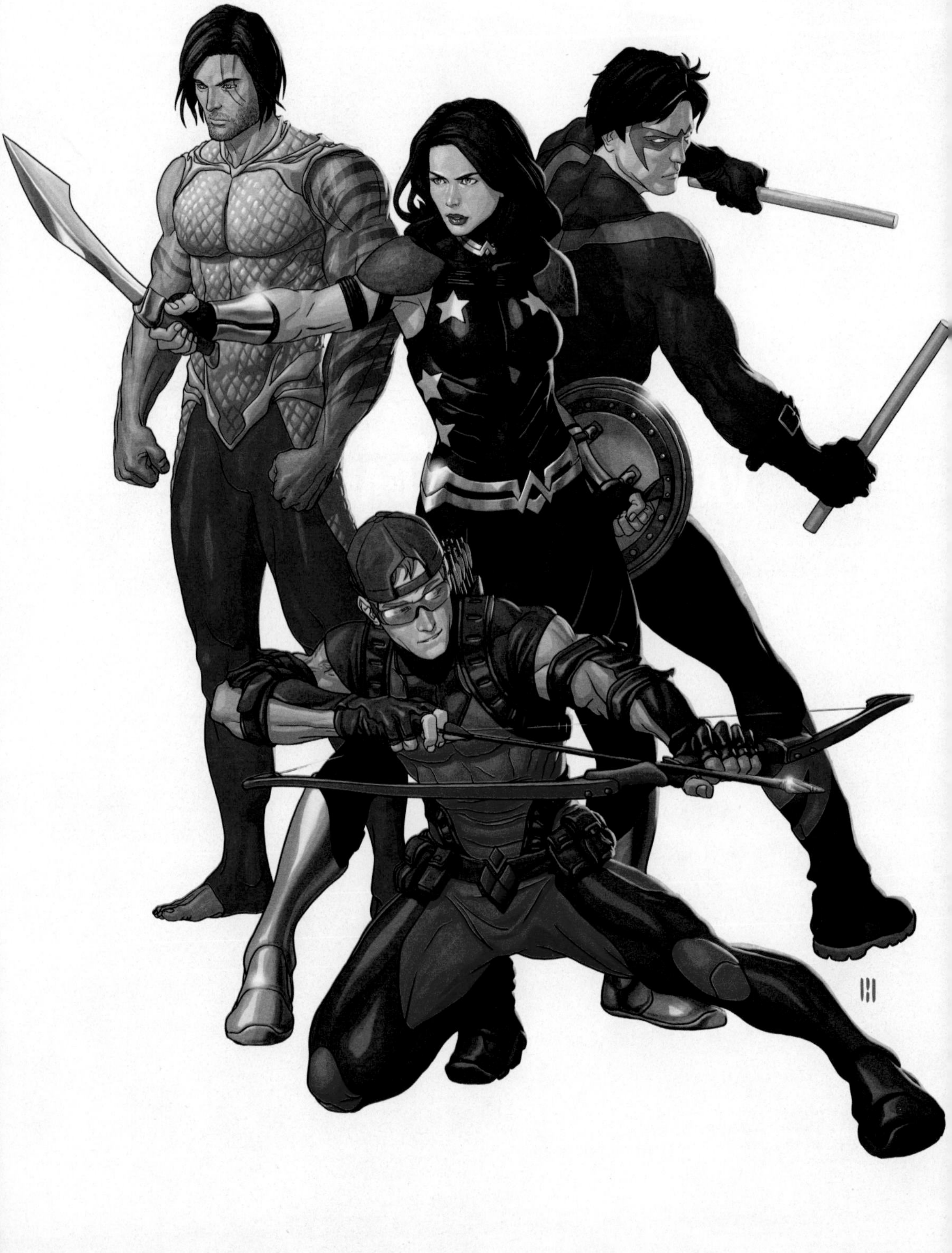

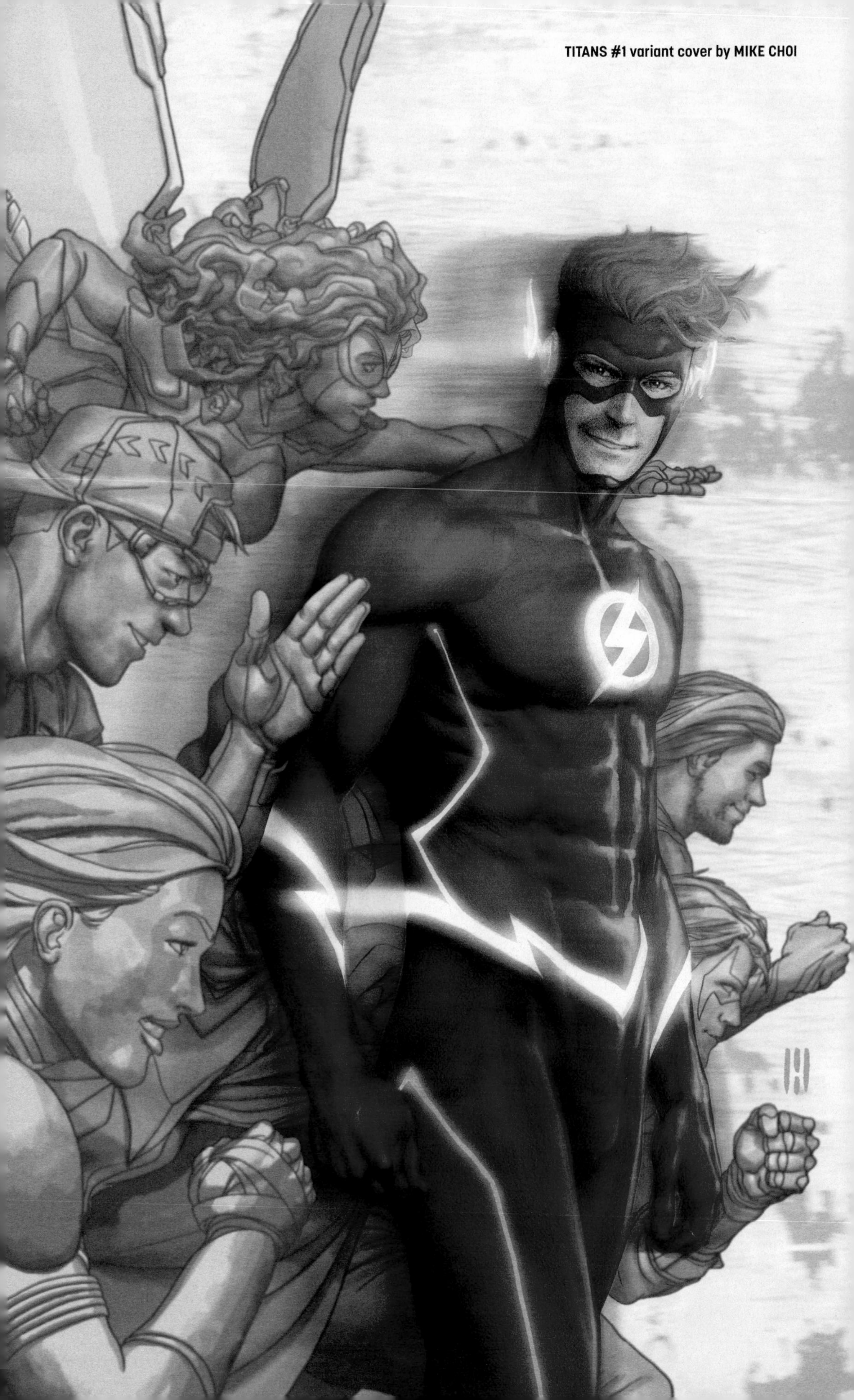

TITANS #1 variant cover by MIKE CHOI

TITANS #2 variant cover by MIKE CHOI

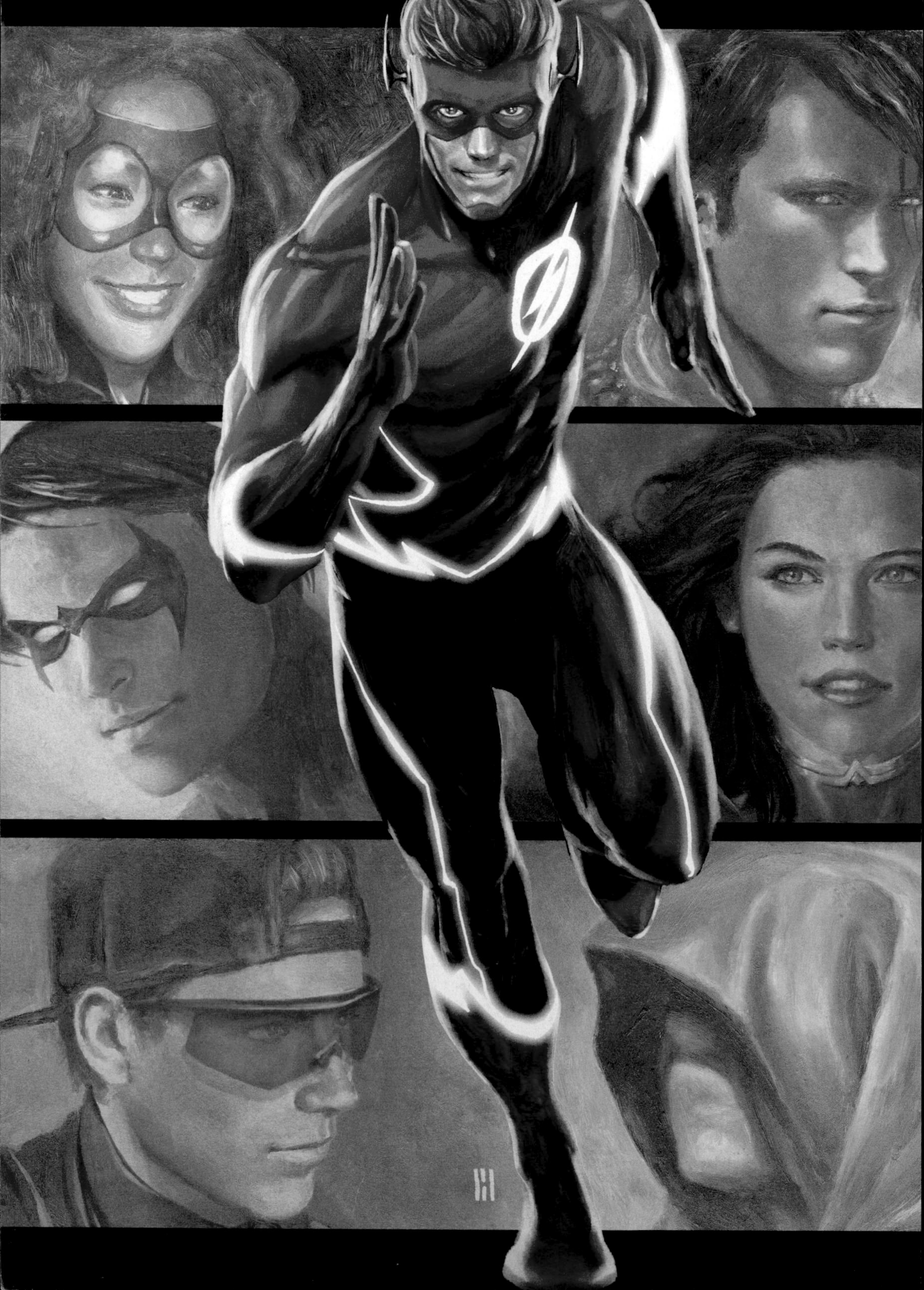

TITANS #3 variant cover by MIKE CHOI

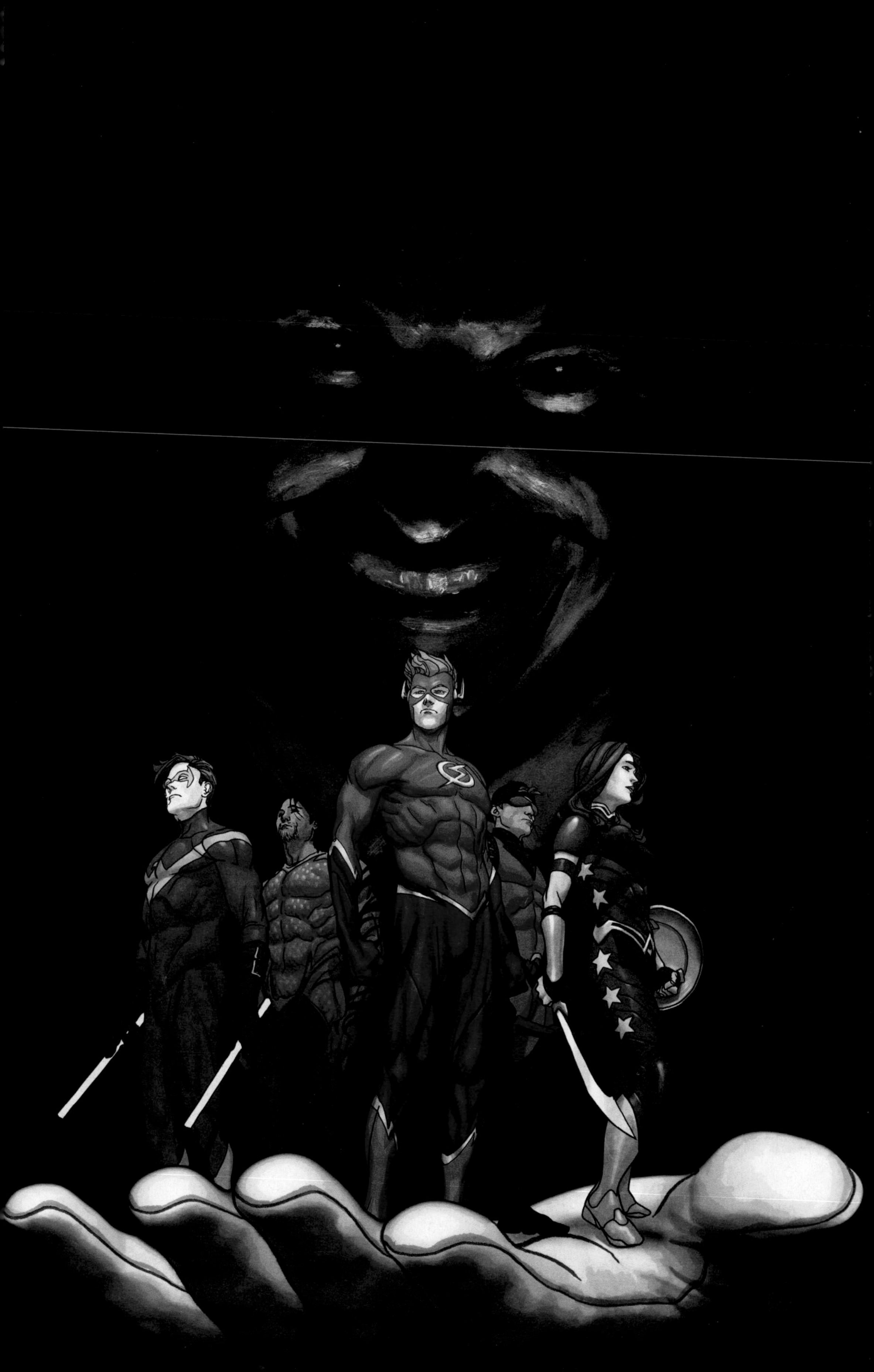

TITANS #4 variant cover by MIKE CHOI

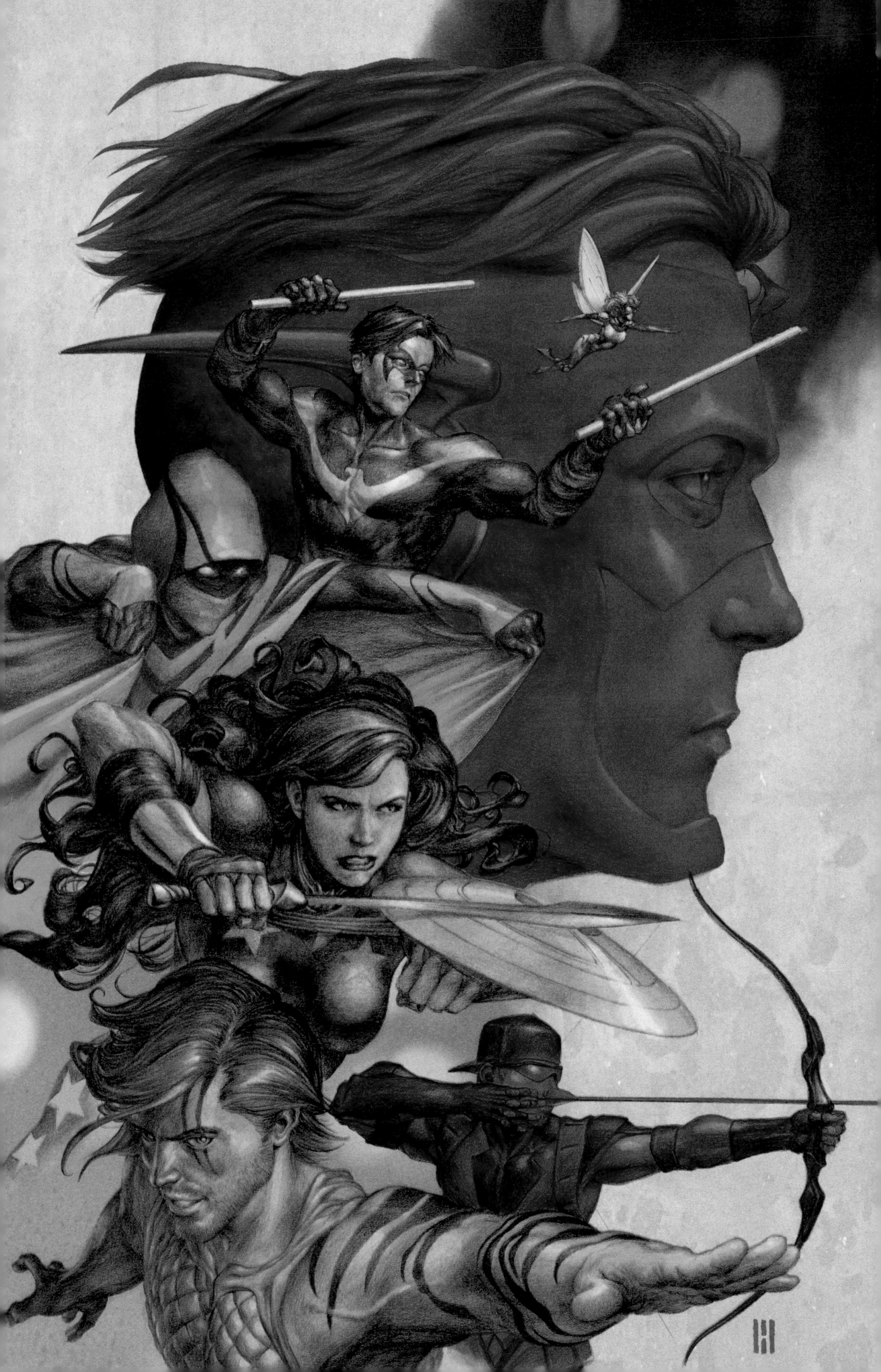

TITANS #5 variant cover by MIKE CHOI

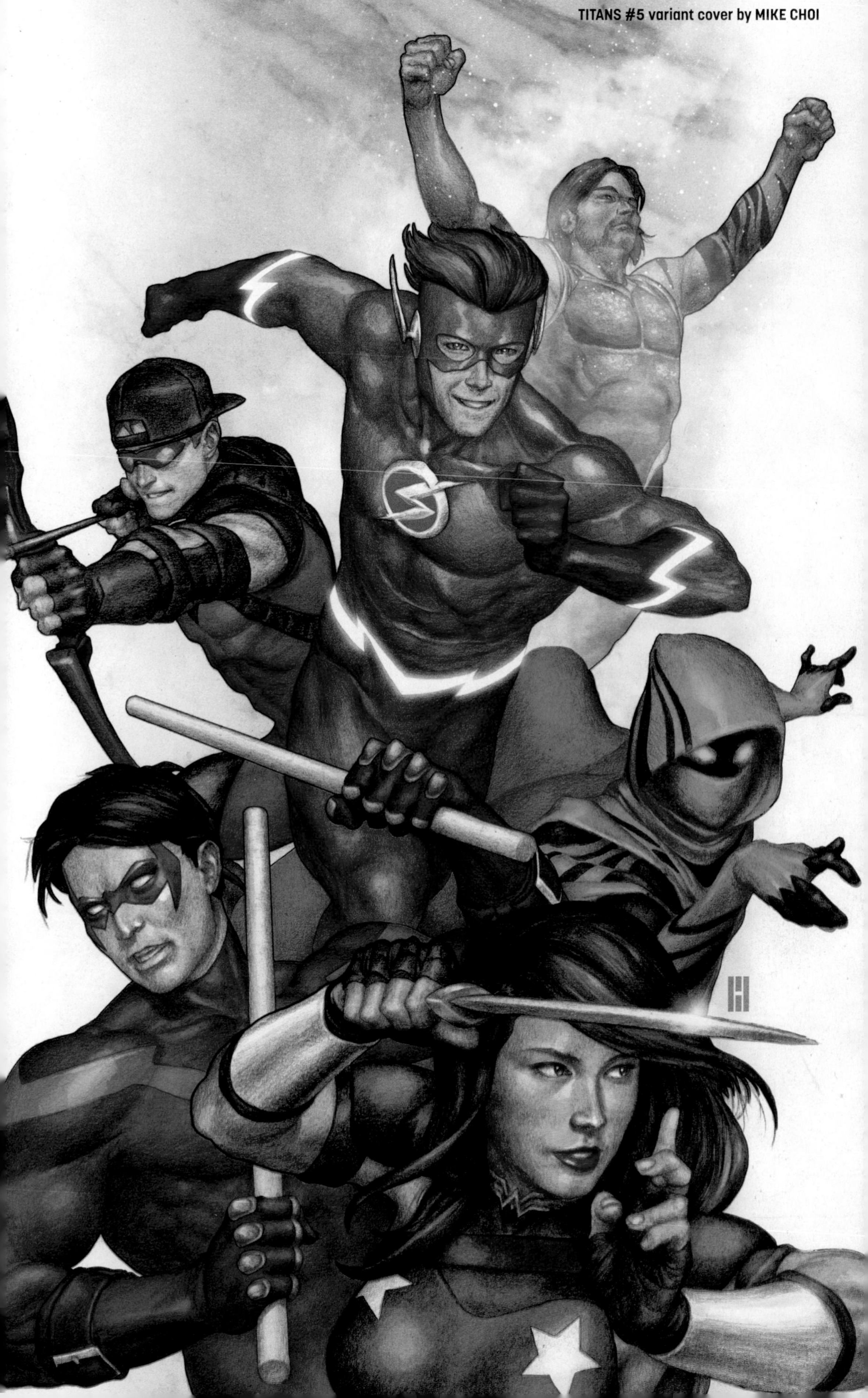

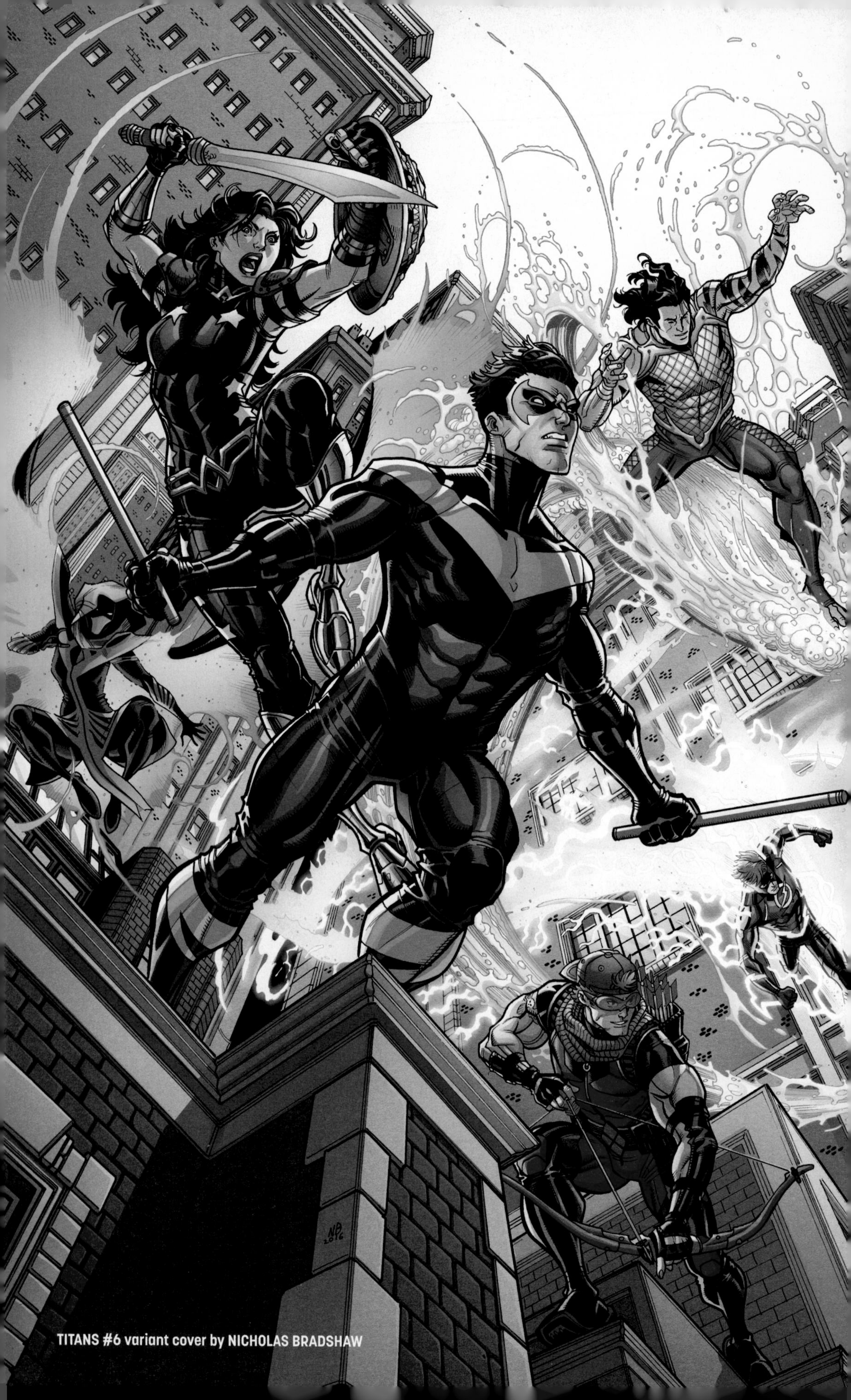

TITANS #6 variant cover by NICHOLAS BRADSHAW

TITANS: REBIRTH #1 COVER SKETCHES AND PENCILS
by BRETT BOOTH

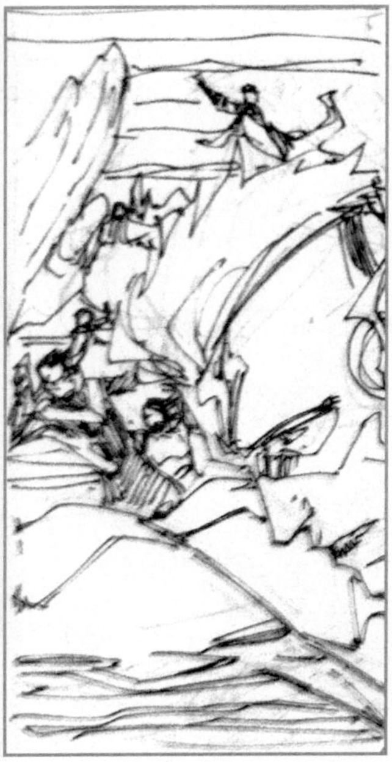

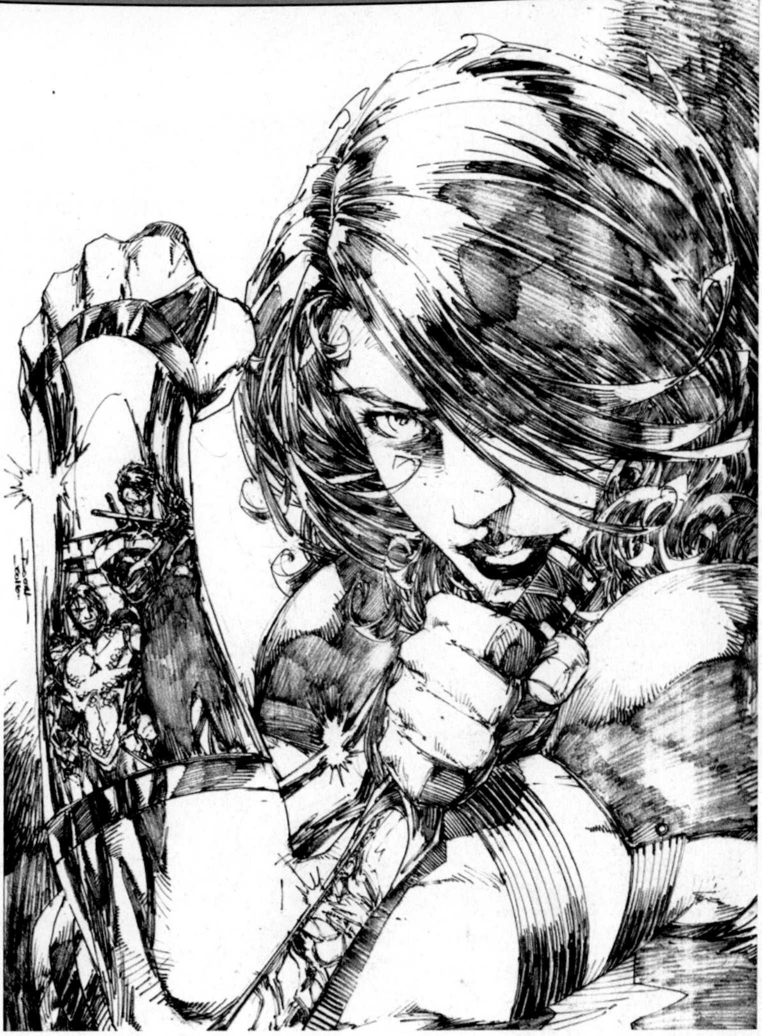

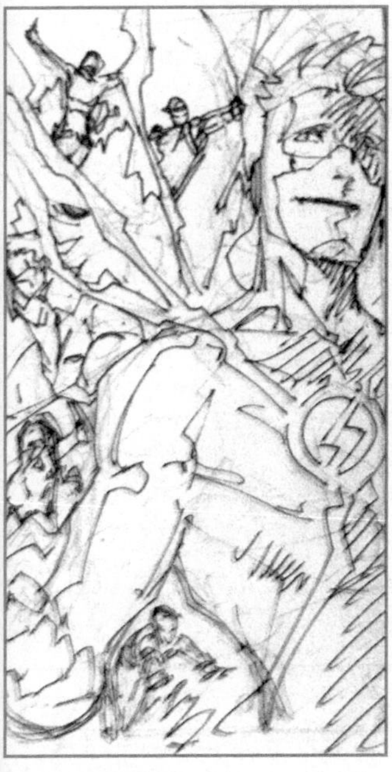

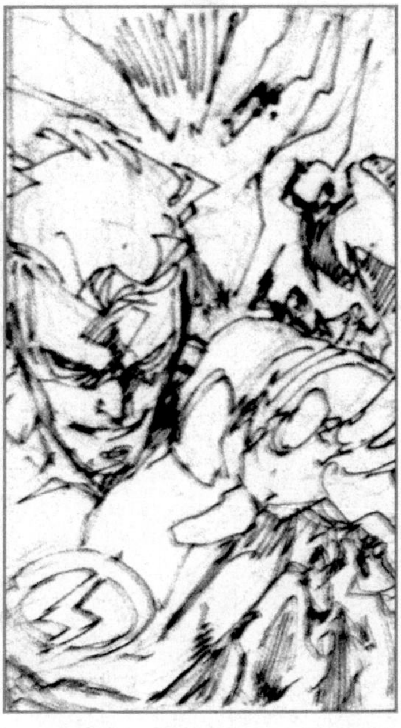

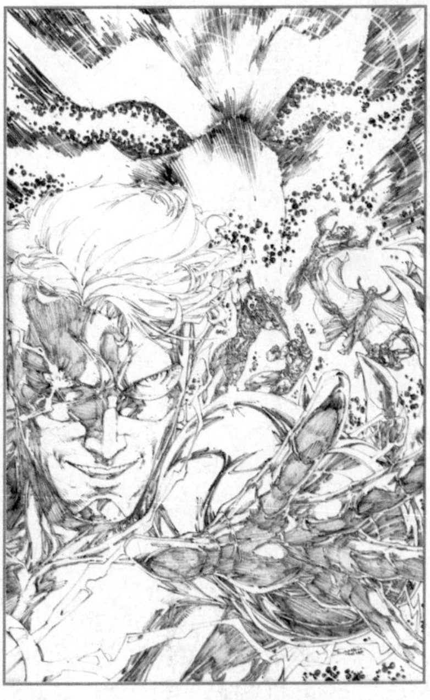

COVER SKETCHES AND PENCILS FOR TITANS #2-4
by BRETT BOOTH

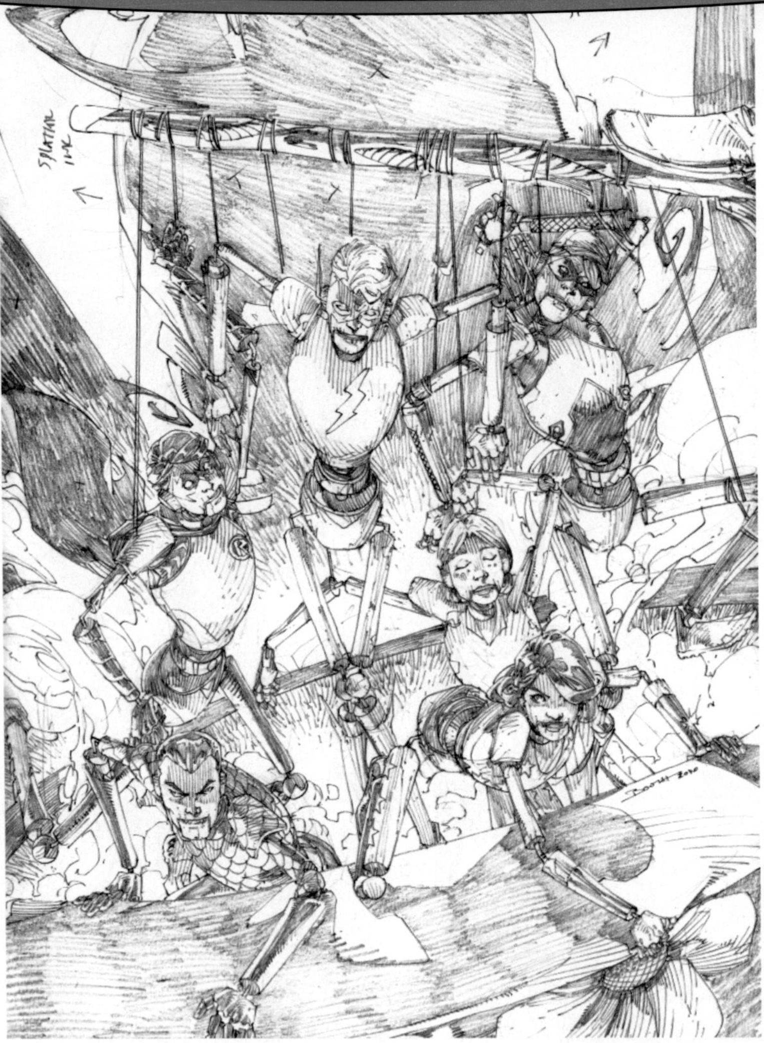

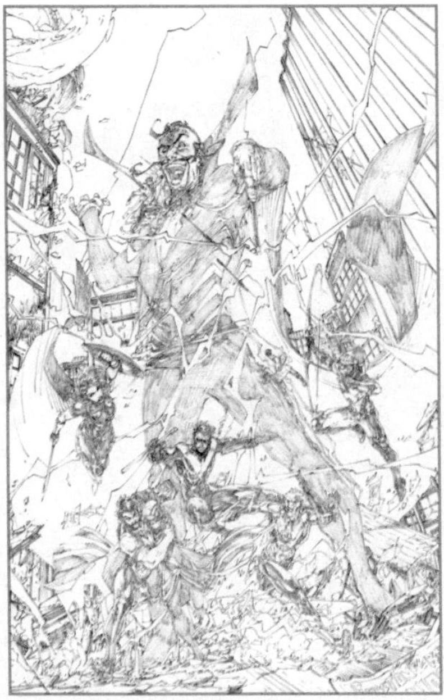

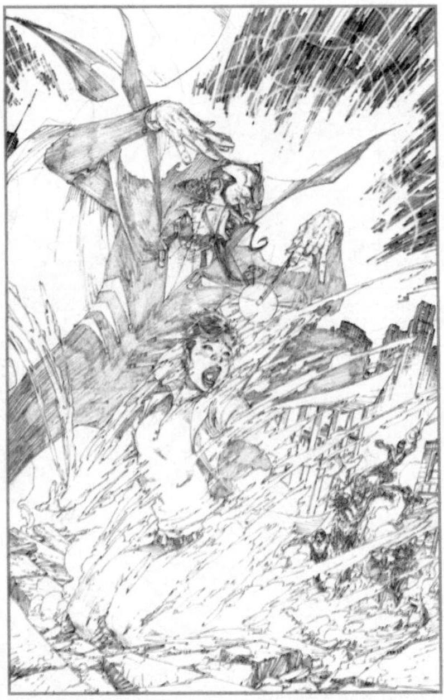